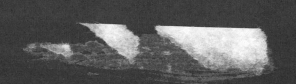

# THE STORY OF
# PHILOSOPHY

# THE STORY OF
# PHILOSOPHY

## BRYAN MAGEE

**DORLING KINDERSLEY**

LONDON • NEW YORK • SYDNEY • MOSCOW

www.dk.com

A DORLING KINDERSLEY BOOK

www.dk.com

**Project editor** Neil Lockley
**Senior project art editor** Rowena Alsey
**Editor** Lara Maiklem
**Senior editor** Luci Collings
**Senior art editor** Claire Legemah
**Managing editor** Anna Kruger
**Deputy art director** Tina Vaughan
**Senior managing editor** Sean Moore
**Picture researchers** Frances Vargo, Melissa Albany
**Production controllers** Meryl Silbert, David Proffit

**Author's dedication**
*I dedicate this book with love
to my daughter Gunnela
and her husband Santiago*

Published in Great Britain in 1998
by Dorling Kindersley Limited,
9 Henrietta Street, London WC2E 8PS

4  6  8  10  9  7  5  3

Copyright © 1998 Dorling Kindersley Limited, London
Text copyright © 1998 Bryan Magee

A CIP catalogue record of this book is available from the British Library

ISBN 0 7513 05901

Colour reproduction by Colourscan, Singapore

Printed and bound in China by Toppan

# CONTENTS

## INTRODUCTION
An Invitation to Philosophy 6

## THE GREEKS AND THEIR WORLD

SOCRATES (C. 470–399 BC)

## CHRISTIANITY AND PHILOSOPHY

SAINT AUGUSTINE
(AD 354–430)

## THE BEGINNINGS OF MODERN SCIENCE

MODEL OF THE SOLAR
SYSTEM (1712)

# An INVITATION to PHILOSOPHY

## QUESTIONING THE FUNDAMENTALS WE NORMALLY TAKE FOR GRANTED

THE DAILY LIVES OF MOST of us are full of things that keep us busy and preoccupied. But every now and again we find ourselves drawing back and wondering what it is all about. And then, perhaps, we may start asking fundamental questions that normally we do not stop to ask.

This can happen with regard to any aspect of life. In politics, for example, people are all the time bandying around terms like "freedom", "equality", "social justice", and so on. But every now and again somebody comes along who asks: "Yes, but what do we actually mean by freedom? And what do we mean by equality?" Such questioning can become challengingly awkward. The person may say: "Surely freedom and equality are in conflict with one another? If we're all free to live our lives as we like, aren't we bound to end up in a whole lot of different and very unequal situations? And isn't that something that can be prevented only by government interference? If that's true, then it's no good us saying we're in favour of freedom and equality and just leaving it at that. There's an element of contradiction involved." It is when people start to talk like this that they are beginning to think philosophically. In this case they are embarking on what is known as political philosophy.

People can subject any field of human activity to fundamental questioning like this – which is another way of saying that there can be a philosophy of anything.

REMBRANDT, *THE TWO PHILOSOPHERS* (1628)
*Discussion, argument, debate, are crucial to philosophy, because everything that is said must lie open to question and criticism. So one might say it takes two to philosophize, and philosophy is a shared search for truth.*

## "PHILOSOPHY BEGINS IN

Lawyers are referring constantly to guilt and innocence, justice, a fair trial, and so on. But if one of them says: "When we talk about justice, do we mean the same as what the politicians mean when they talk about social justice, or are we talking about something different here?" he is beginning to do philosophy of law. The doctor who asks himself: "Is there ever such a thing as perfect health – if not, what do we mean by cure?" is beginning to do philosophy of medicine. In every field of activity there is a philosophy of it that involves questioning its fundamental concepts, principles, and methods. So there is philosophy of science, philosophy of religion, philosophy of art, and so on. Nearly always, some of the best practitioners in each field are interested in its philosophy.

It is important to realize that when the political philosopher asks: "What is freedom?" he is not just asking for a definition of the word. If that were all he wanted he could look it up in the dictionary. His question goes far beyond that. He is seeking an altogether deeper understanding of the concept, and of how it actually functions in our thoughts and our lives, and of other ways in which it might also be used, and of the possible dangers of its use, and of how it does or could relate to other key political concepts such as equality. He is trying to clarify his mind and ours on a subject that has important practical implications for us and yet which bristles with difficulties.

THIS ELUCIDATION OF CONCEPTS, though, fascinating as it is, is the mere surface of philosophy. The greatest philosophers have gone much deeper than that and questioned the most fundamental aspects of our existence and our experience. We human beings find ourselves in a world we had no say about entering. In its most obvious and basic features it consists of a framework of space and time – three dimensions of space and one dimension of time – inhabited by a large number of widely differing material objects, some of which are people like ourselves. And philosophers have raised questions like: "What is time?" and "Is everything that actually exists, including people, a material object and nothing more? Can something that is not a material object have real existence? If so, what is the nature of that existence?" In asking questions like this they are not just trying to achieve a deeper understanding of concepts. They are striving towards a fundamental understanding of whatever it is that exists, including ourselves. And they are trying to do this without making it a question of

# WONDER" PLATO

religious faith, or appealing to the say-so of an authority. They may as individuals have religious beliefs - most great philosophers have had, though some have not – yet as good philosophers they do not attempt to support their philosophical arguments with appeals to religion. A philosophical argument is one that carries its own credentials with it, in the form of reasons: it asks you

for your rational assent, not for faith or obedience. Philosophy tries to see how far reason alone will take us.

Because philosophy is a quest for rational understanding of the most fundamental kind it raises important questions about the nature of understanding and hence of enquiry and knowledge. How are we to go about finding answers to all these questions of ours? Can we ever really know, in the sense of being sure of, anything? If so, what? And even if we do know, how will we be able to be sure that we know; in other words can we ever know that we know? Questions like this have themselves come to occupy a place near the centre of philosophy. Alongside questions about the world around us, the philosopher asks questions about the nature of human perception, experience, and understanding.

So, put at its most basic, philosophy has developed in such a way that two fundamental questions lie at its heart: the first is "What is the nature of whatever it is that exits?" and the second is "How,

AUGUSTE RODIN,
*THE THINKER* (1880)
*The nakedness of Rodin's famous statue of a solitary thinker deeply wrapped in thought suggests that man is a uniquely reflective and self-aware animal, and that this is something fundamental to the human condition.*

if at all, can we know?" Investigation into the first question, about what exists and the nature of existence, constitutes the branch of philosophy known as ontology. Investigation into the second question – about the nature of knowledge, and what, if anything, we can know – is called epistemology. It is the development of these two over the centuries – and of all the subsidiary questions that arise out of them – that constitute the mainstream of philosophy's history.

Into this mainstream flow all the important tributaries, such as moral and political philosophy, philosophy of science, aesthetics, philosophy of religion, and the rest. All these have their place in philosophy as a whole, but questions about what exists, and how we can know, are logically prior to questions raised in these other branches.

It may be that to some of our most important questions we shall never find the answers. But that is itself not something we can know in advance. So we

## "THE BUSINESS OF IS NOT TO GIVE RULES, BUT THE PRIVATE OF COMMON

WILLIAM BLAKE, *THE ANCIENT OF DAYS* (1794)
*Regularity is found at every level in the known universe, from the very biggest to the very smallest, and usually in forms that can be expressed in mathematical equations. It is as if the universe itself embodies rationality. It is as if, somebody once said: "God is a mathematician."*

shall want to mount assaults on all the problems that interest us. If in the course of doing so we discover good reasons to believe that a particular question is not susceptible of an answer we shall have to find a way of coming to terms with that. It is a conclusion which – like all other philosophical conclusions – we shall require good reasons for believing. We shall not be willing just to accept it on spec, or on faith, or because we have an intuition to that effect: we shall want to know why we should believe it to be true.

THIS INSISTENCE ON REASONS is one of the hallmarks of philosophy. It distinguishes philosophy from, for example, both religion and the arts. In religion, reasons are appealed to sometimes, but also faith, revelation, ritual, and obedience have indispensable roles, and reason can never take a person the whole way. The creative artist, like the philosopher, is fully committed to a truth-seeking activity, trying to see below the surface of things and acquire a deeper understanding of human experience; however, he publishes, or publicly presents, his insights in a different form from the philosopher, a form that relies on direct perception and intuition rather than on rational argument.

A different sort of frontier runs between philosophy and the sciences. Again, the scientist like the philosopher and the creative artist, is engaged in truth-seeking enquiry, trying to make new discoveries about the world and the nature of our experience of it, and to make sense of these, and to publish his findings. And he, like the philosopher, is much concerned to be able to provide rational backing for everything he says. In his case the key difference from the philosopher is that the scientist

# PHILOSOPHY TO ANALYSE JUDGEMENTS REASON"

IMMANUEL KANT

is concerned with questions that can be decided by experiment or observation. And there are no experiments or observations that will tell us whether or not time had a beginning, or what "rights" are. Questions like that, which are amenable to rational enquiry but not amenable to the methods of science, are typical of the questions that get bequeathed to philosophers.

IT IS ESSENTIAL TO REALIZE that philosophy, science, and art are not at odds with one another. They have much more in common than appears at first sight. In fact, as we shall see in this book, it was out of philosophy that science was born. It is the same world that philosophy, science, and art are all exploring. All three confront the mystery of the world's existence, and our existence as human beings, and try to achieve a deeper understanding of it. All three make perpetual use of both inspiration and criticism. And all three make their findings public so that they can be shared. But because they use different methods, and follow different paths, they may sometimes appeal to different temperaments. Yet they share the goal of exploring human knowledge and experience, and trying to bring what is hidden to light, and organize their findings into publicly articulate

form. They enrich one another, and a fully rounded human being will find himself becoming naturally interested in all three. This book tells the story of one of them, philosophy. Like the other two, it is among the most fascinating and valuable things that civilization has produced. And, like the others, its future is likely to be richer than its past.

SALVADOR DALÍ,
*HOMAGE TO NEWTON* (1969)
*Man has the ability not only to explore space outside himself but to relate his discoveries to his own inner spaces of thought and feeling. Here the sciences, philosophy, and the arts may meet and fructify one another.*

# The GREEKS & Their WORLD

PHILOSOPHY BEGINS WHEN HUMAN BEINGS START TRYING TO UNDERSTAND THE WORLD, NOT THROUGH RELIGION OR BY ACCEPTING AUTHORITY BUT THROUGH THE USE OF REASON. THIS SEEMS TO HAVE BEGUN AMONG THE EARLY GREEKS, IN THE 6TH, 5TH, AND 4TH CENTURIES BC. THEIR EARLIEST QUESTIONS WERE: "WHAT IS THE WORLD MADE OF?" AND "WHAT HOLDS THE WORLD UP?" BUT THEN CAME SOCRATES, THE MOST FAMOUS OF ALL GREEK PHILOSOPHERS, WHO SAID THAT WHAT MATTERS MOST IS HOW WE OUGHT TO LIVE. HIS BASIC QUESTION WAS: "WHAT IS JUSTICE?" HIS PUPIL PLATO WAS THE FIRST WESTERN PHILOSOPHER WHOSE WRITTEN WORKS HAVE SURVIVED, AND THESE ARE NOW STUDIED IN UNIVERSITIES ALL OVER THE WORLD. PLATO'S PUPIL ARISTOTLE WAS OF SIMILAR GENIUS.

**BRONZE HEAD OF APHRODITE**
*This bronze head was found at Satala, Turkey. It was sculpted in the 2nd or 1st century* BC *and is now in the British Museum, London.*

# BEFORE SOCRATES
## THE EMERGENCE OF RATIONAL THINKING

*The very earliest Western philosophers, those before Socrates, produced large-scale theories about the world, some of which were wildly mistaken but some profound enough to be influential down to our own day.*

**CONNECTIONS**
Chalenas, a Greek soothsayer of the 4th century BC, examines an animal's liver. He was not studying anatomy, however, he was trying to predict the future by examining entrails. Everywhere, magical thinking came before rational thinking, and sometimes led to it. For this reason it is a mistake to think of the two as necessarily opposed: they are often contiguous.

THE FIRST PHILOSOPHERS were making two great breaks with the past simultaneously. In the first place they were trying to understand the world by the use of their reason, without appealing to religion, or revelation, or authority, or tradition. This in itself was something wholly new, and one of the most important milestones in human development. But at the same time they were teaching other people to use their own reason too, and think for themselves; so they did not expect even their own pupils necessarily to agree with them. They were the first teachers who did not try to pass on a body of knowledge pure and unsullied, inviolate, but instead encouraged their pupils to discuss and argue, debate, put forward ideas of their own.

These two developments in the mental life of mankind, both of them revolutionary, are linked, which is why they appeared on the scene together. They form the foundations of what we now call "rational thinking". Once they had been introduced they launched an unparalleled rate of growth in human knowledge and understanding.

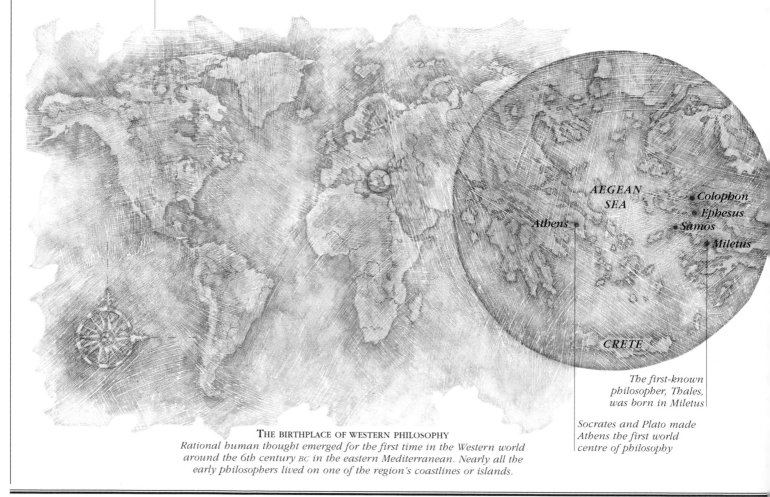

AEGEAN
SEA

*Colophon*
*Ephesus*
*Samos*
*Miletus*

Athens

CRETE

*The first-known philosopher, Thales, was born in Miletus*

*Socrates and Plato made Athens the first world centre of philosophy*

**THE BIRTHPLACE OF WESTERN PHILOSOPHY**
*Rational human thought emerged for the first time in the Western world around the 6th century BC in the eastern Mediterranean. Nearly all the early philosophers lived on one of the region's coastlines or islands.*

**THALES**
*While he realized that the material world was reducible to a single element, Thales mistakenly supposed this to be water.*

The first thinkers of this kind emerged in the ancient Greek world in the 6th century BC. The one usually thought of as the very first, Thales, was a Greek who lived in the town of Miletus, on the Asia-Minor coast of what is now Turkey. After the name of the town, he and his followers have become known as the Milesian school. We do not know his dates of birth and death, but we know he was active and flourishing in the 580s BC, because he accurately predicted an eclipse of the sun that took place in 585 BC. He was also an early civil engineer, one who carried out the feat of diverting the waters of the river Hylas to enable King Croesus to pass.

## WHAT ARE THINGS MADE OF?

The question that most obsessed Thales was: "What is the world made of?" It seemed to him that it must ultimately all be made from a single element. Now this is an amazing insight, extremely unobvious, and one we now know to be true: we now know that all material objects are reducible to energy. But this thought could not have occurred to Thales – the physics that leads up to it had not yet been done. He came to the conclusion that everything was water in one form or another. He could see that at very low temperatures water becomes rock, at very high temperatures air. Every time the rains come down plants spring out of the earth, so they are evidently water in another form. All living things need a huge and constant intake of water to go on living. (Our bodies are in fact some 60 per cent water.) Every landmass comes to an end at the water's edge; so Thales thought this meant that the whole earth is floating on water, and so has emerged out of water, and so is constituted of water.

Thales had a pupil called Anaximander, who was born in Miletus in 610 BC and lived to about 546 BC. He realized that if, as Thales said, the earth was supported by the sea, the sea would have to be supported by something else – and so on, *ad infinitum*: you would find yourself in what is known as an infinite regress. He solved this problem with the astounding idea that the earth is not supported by anything at all. It is just a solid object hanging in space, and is kept in position by its equidistance from everything else. Anaximander did not think of the earth as being a globe, because it seemed to him self-evident that we live on a flat surface, so he thought of it as cylindrical. "The earth… is held up by nothing, but remains stationary owing to the fact that it is equally distant from all other things. Its shape… is like that of a drum. We walk on one of its flat surfaces, while the other is on the opposite side."

This was too much for his pupil Anaximenes, who considered it self-evident that the earth was flat, and also that it must be held up by something. He came to believe that it floated on air in the sort of way the lid of a boiling saucepan sometimes floats on the steam. It is salutary to realize that for many generations after their deaths Anaximenes remained a more respected and more influential philosopher than Anaximander. This means that throughout those generations there were thinkers using Anaximenes as their starting point when in fact there had already been another thinker before him who had come up with something much better. This sort of thing has

**HARVESTING OLIVES**
When Thales was taunted for his poverty, he put down all the money he had on deposit to rent the olive presses during the next harvest season. He was then able to charge whatever he liked when people needed the presses. This was to show that philosophers can make money if they want to, but are interested in other things.

**ANAXIMANDER, THE FIRST MAP MAKER**
*Anaximander was the first to make a map of the known world, and to realize that the earth was hanging unsupported in space. Despite this amazing discovery, however, belief in a flat earth persisted for a long time.*

*"This world
is a comedy to
those that think,
a tragedy to
those that feel –
a solution of
why Democritus
laughed and
Heraclitus
wept "*
HORACE WALPOLE

**HERACLITUS: THE FIRST OF THE HIGHLY QUOTABLES**
*Among Heraclitus' sayings is that a man's character is his
destiny. This perceptive insight was to be seconded by
Sigmund Freud more than two thousand years later.*

to make up the world. If you did away with
contradiction you would do away with reality.
But this in turn means that reality is inherently
unstable. Everything is in flux all the time. And
this is the second idea that has been permanently
associated with Heraclitus. "Everything is Flux."

Nothing in this world of ours just permanently
*is*. Everything is changing all the time. Things come
into existence in their different ways, and are never
the same for two moments together so long as they
exist, until eventually they go out of existence
again. We ourselves are like this. Everything in the
universe is like it – perhaps the universe itself is
like it. What we think of as "things" are not actually
stable objects at all, they are in perpetual transition.
Heraclitus likened them to flames in this respect:
flames *look* as if they are objects, but they
are not so much objects as
processes. This is a
profound idea. But it is
also disconcerting.
Human beings

continued to happen throughout the history of
philosophy. It does not develop in a straight line, but
rather in a two-steps-forward-followed-by-one-step-
back sort of way. If it should happen that we
ourselves are living in a one-step-back period, we
have especially much to learn from the past.

## THE WAY UP IS THE WAY DOWN

A philosopher better known today than any of the
Milesians is Heraclitus. He was from Ephesus, a
town on the same stretch of coast as Miletus, and
at his peak in the early 6th century BC. He is famous
for two ideas in particular, both of which have had
great influence.

The first is the unity of opposites. He pointed
out that the path up the mountainside and the
path down the mountainside are not two different
paths running in opposite directions, they are one
and the same path. The young Heraclitus and the
old Heraclitus are not two different individuals,
they are the same Heraclitus. If your drinking
companion says your bottle of wine is half full and
you say it is half empty you are not contradicting
him, you are agreeing with him. Everything
(Heraclitus thought) is a coming together of
opposites, or at least of opposing tendencies.

This means that strife and contradiction are not
to be avoided. Indeed, they are what come together

A
MARITIME
OUTLOOK
*The world of the
ancient Greeks was
waterborne, a world
of coasts and islands,
thus leading them at first
to believe that the whole
earth was floating on water.*

ave always tried to find something stable to believe in, something reliable that would last and not pass away. And Heraclitus is telling us that there is no such thing. Change is the law of life and of the universe. It rules over all. We can never escape it.

## THE KEY IS MATHEMATICS

Perhaps the most famous of all the pre-Socratic philosophers, better known even than Heraclitus, is Pythagoras. He was born on Samos, an island off the coast from which all the philosophers came that we have discussed so far; and he lived from about 570 BC to about 497 BC. He was a many-sided genius, one of his gifts being for mathematics – many of us in the 20th century have had to learn Pythagoras' Theorem at school. It was he who introduced the idea of the "square" and the "cube" of a number, thus applying geometrical concepts to arithmetic. Through his teachings the word "theory" acquired its now

### PYTHAGORAS
*This Greek philosopher and mathematician was the first person to have the idea that all the workings of the material universe are expressible in terms of mathematics.*

familiar meaning. He is thought to be the person who invented the term "philosophy", and who first applied the word "cosmos" to the universe. His direct influence lasted for generations.

He was the first great thinker to bring mathematics to bear on philosophy. This was one of the most fruitful notions that any human being has ever had. Ever since his day, mathematics has developed in symbiotic relationship with philosophy and the sciences, and some of the very greatest philosophers have also been great mathematicians – Descartes, for instance, invented not only the graph but the whole subject of analytic geometry, and Leibniz discovered calculus; to take only two examples.

## "EVERYTHING IS FLUX"

### HERACLITUS

We are now used to the idea that mathematics plays an indispensable role in our understanding of the universe. The fact that the cosmos at every level, from the outermost galaxies down to the interior of the individual atom, is saturated with structure of a kind that is expressible in mathematical

### PENNY-WISE
Coins transmit not only value but information and propaganda, even religious images. Their use began in the same geographical area as rational thinking. By the time of the pre-Socratic philosophers many Greek city states had their own mints, and these began to stamp their coins with their own distinctive devices: Athens chose that of an owl, the bird of wisdom.

*" Thou almost makest me waver in my faith To hold opinion with Pythagoras "*
WILLIAM SHAKESPEARE,
THE MERCHANT OF VENICE

### PYTHAGORAS' THOUGHTS
*Pythagoras originated more of the fundamental ideas of Western philosophy than any thinker before Plato. Indeed, much that is often attributed to Plato was adapted by him from Pythagoras, including the idea that we remember a good deal of what we know from a previous life, and the idea that mathematical order pervades the physical world.*

**ALLEGORY OF THE LIBERAL ARTS**
*In this Renaissance painting, created two thousand years after his death, Pythagoras was still seen as being at the summit of the liberal arts for his mathematics. Aristotle – on the first tier holding a book – is also still in the picture for his logic.*

terms is so familiar to us that it is in danger of appearing obvious, but in truth it is not obvious at all, it is utterly astonishing. It is what has led so many of the greatest scientists of all, such as Einstein, to believe

that there must be some sort of intelligence behind the universe, if not necessarily a God in the conventional Judaeo-Christian sense. The very first person to have this insight about the expressibility of the whole universe in terms of mathematics was Pythagoras, and he also was led by it into some sort of mysticism.

Pythagoras developed the philosophical consequences of these insights over a broad area; but since nearly all his most important ideas were taken up and developed still further by Plato we shall (to avoid repetition) wait until we get to Plato before going into them further.

## WE MAKE OUR KNOWLEDGE

One of the most attractive of the pre-Socratic philosophers is Xenophanes, who flourished in the later part of the 6th century BC. Like Pythagoras he was born on the Greek litoral (Colophon, Ionia) of Asia Minor but spent most of his time in southern Italy. He seems to have understood in a rather deep way that human views of things are human creations, including what we take to be our knowledge. By learning more and more, and changing our ideas in the light of what we learn, we may get nearer and nearer to the truth, but our ideas remain always ours, and there is always an element of guesswork involved. He said

> *... as for certain truth, no man has known it,*
> *Nor shall he know it, neither of the gods*
> *Nor yet of all the things of which I speak,*
> *For even if by chance he were to utter*
> *The final truth, he would himself not know it:*
> *For all is but a woven web of guesses.*

Xenophanes was shrewd, indeed witty, on the subject of gods:

> *The Ethiops say that their gods are flat-nosed*
> *    and black.*
> *While the Thracians say that theirs have blue*
> *    eyes and red hair.*
> *Yet if cattle or horses or lions had hands and*
> *    could draw*
> *And could sculpture like men, then the horses*
> *    would draw their gods*
> *Like horses, and cattle like cattle, and each*
> *    would then shape*
> *Bodies of gods in the likeness, each kind,*
> *    of its own.*

These translations of Xenophanes were made by the 20th-century philosopher Karl Popper. The idea that all of our so-called scientific knowledge is in fact conjecture, and is in principle always replaceable by something that may be nearer to the truth, is central to Popper's philosophy; and he regarded Xenophanes

### THE BASIC ELEMENTS
*Two thousand years after Empedocles first formulated the idea that the world consists of the four elements of earth, water, air, and fire the notion still persisted. The idea is represented in this medieval painting.*

...s the first person ever to have expressed that thought. There is a tradition that the next philosopher we come to consider, Parmenides, was a pupil of Xenophanes. He flourished in the first half of the 5th century BC, and he provides us with our first link to Socrates. Plato has an account of Parmenides as an old man, Zeno (a disciple of Parmenides) as a middle-aged man, and the young Socrates, meeting for a philosophical discussion. Both Socrates and Plato were conscious of having learnt from Parmenides.

## ALL IS ONE

Parmenides considered it self-contradictory to say of nothing that it exists. There can never, he thought, have been nothing, and therefore it cannot be true to say that everything – or, indeed, anything – came out of nothing. Everything must always have existed. For a similar reason it is not possible for anything to pass into nothing. Therefore not only must everything be beginningless and uncreated, it must also be eternal and imperishable. For similar reasons, too, there cannot be any gaps in reality, parts of reality where nothing is: reality must be continuous with itself at all points; all of space must be full, a plenum. This gives rise to a view of the universe being really a single unchanging entity. All is One. What appears as change, or movement, is something that occurs within an enclosed and unchanging system.

Surprisingly, perhaps, this is strikingly like the scientific view of the universe that developed between Newton in the 17th century and Einstein in the twentieth. Two things about that view made

it reminiscent of Parmenides. First, it was deterministic, so everything was seen as being inescapably and necessarily as it is. Second, it was believed that only from the subjective standpoint of an observer could there be a "now": objectively speaking, all time-instants were equally significant. When two of the greatest minds of the 20th century found themselves having an argument about this, the name of Parmenides came up in the discussion. The two were Einstein and Popper, and in the account the latter gives of it in his autobiography *Unended Quest* he writes: "I tried to persuade him to give up his determinism, which amounted to the view that the world was a four-dimensional Parmenidian block universe in which change was a human illusion, or very nearly so. (He agreed that this had been his view, and while discussing it I called him 'Parmenides.')" Nothing could illustrate more vividly than this the fact that the ideas of Parmenides have been a living point of reference for thinkers down to our own day.

## THE FOUR ELEMENTS

The most colourful personality among the pre-Socratic philosophers was Empedocles, who lived for roughly the first half of the 5th century BC. He was a democratic political leader, no doubt a demagogue, who was credited with miraculous powers, and died by throwing himself into the crater of the volcano Mount Etna – which must be the most melodramatic, not to say operatic, death of any famous philosopher.

Empedocles tried to reassert the reality of the ever-changing world of sensory experience, and also the plurality of this world, as against Parmenides, while conceding some of Parmenides' insights. He admitted that matter cannot come into existence out of nothing, or pass away into nothing, but he held that everything was made up of four different elements that are perennial: earth, water, air, and fire. (The fire accounts for the heavenly fires of sun and stars.) This doctrine of the four elements

> *"Each man believes only his experience"*
> EMPEDOCLES

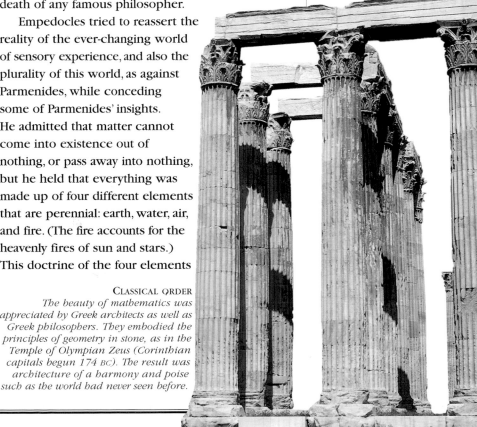

### CLASSICAL ORDER
*The beauty of mathematics was appreciated by Greek architects as well as Greek philosophers. They embodied the principles of geometry in stone, as in the Temple of Olympian Zeus (Corinthian capitals begun 174 BC). The result was architecture of a harmony and poise such as the world had never seen before.*

was taken up by Aristotle, and played an important role in Western thinking until the Renaissance. Indeed, it is still quite often alluded to in Western literature.

Among the most insightful of the pre-Socratic philosophers were those known as "the Atomists", by which term is meant chiefly two people, Leucippus and Democritus. Leucippus had the fundamental idea that everything is made up of atoms that are too small to be seen, or even sub-divided any further – the word "atom" comes from the Greek words meaning "cannot be cut". All that exists, he taught, are atoms and space; and all the different objects that there are consist simply of different collections of atoms in space.

The atoms themselves are uncreated and indestructible, and all change in the universe consists of atoms altering either their formations or their locations. The interpretation that he and Democritus put on change was essentially causal, and this is notable because they made no attempt to explain natural phenomena in terms of purposes. Democritus once said: "I would rather discover one cause than gain the Kingdom of Persia." Yet another basic doctrine they taught is that the universe is not a continuum, as Parmenides said it was, but consists of separate entities. Between them they seem to have originated atomic physics. Altogether these two thinkers made astonishing strides. We must not fall into the error of attributing to them developments of their ideas which came later; but when all is said and done there remains something profoundly original about their insights.

### PHILOSOPHY COMES TO ATHENS

Our consideration of the Greek philosophers before Socrates has been selective, and has by no means exhausted the catalogue of interesting and important figures. We have discussed only the most influential of them; but there remains, for example, Anaxagoras, who introduced philosophy to Athens itself, and Protagoras, who is still often quoted for his phrase: "Man is the measure of all things."

If we stand back and view them as a whole we find that before Protagoras they all had certain striking features in common. First, they were concerned primarily to understand the nature of the world around us rather than human nature – indeed, it is doubtful whether they even had such a concept as "human nature". Second, they uninhibitedly went in for bold theorizing on the largest possible scale. Inevitably, given that they

## " MAN IS THE MEASURE OF ALL THINGS "

PROTAGORAS

were the very first thinkers to do so, much of what they came up with may seem wild and woolly. But the impressive thing is how many good ideas they had, ideas destined to bear rich fruit in the subsequent development of the attempts we human beings have made over the centuries to understand the world in which we find ourselves.

**SOPHISTS**

*Professional teachers, Sophists began to appear in the period just before Socrates. They trained young men in the arts needed for public life, in particular public speaking. Because they taught their pupils how to make the best of any case, regardless of what their own private convictions might be, they drew opprobrium from the intellectually fastidious; the word "sophist" consequently acquired a derogatory connotation that it has kept to this day. The first and most famous of the Sophists was Protagoras.*

THE WISDOM OF CLASSICAL PHILOSOPHY

*Philosophers of classical antiquity were frequently portrayed in medieval and Renaissance art. They represented a secular ideal of wisdom and learning. Often their presence in an otherwise religious context was meant to indicate that faith was not hostile to reason, but harmonious with it.*

# ACHILLES *and* *the* TORTOISE

One of Parmenides' pupils was a clever young man called Zeno (known as Zeno of Elea to distinguish him from the founder of Stoicism, Zeno of Citium). This Zeno was brilliant at producing paradoxes, some of which have puzzled people ever since.

Among these is the story of Achilles and the tortoise. Achilles and the tortoise decide to have a race. Because Achilles can run twice as fast as the tortoise he gives her a long start. Now, says Zeno, by the time Achilles reaches the tortoise's starting point she will have moved ahead by half the distance of her lead. And by the time Achilles reaches that point she will have moved on by half of that distance. And so on, and so forth, *ad infinitum*. Achilles is never able to catch up with the tortoise, because, at each point, by the time he has covered the distance between them she will always have moved on further by half of that distance. So Achilles never overtakes the tortoise.

"Hang on!", you may cry: "But Achilles does overtake the tortoise. Of course he does. This is all nonsense." If you say that you will be

missing the point – and it is important to be clear what the point of this story is. It is not to convince you that Achilles never

## AN IMPECCABLY LOGICAL ARGUMENT THAT LEADS TO A FALSE CONCLUSION

## THE PARADIGM OF A PHILOSOPHICAL PUZZLE

actually overtakes the tortoise. He does, and you know perfectly well that he does, and so does Zeno. The point is that here is an impeccably logical argument that leads to a false conclusion. And what are we to say about that?

If it is possible for us to start from unobjectionable premises, and then proceed by logical steps, each of which is without fault, to a conclusion which is manifestly untrue, this threatens with chaos all our attempts to reason about the world around us. People have found it terribly disconcerting. There must be a fault in the logic, they have said. But no-one has yet been wholly successful in demonstrating what it is.

For this reason, one of the well-known philosophers of the 20th century, Gilbert Ryle, has written of the parable of Achilles and the tortoise: "In many ways it deserves to rank as the paradigm of a philosophical puzzle." Perhaps one day it will be solved, as someone has recently solved the problem of Fermat's Last Theorem.

# SOCRATES
## THE MASTERLY INTERROGATOR

*Socrates was in effect the founder of moral philosophy. He also established the method of trying to get at truth by persistent questioning.*

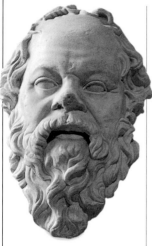

**CENTRE OF ATTRACTION**
Socrates was far from handsome. All the descriptions and images we have of him portray him as snub-nosed and pug-faced. But he possessed great irony and humour. He also had a powerful personal charisma. People who were themselves of the highest ability were attracted to him, and formed a brilliant circle with him at its centre.

SOCRATES WAS THE FIRST great Greek philosopher to be Athenian by birth, and he lived in what has been called that city's golden age. He was born around 470 BC and died in 399 BC, leaving behind him a wife and three children. As a young man, he studied the then-fashionable philosophies of what are now called the "pre-Socratic philosophers", which in their different ways were trying to understand the natural world around us. Two things above all impressed him about them, both of which he thought were to their disadvantage.

The first was that they were at odds with one another. They were a welter of conflicting theories. And there seemed to be no satisfactory way of deciding between them. They propounded exciting ideas about the world, but without much apparent regard for critical method; so it was impossible to tell which of them, if any, was true. But his second objection was that it would make little practical

***THE SCHOOL OF ATHENS***
*This magnificent fresco in the Vatican, painted by Raphael during the years 1508–11, portrays the most famous thinkers of ancient Greece. At the very centre, side by side, stand Plato and Aristotle, Plato on the left, Aristotle on the right. To the left of them Socrates is addressing a group of bystanders.*

difference, anyway, even if we could discover which of them were true. What effect did it have on our actual lives to know how far the sun was from the earth, or whether it was the size of the Peloponnese or bigger than the whole world? Our behaviour could in no way be affected by such knowledge. What we needed to know was how to conduct our lives and ourselves. For us, the urgent questions were more like: What is good? What is right? What is just? If we knew the answers to those questions it would have a profound effect on the way we lived.

Socrates did not think he knew the answers to these questions. But he saw that no-one else knew them either. When the oracle at Delphi declared him to be the wisest of men, he thought this could mean only that he alone knew that he did not know anything. There was no such thing at that time as securely based knowledge of the natural world, and not much knowledge about the world of human affairs either.

**THE OMPHALOS STONE**
Delphi was regarded as the centre of the world. The Greeks placed a huge stone there to be, as they put it, the world's navel – and then revered it as a holy object.

***THE TEMPLE AT DELPHI***
*The oracle at Delphi was generally regarded as the ultimate source of wisdom about the true nature of things.*

New portraits of Socrates continue to be made to this day. This picture of him walking through the streets of Athens dates from 1897.

This Socratic questioning became famous. And it killed two birds with one stone. It exposed the ignorance of people who thought they knew – but who in fact, as the Delphic oracle had told Socrates, knew no more than he did. And it aroused in the bystanders an interest in a fundamental philosophical question, and got them launched on a discussion of it. Although Socrates seldom came up with any final answers himself (and in any case it would have been part of his method to insist that any such answer should itself be probed and questioned, and therefore could not be relied on to be "final"), he stimulated an excited interest in the problems he raised, and made people appreciate more fully than they had before the difficulties involved in trying to solve them.

## WHAT LIES BEHIND THE WORDS?

When Socrates asked a question like "What is justice?" he was not asking for a mere verbal definition. The fact that we apply the word "just" to all sorts of different people, decisions, laws, and sets of arrangements meant, he believed, that there was something common to them, a common property called "justice" which they all shared; and it was the character of this common property that he was trying to uncover. In other words, he believed that something exists called "justice", and that its existence is real, although

So he went around Athens raising the basic questions of morality and politics with anyone who would listen to him. Such was the interest of the discussions he raised – and he was obviously a charismatic personality as well – that people gathered round him wherever he went, especially the eager young. His procedure was always the same. He would take some concept that was fundamental to our lives and ask, "What is friendship?", or "What is courage?", or "What is religious piety?" He would challenge a person who thought he knew the answer, and then subject that answer to examination by asking the person a series of searching questions about it. For instance, if the person claimed that courage was essentially the capacity to endure, Socrates might say, "But what about obstinacy, then? Obstinate people can show extraordinary persistence, and therefore endurance. Is that courage? Is it even admirable?" And so the other person would be driven to retract his answer, or at least qualify it. Under interrogation it always emerged that the original answer was defective. This showed that although that interlocutor – and what is more the bystanders – had thought they knew what, let us say, "courage" was, actually they did not.

**ANCIENT AND REVERED**
*By the time this mural painting of Socrates was made in a Roman villa during the 1st century AD, he had become a cultural hero in intellectual circles of the Roman Empire.*

*"If you will take my advice, you will think little of Socrates, and a great deal more of truth"*
SOCRATES

**CARELESS OF FAME**
*Socrates took no steps to ensure the survival of his own work or name. Socrates never, so far as we know, wrote anything down. All the knowledge we have of him comes from other people. The chief of these is his pupil Plato, who wrote an immortal series of dialogues with Socrates as the main speaker. In Plato's early dialogues, at least, we get the views of the historical Socrates. Later, Plato begins putting his own views into Socrates' mouth.*

**SOCRATES INTERROGATED**
In a scene from the play *The Clouds* (423 BC) by the comic dramatist Aristophanes (c. 448–380 BC), who satirized issues such as the new learning of Socrates, Socrates is shown suspended in a basket over peoples' heads. He is being questioned by Strepsiades, another character in the play.

not material, perhaps some sort of essence; and that he was trying to discover the nature of this abstract reality. This view of his was to be developed in the work of his disciple Plato into a belief in abstract Ideas as the perfect and permanent forms of all the entities and characteristics to be found in this imperfect and impermanent world of our daily lives.

# "WHAT IS JUSTICE?"

SOCRATES

The very nature of what Socrates did made him a disruptive and subversive influence. He was teaching people to question everything, and he was exposing the ignorance of individuals in power and authority. He became a highly controversial figure, much loved but also much hated. At one of the city's public festivals he was caricatured in the theatre in front of the whole population of Athens by the comic dramatist Aristophanes, in a play called *The Clouds* (423 BC). In the end, the authorities arrested him on charges of corrupting the young, and of not believing in the gods of the city. He was tried, and condemned to die by poison. The detailed story of his trial and death is one of the most inspiring tragedies in the history of human thought. What has made Socrates in some ways the best known of all philosophers is that it was he who began the relentless questioning of our basic concepts that has been characteristic of philosophy ever since. He used to say that he had no positive teachings to offer, only questions to ask. But this was disingenuous. From certain lines of questioning to

**ARISTOPHANES**
*The immortal comedian Aristophanes was the greatest comic playwright of ancient Greece. In one of his plays he caricatured Socrates on the stage. This indicates how well known to the public Socrates had become.*

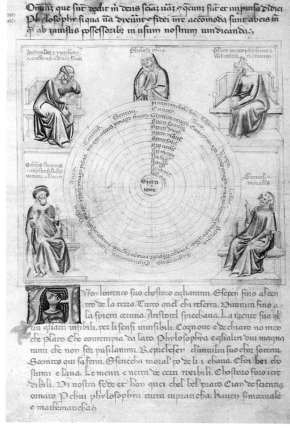

**FOUR GREAT PHILOSOPHERS**
*This medieval Italian manuscript shows the four philosophers most revered by the time of the Renaissance: Aristotle (top left), Plato (top right), Seneca (bottom right), and Socrates (bottom left).*

which he continually reverts, it becomes clear that there are certain cherished beliefs that underlie much of what he says.

One is that to a man who preserves his integrity no real, long-term harm can ever come. The uncertainties of this world are such that it can happen to anybody that he is stripped of all his possessions and thrown into prison unjustly, or crippled by accident or disease; but these are chance happenings in a fleeting existence that is going to end soon anyway. Provided your soul remains untouched, your misfortunes will be comparatively trivial. Real personal catastrophe consists in corruption of the soul. That is why it does a person far, far less harm to suffer injustice than to commit it. We should pity the perpetrator of injustice, not the victim of injustice.

This belief of Socrates made him a hero to the Stoics, who hundreds of years later turned him into a sort of secular patron saint. Another basic belief of Socrates was that no-one really knowingly does wrong. His point here was that if you really do in the fullest sense understand that it is wrong to do something, then you do not do it. Conversely, if you do do it, this shows that you have not properly grasped, deep down, that it is wrong. This view has the consequence that virtue becomes a matter of knowledge. This conviction on Socrates' part provided a great deal of the drive behind his tireless pursuit of questions like "What is justice?": he believed that if only we knew the answer to that question we would be bound to behave justly. In such cases, the pursuit of knowledge and an aspiration to virtue are one and the same thing.

## BE TRUE TO YOURSELF

It is doubtful whether any philosopher has had more influence than Socrates. He was the first to teach the priority of personal integrity in terms of a person's duty to himself, and not to the gods, or the law, or any other authorities. This has had incalculable influence down the ages. Not only was he willing to die at the hands of the law rather than give up saying what he believed to be right, he actually chose to do so, when he could have escaped had he wished. It is a priority that has been reasserted by some of the greatest minds since – minds not necessarily under his influence. Jesus said: "What will a man gain by winning the whole world, at the cost of his true self?" And Shakespeare said: "This above all: to thine own self be true."

In addition to this, Socrates did more than any other individual to establish the principle that everything must be open to question – there can be no cut and dried answers, because answers, like everything else, are themselves open to question. Following on from this, he established at the centre of philosophy a method known as dialectic, the method of seeking truth by a process of question and answer. It has remained there ever since, and is used particularly as a teaching method – which is after all what Socrates himself used it for. It is not equally appropriate for all forms of teaching – it is not, for example, a good way of imparting pure information – but as a way of getting people to re-examine what they think they already know, it is incomparable. To be most effective it calls for a sympathetic personal relationship between teacher and pupil, one in which the teacher truly understands the pupil's difficulties and prompts him step by step in the right direction. This is often still called "Socratic method".

USING THE NAME
*Socrates has given his name to the archetypal notion of a wise and dominant figure outside the realm of politics. If we say of a person "He is the Socrates of present-day Paris" everyone knows what we are meaning. We do not use the name of any other philosopher like this.*

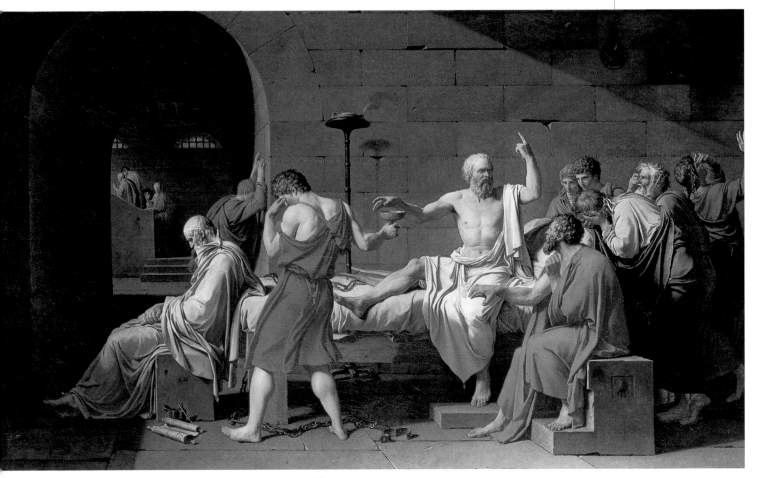

*THE DEATH OF SOCRATES*

*This famous painting by the French artist David, completed in 1787, shows Socrates about to drink the hemlock that killed him. (In ancient Athens prisoners condemned to death were required to take poison themselves or be killed.) He points to the higher realm which he considers his final destination.*

# PLATO
## BRIDGING THE HUMAN AND ABSTRACT WORLDS

*There is a well-known saying that the whole of Western philosophy is footnotes to Plato. This is because his writings have set an agenda which philosophy as a whole – and not only moral philosophy – can be said roughly to have followed ever since.*

**A WRITER BUT NOT A RULER**
Plato was a genius in more ways than one. His dialogues, in the finest Greek prose ever written, were works of art as well as works of philosophy. When he tried to influence practical politics, however, he was not successful.

**KEY WORKS**
*The* Republic *for an overview of Plato's whole philosophy.*
*The* Symposium *for his views on love.*
*The* Apology, *the* Phaedo *and the* Crito *for his portrait of Socrates.*

NONE OF THE PHILOSOPHERS we have considered up to now left written works which have survived. So everything we know about them comes from references and quotations in the writings of other and later thinkers, who knew them or their works, works that have since been lost. Some of the references and quotations are extensive but nevertheless they are incomplete, and second-hand. Socrates wrote nothing at all, and so it is only through the writings of others that we know anything at all about him. Yet we have a vivid sense of his character.

Our chief source here is Plato, who was one of his pupils. Plato was the first Western philosopher who wrote works that survive intact. What is more, we have reason to believe that we possess pretty well his entire output. As with his teacher Socrates, there are many people who regard him as the greatest philosopher of all time.

### SOCRATES' PLATO AND PLATO'S SOCRATES
Plato was about 31 when Socrates was executed in 399 BC. He was in the courtroom throughout the trial. That whole sequence of events seems to have come as a traumatic experience to him, for he regarded Socrates as the best and wisest and most just of all human beings. After the death of Socrates, Plato started to circulate a series of philosophical dialogues in which the protagonist is always Socrates, quizzing his interlocutors about the basic concepts of morals and politics, tripping people up with his questions. Plato seems to have had two main motives for doing this. One was defiant, to reassert the teachings of Socrates in spite of their having been officially condemned; the other was to rehabilitate his beloved mentor's reputation, showing him to have been not a corrupter of young men but their most valued teacher.

It is generally agreed among scholars that the chief source of the ideas in Plato's dialogues changed as the years went by. The early dialogues contain a more or less accurate portrait of the historical Socrates, if we allow for the usual artistic or journalistic licence. The subjects raised were the subjects raised by the real Socrates, and things that Plato had heard him say were put into his mouth. But by the time Plato had come to the end of this material he found he had created an enthusiastic reading public that was eager for more. So, having plenty more to say, he went on writing and publishing dialogues, in what was by now a

## "LET NO-ONE ENTER HERE WHO IS IGNORANT OF MATHEMATICS"
PLATO

popular and accepted form that features Socrates as the protagonist; but now he was putting his own ideas into that figure's mouth. Inevitably, this creates a problem for scholars about where the real Socrates ends and Plato begins. Perhaps this can never be satisfactorily solved. But there is little room for doubt that the earlier and later dialogues of Plato present us with the philosophies of two different philosophers, the earlier being Socrates and the later being Plato.

The earlier is solely concerned with the problems of moral and political philosophy, and is dismissive of philosophical problems about the natural world. One of this earlier philosopher's

THE SCHOOL OF PLATO

*Ancient Greece was the first society in which students were taught to think for themselves – to discuss, debate, argue, and criticize – and not just to parrot the views of their teacher. It led to the most rapid expansion of understanding there had ever been, and to the idea that knowledge can actually grow through criticism.*

most committed beliefs is in the identification of virtue with knowledge; and he pursues knowledge entirely through discussion and argument.

None of these things is true of the later philosopher. This one, Plato, is passionately interested in philosophy right across the board, every bit as much applied to the natural world as to how we should conduct our personal lives. No aspect of reality fails to arouse his interest. Far from being unconcerned with mathematics or physics, he regards these as the keys to understanding the natural world. Over the door of his academy he inscribed the words: "Let no-one enter here who is ignorant of mathematics." Many of his most important

> "*The wise Plato
> saith, as ye
> may read
> The word
> must needs
> accorde with
> the deed*"
>
> GEOFFREY CHAUCER

### CRADLE OF WESTERN CULTURE

*Plato knew Athens in
its golden age in the
5th and 4th centuries
BC, when this one city
was producing not
only great philosophy
but great physics,
mathematics,
astronomy,
history – and also
great sculpture,
architecture, and
drama. In addition
to all this it was the
first democracy.*

doctrines are expounded in long explanations that
are not discussions or dialogues in any real sense
but only in a purely token form, with a cardboard
character chiming in every now and again with a
"Yes indeed" or "That has to be admitted." And he
rejects the doctrine that virtue is solely a matter
of knowing what is right.

Where Plato never parts company with Socrates
is in his commitment to the view that the only real
harm that can come to a person is harm to the soul,
and therefore that it is better to suffer wrong than
to commit it; and also in his commitment to
thinking for oneself, taking nothing for granted,
being ready to question everything and everybody.
It was this latter belief that carried him forward
over the years from expounding the ideas of
Socrates to expounding his own ideas. After all,
to think in Socrates' way, the way Socrates taught
other people to think, is to think for oneself

independently of any authority; so for Plato this
meant thinking for himself, independently of Socrates.
By departing from Socrates he followed Socrates.

### THE FIRST PROFESSOR

Plato lived for half a century after the death of
Socrates, dying at the age of 81. During this time
he published some two dozen dialogues which
vary in length from 20 to 300 pages of modern
print. The most famous of all of them are the
*Republic*, which is chiefly concerned with the
nature of justice, and which attempts, among other
things, to set out a blueprint for the ideal state, and
the *Symposium*, which is an investigation into the
nature of love. Most of the rest are named after
whoever appears in them as the chief interlocutor
of Socrates. Thus we have the *Phaedo*, the *Laches*,
the *Euthyphro*, the *Theaetetus*, the *Parmemides*,
the *Timaeus*, and so on.

These dialogues are among the world's great
literature. In addition to containing some of the
best philosophy ever produced they are beautifully
written – many language scholars think they
contain the finest of all Greek prose. Perhaps the
most moving of all, and therefore the best to read
first, are those most directly to do with the trial
and death of Socrates: the *Crito*, the *Apology*, and
the *Phaedo*. The *Apology* purports to be the
speech made by Socrates in his own defence at
his trial, and is his *apologia pro vita sua*, his
justification for his life.

A SCENE FROM THE *SYMPOSIUM*
*Alcibiades the statesman arrives at the house of Agathon the
poet for an evening of conversation that will last for ever.*

Plato is to be considered as an artist as well as a philosopher. Also, it was he who established the prototype of the college. "Academy" was simply the name of his house, and because he taught grown-up pupils there the word came to be used for any building in which young people of mature years receive a higher education.

## IDEAL EXISTENCE

The doctrine for which Plato is best known is his theory of Forms or Ideas, by which for these purposes he meant the same thing. (In this context, the words Form and Idea are usually spelt with a capital letter to make it clear that they are being used in Plato's sense.)

Reference has been made to the fact that when Socrates asked "What is beauty?" or "What is courage?" he regarded himself not as trying to pin down the definition of a word, but as trying to discover the nature of some abstract entity that actually existed. He regarded these entities not as being in some place, or at any particular time, but as having some kind of universal existence that was independent of place and time. The individual beautiful objects that exist in our everyday world, and the particular courageous actions that individual people perform, are always fleeting, but they partake of the timeless essence of true beauty or true courage; and these are indestructible ideals with an existence of their own.

Plato took up this implied theory about the nature of morals and values and generalized it across the whole of reality. Everything, without exception, in this world of ours he regarded as being an ephemeral, decaying copy of something whose ideal form (hence the terms Ideal and Form) has a permanent and indestructible existence outside space and time.

Plato supported this conclusion with arguments from different sources. For example, it seemed to him that the more we pursue our studies in physics, the clearer it becomes that mathematical relationships are built into everything in the material world. The whole cosmos seems to exemplify order, harmony, proportion – or, as we would now put it, the whole of physics can be expressed in terms of mathematical equations. Plato, following Pythagoras, took this as revealing

THE CLARKE PLATO
Before the invention of printing, the only way writings could be circulated was through being re-copied by hand. Thus a work's being known and studied, perhaps even its very survival, depended on copying, as in the case of the Clarke Plato (895 AD). Throughout the Middle Ages this was one of the chief occupations of scholars and churchmen. So it is through the medieval church that a great deal of pre-Christian culture has been transmitted to the modern world.

### RATIONAL ORDER IN ALL, FROM MATHEMATICS TO LAW

*Plato continues to crop up in images from his time to our own. This 16th-century fresco in a Romanian monastery shows him in the company of the mathematician Pythagoras and Solon, the great Athenian reformer and legislator.*

**AN AUSTERE REGIME**

*Sparta, the ancient Greek city state that dominated the southern Peloponnese, was flourishing as a rival to Athens when Plato was in the prime of life – but he lived to see its downfall. Its social structure was essentially a military one, and by contrast with cultured, democratic Athens its way of life was disciplined and austere. The word "Spartan" remains in use to this day as a byword for a harsh regime.*

## THE REPUBLIC

*Plato's* Republic *begins as an enquiry into the nature of justice, but broadens out into a consideration of human nature as a whole, including the nature of man's social life, until by the end it has addressed most of the main questions of philosophy. It also contains the first known blueprint for an ideal society. For all these reasons it has now come to be thought of as Plato's masterpiece, the dialogue providing the best overview of his mature philosophy.*

**THE GREEK IDEAL**
The Greek genius for combining order with emotion found expression in their way of life, from their politics to their art. Even their vases show an ideal blend of form and feeling. This balance has been regarded as an ideal ever since, and is known as "the Greek ideal", but no subsequent society has succeeded in achieving it.

that, underlying the messy, not to say chaotic surface of our everyday world, there is an order that has all the ideality and perfection of mathematics. This order is not perceptible to the eye, but it is accessible to the mind, and intelligible to the intellect. Most important of all it is there, it exists, it is what constitutes underlying reality. In pursuit of this particular research programme he drew into the Academy some of the leading mathematicians of his day, and under his patronage great strides were made in the development of various aspects of mathematics and what we now think of as the sciences. All were then part of "philosophy".

## PLATO AND CHRISTIANITY

This approach, developed by Plato with great richness across a wide area of subject matter, resulted in a view of total reality as being divided into two realms. There is the visible world, the world as it is presented to our senses, our ordinary everyday world, in which nothing lasts and nothing stays the same – as Plato liked to put it, everything in this world is always becoming something else, but nothing ever just permanently is. (This formulation became shortened to "everything is becoming, nothing is.") Everything comes into existence and passes away, everything is imperfect, everything decays. This world in space and time is the only world that our human sensory apparatus can apprehend. But then there is another realm which is not in space or time, and not accessible to our senses, and in which there is permanence and perfect order. This other world is the timeless and unchanging reality of which

## "EVERYTHING IS BECOMING, NOTHING IS"

PLATO

our everyday world offers us only brief and unsatisfactory glimpses. But it is what one might call real reality, because it alone is stable, unshakeable – it alone just is, and is not always in the process of sliding into something else.

The implications of the existence of these two realms are the same for us human beings considered as objects as they are for everything else. There is a part of us that can be seen, while underlying

**IDEALS THAT LAST**
*The* Venus de Milo *(c. 200 BC) is perhaps the most famous statue in the world. It shows the Greek goddess Aphrodite as the ancient Greeks' ideal of feminine beauty.*

this is a part that cannot be seen but of which our minds are capable of achieving awareness. The part that can be seen consists of our bodies, material objects that exemplify the laws of physics and inhabit the realm of space and time. These physical bodies of ours come into existence and pass away, are always imperfect, are never the same for two moments together, and are at all times highly perishable. But they are the merest and most fleeting glimpses of something that is also us and is non-material, timeless, and indestructible, something that we may refer to as the soul. These souls are our permanent Forms. The order of being that they inhabit is the timeless, spaceless one in which exist all the unchanging Forms that constitute ultimate reality.

Readers who have been brought up in a Christian tradition will at once recognize this view as familiar. That is because the school of philosophy that was dominant in the Hellenistic world in which Christianity came on to the scene and proceeded to develop was the tradition of Platonism. The New Testament was, of course, written in Greek; and many of the deeper thinkers among the early Christians were profoundly concerned to reconcile the revelations of their religion with Plato's main doctrines. What happened was that the most important of these doctrines became absorbed into orthodox Christian thinking. There was a time when it was quite common for people to refer to Socrates and Plato as "Christians before Christ". Many Christians seriously believed that the historic mission of those Greek thinkers had been to prepare the theoretical foundations for some important aspects of Christianity. The detailed working out of these connections was something that preoccupied many scholars during the Middle Ages.

Plato, to state the obvious, was neither Christian nor Jew, and arrived at his conclusions in complete independence of the Judaeo-Christian tradition. In fact, he arrived at them by philosophical argument.

They do not call for any belief in a God, or in religious revelation, and during the period since him they have been accepted in whole or in part by many who were not religious. Plato himself did in fact come to regard the Ideal Forms as divine, because perfect; and he also came to believe, as Pythagoras had done, in reincarnation; but the bulk of his philosophical influence has been on thinkers who declined to go along with him in either of those respects, some completely irreligious.

## PLATO'S HOSTILITY TO THE ARTS

Plato believed that for an intelligent person the ultimate aim in life should be to pierce the surface of things and penetrate to the level of underlying reality. This may in turn be understood as a kind of intellectual mysticism, for it means acquiring an intellectual grasp of that world of Ideas in which the soul exists already, and will go on existing for all eternity. In this sense it is rather like rehearsing for being dead – which is exactly what Socrates is quoted in the *Phaedo* as saying the philosopher does.

To achieve this, clearly, the individual needs to see through (in both senses) the decaying ephemera that constitute the world of the senses, to free himself from their attractions and seductions. It is this requirement that leads Plato to be hostile to the arts. He views the arts as being of their nature representational, and as making a powerful appeal to the senses – and of course the more beautiful the art the more powerful this appeal is bound to be. Works of art are, in his view, doubly deceptive, for they are illusory semblances of things that are illusory semblances. They glamorize the fleeting things of this world, and they enrich our emotional attachment to them, thereby holding us back from our true calling, which is to soar above their level altogether to the timeless and non-sensory reality beyond. So they are a danger to our souls. In an ideal society they would not be allowed. This doctrine of Plato's has since helped to give confidence to people wishing to ban or control the arts.

**DANCE BEFORE THE GOD DIONYSOS**
The Greek world in which Plato was philosophizing was one in which religious rituals were widespread. For a prominent person to deny the existence of certain pagan gods was for him to put his life in danger. This makes it difficult to be sure to what extent, if at all, Plato really believed in them.

**IMAGINARY LIKENESS**
*Manuscripts, before the age of printing, were often illuminated with illustrations. These are one of our chief sources of portraits of the philosophers of antiquity, as in the picture of Plato (top left) above. But usually there was nothing on which to base a likeness of the original.*

**GREEK TRAGEDY**
*Greek tragedy dealt with some of the deepest of all human concerns, and was therefore of interest to many philosophers. The three outstanding tragedians were Aeschylus, Sophocles, and Euripedes, all of whom are still performed. One of the perennial themes was the conflict between the individual's private desires or relationships and his duty to society as a whole: an individual who comes into head-on conflict with society almost always ends by being destroyed.*

*"If a man seeks from the good life anything beyond itself, it is not the good life that he is seeking"*

PLOTINUS

PLATO AND CHRISTIANITY

*Plato had more influence on the development of early Christian thought than any other non-Christian. Greek was still the language of international culture and scholarship in the world into which Jesus was born; and the best-known philosophy in that world was Plato's. The New Testament was written in Greek.*

Plato sees the human individual as made up of three conflicting elements: passion, intellect, and will. And he deems it essential for the intellect to be in control, governing passions through the will. From this appraisal of persons, he extrapolates a corresponding view of society as a whole. In his ideal society, an intermediate police class, which he calls the auxiliaries, would keep the masses in order under the direction of a philosophically aware governing class, who would act as the guardians of society as a whole. Put like this, it sounds not unlike a description of the communist societies of the 20th century; and it was indeed to be the case that Plato's political ideas had an immense influence down the centuries, and not least on the utopian totalitarian philosophies of Left and Right that characterized the 20th century.

## DISCIPLES OF GENIUS

The writings of Plato, plus those of philosophers who developed under his influence, were to dominate philosophy in Europe for six or seven hundred years – until, that is, the rise of Christian thought to a position of comparable and then greater pre-eminence.

The most gifted of Plato's successors was one of the most immediate, his pupil Aristotle, whose work is of such importance that it will receive extended consideration in its own right. Aristotle founded a tradition in philosophy that was different from Plato's, and often at odds with it – yet, even so, he several times says "we" to describe the disciples of Plato. Apart from Aristotle, the outstanding philosopher to emerge directly

from under the influence of Plato's teaching came hundreds of years later, towards the end of its period of dominance, in the 3rd century AD. He was Plotinus, who was born in 204 AD and died in 269 AD.

Plotinus, though an Egyptian (with a Roman name), wrote in Greek, and can be thought of as the last of the great Greek philosophers, the end of a line of succession that had begun with Thales in the 6th century BC, and indeed the last great philosopher of antiquity altogether. His thought developed the mystical strain in Plato's and came to be known as Neo-Platonism. He was not a Christian and he never mentioned Christianity in his writings, yet his philosophy stands recognizably close to those of the two greatest Christian philosophers of the next thousand years, St Augustine and St Thomas Aquinas. His influence on the development of Christian thought was enormous. The famous 20th-century Christian writer Dean Inge refers to him as "the great thinker who must be, for all time, the classical representative of mystical philosophy. No other mystical thinker even approaches Plotinus in power and insight and profound spiritual penetration."

## THE PHILOSOPHER-MYSTIC

Plotinus' work, more than that of anyone before him except for Plato himself, made Platonic philosophy central to the intellectual development of Christianity. Plotinus taught that since ultimate reality consists of Plato's Ideal Forms, what exists is ultimately mental, and therefore for something to be created is for it to be thought. There are, he believed, three ascending levels of being.

The lowest, on which human beings are, is soul. The next level up, on which the Ideal Forms are apprehended, is intellect. The highest level is the good. Reflective human beings are engaged in an attempted ascent towards one-ness with the good. Christians translated this into their doctrines that the world has been created in the mind of God, and that human beings are aspiring to one-ness with God, who is perfect goodness.

**APPROVED PAGAN PHILOSOPHER**
*Though not a Christian, Plotinus' ideas found sufficient approval for his sarcophagus to be housed in one of the Vatican's museums.*

# *The* MYTH *of* *the* CAVE

The most famous passage in all Plato's writings occurs in the *Republic*, and is known as the Myth of the Cave. In it Plato puts into symbolic form his view of the human condition, and especially of human knowledge, in relation to reality as a whole.

Imagine, he says, a big cave, connected to the outside world by a passage long enough to prevent any daylight from penetrating into the cave itself. Facing the far wall, with their backs to the entrance, is a row of prisoners. Not only are their limbs chained, they are also fastened by the neck so that they cannot move their heads, and therefore cannot see one another, indeed cannot see any part of themselves. All they can see is the wall in front of them. And they have been in this situation all their lives, and know nothing else.

In the cave behind them is a bright fire. Unknown to them there is a rampart as high as a man between the fire and them; and on the other side of this rampart are people perpetually passing to and fro carrying things on their heads. The shadows of these objects are cast on to the wall in front of the prisoners by the light of the fire, and the voices of the people carrying them are echoed back from this wall to the prisoners' ears. Now, says Plato, the only

entities that the prisoners ever perceive or experience in the whole of their existence are those shadows and those echoes. In these circumstances it would be natural

for them to assume that shadows and echoes constitute all the reality there is; and it would be to this "reality", and to their experiences of it, that all their talk would refer.

# ALL THEY CAN SEE IS THE WALL IN FRONT OF THEM

If one of the prisoners could shake off his chains, so cramped would he be by a lifetime of entrapment in the half-dark, that merely to turn around would be painful and awkward for him, and the fire would dazzle his eyes. He would find himself confused and uncomprehending, and would want to turn back again to face the wall of shadows, the reality he understood. If he were dragged up out of the cave altogether into the world of blazing sunlight he would be blinded and bewildered, and it would be a long time before he was able to see or understand anything. But then, once he was used to being in the upper world, if he were to return to the cave he would be temporarily blinded again, this time by the darkness. And everything he said to the prisoners about his experiences would be unintelligible to those people whose language had reference only to shadows and echoes.

The way to begin understanding this allegory is to see us human beings as imprisoned in our own bodies, with only other such prisoners for company, and all of us unable to discern the real selves of one another, or even our own real selves. Our direct experience is not of reality, but what is in our minds.

# ARISTOTLE

## THE MAN WHO MAPPED OUT SCIENCES AND FORMULATED LOGIC

*Aristotle was the founder of an approach to philosophy
that starts from observation and experience,
prior to abstract thinking.*

**GENIUS UNDIMMED**
Aristotle is regarded by
virtually all serious
students of philosophy as
one of the three or four
greatest giants of the
subject. Today his
*Metaphysics* and his
*Ethics,* in particular, are
studied in universities
all over the world.

*"Plato is dear
to me, but
dearer still
is truth"*
ARISTOTLE

JUST AS PLATO HAD been a pupil of Socrates, so
Aristotle was a pupil of Plato. And Aristotle himself
became tutor to Alexander the Great, so there is a
direct line of intellectual succession here through
four generations of tremendous historical figures.

Aristotle's father was court physician to the king
of Macedon, which is how he later came to be tutor
to Alexander, son of Philip of Macedon. Aristotle
himself was born in the city of Stagira in 384 BC.
His father died when he was still a boy, so he was
brought up by a guardian, who sent him to Athens
when he was about 17 to be educated at Plato's
Academy. Aristotle stayed at the Academy for
something like 20 years. Later in life, in about 335 BC,
he founded a school of his own in Athens called the
Lyceum: its archaeological site was recently
discovered, to great international excitement, in
1996. He died in the year 322 BC at the age of 62.

### PHILOSOPHER OF THIS WORLD
Aristotle fully acknowledged Plato's
genius, and his own indebtedness
to him, but rejected something
fundamental to Plato's philosophy,
namely the idea that there are two
worlds. As we have seen, Plato
taught that there can be no such
thing as reliable knowledge of this
ever-changing world that is
presented to our senses. The objects
of true knowledge inhabit, he said,
another world, an abstract realm
independent of time and space,
accessible only to the intellect.
As far as Aristotle was concerned,
there is only one world that we can
do any philosophizing about, and that
is this world we live in and
experience. To him this is a world of
inexhaustible fascination and wonder.
Indeed, he believed that it was this

sense of wonder that caused human beings to
philosophize in the first place, whether as
individuals or as a species; that *this* is the world
they want to get to know and understand.

Furthermore, Aristotle did not believe that
we could find any firm ground outside this world
on which to stand, and from which to pursue

## "WHAT IS BEING?"
ARISTOTLE

philosophical enquiries. Whatever is outside all
possibility of experience for us can be nothing
for us. We have no validatable way of referring to
it, or talking about it, and therefore it cannot enter
into our discourse in any reliable way: if we stray
beyond the ground covered by experience we
wander into empty talk. From this standpoint
Aristotle was dismissive of Plato's Ideal Forms:
he simply did not believe that we have any good
reasons to believe that they exist, and what is
more he did not believe that they do exist.

Aristotle's desire to know about the world of
experience was like an unslakable lust. Throughou
his life he poured himself into research with
gargantuan passion and energy across an almost
incredibly wide range. He mapped out for the first

**ARISTOTLE AND ALEXANDER**
*Aristotle the philosopher tutoring his gifted
young pupil Alexander the Great, who went
on to conquer the whole of the known world.*

PLATO AND ARISTOTLE – PHILOSOPHY'S TWO WORLE
*Plato on the left, holds the* Timaeus, *a work of abstra
metaphysics, and points to higher things. Aristotle clutch
his* Ethics, *and says by his gesture that we should keep ou
feet on the ground. These two opposing tendencies i
philosophy have been in conflict throughout its histor*

**DANTE, PUPIL OF GENIUS**
*Dante was the pre-eminent poet of the late Middle Ages. He regarded Aristotle as the ultimate authority on matters which Christian doctrine did not address.*

these different forms of inference names. For two thousand years the study of logic was to mean the study of Aristotle's logic.

Before this sort of intellectual accomplishment one can only stand in awe. The human race was not to produce a thinker of Aristotle's calibre for another two thousand years. Indeed, it is doubtful whether any human being has ever known as much as he did.

# "THE TEACHER OF THOSE WHO KNOW"

DANTE ON ARISTOTLE

During the Dark Ages, following the fall of the Roman Empire, knowledge of his work died out in Europe, but was kept alive in the Arab world. From there it made its way back into Europe during the late Middle Ages, and became the biggest single body of scientific, or quasi-scientific, knowledge that Europeans possessed. Inevitably, those parts of it that were to develop as separate sciences eventually outgrew not only Aristotle's own research but also his conceptions and his methods. Nevertheless, in the 14th century we find the Italian poet Dante (1265–1321) referring to Aristotle as "the teacher of those who know". His biology was important until the 19th century, and so was his logic. His general philosophy, including his political and moral theory and also his aesthetics, remain influential to this day.

## THE NATURE OF BEING

The key question from which Aristotle started out was: What *are* the objects in this world? What is it for something to exist? In his own words, "The question that was asked long ago, is asked now, and is always a matter of difficulty [is] What is being?"

His first important conclusion was that things are not just the matter of which they materially consist. He uses the example of a house. If you commissioned a builder to build a house on your

---

**METAPHYSICS**
*The word "metaphysics" comes from the Greek words meaning "after physics", and was simply the name of that book in Aristotle's collected works which came after the book about physics. It denotes the study of the most underlying features of reality – time, space, material substance, and so on.*

time many of the basic fields of enquiry, and his own work on them provided the names for them that are used to this day: among these are logic, physics, political science, economics, psychology, metaphysics, meteorology, rhetoric, and ethics. This is an almost unbelievable achievement for one individual. He also invented technical terms in those fields that have been used ever since, the words in other languages being derived either from his Greek terms or from their subsequently Latinized equivalents. Such terms include energy, dynamic, induction, demonstration, substance, attribute, essence, property, accident, category, topic, proposition, and universal. On top of all this he systematized logic, working out which forms of inference were valid and which invalid – in other words, what really does follow from what, and what only appears to but doesn't really; and he gave all

nd, and his trucks
nloaded on to the site the
ricks, the tiles, the wood
nd so on, and he said to
ou: "Here you are, here's
our house", you would
hink it must be a joke, and
bad one. There would be
ll the constituent materials
f a house, but it would
ot be a house at all – just
higgledy-piggledy heap of
ricks and so on. To be a
ouse, everything would
eed to be put together in
ertain ways, with a very specific and detailed
tructure, and it would be by virtue of that
*tructure* that it was a house. Indeed, the house
vould not need to be made of those sorts of
naterials at all, it could be made entirely of other
hings – concrete, glass, metal, plastics. It does of
ourse (and this retains a certain importance)
ave to be made of *some* material, but it is not the
naterials that make it a house, it is the structure
nd the form. Aristotle's most striking example
f this is human beings. Take Socrates, he says.
he matter of which his body
onsists is changing
very day, and

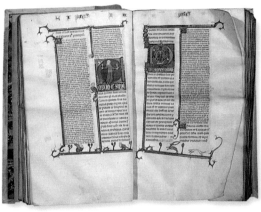

ARISTOTLE'S *PHYSICS*
*It is from the title of this work by Aristotle that
the subject of physics gets its name.*

it changes in its entirety
every few years; yet
throughout his life he goes
on being the same Socrates.
Therefore it cannot possibly
be contended that Socrates
is the matter of which his
body consists. Aristotle
extends this argument to
whole species. We do not
call all the different kinds
of dogs dogs because they
are made of some distinctive
material. They are dogs by
virtue of a distinctive
organization and structure which they share, and
which differentiate them from other animals that
are likewise made of flesh, blood, and bone.

These arguments of Aristotle's against the kind
of crude materialism which asserts that only matter
exists are devastating, and have never been properly
answered. Yet from his day to ours there have
continued to be some people who are crude
materialists. However, until they can answer
Aristotle's objections their position would seem
to call for little further consideration. Aristotle,
then, has established that a thing is
whatever it is by virtue of
its form. This brings

OUT OF FAVOUR
A reaction against
Aristotle's world view
came eventually in the
16th and 17th centuries.
Here, in a book of 1616
about different types
of human character,
Aristotelian man is
compared to an ass.

*"Men are
good in
one way,
but bad
in many"*
ARISTOTLE

LOOKING CLOSELY AT THE FACTS
*mong Aristotle's most valuable contributions were those to*
*iology and physiology. As always, he tried to base his theories*
*on careful observation of the facts. This 4th-century fresco*
*is thought to show him leading pupils in an anatomy class.*

KEY WORKS
Nicomachean Ethics
Politics
Poetics
Rhetoric
Posterior Analytics
Physics
Metaphysics
On the Soul

him straight up against his next problem: What exactly is *form* in this sense? We have established that it is not material, so what is it? Aristotle has already rejected Plato's theory of Forms, so he has ruled out the possibility that form is some sort of other-worldly entity existing outside space and time. To satisfy him it has got to be this-worldly.

### THE FOUR BECAUSES

We have seen that, according to Aristotle, form is that which causes something to be the thing it is. This leads him to examine the notion of "cause" in this context; and he ends by breaking the concept of "form" down into four different and

*RHETORIC*
In this book Aristotle analyses and teaches the art of persuasion – not only how to construct a speech but also how to make a personal impression on the audience, the tricks of the orator's trade.

*"The weak are always anxious for justice and equality. The strong pay no heed to either "*
ARISTOTLE

### WISE WORDS
*In 1545 Roger Ascham (1515–68), the English scholar and humanist, made the following observation: "He that will write well in any tongue must follow this counsel of Aristotle, to speak as the common people do, to think as wise men do; and so should every man understand him."*

FORM AND INTENTION
*In Michelangelo's unfinished sculpture,* The Awakening Slave *(c. 1525–30), a human figure emerges from obscurity. The artist's intention, his concept, and his carving are just as indispensable to the statue as his marble.*

complementary kinds of "cause". Since what he then calls "the four causes" constitute the reasons why a thing is as it is, it can be helpful to think of them as the four "*be*-causes", in short the four becauses. Form is the *explanation* of things.

Let us take his example of a marble statue. For this to be the thing it is there needs first of all to be the marble. This would be called by Aristotle the material cause, the *what-is-it-made-of?* cause. We have already learnt from Aristotle that this is not enough in itself to make the statue, which requires no fewer than three other causes, yet nevertheless the material is necessary, even though not sufficient. For the statue to come into being it needs to have been hewn out of a block of marble by a hammer and chisel: this hewing is what Aristotle calls the efficient cause, the *what-actually-does-or-makes-it?* cause. But again, to be the thing that it is, the statue needs to take the shape that it

## "ALL MEN BY NATURE DESIRE TO KNOW"
ARISTOTLE

does, that of a horse or a man or whatsoever – a block of marble hacked at random is not a statue. Aristotle calls this shape the formal cause, the *what-gives-it-the-shape-by-which-it-is-identified?* cause. Then, finally, all of this only happens at all because a sculptor has set out to make a statue in the first place. All three of the other causes have been called into operation in order to realize an intention: the overall reason for the statue's existence is that it is the fulfilment of a sculptor's purposes. Aristotle calls this the final cause, the *ultimate-reason-for-it-all* cause.

Aristotle's four causes, then, are as follows: material cause, efficient cause, formal cause, and final cause. Of the second, third, and fourth of these, any two or more may be the same in an individual case. This is particularly germane in the life sciences: the formal cause of the oak tree that has grown out of the acorn is also its final cause:

### THE FATHER OF LOGIC

*Aristotle's logic remained at the centre of a Christian higher education throughout the Middle Ages, and well beyond.*

*This painting of 1502 in the Cathedral of Le Puy, depicts Aristotle's Logic, Cicero's Rhetoric, and Tubal's Music.*

the ultimate shape achieved is also the ultimate point of the process. (In this case the material cause would be the wood, bark, and leaves of which the tree consists, and the efficient cause would be the indispensable nourishment of it by earth, water, air, and the light from the sun's fire.)

Through this analysis we begin to understand the nature of Aristotle's conception of form, as against Plato's. According to Aristotle an object's form, though not something material, is inherent in the this-worldly object, and can no more exist separately from it than a man's build can exist separately from his body. Something of utmost significance that this illustrates is that in our understanding of the world we are not compelled to choose between a materialist analysis and an other-worldly analysis: it is possible to develop an understanding of the world that gives full rein to non-materialist considerations while remaining this-worldly. Aristotle always saw the true essence of any object as consisting not in the matter of which it is made but in the function it performs: he once said that if the eye had a soul it would be seeing. He applied this principle also to inanimate objects: he said that if an axe had a soul it would be cutting. The real point of everything, according to him,

is what it *does*, what it is for; and it is through understanding this that we learn to understand things. We also come in this way to an understanding of Aristotle's concepts of soul, form, and final cause.

This analysis, in addition to giving Aristotle a solution to the problem of what things are that does away with Plato's Ideal Forms, also provides him with a solution to the problem of change. According to him, change occurs when the on-going material that is part of something acquires a form that it had not previously possessed.

### SAVING THE APPEARANCES

In all attempts to understand the world, says Aristotle, we should never lose sight of the fact that it is *this* world that we are trying to understand. Although we may be in awe of it we should never accept explanations of it that deny the validity of the very experiences we are trying to explain. We should make it a point of method in all our investigations to maintain a firm hold on these experiences, the experiences that actually present themselves to us, and to keep referring back to them at every stage, because it is understanding these that is, so to speak, the final cause of our enquiries. To jettison our hold on them in order

**ARCHIMEDES**
The inventor and mathematician Archimedes (287–212 BC) was among Aristotle's most gifted successors in the development of science. He formulated the principle of the lever, and showed that an irregular body's volume could be measured by the amount of water it displaced.

*"Poetry is more philosophical and more worthy of serious attention than history"*
ARISTOTLE

to embrace belief in something we do not experience is to throw the baby out with the bath water. He called this principle "saving the appearances". The phrase is a rather feeble-sounding one, but it is used by philosophers to this day because of the importance of the principle involved.

Plato and Aristotle are the two archetypes of the two main conflicting approaches that have characterized philosophy throughout its history. On the one hand there are philosophers who set only a secondary value on knowledge of the world as it presents itself to our senses, believing that our ultimate concern needs to be with something that lies "behind" or "beyond" (or "hidden below the surface of") the world. On the other hand there are philosophers who believe that this world is itself the most proper object for our concern and our philosophizing. To take an example much nearer to our own age, the great rationalist philosophers of the 17th and 18th centuries believed that the knowledge of the surface of things that our sensory experience seems to give us only too often deceives us; whereas the great empiricist philosophers of the selfsame period believed that reliable information can be based only on direct examination of observable facts. The opposition between the two tendencies is perennial, and comes out in one way or another in age after age, in different guises.

### THE GOLDEN MEAN

The respective appeals that the two different approaches possess for individuals may have something to do with personal temperament. People of a religious bent, though by no means only they, are likely to find a more Platonic approach congenial, while more down-to-earth, worldly, commonsensical people are likely to prefer an Aristotelian approach. But the reason why both are perennial is that each emphasizes truths which the other undervalues. Therefore the important thing is not to be exclusive in our own approach, but to learn from both. The unique genius of the German philosopher Kant, in the late 18th century, is that he brought the two harmoniously together and fused them in a way that is both coherent and plausible.

So far, our discussion of Aristotle has confined itself to his epistemology (theory of knowledge). But something should also be said about other areas of his philosophy. His writings in ethics have been as influential as anyone's, his key book here being the *Nicomachean Ethics*. Whereas for most of the 20th century moral philosophers tended to take a narrow view of the subject, and to devote themselves to the analysis of moral concepts – *What do we mean by good? What do we mean by ought?* – Aristotle's approach was quite different from this, and very much broader.

## "MAN IS BY NATURE A POLITICAL ANIMAL"

ARISTOTLE

He starts out from the proposition that what each one of us wants is a happy life in the fullest sense of the phrase. What will give us this, he thinks, is the fullest development and exercise of our capacities that is compatible with living in a society. Unbridled self-indulgence and self-assertion will bring us into perpetual conflict with other people, and in any case it is bad for our character – but then so also is inhibition. So he develops his famous doctrine of "the golden mean", according to which a virtue is the midway point between two extremes, each of which is a vice. Thus generosity is the mean between profligacy and meanness; courage between foolhardiness and cowardice; self-respect between vanity and self-abasement; modesty between shamelessness and shyness. The aim always is to be a balanced personality. And this, he thinks, is the way to achieve happiness.

A MODEL EDUCATION
*The Greeks developed the principle of "all-round education" that was to become the ideal for the rest of Europe.*

One striking thing about Aristotle's moral philosophy is how little moralizing there is in it. Its aim is essentially practical. Its doctrine of moderation in all things, and nothing too much, may appeal less to the young and eager than it does to the middle-aged and comfortable; but the young usually come round to thinking more highly of it in the course of time.

## THE FULL LIFE

Aristotle's *Nicomachean Ethics* leads straight into his *Politics* – in fact the two were intended to be the first and second parts of the same treatise. For according to Aristotle the true purpose of government is to enable its citizens to live the full and happy life discussed in his ethics. And one of his first points is that it is only by being a member of a society that an individual can do this – happiness and self-fulfilment are not to be found in personal isolation. This is the point of his much-quoted phrase "Man is by nature a political animal." There are, he insists, inescapable social and political dimensions to any happy personal life. And one of the most influential aspects of his political philosophy has been his *enabling* view of the State, his idea that the function of the State is to *make possible* the development and happiness of the individual.

## PITY AND TERROR

The only other book of Aristotle's that we shall mention is his *Poetics*. This is a discussion of literature and drama. The most important part of it is devoted to poetic tragedy, which Aristotle claims can give us more insight into life than does the study of history. (Most lovers of Shakespeare would agree with that.) The emotional experience we have when we watch a tragedy, Aristotle says, is catharsis, which he defines as purgation, or cleansing, by pity and terror. It was Aristotle who laid it down that a plot should have, in his very own words, "a beginning, a middle, and an end". He also said that the plot of a tragedy "tries as far as is possible to keep within a single revolution of the sun, or only slightly to exceed it". One of his editors

**A** GREEK THEATRE
*The Greeks staged their plays in open air theatres such as this one at Taormina, Sicily. The auditorium was fan-shaped and seating levels were not divided.*

at the time of the Italian Renaissance, a man called Castelvetro who published an edition of the *Poetics* in 1570, expanded this into the famous doctrine of the three unities of time, place, and action. These have come to be known as "the Aristotelian rules" of the drama, and they have had enormous influence, but they are not strictly speaking Aristotle's idea but rather an extension of one of his ideas.

However, so many of Aristotle's ideas have become part of our culture that it is a tragedy that we do not have in their original form the works that he published. These were famous throughout antiquity for their great beauty of style – the Roman writer and orator Cicero called Aristotle's writing "a river of gold". So widely are they referred to in the writings of others that we know quite a lot about them; but the works themselves have been lost. All that now survive are lecture notes, written up either by Aristotle himself or by his pupils, covering something like a fifth of his total output of ideas. These have nothing like the artistic quality of Plato, in fact they are a bit stodgy to read (as one would expect of lecture notes) so in practice it is only devoted students of philosophy who read them. But of their importance to Western civilization there can be no question.

**GREEK DRAMA**
The quality of the best Greek drama has never been surpassed. In Athens the plays were attended by most of the male citizen body, and handled what were widely felt to be fundamental issues. Masks were always worn by the actors to represent the characters they were playing – there was no such thing as make-up.

# THE CYNICS

## THE DROP-OUTS OF THE ANCIENT WORLD

*The Cynics rejected all social conventions. They were the first of four major schools of Greek philosophy which emerged after the fall of Athens.*

**A HARSH WORD**
*Cynic means "like a dog", and the most famous of all the cynic philosophers, Diogenes, explained this nickname: "I am called a dog because I fawn on those who give me anything, I yelp at those who refuse, and I sink my teeth in rascals."
The word "cynic" is still in use today, but has come to mean someone who always takes the lowest possible opinion of the motivations of others.*

*"Truly, if I were not Alexander I would wish to be Diogenes."*
ALEXANDER THE GREAT

ARISTOTLE'S PUPIL Alexander the Great changed history in a way that affected the development of philosophy. In an astoundingly short time he conquered more or less the whole world as it was known to the ancient Greeks, from Italy to India, including most of what is now called the Middle East, together with vast areas of North Africa. The independence of the Greek city states came to an end as they were swallowed up in Alexander's empire, and they lost their cultural dominance.

Everywhere he went, Alexander founded new cities, from which his conquests were to be administered, and these he colonized with Greeks. The colonists mostly married local women, so the populations of these cities quickly became cosmopolitan, but their ruling ethos and language remained everywhere Greek. The upshot was that the whole of the ancient world came to be run from "Greek" cities that were not in Greece, and whose populations were multiracial and multilingual. That world is known as the Hellenistic world. Its most important city was the one which Alexander named after himself, Alexandria, in Egypt. This became the chief international centre of culture and learning, the site of the most important library the ancient world ever possessed. The Hellenistic age of which it was the cultural capital lasted for some three hundred years, from the downfall of the Greek city states in the 4th century BC to the rise of the Roman

Empire in the 1st century BC. During that time the culture and civilization of ancient Greece became propagated throughout the ancient world. These were the circumstances in which the Roman republic emerged, and in which the Roman Empire struggled to establish itself. It was also the world into which Christianity was born, and explains why – although Palestine was a Roman colony – the New Testament was written in Greek.

### THE FIRST TWO CYNICS

Immediately after the death of Alexander his empire broke up into warring factions – so, while the cultural unity that he had created continued, there was incessant strife and conflict at the political level. All four of the new schools of philosophy that flourished during this period – the Cynics, the Sceptics, the Epicureans, and the Stoics – reflect that fact. All of them are concerned with how a civilized man is to live in an insecure, unstable, and dangerous world.

The first of these to appear were the Cynics. They were what we would now call drop-outs. Their progenitor was Antisthenes, a disciple of Socrates and near-contemporary of Plato. Until he was middle-aged he lived a conventional life in that aristocratic circle of philosophers. But with the death of Socrates and the fall of Athens Antisthenes world came to an end, whereupon he decided to opt out and embrace a basic, simple life. He started dressing like a labourer, and living

**THE FIRST INTERNATIONAL LIBRARY**
*Alexandria's library was the world's most valuable for nearly a thousand years, from 290 BC to AD 646.*

**ALEXANDER: PHILOSOPHER AND SCIENTIST**
*Not only a great warrior, Alexander was in part responsible for spreading Greek culture throughout the ancient world. This medieval illumination shows Alexander exploring the sea-bed in a glass diving-bell.*

# "I AM A CITIZEN OF THE WORLD"

DIOGENES

and foreigner – so when asked what his country was he replied: "I am a citizen of the world", and in doing so coined the single Greek word in which he expressed that thought, "cosmopolitan", a concept for which many have been grateful to him.

There are many good stories about Diogenes. The most famous is that when Alexander the Great came to visit him in his filthy hole and stood in the entrance asking if there was anything that he, the ruler of the entire world, could do for him, Diogenes replied "Yes – you can stand out of my light." There is no doubt that he meant this figuratively as well as literally. It is possibly the most eloquent put-down of worldly values that a philosopher has ever managed to deliver.

among the poor, and he proclaimed that he wanted no government, no private property, no marriage, and no established religion.

Antisthenes had a follower who became more famous than himself, a man called Diogenes (404–323 BC). Diogenes aggressively flouted all the conventions, and deliberately shocked people, whether by not washing or by dressing, if at all, in filthy rags, or living in a burial urn, or eating disgusting food, or committing flagrant acts of public indecency. He lived like a dog; and for this reason people gave him the nickname "Cynic" (from the Greek word *kynikos)* which means "like a dog". This is how the word, which we still use, was coined. But its meaning has changed over time.

## THE FIRST COSMOPOLITAN

Diogenes and his followers were not cynics in today's sense of the word. They had a positive belief in virtue. But their basic creed was that the difference between true values and false values was the only distinction that mattered: all other distinctions were rubbish – all social conventions, for instance, such distinctions as those between yours and mine, public and private, naked and clothed, raw and cooked – all that was nonsense. Diogenes had the same contempt for the distinction between Greek

**DIOGENES BEING VISITED BY ALEXANDER**
*In a confrontation of two whole value-systems, the conqueror of the world meets the philosopher who rejected worldly values, preferring to live like a dog.*

# THE SCEPTICS
## THE FIRST RELATIVISTS IN PHILOSOPHY

*Scepticism as a philosophy was launched on its long and influential career by one of Alexander the Great's soldiers.*

**CARNEADES (214–129 BC)**
A formidable debater, Carneades succeeded Arcesilaus both as head of Plato's Academy and as the leading proponent of Scepticism of the day. He was especially effective in criticizing the rival philosophies of the Epicureans and the Stoics.

IN THE BROADEST SENSE of the word "scepticism" there had long been a certain tradition of it in Greek philosophy. Xenophanes had taught that, although we can always learn more than we know, we can never be sure that we have reached any final truth. Socrates said that the only thing he knew was that he did not know anything. However, Socrates did at least believe that knowledge was possible, and, what is more, he was bent on acquiring some, while Xenophanes believed that we could lessen the degree of our ignorance if we made the effort. Both men took a positive attitude towards enquiry and the possibility of learning.

### ARGUING BOTH WAYS

The first person to make scepticism the be-all and end-all of his thought – to adopt it as being in itself a philosophy, so to speak, and one consisting of an active refusal to believe anything – was Pyrrho (c. 365–270 BC).

He launched a whole school of philosophers that became known as Sceptics; and their brand of systematic, all-embracing philosophical Scepticism is to this day sometimes referred to as Pyrrhonism.

Pyrrho had served as a soldier with Alexander the Great, and had campaigned with him as far afield as India. Seeing such a huge diversity of countries and peoples seems to have impressed on him the diversity of opinions that are to be found among human beings. For almost everything believed by the people in one place there seem to be people somewhere else who believe the opposite. And normally the arguments are equally good on both sides – or so it seemed to Pyrrho. All we can do is go by things as they appear to us: but appearances are notoriously deceptive, so we should never assume the truth of one explanation rather than any other. The best thing was to stop worrying and just go with the flow, that is to say swim along with whatever customs and practices prevail in the circumstances we happen to find ourselves in.

Pyrrho had a pupil, Timon of Phlius (320–230 BC), who supported this attitude with more substantial intellectual arguments. In particular he pointed out that every argument or proof proceeded from premises which it did not itself establish. If you tried to demonstrate the truth of those premises by other arguments or proofs then *they* had to be based on undemonstrated premises. And so it went on, *ad infinitum*. No ultimate ground of certainty could ever be reached.

After Timon's death his successor, Arcesilaus (315–240 BC), took over the leadership of Plato's Academy, which then remained in the hands of the Sceptics for two hundred years. Arcesilaus had two main teaching methods: one was to expound equally powerful

**POWER AFFECTS IDEAS**
*Alexander the Great had a bigger side-effect on the way Western philosophy developed than any other ruler: he destroyed the independence of the Greek city states in which philosophy had come to fruition, while making Greek a universal language.*

rguments on both sides of a question; the other
vas to offer to refute any case put forward by
ne of his students. His successor as head of the
Academy, Carneades (214–129 BC), made a great
tir on a visit to Rome by giving a series of public
ectures, in the first of which he forcefully
xpounded the views of Plato and Aristotle
n justice, and then in his second lecture refuted
verything he had said in the first.

## NO ULTIMATE CERTAINTY

cepticism has had a permanently important part
o play in the history of philosophy, from that day
o this. Chiefly it is because certainty is simply not
vailable at the level of argument, demonstration,
r proof – although it was not until the 20th century
hat this became generally acknowledged, so the
ursuit of certainty was destined to play a centrally
mportant role in the historical development of
hilosophy. What a valid argument proves is that its
onclusions follow from its premises, but that is not
t all the same as proving that those conclusions are
rue. Every valid argument starts with an "if": if p is
rue then q must be true. But that leaves open the
question of whether or not p is true. The argument
tself cannot prove that, because it has already

> # BY SCEPTICISM... WE ARRIVE FIRST AT SUSPENSION OF JUDGEMENT, AND SECOND AT FREEDOM FROM DISTURBANCE "
>
> SEXTUS EMPIRICUS

ssumed it, and to have assumed already what it sets
ut to prove would be to move in a vicious circle.
So every "proof" rests on unproven premises; and
his is as true in logic, mathematics, and science as
t is in everyday life. Even so, it does not follow from
his that we have no better grounds for any one set
f beliefs than for any other: to say that would be

**THE ENDS OF THE EARTH**
*Alexander's empire was identified by its inhabitants with
civilization, as if surrounded by a wall of fire. It established
what we know as the Hellenistic world, which lasted
for hundreds of years and within which the universal
language was Greek – which is why the New Testament
was written in Greek.*

untrue. However, the working out of these tricky
distinctions was to be a long and troublesome
business in the history of philosophy.

The most famous Sceptical philosopher of more
recent centuries is the Scotsman David Hume (see
pp.112–17). He qualified his own Scepticism by
pointing out that to live at all we have perpetually
to make choices, decisions, and this forces us to
form judgements about the way things are, whether
we like it or not. Since certainty is not available to
us we have to make the best assessments we can
of the realities we face – and this is incompatible
with regarding all alternatives with equal scepticism.
Our Scepticism therefore needs to be, as he put it,
mitigated. It is indeed doubtful whether anyone
could live on the basis of complete Scepticism –
or, if they could, whether such a life would be
worth living. But this refutation of Scepticism,
if refutation it is, is not a logical argument.

In practical life we must steer a middle course
between demanding a degree of certainty that we
can never have and treating all possibilities as if
they were of equal weight when they are not.

**SEXTUS EMPIRICUS'
*PYRRHONIARUM* (OUTLINES
OF PYRRHONISM)**
The fullest account we
have of the works of
Pyrrho, Scepticism's
founder, is from Sextus
Empiricus (c. AD 200).
Sextus was not himself
an original thinker, but
he set out other peoples'
arguments so well that
his writings became
influential. In the 4th
century St Gregory
publicly denounced him
along with Pyrrho for
infecting people with
"the vile and malignant
disease" of Scepticism.

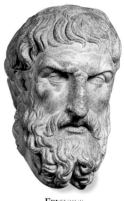

# THE EPICUREANS

## THE EARLIEST SCIENTIFIC AND LIBERAL HUMANISTS

*Like many attitudes of the 20th century, the philosophy of Epicurus was materialistic, pleasure-seeking, and non-religious. It was the first such philosophy to be fully developed intellectually.*

OF THE PHILOSOPHIES that were new in the Hellenistic age, two were outstanding in importance and influence, and they were those of the Epicureans and the Stoics.

Epicureanism was very much the creation of a single thinker, Epicurus (c. 341–270 BC). Its aim above all else was to liberate people from fear, not only the fear of death but the fear of life. In an age when all forms of public life were unpredictable and highly dangerous it taught people to seek happiness and fulfilment in their private lives. "Live unknown" was one of its maxims. This was

**BACCHUS AND MAENAD**
*Bacchus, or Dionysos, was the god of the intoxicating powers of Nature. He was associated with orgies – of which the Epicureans were often accused, but of which they actually disapproved.*

completely at odds with all previous ideas of seeking fame and glory, or even wanting something so apparently decent as honour. But Epicureanism was to an unusual degree a fully worked-out philosophy that tried to embrace all aspects of existence. It began with a view of physics.

First of all, Epicurus accepted the atomism of Democritus. He believed that all there was in the material universe were atoms and space, nothing else.

Since it is impossible for atoms to come into existence out of nothing or pass away into nothing, they are indestructible and eternal. However, their movements are unpredictable, and no combination that they form ever endures. For this reason, physical objects, all of which are combinations of atoms, are ephemeral. Their life is always a story of atoms coming together and then, eventually, dispersing again. All change in the universe consists either of this endlessly repeated process or of the objects thus formed moving in space.

### WOMEN AND SLAVES INCLUDED

We ourselves are among the objects formed in this way. A group of particularly fine atoms comes together to make a body and a mind in the form of a single entity, a human being, whose eventual dispersal is inevitable. But this dispersal is not to be feared. Such a dissolution of the human being means that the entity that we are ceases to exist when we die, and therefore there is no-one to whom being dead happens: so long as we exist, death is not, and when death is, we are not. Nor is there anyone to whom those terrors, that so many religions threaten people with after their deaths, can happen. "Death is nothing to us", says Epicurus and anyone who genuinely grasps that truth, deep down, is liberated from fear of death.

As for the gods, Epicurus manages to get them out of the picture without denying their existence (which would have been a dangerous thing for him to do) by saying that they are far, far away and,

eing gods, they have no desire to become involved
n the perpetual mess and turmoil of human affairs.
o they are inactive as far as we are concerned, and
we have nothing to hope and nothing to fear"
rom them. For us, it is as if they do not exist.

Since non-existence is our own inescapable
estiny we should make the best of the only life
/e have. The good life in this life, happiness in
uis world, should be our aim. The way to achieve
uis is to have nothing to do with the violence
nd uncertainties of public life but to withdraw
ato private communities of like-minded people.
nd because both our physical health and the
aaintenance of good personal relationships require
, we should enjoy our pleasures in moderation,
uough no non-injurious activity needs to be
egarded as forbidden in itself.

# "DEATH IS NOTHING TO US"

EPICURUS

he communities formed by the Epicureans for
uese purposes were in principle open to anyone,
ucluding women and slaves – a fact which drew
 great deal of antagonism towards them from their
urrounding societies. When Christianity came on
ue scene the Epicureans were anathema to
hristians in particular, because of their denial of
nmortality and of the existence of a benevolent
iod, and also because of their affirmation of the
alues of this world.

## POETIC MASTERPIECE

Vhat is striking to us now about Epicureanism
; how similar it is, almost point by point, to the
cientific and liberal humanism of the 20th century.
: was the first thought-through version of an
ttitude to life that has been widely embraced in
ur own age. Its most dramatic and widely read
rticulation was achieved in a long poem written
u the Latin language in the 1st century BC, *On the
ature of Things* (*De Rerum Natura*) by Lucretius
c. 95–52 BC). This is one of the supreme
uasterpieces of Latin literature, and its purpose
as to import Epicureanism into Roman culture.

The poet seems to have been somewhat
desperately seeking salvation in the philosophy
he so passionately embraced, for he himself was
intermittently subject to the terrors of madness,
and he died eventually by committing suicide.
Perhaps because the doctrines of Epicureanism
were to such an unusual degree the creation of
a single thinker, it remained surprisingly
unchanged throughout its long history. In the
Middle Ages it was denounced by Christians as
Antichrist, and then almost petered out; but it was
rediscovered in the 16th and 17th centuries, and
had a significant influence on the beginnings of
modern science and humanism.

**MEMENTO MORI**
The skull was used
by the Epicureans,
as by many others, as
a symbol of mortality.
Its implied message
was: "Enjoy life while
you have it."

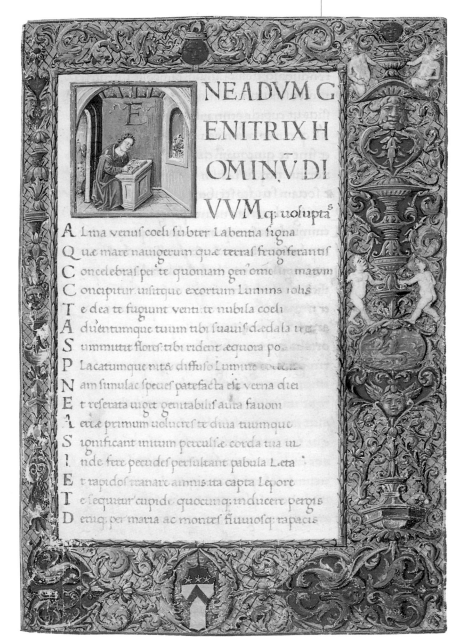

*ON THE NATURE OF THINGS*
*Lucretius, the supreme Epicurean poet, is shown writing at his desk in this illuminated
Christian edition of his pagan masterpiece. The accompanying text is the opening of
Book One, his paean of praise to Venus, the goddess of sexual love.*

**ZENO OF CITIUM**
The founder of Stoicism, Zeno, wrote a much admired *Republic* in which he argued for the rule of law and the universal validity of political institutions. With the exception of scattered quotations, none of his writings survive.

**KEY WORKS**

The *Letters* of Seneca

The *Discourses* of Seneca

The *Discourses* of Epictetus

The *Meditations* of Marcus Aurelius

*Excellent histories of Stoicism in the ancient world were written by Cicero, Diogenes, Laertius, and Sextus Empiricus.*

# THE STOICS

## THE GOVERNING PHILOSOPHY OF THE ROMAN EMPIRE

*Since death and adversity are out of our control, and come to everyone, we should meet them with dignified acceptance.*

**MARCUS AURELIUS**
*This Roman Emperor, who ruled from AD 161 to 180, has symbolized for many generations the golden age of the Roman Empire. As a Stoic and philosophical writer, Marcus Aurelius reveals what it can be like when the man at the very apex of power is also a philosopher.*

STOICISM AS A PHILOSOPHY continued as an organized movement for some five hundred years. With it, and through it, Western philosophy ceased to be specifically Greek and became international. This was a direct result of Alexander the Great's conquests having spread Greek culture throughout the so-called civilized world – the early Stoic philosophers were mostly Syrians, the later ones mostly Romans. The voices of the most famous of them came from the entire gamut of the social hierarchy, one even being a slave (Epictetus) and another a Roman Emperor (Marcus Aurelius). Stoicism seems to have had a special appeal for emperors. According to a leading authority, "nearly all the successors of Alexander – we may say all the principal kings in existence in the generations following Zeno – professed themselves Stoics."

Zeno (334–262 BC) of Citium, in Cyprus, was the founder of Stoicism. (He should not be confused with the pre-Socratic philosopher Zeno of Elea, who was discussed on p.19.) The core of the Stoic philosophy lies in the view that there can be no authority higher than reason. By unpacking the consequences of that belief we arrive at most of the important tenets of Stoic philosophy.

First, the world as our reason presents it to us as being, that is to say the world of Nature, is all the reality there is. There is nothing "higher". And Nature itself is governed by rationally intelligible principles. We ourselves are part of Nature. The spirit of rationality that imbues us and it (and that is to say, everything) is what is meant by God. As thus conceived, God is not outside the world and separate from it, he is all-pervadingly in the world – he is, as it were, the mind of the world, the self-awareness of the world.

### EMOTIONS ARE JUDGEMENTS

Because we are at one with Nature, and because there is no higher realm, there can be no question of our going anywhere "else" when we die – there is nowhere else to go. We dissolve back into Nature. It is through the ethics evolved from this belief that Stoicism achieved its greatest fame and influence.

Because Nature is governed by rational principles there are reasons why everything is as it is. We cannot change it, nor should we desire to. Therefore our attitude in the face of our own mortality, or what may seem to us personal tragedy, should be one of unruffled acceptance. In so far as our emotions rebel against this, our emotions are in the wrong. The Stoics believed that emotions are judgements, and therefore cognitive: they are forms of "knowledge", whether true or false. Greed, for

**SENECA – A PHILOSOPHER AND POLITICIAN**
*One of the later Stoics, Seneca, tutor to Nero, was joint-chief administrator of the Roman Empire from AD 54–62.*

stance, is the judgement that money is a
re-eminent good and to be acquired by every
vailable means – a false judgement. If all our
motions are made subject to our reason they will
mbody none but true judgements, and we shall
hen be at one with things as they actually are.

People who adopted the Stoic philosophy were
ften able to endure life's vicissitudes with calm
nd dignity. But even for them there might come
 time when they would no longer wish to go on
ving – for example in circumstances of personal
uin or disgrace, or in the agonies of a terminal
isease. In those circumstances, they believed,
he rational thing to do was to end one's own life
ainlessly, and this many of them did. So a high
roportion of the well-known Stoics ended their
ves by committing suicide.

The most vivid and compelling of all the
xpositions of Stoicism are to be found in the
ritings of the later Stoics, which were all in Latin.
he outstanding figures here are Seneca
c. 2 BC–AD 65) and Marcus Aurelius (AD 121–180).
hey were not original thinkers in the sense of
dding significantly to already-existing Stoic
octrines, but they were such good writers that
heir works are read to this day by people who
re not academics. It is to them that anyone who
ants to study Stoicism at first hand should turn.

## " EVERY STOIC WAS A STOIC, BUT IN CHRISTENDOM, WHERE IS THE CHRISTIAN? "

RALPH WALDO EMERSON

toic ethics have always been widely found to be
npressive and admirable, even by people who do
ot wholly go along with them. They are not easy
 practise – but perhaps it is bound to be a
haracteristic of any ethics worthy of the name that
ney are difficult to put into practice. They had an
nmistakable influence on Christian ethics, which
ere beginning to spread at the time when Seneca,
pictetus, and Marcus Aurelius were writing. And,
f course, to this very day the words "stoic" and

"stoicism" are in familiar use in our language, with
perhaps grudgingly admiring overtones, to mean
"withstanding adversity without complaint". There
must be many people now living who – even if
they have never consciously formulated this fact to
themselves – subscribe to an ideal in ethics which
is essentially the same as that of the Stoics.

The fact that in recent centuries the best
available school education in many European
countries was based on the study of Latin literature
had, as one of its side-effects, that many generations
of well educated European males absorbed some of
the values of Stoicism. The famous "stiff upper lip"
of the public-school educated Englishman was
precisely an example of Stoicism in practice and
in action, partly rooted in a classical education.

CHOOSING DEATH OVER LIFE
*Suicide was not taboo for the Stoics. On the contrary, they believed in a man's right
to determine his own death as well as his own life.*

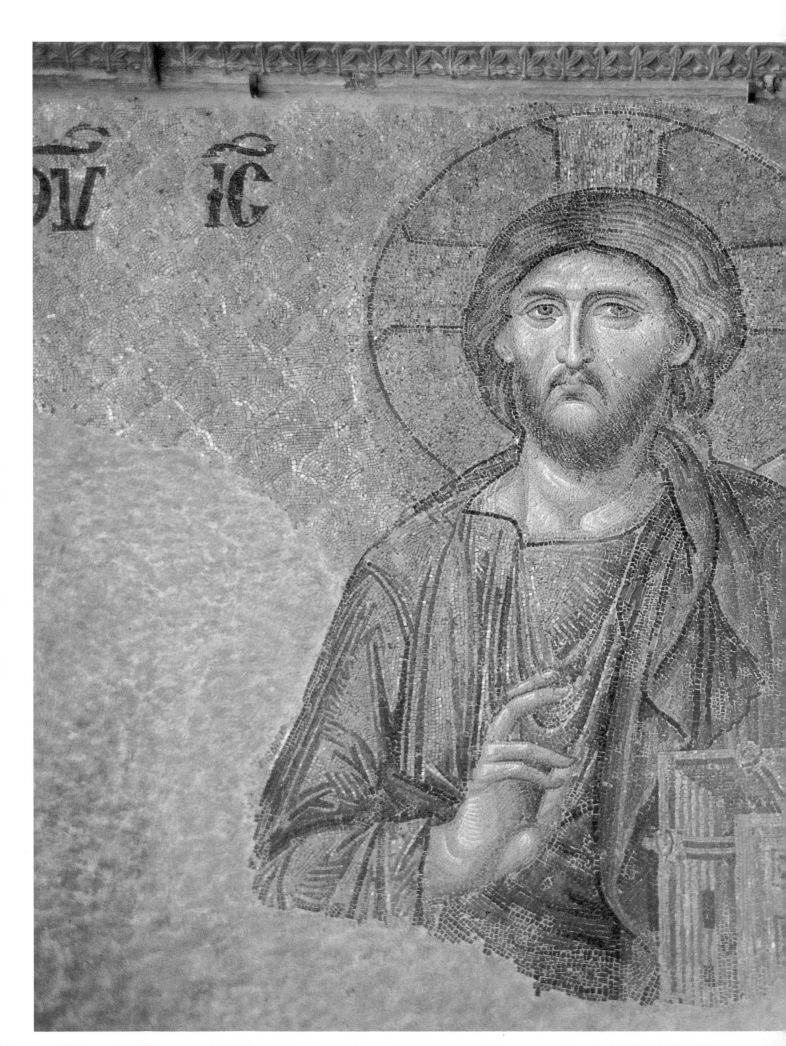

# CHRISTIANITY & PHILOSOPHY

FOR A THOUSAND YEARS BETWEEN THE FALL OF THE ROMAN EMPIRE IN THE 5TH CENTURY AD AND THE DAWN OF THE RENAISSANCE IN THE 15TH CENTURY THE TORCH OF CIVILIZATION IN WESTERN EUROPE WAS CARRIED MAINLY BY THE CHRISTIAN CHURCH. BUT BEFORE CHRISTIANS WERE WILLING TO EMBRACE ANY IDEAS OR DISCOVERIES, THEY NEEDED TO ASSURE THEMSELVES THAT THESE WERE NOT INCOMPATIBLE WITH CHRISTIANITY. SO THE WRITINGS OF THE GREATEST PHILOSOPHERS OF ANTIQUITY WERE SCRUTINIZED TO DETERMINE WHICH OF THEIR IDEAS COULD BE HARMONIZED WITH CHRISTIANITY, AND WHICH WOULD HAVE TO BE REJECTED. THE SUPREME SYNTHESIS WAS ACHIEVED TOWARDS THE END OF THE PERIOD, IN THE WRITINGS OF THOMAS AQUINAS, WHO PRODUCED A VAST, CAPACIOUS WORLD-VIEW HARMONIZING WHAT WERE THEN THE MAJOR THOUGHT-SYSTEMS.

**BYZANTINE ALTARPIECE**
*This detail from the High Altar of San Marco, Venice, is made of gold and silver with precious stones, pearls, and enamel.*

# SAINT AUGUSTINE

## THE FUSION OF PLATONISM AND CHRISTIANITY

*Augustine was arguably the outstanding figure in philosophy between Aristotle and Aquinas, a period of some 1,600 years.*

ONE OF THE MOST ATTRACTIVE personalities in the history of philosophy, Augustine was born in the town of Hippo in North Africa, in what is now Algeria, in AD 354. It was there that he died in AD 430, though between those two dates his travels took him far afield in the Mediterranean world.

His father was a pagan but his mother, whom he loved dearly, was a woman of simple Christian faith. Augustine turned his back on Christianity when he was a teenager. Reading Cicero at the age of 18 or 19 sent him off on a philosophical quest that was to take him through several different intellectual positions before he returned to what he called Catholic Christianity.

He first adopted Manichaeism, a doctrine of the Persian prophet Mani, of about the 3rd century AD, to the effect that the universe is a battleground between forces of good and evil, light and darkness. Matter is evil but spirit is good, and each human being is a mixture of both, with the spark of light that is his soul longing for liberation from the gross material of his body. But Augustine grew sceptical of what seemed to him the unsound intellectual arguments of the Manichaeans, and eventually he became a fully-fledged philosophical Sceptic of the kind that now ruled in the Academy that had been founded by Plato. This seems to have led him to the study of Plato, and of Neo-Platonism in the work of Plotinus; and for a time he came completely under their sway. When finally he returned to Christianity at the age of 32 he carried his Platonism and his Neo-Platonism with him, and fused them with Christianity in a way that was to have consequences of incalculable importance.

He himself tells the story of these development in his wonderful book *Confessions*, which is the first autobiography in the modern sense. It contains a fascinating account of his childhood, a moving character portrait of his mother, and frank confessions of his sexual promiscuity as a young man. Wanting and yet not wanting to escape from his enslavement to sex, he tells us he used to pray to God: "Lord, make me chaste, but not yet."

### ANTICIPATIONS

The most interesting philosophizing in the *Confessions* - appropriately for an autobiography - is about the nature of time. "If no one asks me [what time is] I know; if they ask and I try to explain, I do not know." Augustine's conviction that although the flow of time exists for living creatures it is not a reality for God led him to the conclusion that the flow of time is something that characterizes only experience, and is not something that exists in itself, independently of experience. In this he anticipated the philosophy of Kant (see pp.132-37). In another of his doctrines about time he anticipated Schopenhauer (see pp.138-45), namely the doctrine that the present is the inescapable mode of all existence. He anticipated Schopenhauer again in his view that our whole worldly being, including our intellect, is dominated by our will. Yet another of his impressive anticipations is of Descartes (see pp.84-89): he argued that the Sceptics must be wrong, because, as he explained, to doubt anything, let alone "everything", I must needs exist, and therefore my own existence is something which it is impossible for me to doubt. Since the fact that I exist is a truth that I know with absolute certainty it is untrue to say that we cannot know anything, or that it is impossible for us to be sure of anything or indeed that it is possible for us to doubt

SAINT AUGUSTINE

*In answer to the pagan challenge: "Why did your God create the universe at that arbitrary moment in time?", St Augustine replied: "But that was when he created time too".*

verything, which is the very foundation of the
ceptical position. And this being so, there may
e other things, too, that it is possible for me
o know with absolute certainty.

A SUCCESSFUL MARRIAGE
One thing that made it possible for Augustine
o fuse the Platonic tradition in philosophy
vith Christianity is the fact that Christianity
s not, in itself, a philosophy. Its
undamental beliefs are of a historical
ather than a philosophical nature: for
nstance that a God made our world,
nd then came to live in the world of
iis creation as one of the people in it,
nd appeared on earth as a man called
esus, in a particular part of Palestine,
t a particular time, and lived a life that
ook a certain course, of which we possess
iistorical records. Being a Christian involves,
mong other things, believing such things as
his, and trying to live in the way the God who
reated us told us, partly through the mouth of
his Jesus, that we should. Jesus did indeed provide
s with a good deal of moral instruction, but he was
ot much given to discussing philosophical questions.

**THE BAPTISM OF CHRIST**
*Christianity's beliefs are historical rather than philosophical.
This 5th-century mosaic depicts Christ's Baptism by St John the
Baptist and the subsequent appearance of the Holy Spirit in the
form of a dove, as the voice of God declares Jesus as his Son.*

> ## "LORD MAKE ME CHASTE, BUT NOT YET"
>
> SAINT AUGUSTINE

o it was not the case that there was a Platonic
philosophy on the one hand, and on the other, a
philosophy at variance with it, Christian philosophy –
hus giving Augustine the problem of marrying
he two. It was rather that Christianity (unlike,
ay, Buddhism) was for the most part a non-
hilosophical religion, and Augustine, believing
hat Platonic philosophy embodied important

truths about aspects of reality that the Bible did
not concern itself with, wanted Platonism to be
absorbed into the Christian world-view. In the way
that this was effected, though, it was important not
to take on board any particular aspect of Platonism
that might have as one of its logical consequences
(perhaps not perceived immediately) something
that contradicted Christianity, for Christianity was
the self-revelation of God, and must always have
prior claim to truth. Anything believed by a
Christian in contradiction to Christianity was
heresy. It was with these thoughts in mind that
Augustine brought the detailed analysis of
philosophical doctrines on to his agenda. He always
saw philosophy as playing a secondary role to
religious revelation. But the best of his philosophy
is excellent philosophy nonetheless. In this way
he was largely successful in his aim of getting
Platonic and Neo-Platonic philosophy absorbed
into the church's view of the nature of reality.
Plato's doctrines that true knowledge is of a realm
of timeless and perfect non-material entities with

**KEY WORKS**
*It is rare for one
person to have written
not just one but two
of what are generally
regarded as the world's
greatest books. But
Augustine did. There
is first* The Confessions
*(c. AD 400) the world's
first autobiography,
and still one of the
best. And then there is*
The City of God
*(AD 413–426), still
required reading in
Religious Studies
at universities.*

which our contact is non-sensory; that there is a part of us that is also timeless and non-material which already belongs to that realm, while our bodies are among the fleeting and decaying material objects of the sensory world; that because all the objects of the sensory world are ephemeral and decaying there can be no stable, true, and lasting knowledge of it, consisting as it does of fleeting illusions; all this, and many other Platonic doctrines besides, became so familiar a part of the Christian outlook that many if not most Christians came to assume that these ideas, although nowhere actually stated by Christ, had nevertheless somehow been originated by Christianity, and were to be thought of as a natural part of it.

### SOULS IN HELL

One doctrine of St Augustine's that was never officially accepted by the church but had long-term and in many ways tragic consequences was his doctrine of predestination. This rested on his view that we cannot be saved through the exercise of our own wills independently of God, but that God's intervention and grace are necessary for our salvation. Souls who go to hell are souls for whom God does not intervene. Thus the damned are damned by God's choice. This doctrine was used over subsequent centuries to justify the burning and torture of many heretics – treating them, in other words, as if they were damned souls in hell – and untold thousands died appalling deaths in its name. This is one example – Marxism provides others, and there are more elsewhere –

of theories produced by a philosopher being used to justify mass murder. It demonstrates, if demonstration were needed, the immense practical consequences that can flow from an abstract idea. More than a thousand years later this same idea of Augustine's was still exerting a powerful influence on leading religious thinkers, not Catholics only but also key Protestant church reformers such as Luther, Calvin, and Jansen.

### THE COLLAPSE OF CIVILIZATION

Augustine lived during part of the period of collapse of the Roman Empire. Throughout his life the whole civilized world as he knew it was being steadily destroyed by barbarian hordes. At the very moment when he died in the city of his birth, Hippo, it was being besieged by Vandals, to whom it surrendered after his death. What lay immediately ahead in time was further collapse followed by the period we now call the Dark Ages. There can be little doubt that these circumstances were in part responsible for Augustine's pessimistic view of fallen human nature, and of the sinful character of the world in which we have to live. His great book *The City of God* is about how each individual is a citizen of two different communities simultaneously; on the one hand there is the kingdom of God, which is unchanging and eternal, and based on true values, while on the other there are the highly unstable kingdoms of this world, which come and go with bewildering rapidity and are based on false values. We find ourselves living in both. (The reader will at once see a parallelism between these and the two worlds of Plato.)

Augustine was the last great philosopher of Latin antiquity, and many would consider him the greatest. He was also the first philosopher whose philosophical quest took more the form of digging into his own inner life than of considering the reality outside himself or the society around him. And he contributed not just one but two of the finest books that there are in world literature: the *Confessions* (c. AD 400) and *The City of God* (c. AD 413–426).

**THE FALL FROM GRACE**
Many thinkers in the 4th century ad thought that sexual reproduction was a consequence of the Fall. However, Augustine believed that sexuality was a fundamental part of human nature as intended by God, but was distorted through Adam's sin – Man had fallen by the act of his own will.

**THE SPANISH INQUISITION**
*Augustine believed in the use of some force against dissenters, and his opinion became part of Church law. The Spanish Inquisition, set up in 1478, became powerful after laws were passed in 1492 and 1502 requiring Moslems and Jews to convert to Christianity.*

**THE TORMENTS OF HELL**
*The City of God (AD 413–26) was one of the most influential books of the Middle Ages. Augustine believed that ever since the Fall God had divided mankind into the elect and the damned. In this world the earthly and heavenly worlds are intermingled, but after resurrection only the elect receive God's grace – the damned will burn for eternity in Hell.*

# MEDIEVAL PHILOSOPHY

## A PROLONGED ATTEMPT TO FIT PLATO, ARISTOTLE, AND CHRISTIANITY HARMONIOUSLY INTO THE SAME OUTLOOK

*Because of the subsequent rise of science, medieval philosophy has been unjustly neglected in recent centuries, except by Roman Catholic scholars. It richly rewards attention.*

**MOORISH ARCHITECTURE**
The Moors' conquest of Spain, following their invasions of AD 711, lasted for eight centuries. In the citadel and palace of the Alhambra (1238–1358) the Moorish tradition reached its climax. With its colonnades and courtyard gardens the Alhambra is a fine example of the Islamic heritage running alongside the Christian traditions of European Gothic architecture. This view of the palace shows the Court of Lions.

*"For in every ill-turn of fortune the most unhappy sort of misfortune is to have been happy"*
BOETHIUS

**THE WORLD OF ISLAM**
*By the time of Mohammed's death in AD 632 Islam had spread through much of Arabia. By AD 751 the Islamic empire ranged from the borders of France almost to China in Asia. Islam made great advances in philosophy, mathematics, astronomy, and medicine. In the arts, it produced great architecture, calligraphy, ceramics, and textiles.*

THE COLLAPSE OF THE ROMAN EMPIRE saw the overrunning and occupation of its various territories by other forces, many of them pagan hordes who were often at war with one another. The classical civilization that by now consisted of the accumulated treasures of Greek, Hellenistic, and Roman culture was brought down in ruins, and was succeeded by the period that we call the Dark Ages. Since Europeans have for so long tended to equate civilization itself with European culture it is worth noting that while Europe was going through this dark age – approximately the period between AD 600 and 1000 – there were more highly developed civilizations flourishing in other parts of the world. It was the golden age of Islam, which prospered throughout the eastern part of what had been Alexander's empire, and from there all the way across North Africa to Spain. Chinese civilization reached the high point of the Tang dynasty (AD 618–907), which is considered by connoisseurs to be the greatest period ever of Chinese poetry.

**THE CONSOLATION OF PHILOSOPHY**
*Here we see Lady Philosophy wooing her student Boethius away from "strumpet muses" – Lady Fortune, who is turning a wheel on which four figures are ascending and descending.*

## "A PERSON IS AN INDIVIDUAL SUBSTANCE OF A RATIONAL NATURE"
BOETHIUS

A distinctive Japanese culture was emerging and developing rapidly towards what was to be its classical period. Another half millennium was to pass before Europe began to get itself launched on the process of effectively imposing its power and its culture on the rest of the globe. If anyone in the Dark Ages had suggested that this barbaric, benighted continent would ever one day be able

*A BATTLE BETWEEN ROMANS AND BARBARIANS*

*In the 4th and 5th centuries AD barbarians began to cross the borders of the Western Roman Empire. The poor economies of some barbarian peoples, such as the Goths and the Vandals, had led them to seek new lands and wealth.*

*In AD 410 a Visigothic army commanded by King Alaric laid siege to Rome, a feat repeated in AD 455 by the Vandals. By AD 476 the Western Roman Empire had ceased to exist and Italy was ruled by barbarian kings.*

to do that it would probably have seemed absurd. During that period it was the Islamic world that preserved much of the culture of classical antiquity. The outstanding example of this in philosophy involves the works of Aristotle. Most of these were lost in Europe but preserved in the Arab world, and were not to be reintroduced into Europe until the 13th century. (Cultural contact with the Arab world in the 12th and 13th centuries was to have altogether transforming effect on European intellectual development, and not only with regard to Aristotle.)

The only works of Aristotle's to survive in Europe during the Dark Ages were his logical writings, and this was because they were translated into Latin by Boethius (c. 480 BC–c. 524 BC). This extraordinary man rose to high office under an Ostrogoth ruler of Italy called Theodoric whose principal minister he became for many years; but his enemies conspired against him, and he was imprisoned and executed. While awaiting his death in prison he wrote a book called *The Consolation of Philosophy* which has continued to be read from that day to this. Although he was a Christian the consolations to

which his title refers are not specifically Christian but rather Stoic and Neo-Platonist. His book remained one of the two or three books with most universal appeal throughout the Middle Ages.

## IRELAND AS A BEACON

After Boethius, Europe's reversion to barbarism lasted over a period of several hundred years, throughout which time the individuals and institutions trying to cling to the remnants of civilization were very much on the defensive. Foremost among these institutions was the Christian church, which in the earlier part of the period had to fight every inch of the way for its own survival. So it was not a time in which much could be expected in the way of disinterested and original intellectual work, and scarcely any was done.

The Germanic tribes that destroyed Roman rule in northern Europe invaded and occupied Britain, but stopped at the Irish sea; so Ireland was left unbarbarized. Many of the literate and learned from Britain and the Continent fled there, with the result that an amazing period occurred in Irish history – roughly the 6th, 7th, and 8th centuries – when that island was an outpost of civilization on the edge of an otherwise uncivilized Europe. This is how it came about that the only truly outstanding philosopher to emerge during the Dark Ages was in Ireland. His name, somewhat confusingly, was John the Scot, the Latin name for Ireland in those days being "Scotia". He is also sometimes referred to as John Scotus Erigena. His dates of birth and death are unknown, but he is thought to have been born in around AD 810 and died in about AD 877.

## DIVINE SELF-KNOWLEDGE

Erigena argued that since correct reasoning cannot lead to false conclusions, there can never be any conflict between reason and divine revelation: they are independent ways of arriving at truth, and both are valid. So he set out to demonstrate rationally all the truths of the Christian faith. This was to bring his work under official suspicion on the ground that if he were right it would render both faith and revelation unnecessary. His philosophical approach was that of Neo-Platonism, and as such very much in the tradition of St Augustine; but he was a more rigorous thinker than Augustine – the technical quality of the argumentation is higher, and his intellectual points drive deeper. One of his profoundest arguments was to the effect that since God is unknowable, in the sense of not being the sort of entity that constitutes a possible object of knowledge, it is impossible for God to know himself, to understand his own nature. After many centuries this insight was generalized by Kant into the point that it is impossible for any consciously aware being – not only God but also, for example, a human being – to understand its own nature.

**IRISH CRUCIFIXION PLAQUE**
*Celtic monasteries produced some of the greatest Early Christian art, providing new patronage and new techniques. This 8th-century crucifixion plaque may be one of the earliest representations of the Crucifixion in Ireland.*

Erigena was the only large-scale systematic philosopher to emerge in the West between, on the one hand, St Augustine and Boethius, and on the other, Anselm in the 11th century a period of five or six hundred years. However, once we come to Anselm we find ourselves encountering a succession of gifted philosophers one after another: Peter Abelard in the 12th century, Roger Bacon and Thomas Aquinas in the 13th, followed then by Duns Scotus, then by William of Ockham – by which time the medieval period is itself coming to an end.

## LOVE STORY

Anselm's most influential contribution to the history of thought is the ontological argument for the existence of God. This is explained and discussed on p.57, so at this point we may move straight on to Abelard, whose life (c. 1079–1142) was lived mostly in and around Paris. The tragic story of Abelard and Héloise is one of the great love stories of the world, on a par with that of Tristan and Isolde, or Romeo and Juliet.

Héloise was the niece of Canon Fulbert of Notre Dame; and she and Abelard became secret lovers. She had a child, whereupon they married, still secretly. Seeking revenge, her brothers, organized by the Canon, broke into Peter's room one night and castrated him. The story ends with him becoming a monk and her a nun, and the two of them writing letters to one another which are now an established part of world literature.

In philosophy Abelard's most interesting writings are about the problem of what are called universals, which are terms such as "red" or "tree" that can be applied in exactly the same way to an

**ABELARD AND HÉLOISE**
*Peter Abelard was a theologian, logician, and moral philosopher, whose most important writings address the problem of universals. His love affair with Héloise led to him being castrated by her uncle, Canon Fulbert of Notre Dame. Here, we see Héloise taking the veil from Abelard.*

# Can the EXISTENCE of GOD be PROVED?

*Among the different arguments for the existence of God, three stand out in importance in the earlier history of philosophy, each of which is still encountered in many variations.*

## THE TELEOLOGICAL ARGUMENT

The argument that the universe exhibits design and purpose: the acorn becomes the oak, the stars move in predictable courses, everything seems to be acting out some purpose or plan. An argument of this kind is called a "teleological" argument because a teleological explanation is one that explains something in terms of its aim or goal. The appeal of such arguments has been weakened by the rise of the modern sciences which – whether in the physical or the life sciences – explain natural phenomena in terms of either causes or randomness, and dispense with the notion of purpose in anything to do with non-conscious phenomena. Also, although there is certainly a great deal of order in the universe, there is also apparent chaos, and perhaps the order has been at one time exaggerated. Furthermore, it has been seriously questioned whether it is meaningful to talk of the sum total of everything as having a purpose.

## THE COSMOLOGICAL ARGUMENT

The argument that the universe's being here at all means that someone must have created it – it cannot just have come into existence all by itself, out of nothing – is the "cosmological" argument. Its great weakness is that

it leads to an infinite regress. If the cosmos is so wonderful that its existence needs something else to explain it, then the existence of that something else is even more wonderful, and how shall we explain that? And indeed, if we do hit on an explanation, we shall then have to provide an explanation of that. And so on.

## THE ONTOLOGICAL ARGUMENT

The third great argument for the existence of God is called the "ontological" argument – the word "ontology" applies to any discussion to do with the nature of being. The inventor of this argument seems to have been St Anselm (1033–1109) who was for 16 years Archbishop of Canterbury. Imagine, he says, the greatest, most perfect being possible. If the being you think of has every desirable attribute except that of existence, it is not the greatest or most perfect possible, because obviously a being that exists is both greater and more perfect than one that does not. Therefore the greatest, most perfect possible being must exist. Most reflective people feel that this argument will not do, but – as in the case of Achilles and the tortoise (see p.19) – it is disconcertingly difficult to show what is wrong with it. Kant, in the late 18th century, did this to most peoples' satisfaction. But the matter remains controversial, and in recent years the ontological argument has re-surfaced in philosophy.

*The consensus among philosophers now is that the existence of God cannot be proved. This is not, of course, to say that he does not exist, but only that his existence is not something that can be rationally demonstrated.*

*"Sin consists not in desiring a woman, but in consent to the desire"*
PETER ABELARD

indefinitely large number of different objects. Do these terms denote something that itself exists, or not? Plato had said that they did – that there is an Ideal Form of redness, and that the particular redness of each individual red object is a copy or reflection of that, however imperfect. Aristotle had denied it: there are of course red objects, he said, but redness is not something that exists separately and apart from the actual red objects there are.

The first of these two positions, the more Platonic one, became known as "realism" because it asserted that universals have a real existence. The latter and more Aristotelian position became known as "nominalism" because it asserted that universals are useful names for certain characteristics, but are not things that exist in themselves. The battle between realists and nominalists became one of the running battles of medieval philosophy. This was partly because it was over an issue of genuine difficulty, and partly because it possessed serious implications for theology, for instance, the nature of the Trinity. Abelard was a sophisticated and qualified nominalist; but the problem has still not been solved to the general satisfaction, and although we no longer use the medieval terminology we are still struggling with the same problem.

## MEDIEVAL RENAISSANCE .

The 13th century saw the first really big flowering of European thought and civilization to occur since the collapse of the Roman Empire. It was the period in which the Christian and Islamic cultures had their most fruitful interchanges; the philosophy of Aristotle returned to Europe from the Arab world; the wonderful romantic literature of the Arthurian legends, and the literatures surrounding

**A HAND RISES FROM THE LAKE TO TAKE KING ARTHUR'S SWORD**
*The Arthurian legends came into existence during the 13th century. The story of Arthur assumed its final form in 1485, after the publication of* Morte d'Arthur *by Sir Thomas Malory.*

**HEAVENLY LIGHT**
*The great Gothic cathedrals of the 13th century were a striking symbol of Europe's emergence from the Dark Ages. One of the finest examples of Gothic architecture is the Sainte-Chappelle (1243–48) in Paris, which displays the decorative effect of window traceries, and the lightness and soaring height that typified the style. Vertical shafts and pointed arches led the eye – and the soul – up to heaven.*

Charlemagne and the Nibelungs, came into existence; the great French Gothic cathedrals were built. In England it saw the foundation of the universities of Oxford and Cambridge; also the beginnings of constitutional government with Magna Carta and the House of Commons. Among the earliest people to teach at Oxford was Roger Bacon (c. 1220–c. 1292). He was remarkable not so much for his achievements as for his perception of possibilities. He believed that there could and should be a unified science, based on mathematics, but making use of observation and experiment as well as abstract reasoning. He himself did original work in optics. He was one of a small but growing band of people who were beginning to recognize the importance of practical observation in the pursuit of empirical truth.

But the outstanding philosopher of the 13th century – in most people's view the greatest philosopher since Augustine, 800 years before – was Thomas Aquinas (1225–74). In more recent times there was a long period during which Aquinas held very special place in the minds of Roman Catholics, because in 1879 Pope Leo XIII recommended his philosophy as a model for Catholic thought. For something like a hundred years after that Aquinas was almost what one might call the official philosopher of the Catholic Church, regarded by Catholics with unique veneration. Since the Second Vatican Council of 1962–64, however, this attitude has relaxed, and Catholic thinkers now feel more comfortable about criticizing Aquinas.

## THOMAS AQUINAS

The great achievement of Aquinas was to produce a vast synthesis of all that had been best argued in Western thought up to his time, and show it to be compatible with Christian belief. He even drew on other sources too by including elements of Jewish and Islamic thought. Christian philosophy had developed from the beginning, as we have seen, with a high content of Platonism and Neo-Platonism; but now the philosophy of Aristotle was recovered by Christendom, and this too had to be absorbed. Thomism (which is what the philosophy founded by Aquinas is called) consists for the most part of a highly successful marriage between an already extensively Platonized Christianity and the philosophy of Aristotle. Throughout this large-scale enterprise Aquinas is scrupulous about maintaining

# "THE SOUL IS KNOWN BY ITS ACTS"

THOMAS AQUINAS

the distinction between philosophy and religion, or between reason and faith. For example, he says that as far as rational thought is concerned the questions whether the world had a beginning and will have an end are undecidable: in either case the truth could lie either way. But, he says, as a Christian

he believes (though it is not rationally demonstrable) that the world had a beginning, having been created by God, and will one day have an end.

Basing himself on Aristotle, Aquinas argues that all our rational knowledge of this world is acquired through sensory experience, on which our minds then reflect. There is nothing in the intellect which was not first in the senses. When a child is born its mind is like a clean slate on which nothing has yet been written. (Aquinas uses the Latin term *tabula rasa*, or clean slate, a phrase often accredited to the much later philosopher John Locke.) From these beginnings Aquinas develops a theory of knowledge which is so uncompromisingly empiricist that a modern reader might suppose it to sit

KEY WORKS

*The most famous works of Aquinas are two compendia written for students, by whom they have been used ever since. One is called* Summa Theologiae (Summary of Theology), *and the other* Summa Contra Gentiles (On the Truth of the Catholic Faith). *Unlike Augustine's works, however, they are difficult for the general reader.*

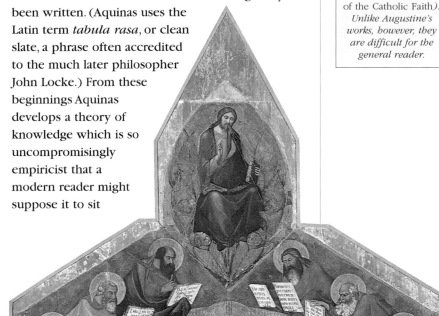

ST THOMAS AQUINAS
*Aquinas was among the first philosophers to introduce the work of Aristotle into Christian thought. In* The Triumph of St Thomas Aquinas, *by the 14th-century Pisan painter Francesco Traini, Aquinas is depicted between Aristotle (left) and Plato (right).*

THE MICROCOSM
The notion of the microcosm dates in Western philosophy from Socratic times. The microcosm is a term designating man as being a little world (as the picture above shows) in which the macrocosm, or universe, is reflected.

uncomfortably with religious belief; but of course Aquinas holds that the world of which we thus gain our knowledge is through and through God's creation, and therefore it is impossible for the knowledge thus gained to conflict with religious revelation.

### ESSENCE AND EXISTENCE

A distinction developed by Aquinas that has played a role in philosophy ever since is between existence and essence. The essence of a thing is *what* that thing is, and this is a separate matter from the question of whether or not it exists. A simple example can make this clear. If a child says to you: "What is a unicorn?" you could reply: "It's a rather elegant horse, usually white, with a long straight or spiral horn sticking up out of its head." If the child then says: "Do unicorns exist?" you would have to say: "No they don't exist." In this example the first of your two answers would have addressed itself to the question of essence and the second to the question of existence. If the child goes on to ask you about tigers you can vividly describe tigers to him, yet however extensive and detailed your description he still has to ask you "Do they exist?", because from the description itself he has no way of knowing whether they exist or not – that is always a separate question, and one which he has to ask you about separately. This distinction was the basis for Aquinas' rejection of Anselm's

GOD CREATING THE WORLD
*This exquisite, 12th-century, Spanish tapestry shows God as the creator. He is surrounded by scenes (from left) of the creation of Eve from Adam, the birds and the fish, and Adam naming the animals.*

ontological argument for the existence of God: Anselm's definition gives us God's essence, but no characterization of essence, however exhaustive, guarantees existence.

Aquinas addressed himself with exceptional insight to the question of what it is for something to exist. If a thing is only essence it has the potential for existence, but its existence is not yet actual. Assuming that God made the world in accordance with his wishes, the world's essence must have preceded its existence. But God's own essence cannot have preceded his existence – so God must be, so to speak, pure existence.

Generations of philosophers were to dispute over the question which is prior, essence or existence. As so often in the history of philosophy, one side of this dispute turned out to have natural affinities with Plato, the other with Aristotle: the notion that essence must always precede existence derived obvious support from Plato's theory of Ideal Forms (see p.27), while the apparently contrary assertion that only from our knowledge of already existing objects can we ever even have derived any notion whatsoever of essences, and that any individual object needs first to exist before it can possibly possess any of the characteristics tributed to it by a knowing subject, fitted in comfortably with an Aristotelian approach. Readers will also notice a parallel between this dispute and the argument over the nature of universals (see p.58).

## OCKHAM'S RAZOR

Positions held by Aquinas were criticized by Duns Scotus (c. 1266–1308), who in some technical ways is the most superior example of a medieval scholastic philosopher. His exposition and dissection of arguments is so meticulous that those who study him are often permanently influenced by that in itself. He always holds honestly to the distinction between reason and faith: for example, though he believes in the immortality of the soul he states that none of the so-called "proofs" of it do in fact succeed in proving it. The outstanding American philosopher C. S. Peirce (see pp.186–87) regarded him as one of the "profoundest metaphysicians that ever lived". It is only too ironical that our word "dunce" should have been coined from his name, by his detractors, after his death.

Some of Duns Scotus' criticisms were pushed further by William of Ockham (1285–1347), who developed such a far-reachingly empiricist approach that in retrospect he seems almost to be a forerunner of the most famous of all schools

## "ENTITIES SHOULD NOT BE POSITED UNNECESSARILY"

WILLIAM OF OCKHAM

of British empiricist philosophy, the succession of Locke, Berkeley, and Hume. Ockham argued that there is such a thing as necessity in logic but not in the natural order of things: in nature even unbroken regularities are contingent, which is to say, they need not have happened, they could have been otherwise. This means we cannot reach any knowledge of the world purely through logical argument or speculation. Instead we have to look and see how things actually are; and it is only observation and experience – which of course we must *then* reason about – that can provide us with a reliable basis for knowledge of the world of nature. With Ockham the path is intellectually

opened to a new approach to human knowledge, an approach we have since come to think of as scientific. The best-known single idea associated with his name is the principle of Ockham's razor, which has been accepted and used ever since. This states that of two alternative explanations for the same phenomena the more complicated is more likely to have something wrong with it, and therefore, other things being equal, the more simple is the more likely to be correct. This being so, we should always, in the course of trying to work out an explanation of something, assume the minimum we need to assume. Entities should not be posited unnecessarily. At first sight it seems counter-intuitive to say that simpler explanations are more likely to be correct than complicated ones; but so it is. The qualification "other things being equal" is crucial here. Einstein hit the point off brilliantly when he said "Everything should be made as simple as possible, but not simpler."

**DUNS SCOTUS**
A Scottish scholastic philosopher and theologian, Duns Scotus became a Franciscan and studied and taught at Oxford and Paris, and finally at Cologne where he died. His philosophy represents a reaction against the ideas of Aristotle and Aquinas.

**THE LADY AND THE UNICORN**
*How can our words have meaning if the thing to which they refer, such as the unicorn, does not exist? The example is unimportant, but it illustrates a fundamental problem about essence and existence which has long puzzled philosophers.*

# The BEGINNINGS of MODERN SCIENCE

SCIENCE DID NOT BEGIN, AS WE MIGHT HAVE EXPECTED, WITH A STUDY OF THOSE MATTERS CLOSEST TO HAND, NAMELY HUMAN AFFAIRS, AND THEN WORK OUTWARDS TOWARDS THE MOST DISTANT THINGS, NAMELY THE STARS. ON THE CONTRARY, SCIENCE BEGAN WITH OBSERVATION OF THE STARS, AND WORKED FROM THERE INWARDS. THE LAST MATTERS TO COME UNDER SCIENTIFIC OBSERVATION WERE HUMAN AFFAIRS. THE KEY TO THE NEWNESS OF MODERN SCIENCE WAS ITS INSISTENCE ON TESTING THEORIES BY DIRECT CONFRONTATION WITH REALITY, CHECKING THEM BY OBSERVING AND MEASURING THE DATA THEY WERE SUPPOSED TO EXPLAIN. BEFORE THEN, THEORIES HAD BEEN TESTED CHIEFLY BY DISCUSSION AND ARGUMENT.

**MODEL OF THE SOLAR SYSTEM**
*This early 19th-century orrery was made to demonstrate the planetary orbits of our Solar System.*

"*Thou hast
fixed the earth
immovable
and firm*"

PSALM 93,
ADDRESSING GOD

# FROM COPERNICUS TO NEWTON

## THE UNVEILING OF THE UNIVERSE

*In the 16th and 17th centuries
the new science brought about the
biggest single change in man's
conception of the universe that
had ever occurred.*

THE SYSTEM OF ASTRONOMY that was developed
over generations by the ancient Greeks came to
be known as the Ptolemaic system, after Ptolemy,
an astronomer who lived in Alexandria in the
2nd century AD and published the first systematic
account of astronomy as it had evolved up to that
time. This remained the basis for astronomy in
Europe until the 16th century. It taught that the
earth was a sphere hanging unsupported in space,
and was the centre of the universe, with the planets
and stars moving around it in vast circles.

### AUTHORITY THREATENED

During the Middle Ages the Catholic Church
incorporated the Ptolemaic system into the
Christian view of the world, as part of its general
programme of combining the wisdom and learning
of the ancients with the Christian religion. On this
view God had made the world to be at the centre
of everything. And to be the master of this world
he had created man in his own image. In the
heavens, he had established his paradise, as being
the realm to which the souls of human beings
would go after their bodies died.

Psychologically, this picture was fairly simple.
The observable part of it seemed more or less
obvious, even if the mathematics required to
support it were disconcertingly complicated.
But in the 16th century a Polish churchman called
Copernicus (1473-1543) pointed out that many
of the most fearsome mathematical difficulties
would melt away if, instead of assuming that the

THE COPERNICAN SYSTEM
*The Polish astronomer Nicolaus Copernicus, founder
of modern astronomy, proposed the idea that the sun,
not the earth, is at the centre of our solar system.
The Copernican system, with the sun circled by the
six known planets, is shown in this print.*

earth were at the centre, we treated the sun as the
centre. When we did this, he showed that planetary
movements that were becoming increasingly
difficult to explain suddenly made good, clear
sense. Copernicus kept insisting that this was only
a hypothesis. He had some idea of the trouble his
ideas would cause, and so he delayed their
publication until what turned out to be the year
of his death, 1543; and even then he dedicated
his book to the Pope.

As usual with new ideas, it took some time
for his to get through. But when they did – one
is tempted to use the phrase "all hell broke loose".
For Copernicus' hypothesis meant that the earth
moved round the sun, and not vice versa; and not
only did this deny something the church had been
teaching for a thousand years, it flatly contradicted

# "WHO WILL VENTURE TO PLACE THE AUTHORITY OF COPERNICUS ABOVE THAT OF THE HOLY SPIRIT?"

JOHN CALVIN

with an impersonal concern for truth. What people were more aware of was the fact that if his theory was right then the most revered of all authorities were wrong, the whole lot of them – the Bible, the church, the wisest men of the ancient world. And if the authorities were wrong about this they might equally well be wrong about other things. The whole established order was under threat, even the very idea of authority itself.

## MOVING IN THE WRONG CIRCLES

Another consequence of Copernicus' ideas that was to be seismic in its effect was the removal of man from his privileged position in the universe. We humans were no longer the centre of everything. It no longer appeared that everything else revolved around us. When this realization spread it was earthquake-like in its consequences for human attitudes, not least peoples' attitudes towards religion.

If no authority could be accepted uncritically this was bound to apply to Copernicus himself. Astronomers who came after him criticized his theory, and checked it

...e Bible itself. Psalm 93 says (addressing God): ...Thou hast fixed the earth immovable and firm." ...is scarcely surprising that, in the century after ...s publication, Copernicus' theory was officially ...ondemned by the church.

But not only the Catholic Church was outraged. ...eading Protestants were just as scandalized. ..."People give ear", protested Luther, "to an upstart ...strologer who strove to show that the earth ...evolves, not the heavens or the firmament, the ...un and the moon...This fool wishes to reverse the ...ntire science of astronomy; but sacred scripture ...lls us that Joshua commanded the sun to stand ...ill and not the earth." Calvin, similarly, said: ..."Who will venture to place the authority of ...opernicus above that of the Holy Spirit?"

The question of authority was central to the ...hole furore. Of course Copernicus was offering ...s fundamental insights into the nature of the ...niverse, insights whose development and ...nplications have been of historic importance. ...it the outcry over his ideas had little to do

NICOLAUS COPERNICUS
*It was while he was studying mathematics and classics at the University of Cracow that Copernicus first developed an interest in astronomy.*

**Jupiter**

MUSIC OF THE PLANETS
Kepler discovered a relationship between the velocities of the planets in their elliptical orbits and musical harmony. He then calculated musical scales from the velocities of the planets when closest to and furthest from the sun. The example above is from his *Harmonies of the World*.

TYCHO BRAHE IN HIS OBSERVATORY
*When Danish King Frederick II gave Tycho Brahe, the greatest of the pre-telescope astronomers, the island of Hven, Tycho built an observatory for the accurate measurement of the stars. The instruments he used for these observations were large metal sextants and quadrants.*

against observable reality. The Danish astronomer Tycho Brahe (1546–1601) built up the biggest and most accurate body of measured observations that was ever made before the invention of the telescope – and then handed all this material over to a figure of genius, the German astronomer Johannes Kepler (1571–1630).

Copernicus had taken it for granted that the motions of all heavenly bodies were circular and uniform, but Kepler destroyed both of these assumptions. He showed that the planets move in ellipses, not circles, and that their motions are faster in some parts of their orbit than in others. This in turn destroyed the deep-rooted assumption that all celestial movements must make symmetrical patterns – an assumption which had started out on an aesthetic basis with the

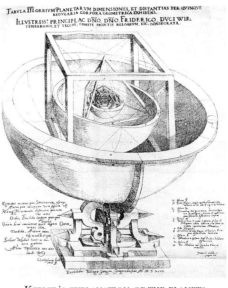

KEPLER'S EXPLANATION OF THE PLANETS
*Johannes Kepler applied mathematics to the study of planetary orbits and based his laws of planetary motion entirely on observation.*

ancient Greeks and then acquired a religious basis in the Middle Ages. This was yet another demolition of age-old conceptions of the universe – and of the authority of the authorities.

## GALILEO, THE GIANT FROM PISA

The first of the founding fathers of modern science to come into personal conflict with the power-wielding authorities of this world was Galileo (1564–1642). He was condemned by the Inquisition – a tribunal formed by the Roman Catholic Church to uncover and suppress heresy – first privately in 1616, then publicly in 1633. His crime was the two-fold one of asserting that the earth rotates on its axis and that it revolves round the sun. These ideas were by now nearly a century old, having been got by Galileo via Kepler from Copernicus; but they almost cost Galileo his skin. To save himself he recanted, and promised never again to uphold the sinful view that the earth moves. However, as he came away from the table on which he had signed his recantation he was heard to mutter under his breath: "But it still moves, just the same."

Galileo was a wonderful scientist, and more than a scientist. It is disputed whether or not he invented the telescope, but he was certainly the first person to look through one at the stars, and this development transformed the whole nature of astronomy. He discovered the principle of the pendulum, and this transformed both the manufacture and the accuracy of clocks. He invented the thermometer. Everyone up to his time had believed that the heavier a body is the faster it will fall, but he made the astonishing discovery that all bodies fall at the same velocity regardless of their weight, provided they are not interfered with by some other pressure. He discovered furthermore, that this velocity accelerates at a uniform rate of 32 feet per second per second. He established that every projectile moves in a parabola (thus launching the science of gunnery). And he showed that – far from it being natural for heavenly bodies, or any other bodies, to move in circles or ellipses – the natural thing was for a moving body to carry on moving in a

**THE TRIAL OF GALILEO**

*[G]alileo's* Dialogue On the Two Chief World Systems – *[Pt]olemaic and Copernican, published in 1632, argued for [th]e new cosmology. As a result, Galileo was called before the Inquisition to explain exactly why he was questioning traditional beliefs. Eventually, Galileo was forced to declare that the earth was the immovable centre of the universe.*

...[st]raight line unless and until some other force acted [o]n it. He discovered that if several different forces [ac]t on a moving body at the same time, the effect [o]n its movement is the same as if they had acted [se]parately and successively. This particularly rich [di]scovery opened the door to the whole new [sc]ience of dynamics. It was Galileo who consciously

# "BUT IT STILL MOVES, JUST THE SAME"

### GALILEO GALILEI

[fo]rmulated for the first time the principle of [ob]jectivity in science, the idea that even the most [im]mediate and direct physical experiences such as [co]lours and smells should systematically be left out [of] the recorded observations of scientists as being [pe]rsonal to the observer.

This cursory list of his achievements, incomplete [th]ough it is, must make it clear that Galileo was one [of] the most original and creative geniuses of all time.

The consequences of his work for man's understanding of the world, and hence for human thought processes, is beyond all calculation. Despite the precariousness of his situation, he proclaimed, when he dared, the principle that power and authority, including the authorities of the Christian religion, should have no right to interfere with the truth-seeking activities of science. "Why," he said: "this would be as if an absolute despot, being neither a physician nor an architect, but knowing himself free to command, should undertake to administer medicines and erect buildings according to his whim – at grave peril of his poor patients' lives, and speedy collapse of his edifices." *Keep out!* was his message to the authorities. And the slow but eventual spread of this attitude was to bring about revolutionary changes in European intellectual and social life.

## ISAAC NEWTON – SUPREME SCIENTIST

The greatest genius of all in this unfolding story – indeed, possibly the greatest scientist of all time – was an Englishman, Isaac Newton (1642–1727). Just for starters, between the ages of 23 and 24, he correctly analyzed the constituent properties of light, invented calculus, and not only formulated the concept of gravity but worked out the law of

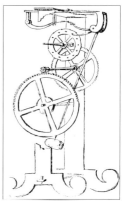

**THE PENDULUM CLOCK**
Galileo observed that a pendulum appears to take the same time to swing back and forth. He later designed a clock that operated on this principle. This design, drawn by his pupil Vicenzo Viviani, was not built until the 19th century. Pendulum clocks were much more accurate than their more primitive forerunners.

Only 54 years earlier the Pope had publicly condemned Galileo for asserting that the earth moved, and now Newton was providing mankind with an accurate working model of the entire planetary system.

The name given to this kind of enquiry was "natural philosophy", because it was the attempt to understand the workings of nature. The distinction had not yet been made, and was not to be made until the following century, between philosophy and science. Meanwhile natural philosophy brought about one of the biggest revolutions in general thinking that had ever occurred. Pythagoras' insight that the whole material universe was susceptible of explanation in terms of mathematics had at last, after two thousand years, been given its vindication and its proof.

For it was now established that the workings of the physical universe were indeed

**THE ROYAL OBSERVATORY**
*Founded by Charles II in 1675 and designed by Sir Christopher Wren, the purpose of the Royal Observatory in Greenwich, England, was to improve knowledge of celestial bodies as an aid to navigation.*

gravitation – all in a single year at the outset of his career. His work enabled him to revise and correct that of Kepler and Galileo – for instance he reformulated Kepler's three laws of planetary motion into what became known ever after as

**NEWTON'S MOMENT OF DISCOVERY**
Newton is said to have realized the wider importance of gravity in 1666 when he saw an apple fall from a tree in his garden. The falling apple made him question whether the force exerted by the earth in making the apple fall was the same force that made the moon fall towards the earth, and so pull it into an elliptical orbit round the earth.

## "IF I HAVE SEEN FURTHER IT IS BY STANDING ON THE SHOULDERS OF GIANTS"

ISAAC NEWTON

Newton's laws of motion – and gradually built up a system of mathematical physics that enabled him to give a complete and accurate picture of the planetary system. The book in which he did this was published in 1687, and is usually known as his *Principia*, short for a much longer Latin title. The intellectual achievement is awe-inspiring.

bject to laws, that these laws were discernible by uman beings, and that they were expressible in quations. Because of their constancy, these quations gave man for the first time the power of cientific prediction. Given a full description of the resent state of any physical system one could, with he aid of Newton's laws, accurately predict what s state would be at any future time. This in turn ave many of the people who understood the new cience an unprecedented sense of mastery, the eeling that they had somehow tamed the universe vith their understanding. This feeling was to be reatly enhanced over ensuing generations, when Newtonian mechanics was put to work in the evelopment of machinery that made the Industrial evolution possible. It seemed that man was indeed becoming the master of nature, not just in his theoretical understanding but in the most direct practical

NEWTON'S *PRINCIPIA*
*Newton's most important book, the one-volume* Principia, *explains his three laws of motion and his theory of gravity, as well as demonstrating that it is the force of gravity that keeps the planets moving in orbits around the sun.*

terms of domination and exploitation. However, with the earth no longer seen as the centre of the universe but a minor planet of a minor star it became difficult for many to believe that the existence of the entire cosmos must have a purpose connected with man. There began that rapid spread of disbelief in the existence of God that conspicuously characterizes the West over the following three centuries, as more and more people came to think of man himself as lord of the known universe.

## A NEW WORLD-VIEW
The consequences of all this for traditional thought-structures and authorities were cataclysmic. It came to be believed increasingly widely that, in matters of truth-seeking, tradition was an encumbrance and authority had no place. Any statement of the form "x is true" was met no longer with the question "Which authority is it that says so?" but with the question "What is your evidence for that – where is your proof?"; and authorities came eventually to be seen as being as open to critical questioning, as accountable, as others.

These great intellectual movements took time to work themselves out, of course, but they played a central role in helping to bring about the end of

*"Where the statue stood Of Newton, with his prism and silent face, The marble index of a mind for ever Voyaging through strange seas of Thought, alone"*
WILLIAM WORDSWORTH

THE CLOCKWORK UNIVERSE
*This clockwork model of the solar system, with the sun in the centre orbited by the earth and the moon, was built in 1712 by John Rowley. Known as an orrery, after the fourth Earl of Orrery, for whom it was made, it reflects Newton's view of the universe as a giant machine.*

*The gardens of Vaux-le Vicomte (1656–61) by André Le Nôtre have a strong axial emphasis. The restrained details and geometrical design, derived from mathematical formulas, express the philosophical thought of the 17th century.*

### ANDRÉ LE NÔTRE

*The French landscape architect André Le Nôtre (1613–1700) perfected the classical style of gardening. His gardens at Versailles and Vaux-le-Vicomte are the perfect symbol of the age. They are balanced and geometrical with a broad terrace and the main axis running from the principal doorway of the house. Features such as balustrades, fountains, and statues are organized on a symmetrical plan.*

what we call the Middle Ages. The Catholic Church lost its control over the intellectual and cultural life of Europe – completely so in those countries that went Protestant, but to some degree even in those countries that remained Catholic, where in the longer run they were also to lose it almost completely. At the scientific level the world-view that was thus overthrown was in essentials Aristotelianism. We have seen how in the later

# "THE LAST ENCHANTMENTS OF THE MIDDLE AGE"

MATTHEW ARNOLD

centuries of the Middle Ages thinker after thinker, culminating in Thomas Aquinas, struggled to incorporate the work of Aristotle within the world-view of the Catholic Church (see p.59). To the very extent that they succeeded, one of the inevitable consequences was that when – throughout the subsequent period covered by, first, the Renaissance, then the Reformation – many of the leading figures of European intellectual and cultural life began to throw off or disregard the dominance of the Christian churches this meant rejecting not

only ecclesiastical and biblical authority but also the authority of Aristotle. So the new scientific view of the world had to struggle for several generations to establish itself *against* the world-view of Aristotle.

*By the end of the Middle Ages the Catholic Church had lost its authority over the attitudes and values of intellectual life in Europe – Man was in charge of his own destiny.*

# "*God said,* LET NEWTON BE!"

Isaac Newton is generally acknowledged to be the greatest scientist who ever lived, the only possible exception being Einstein. Among many other things, he was the first human being to provide a largely accurate account of the movements of the earth through space, and of the workings of the planetary system of which the earth is part.

After human beings had lived on the earth's surface for hundreds of thousands of years without understanding the nature of their home in space, Newton revealed it. It was a unique moment of revelation in human history. As the poet Alexander Pope famously put it:

> *Nature and Nature's laws lay*
> *hid in night:*
> *God said, Let Newton be! and*
> *all was light.*

But not only was it the grand scheme of things that Newton unveiled. His laws applied to the movements of all objects on the earth's surface. He brought to perfection the sciences of statics and dynamics. The application of these through technology was to make the Industrial Revolution possible, and thus to transform the face of the earth – not to mention the nature of human societies.

The consequences of Newton's work for philosophy were immense. Henceforth, every philosopher had

to take full account of the new science, in that any description of reality had to incorporate in a plausible way the reality revealed by science. Not only that: any

## HOW COULD BELIEF IN GOD BE RECONCILED WITH THE REVELATIONS OF SCIENCE?

account of the nature of knowledge itself, and of the way it was arrived at, and its foundations, had to apply to science if it was to command credibility.

As far as science was concerned, the age-old authorities of Church and State simply did not exist. What the truth was did not depend on

what they said at all: truth was now to be established by methods that operated independently of them. So established authorities lost their place in society's intellectual life.

People began to question the fundamentals of their own beliefs. If the movements of all matter in space are known to be subject to scientific laws, what about our own bodies? Are all their movements subject to scientific laws? If so, does this mean there is no such thing as free will? Are we not in control of our own bodies? If there is no such thing as free will, does this mean there is no such thing as morality? And if an exhaustive and accurate explanation of all physical phenomena can now be provided by science, what need is there to believe in God any more?

For well over a hundred years after Newton, some of the greatest of philosophers addressed themselves to these questions. How could belief in God be reconciled with the revelations of science? How could morality function in a world governed by scientific laws? How could there be free will in a deterministic universe? Newton's work set out the agenda not only for the science of the age following him but also for the philosophy.

# MACHIAVELLI
## THE TEACHER OF PRINCES

*Machiavelli was the first person to study objectively, with what we might now call a scientific attitude, politics and government as they are actually practised.*

**KEY WORKS**

The Prince *(1513) discusses how a new prince can build up his power. It applied to politics the methods of experimental science.*

*In his* Discourses *(1513) Machiavelli discusses the arguments for and against different forms of government.*

THE EXCITING STORY OF the emergence of modern science has such a narrative sweep – from Copernicus, through Kepler, and then Galileo, to its culmination in Newton – that we wanted to follow it through, and this has carried us ahead of related developments in other fields. So we now have some catching up to do with parallel developments in other areas. One of the most important of these is political philosophy. The Renaissance threw up an outstanding genius in this field, Niccolò Machiavelli (1469–1527). It will be noted that he was born only four years before Copernicus.

Just like the new scientists in their quite different field, Machiavelli tried to brush aside whatever had been the established ways of talking about politics and to see the facts as they really are, head on. As he puts it in his most famous book, *The Prince*, published in 1513: "Since my intention is to say something that will be of practical use to the enquirer, I have thought it proper to represent things as they are in real truth, rather than as they are imagined." Before him, theorists of politics had written about such things as the duties of the ruler, and what sort of person would constitute an ideal prince, and what would be the most desirable form of society; but however wise and deep the best of such writings were they were not about the day-to-day activities of politics. By contrast with all this Machiavelli set out to tell it like it is. From that day to this some people have found what he says in his book shocking – so much so that the very word "Machiavellian" has come into widespread

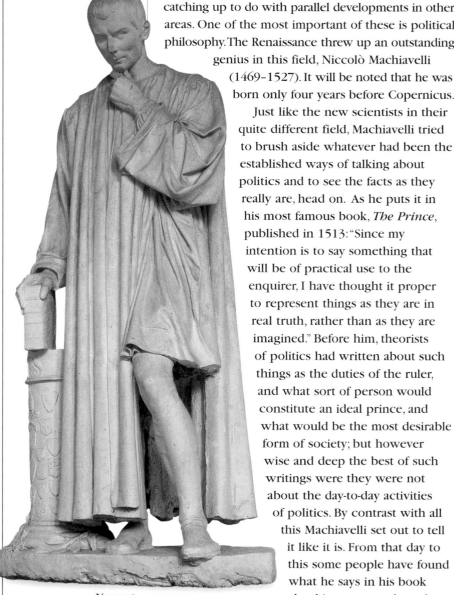

NICCOLÒ MACHIAVELLI
*The Italian statesman and political philosopher Machiavelli was descended on both sides from aristocratic Florentine legal families.*

use as a derogatory term meaning cunning, amoral, opportunist, and, above all, manipulative. But all Machiavelli was doing was to bring intellectual honesty to bear on the realities of politics. Just as the new scientists tried consciously, against the whole weight of Christian tradition, to develop a value-free science, so Machiavelli was trying to develop a value-free political understanding

## THE GREAT TRUTH-TELLER

With great insight and truthfulness he described th things that human beings do to get power, and to keep it – and also the various ways in which they lose it. With disconcerting directness he deals with the central role in all politics of force or the threat of force; with the importance of appearances, and therefore of image-making; with the question of whe it is advantageous for a politician to keep his word, and when it is advantageous for him to break it; with which sorts of plot can be expected to succeed and

> "IT IS MUCH SAFER FOR A PRINCE TO BE FEARED THAN LOVED"
>
> NICCOLÒ MACHIAVELLI

which to fail. *The Prince* has been called the bible of *Realpolitik* (the German word now in use, even in English, for "real", hard-nosed politics). One of its chapters is headed: "On those who came to Power by Crime". Never at any time does Machiavelli base an argument on whatever it is that people are *supposed* to do, still less on any Christian or biblical exhortation What he provides is an accurately observed and superbly written account of what actually happens And it is not only those of us in the 20th or 21st centuries who have studied the careers of Hitler and Stalin who have seen his insights confirmed in modern times. So universal and valid are the best of these insights that one sees them confirmed wherever human beings jockey for place and preferment, not only in politics but in professional associations of any kind, or industrial companies, or service organizations; even, come to that, in churches and clubs and other voluntary bodies.

In Machiavelli's other great work, the *Discourses* (written at the same time as *The Prince*, and also published in 1513), he compares with a similar penetration and honesty the pros and cons of different forms of government, and reveals it as his view that a republic, where it has genuine popular support, is likely to be the best and most stable.

Of course Machiavelli's honest descriptions of what goes on in politics are shocking. So would any such descriptions be of what goes on in our own day. But readers were quite wrong, most of the time, to

FLORENTINE STATESMAN
*Machiavelli was employed as an envoy by the Florentine Republic at a time when Europe's political order appeared to be breaking down.*

accuse him of advocating these wicked practices he wrote about, or to talk of him as if he were the devil himself. There are places in his writings where he says, in effect, that if the ruler is to save the state in a particular sort of crisis, or retain his own position in power, then he must be prepared to act against this or that moral principle; but even in these passages he is, usually, only stating an unpalatable truth, at least in the political circumstances of his time and place, which was Renaissance Italy.

His revelations were hugely appreciated even from the beginning by the perceptive, who saw him, correctly, as clearing away the cant of centuries. He rapidly achieved international fame. Shakespeare refers to him in one of his plays, and the most famous of all English lord chancellors, Francis Bacon, wrote: "We are much beholden to Machiavel and others, that write what men do, and not what they ought to do."

NICOLAI
MACHIAVELLI
PRINCEPS.
EX
SYLVESTRI TELII
FVLGINATIS TRADVCTIONE
diligenter emendata.

*Adiecta fut eiusdem argumenti, aliorum quorundam contra Machiavellum scripta de potestate & officio Principum, & contra tyrannos.*

BASILEAE
Ex officina Petri Pernæ.
M D XXC.

***THE PRINCE***
Intended as a handbook for rulers, *The Prince* (1513) contained advice on what to do and what to say to achieve political success. It is believed by many that Machiavelli's model of the ideal prince was the clever and unscrupulous Cesare Borgia.

---

THE BORGIAS

*Originally Spanish nobles, the Borgia family first came to Italy in 1443 and rose to great prominence in the 15th century. Rodrigo, who later became Pope Alexander VI, was anxious to extend his power and further his children's interests. His illegitimate children, Cesare (1475–1507) and Lucrezia (1480–1519), were notorious for their many crimes and moral excesses.*

***CESARE BORGIA LEAVING THE VATICAN***
*Cesare Borgia was a clever, ambitious, and unscrupulous opportunist in love with political power. But he was an able ruler and was cited by Machiavelli as the model of the ideal prince. In this painting of 1877 by Giuseppe-Lorenzo Gatteri, Cesare is shown being carried from the Vatican after visiting his father, the controversial Pope Alexander VI.*

# FRANCIS BACON

## A NEW METHOD FOR THE NEW SCIENCE

*Bacon saw the vast possibilities of the newly emerging science, and put forward programmes for its development at every level, from the theoretical to the institutional.*

**KEY WORKS**
Essays (1597) deals
with how men live:
what men do and
what men ought to do.

The Advancement of
Learning (1605) is a
review of the state
of knowledge of
Bacon's own time.

In Novum Organum
(1620) Bacon
presented his
scientific method.

**Eſſayes.**

Religious Meditations.

Places of perſwaſion and
diſſwaſion.

Scene and allowed.

AT LONDON,
Printed for Humfrey Hooper, and are
to be ſold at the blacke Beare
in Chauncery Lane.
1 5 9 7.

**BACON'S *ESSAYES***
In his *Essayes* (1597),
Bacon gives his views on
various subjects – political
and personal. In lucid
prose he studies the
natures of such things
as ambition, revenge,
and love.

FRANCIS BACON (1561–1626) was a true
polymath, a man distinguished in politics, law,
literature, philosophy, and science. His whole life
was lived in and around the English court, the
centre of political power, under Queen Elizabeth I
and King James I. His father, Sir Nicholas Bacon, was
Lord Keeper of the Great Seal to Elizabeth. Francis
was educated at Cambridge, where he acquired an
abiding hostility to Aristotle, and then went into
law. He became a Member of Parliament at the
age of 23, and eventually, in succession, Solicitor-
General, Attorney-General, Lord Keeper of the
Great Seal (like his father), Lord Chancellor, as well
as becoming a baron and a viscount. At the age
of 36 he published the
collection of

essays that has been his most popular book ever
since. But throughout his adult life he was producin
writings that were to have a historic influence on th
direction taken by Western science and philosophy
Given that he had a public career so overcrowded
with work and achievements, to suggest that in
addition to all this he also wrote Shakespeare's
plays is about as probable as that George Bernard
Shaw's plays were written by Einstein.

### GODFATHER OF SCIENCE

Bacon wanted to use his political influence for
the advancement of science. He tried to persuade
James I to establish a royal institution that
would take the lead in this, and to
found a college for the study of the
experimental sciences. He also
wanted to see professorships of th
new science founded at Oxford
and Cambridge. None of that came
about in his lifetime. But when James'
grandson, Charles II, founded the Royal
Society in 1662 its members were largely
Baconian in their scientific approach, and
regarded Francis Bacon as the intellectual
godfather of the society.
The most important
of all subsequent
British scientists,

**GRESHAM COLLEGE – THE EARLY HOME OF THE ROYAL SOCIETY**
*Gresham College in the City of London was the birthplace of the Royal
Society, and its home from 1662–1710. The College was founded by Sir
Thomas Gresham (1519–79), one of the great Elizabethan merchants.*

*Gresham College had seven resident professors who gave public lectures i
English as well as Latin. Some of these dealt with practical scientific subject
such as astronomy, which were not then on any university curriculum.*

rationalistic thinkers were like spiders who spin their webs out of matter secreted inside their own bodies: their structures are impressive but everything comes from within, and lacks sufficient contact with external reality. The more empirical thinkers, on the other hand, were likes ants, who mindlessly collect data but have only limited ideas about what to do with it. The traditional logic of

# "THE WISEST, BRIGHTEST, MEANEST OF MANKIND"

ALEXANDER POPE ON FRANCIS BACON

Aristotle was useless as a tool for discovery: it compels assent after the fact, but reveals nothing new. Similarly with definitions: the idea that definitions advance knowledge is an illusion. "Words are but the images of matter", said Bacon: "To fall in love with them is to fall in love with a picture".

What is required in order to advance our knowledge of the natural world, said Bacon, is the following controlled and systematic procedure. First, we must observe the facts, record our observations, and amass a body of reliable data, the more the better. This is more effectively done by many people working in communication with one another than by individuals working alone – hence the need for scientific societies and colleges. At this stage we must be careful not to impose our ideas on the facts, but to let them speak for themselves. When we have amassed enough of them they will begin to do so: regularities and patterns will begin to emerge, causal connections will reveal themselves, and we shall start to perceive the

**ROYAL SOCIETY**
*The Royal Society of London for the Improvement of Natural Knowledge, one of the oldest scientific societies in Europe, was formed in 1662 when a small number of academies were incorporated under royal charter. The organization was to have considerable influence on scientific developments. Among its founding members were the architect Sir Christopher Wren and the physicist Robert Hooke.*

**SIR FRANCIS BACON**
*Bacon became the Lord Chancellor of England. However, [h]e is renowned more as a philosopher and a writer than for his legal and political achievements.*

[N]ewton and Darwin, acknowledged their [in]debtedness to him; and his influence became [a]s great in France as it was in England.

When he was at the height of his career and his [p]ower, 60 years old and Lord Chancellor, he was [ac]cused of accepting bribes. He was tried, found [g]uilty, and dismissed in disgrace from all offices [u]nder the crown. He spent the remaining years [o]f his life writing philosophy and working out yet [f]urther schemes for the advancement of science. [T]hroughout his career he mixed the highest genius [in] theoretical matters with a shabby weakness in [p]ractical affairs. The poet Alexander Pope described [h]im as "The wisest, brightest, meanest of mankind".

## [S]CIENTIFIC METHOD
[B]acon was one of the first to see that scientific [k]nowledge could give men power over nature, [an]d therefore that the advance of science could be [u]sed to promote human plans and prosperity on an [u]nimaginable scale. But he thought that no one had [ye]t gone about this in the right way. The more

**QUEEN ELIZABETH I**
*The Queen did not like Bacon, who was adviser to the Earl of Essex, her favourite. When, however, Essex was arrested for plotting against the Queen, it was Bacon, as one of Her Majesty's counsel, who took part in the prosecution which led to his execution.*

laws of nature at work in the particular instances. At this stage, however, it is important for us to keep our eyes skinned for contrary instances. We are all inclined to leap to conclusions based only on the evidence that fits them: for example, if a man has a dream that then comes true he will often announce that this proves dreams to be prophetic, thereby simply ignoring the countless number of his dreams that have not come true. Negative instances are as important as positive ones in guiding us to the right conclusions. However, if we are self-disciplined in this respect we shall begin to perceive the general laws exemplified in the individual instances. When we have formed a well-based hypothesis of this kind our next task is to test it by crucial experiment. If experiment confirms the hypothesis we shall indeed have discovered a law of nature; and once we have done that we can confidently deduce individual instances from it, in other words make accurate predictions. So in the process of discovering a scientific law we are moving from the particular to the general, a process known as induction; whereas in applying the law once we have got it we move from the general to the particular, a process known as deduction. (Readers of the Sherlock Holmes stories will note that the standard method of the great detective, always referred to by him as deduction, is in fact induction, usually of the unreliable kind against which Bacon warned us.)

This formulation of scientific method was to have a simply immense influence from the 17th century to the twentieth. Generation after generation of scientists were guided by it; and many generations of philosophers, including some of the greatest, looked on Bacon as having set humanity on the right path for distinguishing scientific knowledge from all other sorts of knowledge – Kant placed a quotation from Bacon at the front of the revised edition of his *Critique of Pure Reason*. In the 18th century Voltaire and the French

### THE BACON FAMILY
Francis Bacon was the younger of the two sons of statesman Sir Nicholas Bacon (1509–79), Lord Keeper of the Great Seal to Elizabeth I, a staunch anti-Catholic, and an irreconcilable opponent of Mary, Queen of Scots. In 1606 Francis married Alice Barnham, a London alderman's daughter, but their marriage was childless. He is widely rumoured to have been homosexual – perhaps bi-sexual.

### WILLIAM HARVEY
*The English physician William Harvey (1578–1657) was the discoverer of the circulation of the blood. He studied medicine at Cambridge, and at Padua University, under Hieronymus Fabricius. Harvey's book* De Motu Cordis et Sanguinis *(On the Motion of the Heart, 1628) led to great advances in anatomy and physiology. Harvey was Bacon's personal physician.*

> ## "WORDS ARE BUT THE IMAGES OF MATTER, TO FALL IN LOVE WITH THEM IS TO FALL IN LOVE WITH A PICTURE"

FRANCIS BACON

Encyclopedists regarded him as having inaugurated the critical, scientific kind of thinking that they spent their lives propagating on the continent of Europe. It was not to lose this position until Einstein and Poppe introduced a new attitude to science in the 20th century.

### FALSE IDOLS
Having proposed this powerful and highly disciplined method for acquiring reliable knowledge Bacon warns us against the influences on our thinking that seduce us away from it. Because these are false notions to which we are too inclined to pay reverence he calls them "idols",

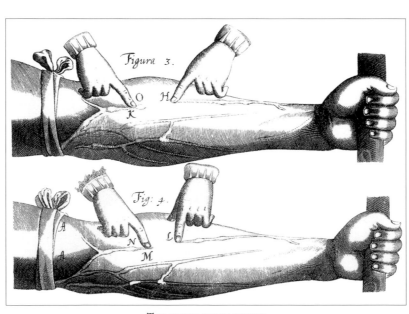

### THE CIRCULATORY SYSTEM
*The discovery of the circulation of blood was one of the first medical advances to come out of the scientific empiricism associated with Bacon. This illustration from Harvey's* De Motu Cordis et Sanguinis *(1628) demonstrates the existence of valves in the veins.*

THE POWER OF SPEECH

*The exchanges between human beings are mediated mostly by language. Words can mean different things to different people, and human beings can often confuse language with reality (Bacon's "idols of the market place"). Nowhere are the confusions and deceptions of language more apparent than in the hurly-burly world of politics – as depicted above in Egbert van Heemskerk's 1637 painting of* The Election in the Guildhall, Oxford.

### SIR WALTER RALEIGH

*An English soldier, seaman, courtier, writer, explorer, and favourite of Queen Elizabeth I, Sir Walter Raleigh (c. 1552–1618) was one of the spectacular figures of the Elizabethan age. His love of adventure and learning typified Elizabethan England. Raleigh quoted Bacon, with approval, in his* History of the World *(1614). Accused of treason against Elizabeth's successor, James I, Raleigh was imprisoned in the Tower of London from 1603 to 1616, and was eventually put to death.*

and he names four as being especially dangerous. First there are what he calls "idols of the tribe", because they are common to all mankind. These are the distorting factors inherent in our nature as human beings: our tendency to believe the evidence of our senses when in fact it often deceives us, and to allow our judgements to be coloured by our feelings, and to impose interpretations based on our own ideas and expectations on what we perceive. Then there are "idols of the cave", a reference to Plato's myth of the cave (see p.31): each separate individual "has his own private den or cavern, which intercepts and colours the light of nature" according to his own "peculiar and singular disposition". Thirdly, there are "idols of the market place", which come from exchanges between human beings, and are therefore mediated chiefly by language. There are two special ways in which words deceive. First, the same word means different things to different people. Second, human beings have a marked

tendency to confuse language with reality. Finally, there are "idols of the theatre". These are systematic representations of reality which are in fact not reality at all. What Bacon has chiefly in mind here are all the various systems of philosophy in terms of which people mistakenly look at reality, perhaps especially the sort that we nowadays term ideologies, the creators of false consciousness.

## QUALITY OF THE MIND
Bacon was a wonderful thinker. He systematically separated science from metaphysics (the things we have to assume before we can do any thinking at all), and saw clearly that scientific explanations were essentially causal explanations, not explanations in terms of purposes or goals. Of special and permanent value were his assertions of the centrality of observation and experiment to the acquisition of knowledge about the world, and his insistence on the never-to-be-forgotten importance, when drawing conclusions, of the negative instance.

# HOBBES

## THE FIRST MODERN MATERIALIST

*Hobbes put forward the view that physical matter is all there is, and that everything can be explained in terms of matter in motion.*

*"The value
or worth of a
man is, as of
all things,
his price"*
THOMAS HOBBES

THOMAS HOBBES (1588–1679) was born prematurely because his mother panicked when she heard that the Spanish Armada was approaching. "Fear and I were born twins", he used to say, referring to his own anxious personality. In spite of it, though, he was a trenchant and aggressive writer, and an exceptionally independent thinker.

He grew up in England during the reign of Queen Elizabeth I, and after her death his long life covered most of the period of Stuart rule plus the whole of the English Civil War. After being educated at Oxford he became tutor to the son of the future Earl of Devonshire, and this gave him three things

THOMAS HOBBES
*Hobbes lived from Elizabeth I's reign well into the reign of Charles II, during which time England faced the many challenges caused by the Reformation and the Civil War.*

that were greatly to promote his intellectual development: access to a first-class library, extensive foreign travel, and the opportunity to meet unusually interesting people at home and abroad. He formed connections at the highest level that were both personal and intellectual: he used to visit Francis Bacon during Bacon's years of retirement; in France he moved in the same circle as Descartes, with whom he corresponded about philosophy, and the mathematician Gassendi, who became a good friend; and in Italy he visited Galileo. For two years he was mathematics tutor to the future King Charles II. Personally timorous he may have been, but he never showed any lack of intellectual self-confidence.

### THE MIND AS MACHINE

In an age dominated by religion, and by religious faction, when to deny belief in God brought a man foul of the law and might endanger his life, Hobbes boldly came out with a philosophy of complete materialism: "The universe, that is the whole mass of things that are, is corporeal, that is to say body; and hath the dimensions of magnitude, namely, length, breadth, and depth. Also every part of body is likewise body, and hath the like dimensions. And, consequently, every part of the universe is body and that which is not body is no part of the universe. And because the universe is all, that which is no part of it is nothing, and, consequently nowhere."

CHARLES II AS THE PRINCE OF WALES WITH A PAGE
*Thomas Hobbes was mathematics tutor to the future Charles II (1630–85), who became king in 1660 when Parliament accepted the restoration of the monarchy.*

e went on to argue that such philosophers' and theologians' concepts as "incorporeal substance" were self-contradictory, and could mean nothing at all. When challenged to say what, in the light of all this, his conception of God was, he replied that it was far beyond the abilities of any mere human being to form a conception of God or his attributes.

This was typical of Hobbes' strategy for securing free speech for himself. He never soft-pedalled his views, but when challenged to explain how they could possibly be made compatible with what was acceptable in the society of his day he gave an answer which would have caused the objectors embarrassment to deny. One of his favourite ploys was to say that a question was one for the sovereign to decide; and he would assert this just as disconcertingly of metaphysical or religious questions as of political or legal ones. It made him, not surprisingly, popular with King Charles II, who knew him well anyway,

> ## "WORDS ARE WISE MEN'S COUNTERS... BUT THEY ARE THE MONEY OF FOOLS"
>
> THOMAS HOBBES

and enjoyed his company; and this secured his safety. To us looking back it is obvious that this was, at least in part, a clever and cynical manoeuvre.

It was obvious to some of his contemporaries too, though, and in consequence of this one of his early books did indeed put his life in danger, whereupon he fled to the Continent; and on another occasion his writings were banned. In spite of these threats, he lived to be 91, writing almost to the end.

Developing his assertion that only matter existed, Hobbes came to look at every moving object, including human beings, as some sort of machine, indeed at the whole universe as a vast machine. Thus, in addition to being what one might call the founder of modern metaphysical materialism, he was the first philosopher to put forward an out-and-out mechanistic view of nature. As part of this he developed a mechanistic psychology. This was something wholly new, to

**AN AGE DOMINATED BY RELIGION**
*Hobbes' philosophy of complete materialism was at odds with the God-fearing spirit of his day. St Peter's in the Wardrobe is one of 52 churches built by Sir Christopher Wren in the City of London after the City had been destroyed by the Great Fire of London in September 1666.*

look at the human mind as a machine – a soft machine, of course; but nevertheless, in Hobbes' view, all mental processes were to be understood as consisting of movements of matter inside an individual's skull. All these ideas – the materialism, the mechanism, and the purely physical psychology – were to be produced and developed by many thinkers over the three ensuing centuries, and were to have great influence. For someone who is out of sympathy with them it may be difficult to appreciate how original Hobbes' ideas were, but they were important because even if ultimately mistaken they helped to further key developments in human understanding. It is, for instance, now widely agreed that there is, at the very least, an indisputable physical basis to mental processes, which therefore cannot be understood without reference to the physical level; and Hobbes did much to stop people thinking of mind as something purely abstract.

Hobbes became fascinated by motion, especially after his visit to Galileo. According to the old Aristotelian world view, which Galileo was now fighting to overthrow, rest was self-evidently

SECURITY AND LIBERTY

*In Hendrik Steenwyck's (1550–1603)* View of a Market Place *we see a society at peace. Hobbes believed that it is the fear of death that causes us to form societies. Without societies* *we are in a "state of nature" with no rules or order. To crea[t]e a situation in which it is not in anyone's interest to break la[w] we must agree to hand over power to a central authority.*

*LEVIATHAN*
In his masterpiece, the *Leviathan* (1651), Hobbes advocates absolutist government as the only means of ensuring order. This title-page shows Leviathan, made up of all the members of the community, dominating the State. Below are the symbols of ecclesiastical and civil rule.

the natural state for physical bodies to be in. But according to Galileo all physical bodies without exception were in motion, including the earth itself (and therefore everything on the earth), and the natural thing was for any such body to go on moving in a straight line unless acted upon by a force. Hobbes, according to his own account, found this idea haunting. It opened up for him the idea of total reality as consisting of matter in motion, and this became his overall conception. If one were to separate out from this view of things the element that carried the greatest weight with him it was not matter but motion. He has been called a motion-intoxicated man. All causality in his material and mechanical world took the form of push; and that was how all change occurred, he believed.

He carried this over into his psychology. All psychological motivation was seen by him as some sort of push, whether in the form of an on-going drive or in the form of a repulsion. One could dub these two directions of motivation appetite and aversion. There are many familiar forms of them: liking and disliking, love and hate, joy and grief, and so on. The first halves of such pairs denote the inherently unsatisfiable, and therefore endless, needs and wants of human beings, which cannot cease unless and until life itself ceases. The overwhelmingly dominant form of the other, aversion, and indeed a repulsion far more powerful

and effective than any other, is the fear of death. Death is something that most of us will do more or less anything to avoid.

This basic view of human psychology was carried over in turn by Hobbes into his political philosophy. And it was his political philosophy which turned out in the long run to be the most influential aspect of his thought.

## FORCE AND FRAUD
Hobbes believed that at bottom it is the fear of death that causes human beings to form societies. Without society, in what he calls the state of natur[e] where there are no rules, order, or justice, life is "war of every man against every man", and all outcomes are determined by violence and cunning or, as he puts it, "force and fraud". In his best-know[n] book, *Leviathan* (1651), he paints a grisly picture of what such a state of affairs would be like, ending with words that are still quoted: "and which is wors[e] of all, continual fear, and the danger of violent death, and the life of man, solitary, poor, nasty, brutish, and short". Individuals might try to get out of this by entering into agreements or alliances with one another; but, as Hobbes says, "covenants without the sword are but words, and of no strength to secure a man at all". Anyone who can get away with breaking them will break them as soon as he finds it in his interests to do so. The only way

escape from the dilemma is to establish a situation in which it is not in anyone's interest to break laws.

The way to do this, says Hobbes, is for everyone to agree to hand over power to a central authority whose job it is to impose law, and to punish severely any law-breakers. For such an authority to be effective it must possess more power than any individual, or association of individuals, within the society can hope to attain, and therefore to have – in effect, and as far as they are concerned – absolute power, which it is hopeless to defy. This is the only way to maximize both the liberty and the security of the individuals who make up the society; but it does mean that each man "must be contented with so much liberty against other men as he would allow other men against himself".

## "I AM ABOUT TO TAKE MY LAST VOYAGE, A GREAT LEAP IN THE DARK"

THOMAS HOBBES' LAST WORDS

Hobbes is always careful to make it clear that this supreme authority can equally well be an individual or a group of individuals, and that in either case it holds its power not from God, or from any ancient or higher authority, but from the people themselves, the commonwealth; and that the people place this power in its hands because to do so maximizes their interests, in particular their personal freedom and their safety (in ascending order of importance). Absolute power is given to the sovereign not for the gratification of the sovereign but for the good of all.

## CHAOS WORSE THAN TYRANNY

Hobbes' fundamental political insight is that what populations fear most of all – more even than the most iron-fisted dictatorship – is social chaos, and that they will submit to almost any tyranny in preference to that. It must be remembered that he lived and wrote during the years of the English Civil War, when a king who believed himself to rule by divine right was executed, and the country descended into violent disorder, and peace was

RIGOROUS PUNISHMENT
*It was Hobbes' view that it is the responsibility of a central authority to punish law-breakers severely. This woodcut shows the execution of the regicides responsible for the death of Charles I, after the restoration of Charles II in 1660.*

restored only by a military dictatorship – and that Hobbes was personally close to some of the important figures in these events. He was himself in political exile in France when he wrote *Leviathan*. When it was published in 1651, Oliver Cromwell was at the height of his power as dictator of England. In the same year, Hobbes, in keeping with his published views, was reconciled with Cromwell and returned to live in England. But his happiness was very much greater when the monarchy was restored in 1660 and his former pupil, Charles II, ascended the throne as King of England.

**OLIVER CROMWELL**
*After serving as one of the leading generals of the Parliamentary forces in the English Civil War, Cromwell (1599–1658) became chairman of the Council of State of the new republic. From 1653, after first forcibly dissolving Parliament, Cromwell became lord protector of England, Scotland, and Ireland, and remained so until his death in 1658. This made him, in effect, dictator of Britain.*

THE BATTLE OF MARSTON MOOR
*In 1682, when in his 80s, Hobbes published* Behemoth, The History of the Causes of the Civil Wars of England. *The battle of Marston Moor, 2 July 1644, was one of the decisive battles of the English Civil War and gave the north of England to Parliament.*

# The GREAT RATIONALISTS

WHEN THE CHURCH'S AUTHORITY OVER THOUGHT
WAS FINALLY LOOSENED, MANY PEOPLE CAME TO
BELIEVE THAT KNOWLEDGE OF THE WORLD COULD
BE GAINED BY THE USE OF REASON ALONE.
IN PHILOSOPHY THIS DEVELOPMENT IS KNOWN AS
RATIONALISM. IT WAS LAUNCHED BY DESCARTES,
AFTER WHOM THE OUTSTANDING FIGURES IN
RATIONALIST PHILOSOPHY WERE SPINOZA AND
LEIBNIZ. DESCARTES AND LEIBNIZ WERE AMONG
THE MOST GIFTED OF ALL MATHEMATICIANS, AND
FOR THEM MATHEMATICS SEEMED TO PROVIDE THE
IDEAL MODEL FOR TRULY RELIABLE KNOWLEDGE.
THEY BELIEVED THAT IF THE METHODS BY WHICH
MATHEMATICIANS SUCH AS THEMSELVES WERE
MAKING NEW DISCOVERIES AND ACQUIRING NEW
KNOWLEDGE COULD BE APPLIED TO HUMAN
ATTEMPTS TO UNDERSTAND THE WORLD, THE
WORLD COULD BE FULLY EXPLAINED.

**AN EARLY CALCULATOR**
*The French philosopher and mathematician Blaise Pascal invented
this calculator in 1644 to help his father with his tax calculations.*

# DESCARTES

## BACK TO SQUARE ONE

*Descartes placed the question "What can I know?" – and a very determined pursuit of certainty in the answer – at the centre of Western philosophy for three hundred years.*

> *"I was struck by the large number of falsehoods I had accepted as true in my childhood"*
>
> RENÉ DESCARTES

RENÉ DESCARTES WAS BORN in France in 1596. He received an excellent education at the hands of the Jesuits, an education which included philosophy and mathematics; then he took a degree in law at the University of Poitiers, his home town. As a brilliant student he perceived that many of the arguments put forward by the various authorities he was studying were invalid, and often he did not know what to believe. In order to complete his education, he says, he joined the army, and travelled widely in Europe as a soldier, though without seeing any fighting. His travels taught him that the world of human beings was even more varied and mutually contradictory than the world of books. He became obsessed by the question whether there was anything we could be sure of, anything we could know for certain.

He settled down in Holland, which allowed the greatest freedom of expression of any country in Europe, and proceeded to examine the foundations of human thought, his investigations taking the

**RENÉ DESCARTES**
*Descartes had his portrait painted several times during his lifetime. This portrait of Descartes is after a painting by the Flemish-born artist Frans Hals (c. 1580–1666), though Descartes almost certainly never sat for Hals.*

form of philosophy, mathematics and science. For roughly the twenty years between 1629 and 1649 he produced original work of the highest quality. In philosophy his outstanding works were two: *Discourse on Method*, published in 1637, and *Meditations*, published in 1641. In 1649 Queen Christina of Sweden invited him to Stockholm to tutor her in philosophy. In the bitter Swedish winter he contracted pneumonia, and died in 1650.

## CARTESIAN DOUBT

Descartes was a mathematician of genius, and invented a new branch of the subject which consists in the application of algebra to geometry: it is known variously as analytic geometry or co-ordinate geometry. He also invented the graph. Those two familiar lines on a graph are named after him: they are called Cartesian co-ordinates, the word Cartesian being the adjective from the name Descartes. The transparent and utterly reliable certainties of mathematics thrilled him. And he began to wonder whether what gave mathematics its certainty was something that could be taken over and applied in other areas of knowledge. If it could, we would have a ready refutation of the sceptics who maintained that nothing else could be known for certain. But, far more important than that, we would have at our disposal a method for acquiring certain knowledge about the world, a method on the basis of which science in the modern sense could be constructed.

**THE JESUIT COLLEGE OF LA FLÈCHE**
*In 1604 Descartes' father sent him to the Royal College in the small town of La Flèche, north of Touraine. Founded by Henry IV and directed by Jesuits, La Flèche became one of the most distinguished schools in Europe. Descartes remained at the college until 1612, the last few years being given to study of logic, philosophy, and mathematics.*

**TREATISE ON MAN**
Descartes' treatise, published in 1664, looks at the human body as a machine, and attempts to explain physiological processes in terms of the behaviour of microscopic corpuscles. This drawing examines the relationship between heat and pain.

**QUEEN CHRISTINA OF SWEDEN AND DESCARTES**

This painting by Pierre Louis Dumesnil the Younger depicts Queen Christina and members of her court listening to Descartes giving a philosophy lesson. Christina insisted that the lessons be given at five o'clock in the morning, three days a week. The lessons lasted around five hours. The combination of early rising and the exceptionally harsh Swedish winter led to Descartes falling seriously ill, and to his death from pneumonia on 11 February 1650.

**CHRISTINA OF SWEDEN**
Christina of Sweden (1626–89), the only child of King Gustav II Adolphus and Princess Maria Eleonora of Brandenburg, was Queen of Sweden from 1644 to 1654. Independent and intellectually gifted, she was the patron of Descartes, the composer Alessandro Scarlatti, and the architect Giovanni Bernini. Christina converted to Roman Catholicism in 1652 and abdicated because of her faith in 1654.

### THE EXPERIENCE OF OBSERVATION

*Descartes argued that direct observation often deceives us, that one can never be certain that things are as they appear to be, however closely one may be looking at them. These paintings of Rouen Cathedral, part of a series painted by Claude Monet between 1892 and 1894, illustrate how the effects of light can alter the appearance of an object.*

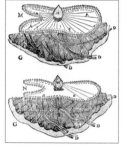

**THE HUMAN BRAIN**
Descartes' *Treatise on Man* (1664) was one of the most widely read texts in the 17th and 18th centuries. The book was an attempt to explain physiological processes along mechanistic lines and interpreted the body as a machine. This illustration shows the human brain awake and asleep.

Descartes came to the conclusion that mathematics owed its certainty to the following set of reasons. Mathematical demonstrations began from a minimal number of premises of the uttermost simplicity, a simplicity so basic and so obvious that it was impossible to doubt them, such as that a straight line is the shortest distance between two points. The demonstrations then proceeded deductively by one logical step at a time, each step being irrefutable, and usually very simple, again indubitable. And then – the thing that entranced everyone who came under the spell of mathematics – you found that in moving only by logical steps, each of which was simple and obvious, from premises each of which was also simple and obvious, you began to reach conclusions that were not at all simple and not at all obvious: whole worlds of unanticipated discoveries started opening up before you, many of them amazing, many of them of great practical usefulness, and all of them reliably true. And there seemed to be no end of these undiscovered worlds: mathematicians were for ever opening up the way to unexpectedly new ones, as Descartes himself had done.

Now, asked Descartes, might it be possible to apply precisely this method to non-mathematical knowledge? If we can find any propositions outside mathematics whose truth it is literally impossible to doubt we can use them as premises for deductive arguments, and then whatever we can logically deduce from them must be true. This will give us the methodological foundations for a body of knowledge on whose discoveries we can one-hundred-per-cent rely. But are there any such premises? Or is it the case (as many people in Descartes' own day were saying) that nothing at all can be known for certain outside mathematics and logic?

In his search for indubitable premises Descartes journeyed through three stages. First, he considered the experience of direct and immediate observation. If I look head-on at this church spire, or that tree dipping in the water, surely I can trust

## "I THINK THEREFORE I AM"

the immediate evidence of my senses? Alas, on investigation it turns out that direct observation deceives us frequently. This church spire that flashes golden in the noonday sun, and glows red at sunset, looks grey the rest of the time. That branch that looks bent at the point where it enters the water turns out to be straight when I lift it out. So I can never be sure that things are in fact as they appear to me, however head-on I may be looking at them, and however awake and alert my state of mind.

## MALICIOUS DEMON

This brings us to Descartes' second set of considerations. Often, he says, he had believed himself with complete certainty to be doing something or other, and then woken to find that he had been dreaming. Sometimes these dreams had been homely dreams about his everyday activities: he had dreamt he was sitting at his fireside reading, or at the desk in his study writing, when all the time he had really been in bed sleeping. How could he be sure he was not dreaming at this very instant? By this token it appeared that he could never be *absolutely* sure he was not dreaming, or hallucinating, or something of that sort.

At this point of apparent despair in his search for indubitability Descartes gave the knife an additional and malign twist, and this was his third phase. Suppose he said, that all the errors and illusions on my part were due to the fact that there exists, unknown to me, a higher spirit whose sole aim is to deceive me, and who can exercise

superhuman power over me – can make me sleep and then dream vividly that I am awake, or make everything I look at look to me like something else, or make me believe that two and two add up to five. Is there anything at all about which even a malignant spirit such as this would be unable to deceive me? And he comes to the conclusion that there is, namely the fact that the deliverances of my consciousness are whatever it is they are. I can always make false inferences from them – I may suppose myself to be sitting beside a fire when in fact there is no fire and I am in bed dreaming, and yet *that* I suppose myself to be sitting beside a fire is an inescapable fact. So the one thing in this and every other case that I can be unshakably sure of is that I am having the experiences I am having. And from this there are things I can infer with absolute certitude. First of all it means I know myself to be some sort of existing being. I may not know my own nature, indeed I may have completely mistaken views about what it is, but *that* I exist is indubitable; and what is more I know with absolute certitude that I am a being which at the very least, if nothing else, has conscious experiences, the particular conscious experiences I have. Descartes encapsulated this conclusion in a Latin tag that has become very famous: *Cogito ergo sum*, usually translated rather ineptly as "I think, therefore I am."

## PURSUIT OF CERTAINTY

So, he says, there actually are things outside mathematics and logic, things about the world of fact, that I can know with absolute certitude. But is there anything that can be inferred from those things with the same degree of certitude? At this point he uses a new version of an old argument, a new version of the ontological argument for the existence of God (see p.57). I know myself, he says, to be a very imperfect being, ephemeral and perishable, and finite, and yet I have in my mind the concept of an infinite being, eternal and immortal, perfect in every way; and it is impossible that anything should be able to create something greater than itself out of its own resources; therefore this perfect being must exist, and must have implanted in me an awareness of itself, like a craftsman's signature inscribed on an example of his handiwork.

The fact that I know that God exists, and is perfect, means that I can put my trust in him: he will not, unlike the malicious demon, deceive me. So provided I play my full part, pay serious attention, and do all the disciplined thinking required of me, I can be certain of the truth of

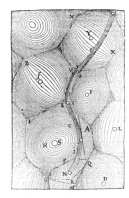

DESCARTES' UNIVERSE
In *The World* (1633), Descartes gives an account of an hypothetical "new world". In the diagram above, he represents the universe as an indefinite number of contiguous vortices. Descartes shows how the matter which filled the universe was collected in the vortices, with a star at the centre of each, often with orbiting planets.

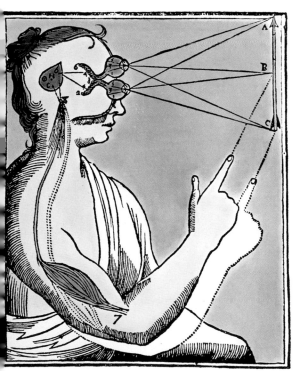

A PHYSIOLOGICAL TEXTBOOK
*Descartes'* Treatise on Man *(1664) is regarded as the first textbook on physiology. This illustration demonstrates the supposed relationship between the sensory perception of an image and muscular action. The image is relayed from the eyes to the pineal gland. The reaction between the image and the pineal gland determines the motor action.*

whatever is then presented clearly and distinctly to me as being true – not by my senses, of course, which I already know to deceive, but by my mind, that part of me that apprehends God and also mathematics, neither of which the senses can do; the mind that I irreducibly am.

## THE BIRTH OF RATIONALISM

Out of this conclusion grew the school of philosophy known as rationalism, which bases itself on the belief that our knowledge of the world is acquired by the use of reason, and that sensory input is inherently unreliable, more a source of error than of knowledge. Rationalism has been one of the abiding traditions of Western philosophy ever since. Its greatest period spanned the 17th and 18th centuries, and its outstanding figures apart from Descartes were Spinoza and Leibniz, but it has never lost an important degree of influence on Western thinking.

Few of the great philosophers after Descartes shared his view of the indubitability of God's existence. But he introduced some fundamental things into Western thought. His belief that the logic of scientific discovery required us to start from indubitable facts and then derive logical consequences from these facts in chains of deductive reasoning became foundational to Western science. Subsequent thinkers came mostly to believe that controlled and disciplined observation (and therefore the use of our senses) had an indispensable role to play in establishing those indisputable facts that we need to stock our premises, but they still thought that Descartes had got the basic method right, namely, to start from reliable facts, then apply logic to those facts and not to let anything intervene that is in the very least degree susceptible to doubt, no matter how far-fetched that doubt might be. Descartes convinced people that this method made possible a mathematically based science that would give human beings reliable knowledge about the world, and indeed that it was the only way of finding out about the world with absolute certainty.

## MIND AND MATTER

Descartes' conclusion that what human beings irreducibly are is minds led him to develop a view of the world as consisting ultimately of two different kinds of substance, namely mind and matter. He saw human beings as experiencing subjects whose world, apart from themselves, consists of material objects which they observe. This bifurcation of nature into two kinds of

entity – mind and matter, subject and object, observer and observed – became a built-in part of Western man's way of looking at the world. To this day it is referred to by philosophers as "Cartesian dualism". Between Descartes and the 20th century there were few leading philosophers who dissented from it, perhaps the most effective being Spinoza and Schopenhauer. Only in the 20th century did dissent from it become widespread and even then it was by no means universal; some leading philosophers continue to subscribe to it.

Even more than Francis Bacon and Galileo, Descartes was a key figure in persuading people in the West that certainty was available in our knowledge of the world. To obtain it you needed to follow the right method, but if you did that you

> " COMMON SENSE IS THE BEST DISTRIBUTED COMMODITY IN THE WORLD, FOR EVERY MAN IS CONVINCED HE IS WELL SUPPLIED WITH IT "
>
> RENÉ DESCARTES

could build up an impregnable science that would give you rock-hard, reliable knowledge. He, more than anyone else, "sold" science to educated Western man. It was largely under his influence that the pursuit of certainty came to dominate intellectual activity in the West, and that considerations of method became central to that pursuit, for he regarded himself not as giving us such knowledge with certainty but as showing us how to get it.

**DESCARTES' SKULL?**
Descartes was buried in Stockholm but his body was later transferred to Paris. The skull which lies with his remains in the church of St Germain-des-Prés in Paris is almost certainly not that of Descartes. It appears that a captain in the Swedish guards who was present at the original exhumation removed the skull and replaced it with another. The skull was resold several times before eventually finding a home in the Musée de l'Homme in the Palais de Chaillot.

**MARIN MERSENNE**
*The French theologian, mathematician, and philosopher Marin Mersenne (1588–1648) was in contact with philosophers and scientists throughout Europe – figures such as Hobbes, Gassendi, and Galileo – and was thus in a unique position to introduce Descartes' work to them and report their comments back. He also discovered a formula ("Mersenne numbers") that attempted to represent all prime numbers.*

SCENES FROM THE LIFE OF DESCARTES

*his engraving depicts Descartes surrounded by scenes of* *Francine, on 7 September 1640. In another (top right),*
*me of the principal events in his life. One scene (top left)* *Descartes is shown as tutor to Queen Christina of Sweden,*
*ustrates the death of Descartes' illegitimate daughter,* *a position he held until his own death on 11 February 1650.*

### KEY WORKS

*In* Discourse on
Method *(1637)*
*Descartes presented*
*his method in*
*simple terms, and*
*summarized his*
*scientific views and*
*metaphysical system.*

*In* Meditations *(1641)*
*Descartes developed his*
*metaphysical doctrine.*

Principles of
Philosophy *(1644)*
*is an attempt to*
*account for all*
*natural phenomena*
*in one single system*
*of mechanical*
*principles.*

will be remembered that the earliest
hilosophers, the pre-Socratics, had taken their
ndamental question to be: "What is there?" or
What does the world consist of?" Socrates had
placed this with a different question, namely
How ought we to live?" These questions and
eir derivations dominated philosophy for many
undreds of years. But then along came Descartes
nd displaced them with one that was different
et again: "What can I know?" It put epistemology,
hich is the theory of knowledge, at the centre
f philosophy, where it remained for three
undred years, so much so that many subsequent
hilosophers came to think of philosophy as being,
ssentially, epistemology. For this reason Descartes
 generally thought of as the first modern
hilosopher, and it often happens that students
oing to university to study philosophy are
quired to begin their course with his work.
here is another reason for this. By using doubt
 a method – systematically suspending
ommitment to anything that it is logically possible
 doubt, thereby stripping away layer after layer
f our accustomed ideas and suppositions – he takes

us right back to square one, and attempts to begin
again from scratch. The first-person-singular form
of the question sharpens its cutting edge – not
"What is it possible for us human beings to know?"
but "What can I know?" This appeals to the young,
and rightly so.

## A PLEASURE TO READ

Descartes is a superlative writer, a wonderfully clear,
jargon-free stylist, and happens to be one of the
only two indisputably great philosophers to have
written in the French language, the other being
Leibniz. But Leibniz had nothing like the stylistic
distinction of Descartes. This makes Descartes
one of France's greatest cultural possessions,
and for this reason he is required reading in the
upper reaches of all secondary schools in France,
the famous French *Lycées*. This in turn means that
every well-educated French man or woman has
read him. He still makes worthwhile reading for
educated people everywhere – and one of the best
ways of introducing oneself to the writings of the
great philosophers is still to read *Discourse on*
*Method* followed by *Meditations*.

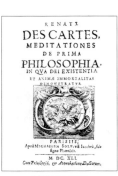

*MEDITATIONS*
Before publication in
1641, the manuscript of
*Meditations* was sent to
Marin Mersenne, who
was given the task of
collecting together
critical opinion,
including that of
Thomas Hobbes and
Pierre Gassendi, to
which Descartes
drafted replies. The
book's publication
made Descartes famous
but also involved him
in controversy. In
Holland the president
of the University of
Utrecht accused him of
atheism, and Descartes
was condemned by the
local authorities.

# SPINOZA
## ALL IS ONE, AND THE ONE IS DIVINE

*Although God is, and is in, everything, this totality is also to be understood in the same way as a system of mathematical physics.*

**BENEDICT SPINOZA**
*Spinoza was born in Amsterdam into a distinguished Jewish emigré family that had fled Catholic persecution in Portugal. He studied non-Hebrew subjects, such as mathematics and linguistics, privately.*

> *"...the noblest and most lovable of the great philosophers"*
> BERTRAND RUSSELL
> ON SPINOZA

SPINOZA WAS JEWISH, the only Jew before Karl Marx to occupy a position in the very front rank of original thinkers among Western philosophers. (There were several great Jewish scholars.) He was born in Amsterdam in 1632. He had an orthodox Jewish upbringing and education; but because of his heterodox opinions he was expelled from the Jewish community at the age of 24. At this time he changed his first name from the Hebrew form Baruch to its Latin form Benedict. He proceeded to live a solitary life, earning his living by grinding and polishing lenses for spectacles, microscopes, and telescopes – at that time a new profession. His writings made him famous even so; but when he was offered a Professorship of Philosophy at Heidelberg University in 1673 he turned it down

because he wanted to be left alone to do his philosophizing "in accordance with his own mind" as he put it.

Apart from his philosophy he was the first scholar of note to examine the scriptures as historical documents that were of problematic authorship and embodied the intellectual limitations of their time. In doing th[is] he inaugurated the so-called higher criticism that was to come to full flower in the 19th and 20th centuries. He was engaged in translating the Old Testament into Dutch at the time of his death in 1677, of a lung complaint which, it was believed, had been brought on by the daily inhalation over many years of powdered glass from his lens-grinding. After his death, but in the same year, 1677, the book by which he is now best known was published. It is called simply *Ethics*, but in fact it covers a whole range of basic philosophical problems in addition to ethical ones.

Spinoza, like so many of the most famous philosophers, was a genuine polymath. For family reasons he was brought up to speak Spanish and

**A JEWISH UPBRINGING**
*This etching and drypoint by Rembrandt, Jews in the Synagogue (1648), depicts a typical scene from Jewish life in 17th-century Amsterdam that would have been familiar to the young Spinoza. Born in Amsterdam of parents of strictly Jewish faith Spinoza received an orthodox Jewish upbringing but was excommunicated from the synagogue and driven out from the Jewish community in 1656 at the age of 24 for his heretical views.*

ortuguese as well as Dutch and Hebrew; and he wrote in Latin. In addition to this and to being a distinguished biblical scholar he was learned in mathematics and what people called "the new science", studying in particular the works of Copernicus, Kepler, Galileo, Hobbes, and Descartes. His professional understanding of microscopes and telescopes gave him a grasp, ahead of his time, of the possibilities of new technology that were being opened up by this new science. His philosophy, it might be said, attempted to bring all these things and their implications together into an integrated and orderly whole.

He was mightily impressed by science, and he accepted from Descartes the view that the right way to build up the edifice of our scientific knowledge was to start from indubitable premises and deduce the consequences of these by logical reasoning. But at the same time he saw that Descartes' philosophy left certain fundamental problems unsolved. If total reality consists of two different sorts of substance that are ultimately distinct, namely material substance and mental substance, or matter and mind, how is it possible for mind to move matter around in space? Descartes' own answer to this was so feeble that no-one was convinced by it, and his successors considered it scarcely worth discussing. But there were other unsolved problems which were of equal moment to Spinoza. He was a deeply moral human being and also, by temperament, a deeply religious

one, and this raised all sorts of difficulties for him as regards the new science. If total reality is the instantiation of a deductive system in which everything that is or happens can be deduced with all the necessity of logic from self-evident

# "GOD IS THE CAUSE OF ALL THINGS, WHICH ARE IN HIM"

BENEDICT SPINOZA

premises, what room is there for moral choice, or indeed free will at all – how can there be free will if everything is scientifically determined?

Also, what place is there for God in such a system? If everything that happens in the universe can be explained in terms of scientific laws and mathematical equations, it would seem that we no longer need God to function as any part of the explanation. He is left outside it all, extraneous to the system so to speak: superfluous. From the 17th century to the 20th many people were deeply upset – and baffled – by questions of this kind. Newton's answer was that it was God who had created the whole universe in the first place; and that he then left it, from outside, to operate all by itself according to the laws which he had laid down, and which we now discover as scientific

**OPTICS**
Spinoza had a deep interest in optics and the new astronomy and was expert at making lenses. He made a living by grinding and polishing lenses for spectacles, telescopes, and microscopes. This illustration shows a microscope and condenser, taken from Robert Hooke's book *Micrographia* (1665).

**BIBLICAL CRITICISM**
*Literary and historical criticism of the Bible, also known as "higher criticism", deals with the historical circumstances out of which the biblical canon developed. It is concerned with three issues: literary structure, date, and authorship. In seeking to study the Bible dispassionately (and dating many Old Testament books later than tradition) Spinoza has been seen as a forerunner of biblical criticism.*

**HEIDELBERG UNIVERSITY**
*Spinoza was offered a Professorship of Philosophy at Heidelberg University in 1673, but chose to turn the offer down. The oldest university in Germany, Heidelberg was founded by Rupert I and chartered by Pope Urban VI in 1386. At the time Spinoza was offered his professorship it was already considered one of the finest universities in Europe.*

laws. But this would not do for Spinoza, who needed a God who was ever-present and all-pervasive. But still the question confronted him: what space was there within a deductive and deterministic system for any such God?

## AGAINST DUALISM

Spinoza's solutions to these problems started with the bold stroke of denying the basic premise, denying the fundamental distinction between mind and matter. We know, he said, for the reasons given by Descartes, that God exists, and is an infinite and perfect being. But if God is infinite then he cannot have boundaries, cannot have limits, for if he had he would be finite. So there cannot be anything that God is not. So it cannot, for instance, be the case that God is one entity and the world quite another, for this would be to place limits on God's being. So God must be co-extensive with everything there is.

> ## "YET NATURE CANNOT BE CONTRAVENED, BUT PRESERVES A FIXED AND IMMUTABLE ORDER"
>
> BENEDICT SPINOZA

There is another good Cartesian reason why this should be so. Descartes had defined substance as that which needs nothing outside itself in order to exist. But Spinoza pointed out that the totality of everything is the only thing that has nothing outside itself. Within this totality everything that we seek to understand has to be explained, at least partially, in terms of something else – our explanations always take, at least to some extent, the form of linking things with other things. The only entity of which this is not, and can not, be so is the totality of everything. This must simply *be*, in and for itself, unexplained by anything else, unconnected with anything else; for there is nothing else. This means that it is the only true substance, the one and only self-subsistent thing, the only

uncaused cause. But these things are what is meant by God. Therefore – again, but for a different reason – God must be co-equivalent with everything.

This means that whether we describe the cosmos in terms of our religious conceptions or in terms of planets and other material objects we are describing the same thing. One set of categories is abstract or mental, the other material, but these are merely two different ways of describing the same reality. The same existent entity is being seen under two different aspects. So God is not outside the world, but he is not in the world either: he is the world. The physical universe is his body, you might

### KEY WORKS

*The* Theological-Political Treatise *was published anonymously in 1670 but was banned in 1674 for its controversial views on the Bible and Christian theology.*

Ethics *(1677), Spinoza's great work, rejects Cartesian dualism in favour of Pantheism.*

### MOSES MAIMONIDES

The foremost intellectual figure of medieval Judaism, Maimonides (1135–1204) was born in Córdoba, Spain. He was a philosopher, jurist, and scientist and his philosophical work, after it was translated into Latin, influenced the medieval scholastic writers. *Guide to the Perplexed* (1176–91), his most famous work, helped introduce the theories of Aristotle into medieval philosophy. Much later, Spinoza found Maimonides' work a source for some of his own ideas.

**THE POWER OF NATURE**

*...uin in Riesengebirge (1815–20), by the German painter ...aspar David Friedrich (1774–1840), depicts a vast and ...esolate landscape through which Friedrich evokes the awesome and sublime power of Nature. His vision stirringly expresses the oneness of Man and Nature and the rationalistic pantheism found in the work of Spinoza.*

**PANTHEISM**

*Pantheism, which literally translates as "all is God", is a mode of thought that regards God as identical to the Universe or Nature. Pantheism affirms the unity of all reality and the divineness of that unity. Religious pantheists are often mystical, claiming to experience God intuitively. Spinoza was a rationalist, he believed that God, man, and the physical world were all part of one substance, and that everything, both physical and spiritual, was an extension of God. Besides Spinoza, other pantheistic philosophers might perhaps include Fichte, Schelling, and Hegel.*

...ay, though that would be merely one way of ...ooking at it: a spiritual apprehension of God ...ould be simply a different way of knowing the ...ame being. We ourselves, although we are finite ...reatures and not infinite, have the same dual ...haracter in one being: we are our physical bodies, ...ut we are also our souls, and these are not two ...ifferent people, they are one and the same person: ...is as if, as an ancient Jewish teaching had it, the ...ody is the soul in its outward form.

This is a compelling vision, and many gifted people since Spinoza have come under its spell. His deification of nature had enormous appeal during the late 18th and early 19th centuries for the Romantic Movement, whose intellectuals made him one of their patron saints. Unlike the Romantics, however, Spinoza saw the actions of the human individual as determined by factors outside his control, though not in any crude, mechanical way. With insights strikingly previsionary of Freud's,

at the same time, unlike Freud, he argued that it was absurd for individuals to be obsessed by their personal problems, these being merely petty concerns: we should try to see our problems as occupying the place they actually do in the totality of things; and when we do that we shall see them as insignificant – and this will greatly help us to bear them. He had a memorable image for the idea that we should look at our own lives through the eyes of eternity: the Latin phrase he uses, *sub speci aeternitatis*, is still often quoted.

## HUMANE VISION

Balance, perspective, toleration – these are the consequences that flow from the social side of Spinoza's philosophy; and they are duly embodied in his political philosophy. One of the books he published during his lifetime, *Theological-Political Treatise* (his Latin title for this, *Tractatus Theologico-Politicus*, was imitated by the 20th-century philosopher Wittgenstein, who called his first book *Tractatus Logico-Philosophicus*), had as its main purpose the defence of free expression. Spinoza argued that freedom of speech, far from being incompatible with public order, was necessary in order to secure it. This view is now a standard part of the liberal-minded attitude, but Spinoza was the first person to put it forward in modern terms. Having said that in a rationally governed society "every man may think what he likes, and say what he thinks"; he then goes on to make the

### FREEDOM OF EXPRESSION
*The Holland of Spinoza's day was a refuge for freethinkers – among them Descartes, whose work greatly influenced Spinoza. Spinoza, too, would not have been allowed to do his philosophical work in any other country. Jan Steen's (1625–79) painting,* Musical Company, *conveys this mood of relative freedom.*

> **"*Men are deceived if they think themselves free*"**
> BENEDICT SPINOZA

Spinoza argues that our everyday sense of being free agents is an illusion based on the fact that we are not for the most part aware of the real causes of our actions; and that acquiring this awareness through reflection can liberate us, not in the sense of making us free agents literally but by giving us understanding and insight, and thus enabling us to come to terms with things as they are. He was the first person in Europe to put forward this idea. But

crucial point: "The real disturbers of the peace are those who, in a free state, seek to curtail the liberty of judgment which they are unable to tyrannize over."

Spinoza's masterpiece, *Ethics* (1677), is laid out like a text-book of geometry. Each demonstration begins with the appropriate definitions and axioms and then there follows the argument itself – at the end of which the letters QED are usually printed. (QED is short for "*quod erat demonstrandum*",

**A CONTROVERSIAL FIGURE**
*Spinoza's determination always to say what he believed on matters of Christian theology, however controversial, had the consequence that he was widely considered the embodiment of ungodliness by his contemporaries.*

hich means "which was to be proved", and is
rinted at the end of every proof in Euclid's
immortal handbook of geometry, *Elements*, written
the 3rd century BC.) All this is in accordance with
pinoza's view, derived from Descartes, that the
ght way to achieve understanding of the world is
apply the methods of mathematics to reality.
his book is often held up as the supreme example
a philosopher's attempt to understand everything
terms of a single interconnected system of
ought. But the Euclidean groundplan in a work
such scope makes for dry reading. And the truth
that most of the logical derivations appear to
llow only if the reader makes assumptions which
ere commonly made in Spinoza's time but are not
ommonly made in ours, for instance that the
xistence of God is self-evident. By the standards
the 21st century, therefore, they are not logical
emonstrations at all. However, the real merits of the
ook lie elsewhere, not in the detailed working out
the proofs but in the conclusions, the overall vision.

**ENIGN INFLUENCE**

pinoza was the supreme pantheist among Western
hilosophers. Although his work was neglected
r something like a hundred years after his death
was revived and treated with veneration by
e Romantics; and ever since then it has had
s admirers, particularly for its religious attitude

towards the totality of what exists. Although
Spinoza was the first great philosopher to follow
Descartes he repudiated Cartesian dualism
(see p.88), a repudiation that was to become
orthodoxy in the 20th century, but not until then.
He was the first great philosopher to set out the
basic case for freedom of speech, which he did a
generation before Locke. And his unaffected yet
lofty, almost mystical attitude to the unimportance
of our personal problems in the overall scheme
of things has brought aid and comfort to many
hard-pressed individuals.

This wide range of vistas has influenced a
correspondingly wide range of people. Subsequent
philosophers who admired him and learnt from
him include Hegel, Schopenhauer, Nietzsche, and
Bertrand Russell. Russell wrote of Spinoza that he
"is the noblest and most lovable of the great
philosophers. Intellectually, some others have
surpassed him, but ethically he is supreme." Not
only philosophers have come under his spell: giant
thinkers in other fields, such as Einstein and Freud,
and also great creative artists, such as Goethe and
George Eliot, have acknowledged themselves in his
debt. He is a major figure in Western culture
generally, as well as in Western philosophy.

This illustrates a point of general importance
about the great philosophers. Fundamental to the
work of each one of them is a vision of total reality.

## "THE TRUE AIM OF GOVERNMENT IS LIBERTY"

BENEDICT SPINOZA

The philosopher is trying to commend this vision
to us with persuasive arguments. He considers
possible criticisms of these arguments that people
might make, and tries to demolish those criticisms
with further arguments. All this argumentation can
become very complicated. Individual arguments can
be technical, and difficult to follow; or, worse, they
can be detailed and boring. But the point of it all lies
not in the arguments but in the vision. Sometimes this
vision is also difficult to grasp; but more often than
not it is simple compared to the arguments.

***ETHICS***
Spinoza's chief work,
*Ethics* (1677), was
published posthumously.
It addresses not only
ethics, but the whole
range of philosophy.
Set out like Euclid's
geometry, Spinoza's
system proceeded from
the premise that
everything could be
demonstrated.

**LITERARY CRITICS**

*Spinoza's reputation
was restored and
made intellectually
respectable by the
endeavours of literary
critics, especially the
18th-century German
writers and critics
G. E. Lessing and
Goethe, and the 19th-
century English poet
Coleridge. Lessing
expressed his belief
in the pantheistic
philosophy of Spinoza
after reading Goethe's
poem* Prometheus.

**GEORGE ELIOT**
The English novelist
George Eliot, pen name of
Mary Ann Evans (1819–80),
developed the method of
psychological analysis
characteristic of modern
fiction. Her *Middlemarch*
(1872) is considered one
of the greatest novels of
the 19th century.

> *"It is one of my most important and best verified maxims that nature makes no leaps. This I have called the law of continuity"*
>
> GOTTFRIED WILHELM LEIBNIZ

# LEIBNIZ
## THE SUPREME POLYMATH

*Logically, Leibniz divided all truths into two sorts, truths of reason and truths of fact. This distinction continues to play an important role in philosophy.*

GOTTFRIED WILHELM LEIBNIZ (1646–1716) was a person of unusually wide genius, even for a great philosopher. He invented calculus independently of Newton, and published it before Newton did, although Newton had invented it earlier. It is Leibniz's notation, not Newton's, that mathematicians now use. He invented the concept of kinetic energy. He invented mathematical logic, although he did not publish his invention: if he had done so the subject would have got going one and a half centuries before it did. And then, in addition to being one of the greatest mathematicians of all time, he was one of the most influential of philosophers.

**GOTTFRIED WILHELM LEIBNIZ**
*Leibniz was born in Leipzig in 1646 and died in Hanover in 1716. As well as being a philosopher, he was a brilliant mathematician, and a pioneer in mathematical logic.*

**LEIBNIZ WITH QUEEN SOPHIA CHARLOTTE OF PRUSSIA**
*Leibniz's book* Theodicy *is dedicated to Queen Charlotte of Prussia. With the Queen's support the German Academy of Sciences in Berlin was founded in July 1700.*

He was the son of a professor of moral philosophy at the University of Leipzig. So outstanding was he as a student that he was offered a professorship at the age of 21; but he turned it down, because he wanted to be a man of the world. Most of his public career was spent as a courtier, diplomat, librarian, and family historian in the service of successive Dukes of Hanover – one of whom, incidentally, became King George I of England. In these various capacities he travelled widely, and this fact together with his published writings made him an admired public figure in his prime, though in old age he became rather neglected and forgotten.

But throughout all this, in the privacy of his study, he was doing solitary intellectual work, not in the form of an ordered writing of books, and not to be published during his lifetime. His description of the disorder in which this writing went on is touching. "When I have done something, I forget it almost completely in a few months, and rather than hunt for it among a chaos of sheets that I have

# "THE ARE TWO KINDS OF TRUTHS: TRUTHS OF REASONING AND TRUTHS OF FACT"

GOTTFRIED WILHELM LEIBNIZ

man, and therefore the neighbour cannot both be a bachelor and have a wife – the statement is self-contradictory, and therefore cannot possibly be true. Leibniz argued that all truths must belong to these two logical types. Either we have to examine the facts in order to find out whether a particular statement is true or false, or we can do that without examining the facts, in which case the statement must be true or false by virtue of the use it makes of its own terms. Because we can determine the truth of statements of this latter type by analyzing them without having to look outside them, they became known later in the history of philosophy as "analytic statements". The other sort became known as "synthetic statements". These two terms are now in common use.

The distinction was developed with great power and sophistication over something like three hundred years. It became central to the empirical

ever had time to sort out and index, I have to do e work all over again." The result of this is that hereas a philosopher like Spinoza presents his stem of thought to the reader as a carefully anned and laid out whole, with Leibniz the reader in the quite different position of having to piece together for himself.

## ASIC DISTINCTION

someone says to us: "My next-door neighbours onsist of a red-haired man and his fat wife" that ould perfectly well be true but it could equally ell be untrue. The only sure way to establish it is carry out a careful investigation to determine hether a man lives next door who is red-haired s against, say, dark-haired, fair-haired or bald), hether he has a fat wife (as against, say, a thin ife or no wife), and whether these two are the ly inhabitants of the neighbouring house. But if meone says to us: "My next-door neighbours onsist of a bachelor and his fat wife" we know ithout further ado that the statement is false. We not need to carry out any investigations at all to tablish this because "bachelor" means unmarried

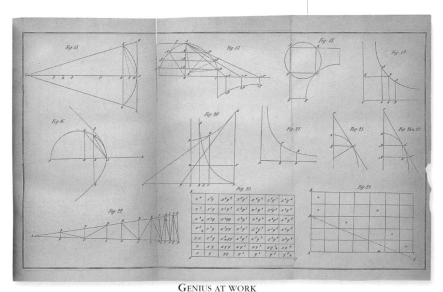

**GENIUS AT WORK**
*By far the most important of Leibniz's mathematical achievements was his discovery of infinitesimal calculus, independently of Newton, in 1676.*

**CAROLINE OF ANSBACH**
The beautiful and intelligent Queen Caroline (1683–1737), wife of King George II of England, sided with Leibniz in the debate about whether it was he or Newton who invented calculus. The argument with Newton made Leibniz unpopular in England, and in spite of Caroline's favour Leibniz remained neglected.

---

### CALCULUS

*In 1676 Leibniz made a visit to London, where his discussions with mathematicians of Isaac Newton's circle were later to lead to a controversy as to whether it was he or Newton who was the inventor of infinitesimal calculus. Leibniz published his system in 1684, Newton published his in 1687, though he could relate it to earlier work. The Royal Society declared for Newton in 1711, but the controversy was never really settled.*

---

tradition of philosophy which arose between Leibniz and Kant, and was then again central to Kant's philosophy. In the 20th century it was fundamental to Logical Positivism. It has often been said that if a student of philosophy does no more than acquire a firm grasp of this distinction then studying the subject will have been worth his or her while. Over time, the whole of both logic and mathematics came to be seen as consisting of analytic statements, while all knowledge claims about the empirical world were seen as synthetic. This profoundly influenced the way knowledge of each kind was envisaged and pursued.

The negative consequences of the distinction are also important. The denial of an analytically true statement is a self-contradiction, and therefore *could not* be true, whereas the denial of a synthetically true statement is not a self-contradiction, it is another synthetic statement that could be true but happens not to be; so the former is an impossibility while the latter is a possibility.

Following on from this, Leibniz introduced into modern philosophy the notion of alternative possible worlds. It would have been perfectly

**"DOCTOR PANGLOSS"**
*Leibniz's view that God chose to create the best possible world was mocked by Voltaire in his novel* Candide *(1759). The character of Doctor Pangloss responds to various misfortunes by saying "All is for the best in the best of all possible worlds."*

possible for us human beings to have had six fingers on each hand, or three; but there is no possible world in which we could have had both at the same time. So although both are possibilities, the actualization of one possibility rules out the actualization of the other. This leads to the notion of "compossibilities" – possibilities which are compatible with one another, as against possibilities that are not. The sum total of any set of compossibilities makes up a possible world – and there is an indefinitely large number of them. Leibniz believed that God could have created any sort of world he chose, provided of course that it was a possible one, but that as a perfect being

> ## "THE SOUL IS THE MIRROR OF AN INDESTRUCTIBLE UNIVERSE"
>
> GOTTFRIED WILHELM LEIBNIZ

himself he chose to create the best possible world. A world containing free will, and in consequence wrongdoing and evil, is better than a world in which free will does not exist; and that is the explanation of why a perfect God has created a world in which there is so much evil.

Voltaire, in his novel *Candide* (1759), lampooned Leibniz immortally as the character Pangloss, a fatuously optimistic philosopher who proclaims that all is for the best in the best of possible worlds. Like most truly marvellous caricatures, it did its victim less than justice, for it gave no indication that there was a serious point behind what Leibniz was saying.

### SUFFICIENT REASON

Another idea that Leibniz made current in philosophy is called the principle of sufficient reason. For everything that is the case, he said, there must be a reason why it is the case. If the truth in question is an analytic one it can be proved without reference to external reality, whether by a logical or mathematical demonstration, or some other form of deductive argument; or, if the matter is one involving meaning, by an appeal to definitions; or, if it is a rule-governed activity, such as a game or astonishingly prescient. But in the 17th century the only vocabulary people had for talking about non-material centres of activity was the vocabulary of minds, or spirits, or souls; and this is how Leibniz tried to express himself. He saw the points of propensity for activity that constitute matter as being like dots of consciousness occupying points in space. He called these "monads", and believed that everything was made up of them. Although he saw all monads as spaceless within themselves he also saw them as differing widely in intensity, from those that go to make up inorganic matter at the lower end of the scale to human minds, each of which is a monad, and then on to God, who is also a monad. Each monad is a point of view in relation to the rest of reality – its own world. In this respect monads do not interact – for example we human beings do not partake of each other's consciousness – we are what Leibniz called "windowless". But all of us monads were created by God to exist together in the same world, so he ordained a harmony of function for us such that the activities of everybody and everything can co-exist. This phrase "pre-established harmony" has become the most generally used description of Leibniz's system.

Leibniz can be described as a philosopher's philosopher: the best of his work is too technical for untrained readers to follow, but his influence on other philosophers has been enormous.

> ### KINETIC ENERGY
> *Everything that moves has energy called "kinetic" energy. The faster an object moves the more mass it has, and the more kinetic energy it has. As early as 1686, more than a hundred years before this discovery was made, Leibniz had introduced the term* vis viva, *meaning "living force". The* vis viva *of an object depended on its mass and speed. The idea caused controversy during the 1700s.*

> *"Why is there something, rather than nothing?"*
> GOTTFRIED WILHELM LEIBNIZ

### THE LEIBNIZ-HAUS
*From 1676 Leibniz took up a post as librarian to the Duke of Brunswick. In 1679 the library was transferred from the Herrenhausen palace to Hanover, and two years later to larger accommodation in a rear wing. From 1698 it was housed in a separate building, with living quarters for the librarian. Known as the Leibniz-Haus, it was destroyed in World War II, but a replica was inaugurated in 1983.*

conventional pursuit, by appeal to rules and conventions. If the truth is a synthetic one involving a factual state of affairs then the sufficient reasons are those physical causes which have had the necessary consequence of bringing about this particular state of affairs. Now to provide an adequate explanation of anything is to spell out the sufficient reason for it: so in a particular case we have first of all to establish which of the different kinds of truth it is, and then search in the area of what would be an appropriate sort of sufficient reason for that kind of truth. This formulation offers a principle of method to researchers that they have made use of ever since.

Leibniz was a surprisingly modern thinker in many ways. Whereas previous thinkers had regarded matter as inert, and motion as caused by this inert matter being given some sort of push, Leibniz saw motion – or at any rate activity, or propensity for activity – as being inherent in the nature of matter. In fact he was convinced that the ultimate constituents of matter were not themselves material but were non-material centres of activity. We now know, of course, that all matter is reducible to energy, so Leibniz's ideas in this respect were

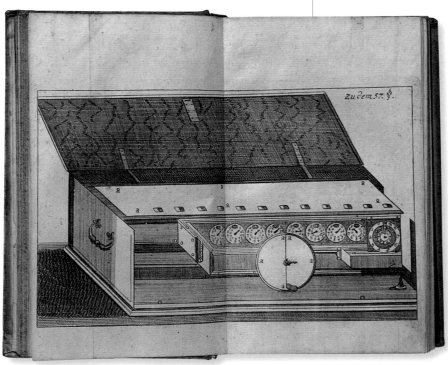

### LEIBNIZ'S CALCULATING MACHINE
*Leibniz devised his calculating machine in 1673. His version was based on an earlier machine developed by Blaise Pascal, the French scientist and writer. Leibniz presented his machine to the Royal Society on his first journey to London, from January to March 1673.*

# The GREAT EMPIRICISTS

THE CHIEF REACTION AGAINST RATIONALISM IN PHILOSOPHY BEGAN IN THE BRITISH ISLES, AND IS KNOWN AS EMPIRICISM. THE RATIONALISTS HAD DOWNGRADED SENSE EXPERIENCE AS A SOURCE OF KNOWLEDGE, MAINTAINING THAT THE ONLY RELIABLE KNOWLEDGE COMES FROM THE USE OF OUR REASON. EMPIRICISTS DENIED THIS. THEY INSISTED THAT INFORMATION ABOUT THE WORLD EXTERNAL TO OURSELVES CAN COME TO US ONLY THROUGH OUR SENSES. THE MIND THEN HAS CRUCIAL WORK TO DO IN APPRAISING AND ORGANIZING THIS INFORMATION, AND DRAWING INFERENCES FROM IT, AND CONNECTING IT WITH OTHER THINGS; BUT THE ORIGINAL SOURCE OF THE DATA ITSELF CAN BE ONLY SENSORY EXPERIENCE. ATTACHMENT TO THIS PRINCIPLE HAS EVER SINCE DOMINATED MOST PHILOSOPHY IN THE ENGLISH-SPEAKING WORLD.

*VIOLA D'AMORE* ("LOVE-VIOL")
*The romantic name of this instrument, made in 1774, refers to the seven sympathetic strings that vibrate in sympathy with the seven melody strings.*

PHILOSOPHICAL

**ESSAYS**

CONCERNING

Human Underſtanding.

By the Author of the

ESSAYS MORAL and POLITICAL.

LONDON:
Printed for A. MILLAR, oppoſite *Katharine-Street*,
in the *Strand*. MDCCXLVIII.

*ESSAY CONCERNING
HUMAN UNDERSTANDING*
John Locke's major
philosophical work was
published in 1689,
but had been developed
over the preceding
20 years. It is a
systematic enquiry into
the nature and scope of
human reason.

**KEY WORKS**

Essay concerning
Human
Understanding *(1689)*

A Letter
concerning Toleration
*(1689)*

Two Treatises of
Government *(1690)*

Some Thoughts
concerning Education
*(1693)*

**WILLIAM III**
Together with his wife,
Mary II, William III
(1650–1702), also known
as William of Orange,
ruled Great Britain and
Ireland from 1689 to 1702.
Although their reign
brought about stability
after a long period of
political unrest, William
was never a popular king.

# LOCKE
## THE SUPREME LIBERAL

*Although not the first empiricist in the history of philosophy,
Locke has ever since his day been regarded as the chief founding
father of empiricism and all that flows from it.*

JOHN LOCKE (1632-1704) was the son of
a West of England lawyer who fought with
the Parliamentarians against the King in
the English Civil War. In 1646 Locke was
sent to Westminster School, at that
time perhaps the best school in
England, and learnt not only
the classics but Hebrew and
Arabic. From there he
passed into Oxford
University, where he
discovered the new
philosophy and the
new science, becoming
eventually qualified
in medicine. He began to get
involved in public affairs at the
level of secretary and
adviser. In 1667 he took up
residence in the household
of the Earl of Shaftesbury,
leader of the parliamentary
opposition to King Charles II, as his personal
physician, though in fact serving him in other
and more political capacities also.

He spent the four years 1675-79 in France,
where he studied Descartes and came into contact
with some of the greatest minds of the age. In 1681
the Earl of Shaftesbury was tried for treason, and
acquitted, but fled the country out of fear for his
safety, and settled in Holland. Things became
dangerous for his associates in England, so in 1683
Locke too left England for Holland. It was there
that he wrote the bulk of his masterpiece *Essay
concerning Human Understanding*, though he had
been working on it since 1671. It was published in
1689. In Holland, Locke became part of a
conspiratorial world of English political exiles.
In the plot to set a Dutchman, William of Orange,
on the throne of England he was one of those
giving advice directly to William. The plot
succeeded. After the Glorious Revolution of 1688,
when King James II fled abroad, Locke personally

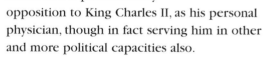

**JOHN LOCKE**
*Locke's chief contributions included a clear
formulation of the social and political principles
that emerged from the turbulence of 17th-century
Britain, and an account of human knowledge.*

escorted the Princess of Orange from
Holland to England, in February 1689,
and there she became Queen Mary to
her husband's King William III. In the
same year Locke published the first
of his important political works,
*A Letter concerning Toleration*.
In 1690 came *Two Treatises
of Government*, and in 1693
*Some Thoughts concerning
Education*. Although he
lived to be 72, and wrote
other things, his most
influential writings all came
out within a period of less
than five years.

Locke derived great
satisfaction from being
involved in practical affairs as
well as philosophy, and was
unusually effective at both.
He never married, but was
much loved, and had many friends: he was warm,
charming, witty, and wise, yet at the same time
modest. Whether in personal relationships, politics,
or philosophy, his supreme attachment seemed to

> ## "NATURE NEVER MAKES THINGS FOR MEAN OR NO USES"
> **JOHN LOCKE**

be to an engaging common sense, even when
this led him into inconsistencies: he would sooner
admit an inconsistency than deny what seemed
to him the obvious and straightforward truth, what
he would often refer to as the plain facts of the

atter. In this he was typically English
ut very un-French, and particularly
n-Cartesian. He had an acute sense of
ow in making our view of things more
onsistent we sometimes distance it
urther from reality.

## OUR LIMITATIONS

ocke is a thinker of the front rank in
wo different areas, theory of knowledge
nd political philosophy. In the former
e launched what many to this day
egard as its most important project,
amely an enquiry into what are the
mits to what is intelligible to humans.
eople before him had tended to assume
at the limits to what could be known
ere set by the limits to what there is –
at in principle, at least, we could go on
nding out more and more about reality
ntil there was nothing left to find out.
here had always been philosophers
ho understood that limits of a different
ort might also exist, namely limits to
hat it is possible for humans to
pprehend, in which case there might
e aspects of reality which humans can
ever know or understand. This
ealization was almost universal among
edieval philosophers. But Locke
ecularized it, and then took it an
mportant stage further. If, he thought,
e could analyse our own mental
culties and find out what they are
apable, and what they are not capable,
f dealing with, we should have
iscovered the limits of what is
nowable by us, *regardless of what
appens to exist externally to
urselves*. No matter how much (or
ttle) exists over and above what is
pprehensible to us, it will have no
ray of getting through to us.

This is why Locke called his masterpiece
*ssay concerning Human Understanding*, and
hy, at the very beginning of the book, he says he
egarded it as "necessary to examine our own
bilities, and see what objects our understandings
ere, or were not, fitted to deal with". In doing
is he launched an enquiry which was taken up
ter him by some of the outstanding figures in
hilosophy – Hume and Kant in the 18th century,
chopenhauer in the 19th; then Russell, Wittgenstein,
nd Popper in the 20th. Each of these individuals

AN ALLEGORY OF THE PROTESTANT SUCCESSION
*The English Baroque painter Sir James Thornhill (1635–1734) was the
most favoured artist of the new regime. His unrestrained depiction of
William and Mary in triumph is to be found on the ceiling of the
Painted Hall at the naval hospital in Greenwich.*

felt a sense of special indebtedness to others who
preceded him in this line of succession, a linked
chain that can be said now to constitute a tradition.

## HOW WE LEARN

What we have direct experience of, said Locke, are
the contents of our own consciousness – sensory
images, thoughts, feelings, memories, and so on,
in enormous profusion. To these contents of
consciousness he gave the name "ideas", regardless
of whether they are intellectual, sensory, emotional,
or anything else: what Locke means by an idea is

> *"It is
> one thing to
> show a man
> he is in error,
> and another
> to put him in
> possession of
> the truth"*
>
> JOHN LOCKE

simply anything that is immediately present to conscious awareness. As regards our knowledge of the external world, he insists, the raw data, the basic input, comes to us through our senses: we are increasingly in receipt of specific impressions of light or dark; red, yellow, or blue; hot or cold; rough or smooth; hard or soft, and so on and so forth; to which in the early stages of our conscious lives, we are not even able to give names. But we register them from the beginning, and remember some of them, and begin to associate some with others, until eventually we begin to form general notions and expectations about them. We start to acquire the general idea of *things*, objects outside ourselves from which we are receiving these impressions; and then we begin the process of learning to distinguish one thing from another. We begin to discriminate, say, a furry object that is always around the place and moves about on four legs and makes a particular kind of noise: eventually we will learn to call it a dog. From beginnings such as these our minds and our memories build up ever more complex and sophisticated ideas on the ultimate basis of our sensory input, and gradually we acquire

an intelligible view of the world; and we develop also the ability to think about it.

One thing Locke emphasizes is that our senses constitute the only direct interface between ourselves and the reality external to us: it is only through our senses that anything of which we can ever become aware is able to get into us from outside. We develop the capacity to do all sorts of marvellous and complicated things inside our head with these data; but if we start performing those operations on material which does *not* come from our (or somebody's) sensory input we have forfeited the mind's only link with external reality. In that case, whatever the mind's operations may or may not be doing, they are not connecting up with anything that exists in the external world. Of course, the mind can produce, from within its own resources, dreams and all sorts of other fictions to which nothing in the external world corresponds; and there are many circumstances in which they do that. But Locke came to the conclusion that our notions about what actually exists – and therefore our understanding of reality, of the world – must always derive ultimately from what has been

KNOWLEDGE OF THE EXTERNAL WORLD

*Locke believed that our knowledge of the external world comes to us through our senses, through which we acquire the idea of objects outside ourselves. The child in Bartolomé*

*Esteban Murillo's* The Holy Family *(1650) exchanges glances with an object that he will eventually, by a process of discrimination, learn to recognize as a dog.*

xperienced through the senses,
r else has to be constructed out
f elements that derive in the end
om such experience.

This is the nub of empiricism.
s usual with any philosophical
octrine, an essential part of the
oint lies in what it rules out. It
enies, for instance, the notion
accepted by Plato) that we are
orn with a certain amount of
nowledge of the world that we
ave acquired in a previous
xistence. Much more germane
o Locke's own time, it denied
escartes' doctrine that, starting
ith nothing but the contents of
ur own consciousness, we can
alidate our conception of the
xternal world. In fact, Locke was
gainst the notion of innate ideas
n any form: he thought there
ere no such things. He believed
at when we are born the mind
like a blank sheet of paper on
hich experience then begins to
rite; and that all our subsequent
nowledge and understanding of
xternal reality develops from these origins.

EDUCATION FOR ALL
*Locke believed that when we are born the mind is like a blank sheet of paper – all future development depends on how an individual is educated. These radical ideas led to a belief that everyone could be liberated by education. This satirical classroom scene,* A School for Boys and Girls, *was painted by Jan Steen in c. 1670, around the time that Locke was beginning work on his* Essay.

 NEW WAY OF IDEAS
his view, or developments based on it, was
ventually to spread throughout the Western world.
oday it is so familiar that many people think of it
s obvious, just plain common sense; but when
ocke put it forward it was new, and not at all
bvious. Some of its social implications were
evolutionary, in fact. If everyone comes into the
orld with a mind that is a blank sheet of paper, a
*bula rasa*, then no-one is superior by birth to
nyone else in this regard: everything for the
dividual depends on how he or she is educated.
ocke's ideas led directly, especially in France, to
e belief that the mass of the people could be
berated from social subjection by education, and
on an equal footing.

Locke's "new way of ideas", as it was called, was
eveloped also hand in hand with the new science,
oth of them placing their central emphasis on
bservation and the checking of general ideas
gainst experience. Locke himself formalized the
stinction between those aspects of material
bjects that could be taken account of by science
e was thinking, inevitably, of the science of his

own day) and those that could not – a distinction
that had been introduced by Galileo. The aspects
of objects that science was able to deal with, said
Locke, were those that were independent of any
individual observer: their length, breadth, height,
weight, position in space, velocity if in motion, and

## " NO MAN'S KNOWLEDGE HERE CAN GO BEYOND HIS EXPERIENCE "

JOHN LOCKE

so on – their measurable, not to say mechanical,
properties. Because independent of any observer,
these properties could be regarded as *objectively*
characterizing an object, and were therefore called
by Locke its "primary qualities". The qualities that
it was not possible for science to deal with were

> *"New opinions
> are always
> suspected, and
> usually opposed,
> without any
> other reason but
> because they are
> not already
> common"*
>
> JOHN LOCKE

### ROBERT BOYLE

*The Irish-born chemist,
physicist, and natural
philosopher Robert
Boyle (1627–91) met
Locke at Oxford and
they became close
friends. Boyle was one
of the most influential
scientists of his day
and is most famous
for arriving in 1662
at a law (Boyle's Law)
which states that the
pressure and volume
of gas are inversely
proportional.
A devout Protestant,
he was one of the first
members of the
"invisible college",
which in 1645 became
The Royal Society.*

those which arose out of the interaction between the object and an observing subject and therefore contained a subjective element which could easily differ from observer to observer - such characteristics as taste, smell, colour, and so on. These characteristics belonged to objects in an ambiguous way that depended on being experienced by a subject, and were therefore called by Locke an object's "secondary qualities". This distinction, having been written into philosophy's constitution by Locke, was never wholly to depart from it.

An essential element in Locke's theory of knowledge is the view that because we are able to observe only an object's observable characteristics and behaviour we have no way of apprehending it independently of those characteristics. In other words, we cannot have any knowledge of what the object is that *has* those characteristics and behaves in that way, the thing in itself: it is an invisible, metaphysical something – a "something I know not what", as Locke himself said. He characterized it as matter, material substance, but was insistent that we could know only its characteristics or properties, we could never know *it*. A similar point applies to the subject. As subjects of knowledge and experience all we can ever find within ourselves are the contents of our awareness, our experiences of every kind: what that entity is, the self or whatever it is, that *has* these experiences, is unknowable to us. So, according to Locke, both the subject and the object of our knowledge are in themselves unknowable. The domain of possible knowledge consists entirely of transactions, or possible transactions, between these mysterious entities.

### LIBERAL REVOLUTION

Because Locke did not believe, as Descartes had, that our scientific knowledge of the world is derived by deductive logic from indubitable premises, he did not believe that it possesses the same certainty as mathematics does. His quite different view that we slowly build up that knowledge on the foundations provided by the input of our senses leaves room for error. We generalize from experience – a process known as *in*duction, not *de*duction – but sometimes our generalizations are mistaken, and we need to allow for that. Occasionally a direct observation turns

out to be erroneous even after it has been checked by others. So even the most carefully constructed knowledge built on observation is not absolutely certain: it is merely probable. It could perhaps occasionally be wrong. So if, says Locke, we are to maintain the principle that our beliefs about things need to be based on the evidence for them, we must be willing to change our beliefs in the light of changing evidence. This calls for a commonsense attitude towards the way we hold our own beliefs, a requirement which is an important part of Locke's philosophy. It connects up in a vital way with his theories about politics, as we shall now see.

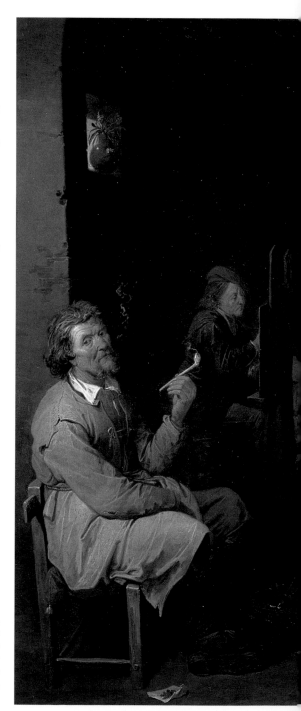

*IN THE EYE OF THE BEHOLDER
Locke claimed that those qualities arising out of the
interaction between an object and an observing subject are
subjective (i.e. "secondary") properties and do not exist
unperceived. One such example is colour, a subjective
element that can differ from observer to observer, as
illustrated in David Ryckaert's* The Artist's Workshop *(1638).*

ankind began, says Locke, in a state of nature. As creature made by God in His own image man was ot, even in a state of nature, a jungle beast, for God ad given him reason and conscience. So Locke's ew of the state of nature is very different from obbes'. Even so, the absence of any such things as overnment or civil order is so greatly to the etriment of human beings that, Locke believed, dividuals came together voluntarily to create ociety. As with Hobbes, the social contract is seen being not between government and the overned but between free men. Unlike Hobbes, owever, Locke sees the governed as retaining their individual rights even after government has been set up. Sovereignty ultimately remains with the people. The securing of their rights - the protection of the life, liberty, and property of all - is the sole legitimate purpose of government. If a government begins to abuse those rights (i.e. becomes tyrannical) or ceases to defend them effectively (i.e. becomes ineffectual) the governed retain a moral right - after seeking redress through normal procedures and failing to obtain it - to overthrow the government and replace it with one that does the job properly. This explains, incidentally, Locke's role in the Glorious Revolution of 1688.

*"All men are liable to error; and most men are, in many points, by passion or interest, under temptation to it"*
JOHN LOCKE

**VOLUNTARY TRANSACTIONS**
*Locke believed that what gives us a right to our property – or a right to dispose of it – is the labour we put into it. It is such voluntary transactions that constitute the elementary foundations of liberal capitalism. The view above shows traders busy at work at Smithfield meat market in the City of London.*

"Where is the man that has incontestable evidence of the truth of all that he holds, or of the falsehood of all he condemns, or can say that he has examined to the bottom all his own, or other men's, opinions? The necessity of believing without knowledge, nay often upon very slight grounds, in this fleeting state of action and blindness we are in, should make us more busy and careful to inform ourselves than constrain others."

## INFLUENCE

Locke did more than any other single thinker to provide the theoretical foundations of liberal democracy. What Americans call their founding fathers, the men who drew up the the Constitution of the United States, had Locke consciously in mind while they were doing so, and referred to him by name in their correspondence with one another. He had a similar influence on French thought throughout the eighteenth century – Voltaire, Montesquieu and the French Encyclopedists found in his work the basis not only for their political but also for their moral, educational, and philosophical ideas. So he was a

Locke believed that what gives us the right to our property is, first of all, the labour we put into it; and then, following on from that, our freedom to do what we like with our own. If I work to produce something, and in doing so do no harm to anyone else, then I have a right to the fruits of my labour. If someone seizes it from me he is, literally, stealing my labour. Given, then, that I have this right to it, I can dispose of it as I wish: I can give it to someone else if I so choose, or sell it to a willing buyer. Thus a society develops that is based on voluntary transactions entered into independently of government. These constitute the elementary foundations of liberal capitalism.

## TOLERATION

One of the ways in which Locke's political philosophy connects up with his theory of knowledge gives rise to a belief in tolerance. It will be remembered that in his view certainty in our knowledge of the empirical world is not available, but only a kind of working probability. This being so, he sees it as both mistaken and morally wrong for political and religious authorities to impose their beliefs. His views in this matter have had such momentous historical influence that it is worth quoting an example of them in his own words.

> "WE HAVE AS CLEAR A NOTION OF THE SUBSTANCE OF SPIRIT AS WE HAVE OF BODY"
>
> JOHN LOCKE

key intellectual influence on the American and the French revolutions. It is doubtful whether any philosopher between Aristotle and Karl Marx has had a greater influence on practical affairs.

# The BEGINNINGS of a MODERN OUTLOOK

Locke has been described as having the first modern mind. This is because he brought together and fused into a single outlook some of the fundamental concerns of post-medieval thought. Part of his basic message could be put into such words as "Don't unthinkingly follow authorities, whether intellectual, or political, or religious. And don't unthinkingly follow traditions, or social conventions. Think for yourself. Look at the facts, and try to base your views and your behaviour on how things actually are." It is difficult for us nowadays to understand just how new this message was. It had revolutionary implications in education, in science, in politics, and in philosophy itself.

It was completely at one with the new demand for observation and experiment in science. Locke influenced Newton, and was influenced by him. In education his attitude was opposed to rote learning, and to the study of a curriculum ossified by time and sanctified by tradition: Locke believed that languages should be learnt not via grammar but through practice and example; and he wanted less emphasis on classical subjects, more on modern ones. He believed that all human beings

## ALL HUMAN BEINGS HAVE THE POTENTIAL FOR DEVELOPMENT

## AN INSISTENCE ON COMMON SENSE

have the potential for development, and that the preservation of their rights and their freedoms is the only legitimate purpose of government.

This outlook carried with it a hostility to all forms of government that failed to meet these criteria. And yet although Locke's philosophy was opposed to arbitrary authority in every aspect of life and thought, its tenor was not at all militant or aggressive but, on the contrary, good-tempered, moderate, and down-to-earth. There was always an insistence on common sense, on not pushing things to extremes, on taking fully into account the plain facts of the matter.

All these aspects of Locke's philosophy tied in with one another, and provided the foundations on which philosophical thought developed in the English-speaking countries over the next two hundred years. They became the basis of a recognizably Anglo-Saxon way of looking at things, but they also had immense influence on developments in the French- and German-speaking worlds. Voltaire in France and Kant in Germany both regarded Locke as having inaugurated the kinds of thought they were advocating.

# BERKELEY
## THE CONSISTENT EMPIRICIST

*Berkeley pointed out that all that can ever be experienced by conscious beings is the contents of their consciousness. Nothing else can be known to exist.*

**TRINITY COLLEGE, DUBLIN**
Founded in 1592 by Queen Elizabeth I, Trinity College, also known as the University of Dublin, is the oldest university in Ireland and was originally built to be one of several colleges. The photograph above shows the famous bell tower, which was built by Sir Charles Lanyon in 1853.

*"Westward the course of empire takes its way"*
GEORGE BERKELEY

GEORGE BERKELEY (1685–1753) was a Protestant Irishman, educated at Trinity College, Dublin. All the philosophical works for which he is now well known were published by him when he was still only in his twenties: *An Essay Towards a New Theory of Vision* in 1709, *A Treatise Concerning the Principles of Human Knowledge* in 1710, and *Three Dialogues between Hylas and Philonous* in 1713. It was more than 20 years after that, in 1734, that he became a bishop; but he has always been referred to since as Bishop Berkeley. He was actively involved in promoting higher education in the New World, and in this pursuit he lived for three years in the American colonies. He left his library and his farm in Rhode Island to Yale University, founded in 1701. One of Yale's colleges is now named after him. The city of Berkeley in California is also named after him. He died at the age of 67 in Oxford, where he lies buried in Christ Church Cathedral.

### BASIC INSIGHT
Most of the famous philosophers of the past have produced a body of work that covers a wide range of problems, but Berkeley is remembered for a single insight which no-one since has been wholly able to ignore. Locke was entirely correct, said Berkeley, in saying that all we can ever directly apprehend are the contents of our own consciousness. But in that case, he asked, what possible warrant can we have for asserting that the existence of these mental contents is caused by things of an entirely and fundamentally different

**GEORGE BERKELEY**
*In 1724 Berkeley was made dean of Derry, but became obsessed with the idea of founding a college in the Bermudas. After years of lobbying he set sail for America i 1728 and spent three years in Rhode Island waiting for grants that never arrived. Berkeley never reached Bermud.*

character from them to which we can never have direct access, namely material objects? If, as people say, we have indirect access to these objects via the sensory images we receive of them, in what sense could that be true? People explain it by saying that our sensory images are "copies" of the objects, but what could this even so much as *mean*? How coul

**JONATHAN SWIFT**
The Anglo-Irish poet and satirist, Jonathan Swift (1667–1745), was born in Dublin and educated at Trinity College. In London he presented Berkeley at court. Swift is best known for *Gulliver's Travels* (1726) in which he satirized the intellectual pretensions of the philosophers, scientists, and politicians of his time.

**YALE UNIVERSITY**
*Located in New Haven, Connecticut, and founded in 1701, Yale is the third oldest university in the United States and has educated some of the most influential people in American history. Berkeley bequeathed his library to Yale, which today has one of the largest libraries in the United States.*

experience such as a colour, or
ound, be a copy of something
at is not an experience, or even
 in any way "like" it? Surely a
lour can be only like, or unlike,
other colour, and a sound only
e, or unlike, another sound?
e whole thing is conceptual
nsense, says Berkeley. Locke is
stulating the existence of a
hole realm of independently
isting, non-sensory, non-mental
ality which we cannot even
nceptualize, which we could
ver have evidence for, and
hose existence could make no
ssible difference to us. What
nceivable grounds are there
 doing this?

We know, said Berkeley, that
periences inhere in a subject,
cause each one of us has
mediate awareness of being such a subject, and
ubject having experiences. But we could never
ossess corresponding grounds for believing that
ese experiences are attached to objects that are
t us. Therefore, said Berkeley, a consistent
npiricism leads us to the conclusion that what
ists are minds and their contents, or subjects
d their experiences. There are no grounds for
lieving in the existence of anything else. We
uld certainly never have grounds for believing in
e existence of inert, independent matter, Locke's

### THE PERCEPTION OF QUALITIES
*In Berkeley's world, what exists are subjects and their experiences, there is
nothing else. He believed that we perceive not things, but qualities, such as
colour, and that these qualities are relative to the percipient. For the cloth dyers
in the picture above, a colour can only be like, or unlike, another colour.*

material substance – which Locke himself admitted
was unconceptualizable. In asserting the existence
of something beyond the bounds of all possible
experience Locke was breaking the fundamental
principle of empiricism.

This is a formidable philosophical argument, and
one that thinkers ever since have found difficulty
in dealing with. Being a Christian, Berkeley fitted
it into a view of total reality as existing in the mind
of God, an infinite spirit who has created us finite
spirits, and who is communicating with us via our
experiences. On this view everything that exists
does so either in our minds or in God's mind – or
else, of course, *is* either us or God. Thinkers who
are not religious have dispensed with this religious

## "TRUTH IS THE CRY OF ALL, BUT THE GAME OF FEW"

### GEORGE BERKELEY

framework; they have pointed out that Berkeley had
insufficient grounds for postulating the existence of
a God, or even of a continuous self. But the rest of
his philosophical challenge remains disconcertingly
difficult to answer.

A

**TREATISE**
Concerning the
**PRINCIPLES**
OF
*Human Knowlege.*

PART I.

Wherein the chief Caufes of Error and Difficulty in the *Sciences*, with the Grounds
of *Scepticifm, Atheifm*, and *Irreligion*, are
inquir'd into.

By *George Berkeley*, M.A. Fellow of
*Trinity-College, Dublin.*

*DUBLIN:*
Printed by AARON RHAMES, for JEREMY
PEPYAT, Bookfeller in *Skinner-Row*, 1710.

**A REJECTION OF
MATERIAL SUBSTANCE**
In his *Treatise
concerning the
Principles of Human
Knowledge* (1710),
Berkeley presents
his arguments against
abstract ideas.
He rejects material
causes, abstract general
ideas, and the belief
in material substance –
affirming spiritual
substance.

# HUME

## A MODIFIED SCEPTIC

*Apart from mathematics we know nothing for certain. But we still have to live: and to live is to act. All actions have to be based on assumptions about reality.*

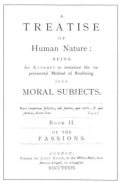

A
TREATISE
OF
Human Nature:
BEING
An ATTEMPT to introduce the ex-
perimental Method of Reasoning
INTO
MORAL SUBJECTS.

*Rara temporum felicitas, ubi sentire, quæ velis, & quæ sentias, dicere licet.* TACIT.

BOOK II.
OF THE
PASSIONS.

LONDON:
Printed for JOHN NOON, at the White-Hart, near
Mercer's-Chapel, in Cheapside.
M.DCC.XXXIX.

***A TREATISE OF HUMAN NATURE***
One of the central texts of British empiricism, Hume's *Treatise* was published anonymously in London in 1739–40. It bore the subtitle, "an attempt to introduce the experimental method of reasoning into moral subjects". It is set out in three books: Book I, on "understanding", aims to explain man's process of knowing; Book II, on "passions", tries to explain in psychological terms the emotional order in man; and Book III, on morals, attempts to describe moral goodness in terms of "feelings" of approval or disapproval.

***ADAM SMITH***
The Scottish economist and philosopher Adam Smith (1723–90) is best known for his book *An Inquiry into the Nature and Causes of the Wealth of Nations* (1776). From 1748 Smith was part of the Edinburgh circle that included David Hume, the biographer James Boswell, and the engineer James Watt.

DAVID HUME (1711–76) is one of the most attractive as well as one of the most important figures in the history of philosophy. Without being in any way sugary he seems to have been loved by everyone. In France, where he lived for several years, he was known as "*le bon David*" and in his native Edinburgh he was known as "Saint David". The Edinburgh street in which he lived is today called St David's Street. Some of his best work was done very young: for eight years he laboured at what is still generally regarded as his masterpiece, *A Treatise of Human Nature* (1739–40), and he was still only 28 when it was published. No-one took any notice of it. In his thirties he developed its ideas further and in what he hoped would be a more popular form; the results were published in two smaller volumes, *An Enquiry concerning Human Understanding* (1748) and *An Enquiry concerning the Principles of Morals* (1751). Still no-one took very much notice.

He turned away from philosophy, or at least he appeared to, and in his forties wrote a six-volume *History of England* (1754–62) which was to remain the standard work on the subject for something like a hundred years, until the appearance of Macauley's five-volume history during the years 1848 to 1861. In his own lifetime Hume acquired a reputation as an economist, and also as an essayist. Among his closest friends was Adam Smith, who is generally thought of as the founding father of economics; and Hume himself produced some original monetarist theories. His chief fame as a philosopher, however, was not to come until after his death in 1776. In 1779 his *Dialogues*

***DAVID HUME***
*In his early years, Hume – shown here in a portrait of 1766 by Allan Ramsay – attended Edinburgh University. Later, against his wishes, he was pressed to study law, and in 1729 he suffered a nervous breakdown.*

*concerning Natural Religion*, on which he had been working in secret, and which undermined all the then most attractive rational arguments for the existence of God, were posthumously published. This book has been considered by some to be his best work.

**A BUNDLE OF SENSATION**
Hume shared with Locke the basic empiricist premise that it is only from experience that our knowledge of the existence of anything outsid ourselves can be ultimately derived, whether the experience be our own or somebody else's. With Berkeley he shared the principle that this premise needs to be employed with consistency. This led him to agree with Berkeley, at least, that we can

## "BEAUTY IN THINGS EXISTS IN THE MIND WHICH CONTEMPLATES THEM"

DAVID HUME

never know with absolute certainty that a material world exists externally to, and independently of, ourselves. However, he took this to be primarily no point about the world but a point about knowledge: certainty, in matters of fact, is not available to us. We deal in hopeful probabilities, not in certainties.

He turned Berkeley's own principle against Berkeley. Who has ever been able to observe his own self, let alone anyone else's? When we introspect, what we find ourselves contemplating are sensory experiences, thoughts, emotions, memories, and so on and so forth, and all these things are fleeting, but we never find ourselves confronting a different sort of entity from these, an experiencing self, *having* these experiences. Therefore, on the principle that we ought not to postulate the existence of anything that is not to be found in experience, we have no grounds for supposing an experiencing self to exist in the way Berkeley does. The experiencing self, the subject of knowledge, is a fiction, says Hume. If you ask, in that case, who or what "I" am, the only answer that can be sustained by experience or observation is that "I" am a bundle of sensations.

## WHAT IS A CAUSE?

A similar argument applies to the existence of God, which Berkeley had also asserted. His existence is a question of fact – either he exists or he does not exist – and questions of fact, or questions of existence, can be settled only by observation. Who has observed God? There is, says Hume, no serious observational evidence for his existence. Hume has little difficulty in showing that what people claim as observational evidence is inferential, indirect, and vague: the most that can be claimed in that direction, he says, is that the degree of order evidenced by the universe could possibly be the manifestation of something remotely analogous to a designing intelligence. But that is a far cry from proof of the existence of a personal God, the God of the Christians or the Jews. And feelings of certainty are not knowledge.

*A LADY AT HER MIRROR,* JEAN RAOUX (1720S)
*Hume argued that when we introspect, what we find ourselves contemplating are experiences, such as thoughts and emotions – we never find ourselves confronting an experiencing self having these experiences. Therefore, Hume believed, we cannot assert that the experiencing self exists.*

With regard to both God and the self, Hume's argument takes the same basic form. To be justified, he says, in claiming the existence of these things we have to be able to point to evidence for it in observational experience, and there is none. This basic form of argument was used by him most influentially of all about the cause and effect relationship, causality itself.

To those coming to philosophy for the first time it is not always obvious why causality is considered so important by philosophers. Causality is of

**KEY WORKS**

A Treatise of
Human Nature
*(1739–40)*

An Enquiry
concerning
the Principles
of Morals
*(1751)*

Dialogues
concerning
Natural Religion
*(1779)*

**CAUSE AND EFFECT**
*For Hume, each causal event is independent of each other such event, and to illustrate this relationship of cause and effect he used the collision of billiard balls. The popularity of the game of billiards in the 18th century is here satirized by the English caricaturist James Gillray (1757–1815).*

Hume pointed out that causal connection - like the self, and like God - cannot be observed. We may *say* that we have observed that Event B was caused by Event A, but all we have actually observed is Event A and then, following it, Event B. We have not observed a third thing, a causal connection, linking the two. But to say that A caused B is not the same as saying that A happened and then B happened; it is saying that A brought B about - that B happened *because* A happened. So all we have observed is a sequence of events, whereas the causal relationship is a necessary connection. You may be tempted to say: "Ah yes, but I can assert that in this case was the cause of B because every time there is an event of type A it is invariably followed by an event of type B. I admit that the causal relationship is not just a simple conjunction of events, but when you get constant and invariant conjunction you know that causal connection is at work." But this will not do either. Every day there has ever been has been followed by a night, and yet day is not the cause of night: day and night are both caused by something else, namely the rotation of the earth on its axis as it goes round the sun. So a connection between two things can be invariant without either of them being the cause of the other. Given this, if constant conjunction is the most that we can ever observe, how are we to distinguish those examples of it in which the connection is causal from those in which it is not?

## WE DON'T KNOW ANYTHING

Since Hume spelt out this problem it has baffled many philosophers. And it has led directly to a further classic problem. If we can never have grounds in experience for asserting that one event necessarily brings about another, how is science possible? It may be that every time in history that water has been heated it has boiled at a temperature of 100 degrees Celsius, but that does

**HUME THE ECONOMIST**
*Hume's economic writings began in the* Political Discourses *(1752), which brought him a degree of fame. His use of evidence, and clear exposition of ideas, made his work ahead of its time; though unlike his friend Adam Smith, he did not work out an economic system. Hume believed that advance beyond an agricultural to an industrial economy was a precondition of civilization.*

fundamental interest to scientists too, incidentally. This is because it appears to be what binds the whole of the known world together: it is why the cosmos is not just a jumble or a chaos. One event causes, or is caused by, another; and there are persistent regularities in many of these happenings, such that different states of affairs connect up with one another in ways that are intelligible to our understanding, thus enabling us to make sense of our environment. If there were no such thing as causal connection our experience would lack intelligibility, in which case human life (as distinct from the life of the lower animals) would be impossible. Common sense takes causal connection for granted, but the scientist is all the time trying to uncover hitherto unknown causal connections, while the philosopher queries the very nature of causality itself and asks: "What is this amazing phenomenon, without which there would not be an intelligible world - what *is* causality?" In other words, because the philosopher's task is to understand reality in terms of its most general features he finds that understanding causality has got to be one of his central preoccupations.

ot *prove* that the heating causes the boiling, and certainly does not prove that the next time I heat ater it will boil at 100 degrees Celsius. Perhaps, ext time, things will be different. For thousands years all the swans that any European had ever bserved had been white, and Europeans took it r granted as a self-evident fact that all swans were

'CUSTOM, THEN, IS THE GREAT GUIDE OF HUMAN LIFE"

DAVID HUME

hite, but when they scovered Australia they scovered black swans. o number of observations white swans, however high, uld ever have guaranteed at all swans were white. d the same principle goes r any other set of observations. owever many Xs I observe d find to have the property that is no proof at all that the ext X I see will be *y*. It may ot be. I may come to *expect* at it will be, but that is a ychological effect, and is mething quite different om a logical proof: it is mere sociation of ideas. Logic is out the relationship between atements, and one statement ay contradict another, but one ct does not contradict another; t if both actually happen.

This raises a deep problem for science. Typical scientific laws are unrestrictedly general statements, which also assert causal connections, statements like "if you heat a body of water at sea-level atmospheric pressure it will boil when its temperature reaches 100 degrees Celsius". Neither the unrestricted generality of the statement nor the causal connection it asserts can be validated by observation or experience. How then, if at all, can either element in the statement be validated? We shall certainly go on expecting water to boil at 100 degrees Celsius, but we have nothing that can seriously be called proof that it will; and therefore we cannot, strictly speaking, say that we *know* that it will.

If we could stop just at this point, Hume would stand before us as an unmitigated sceptic, a man who denied that we could be sure of anything, whether it be the existence of God, or of the external world, or of our own continuous selves, or indeed of any reliable connection between anything and anything else in the world of fact. And he believes this to be the theoretical position. But we do not really have the option, he says, of living in accordance with such a perception of things. The reason why that is so is that our aims in life are not chosen by our intellects. For instance we do not do everything we can to stay alive because we have figured things out and concluded that survival is the best policy to pursue. We do not fall in love, or

EDINBURGH'S GOLDEN AGE
*From the second half of the 18th century and well into the 19th century, Edinburgh was at the height of its influence, becoming a leading centre of the European Enlightenment. The city was home to many of the great intellectual figures of the day, including David Hume, the economist Adam Smith, and the scientist James Hutton, famous as the founder of modern geology.*

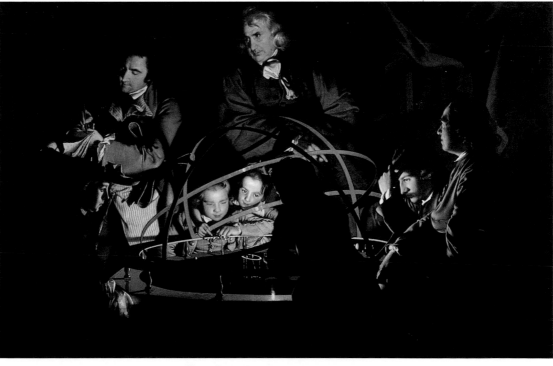

UNDERSTANDING THE LAWS OF SCIENCE
*Using the scientific method of Isaac Newton to describe how the mind worked in acquiring what is called knowledge, Hume concluded that there can be no knowledge of anything beyond experience. The influence of science on contemporary thought is vividly illustrated in Wright of Derby's painting* A Philosopher Lecturing *(c. 1766).*

enjoy music, or lick our lips over strawberries, for *reasons*. The ends of our behaviour are set by our desires, our passions, our emotions, our tastes – our feelings of every sort. And the chief way in which reason then comes in is in adopting and adapting all the various means to secure our ends. In a phrase that has been made famous by Hume, reason is the slave of the passions.

This being so, no-one is going to refuse to eat on the ground that there is no proof that the next time he eats food it will nourish him. We do indeed have no such proof, but we would nevertheless expect anyone who abstained from eating to die. Altogether, we shall carry on doing what we are prompted to do by our emotional drives of every sort; and in choosing the means to those ends we shall follow our accustomed association of ideas. The choices we make will assume that there are

# "REASON IS THE SLAVE OF THE PASSIONS"

DAVID HUME

connections whose existence we are unable to prove. Sometimes we shall come unstuck about this; people quite often eat things that are bad for them, and sometimes eat things that kill them. But even at a level of unattainable theory it is better that we should come unstuck occasionally than abstain from all action on the ground that we cannot be sure of anything – in which case we would have no life at all, literally.

Given that this is the situation, Hume advocated what he himself called "mitigated scepticism". By this he means we should admit to ourselves that conclusive proof plays no part in human affairs outside mathematics. We do not really *know* anything: we have our expectations, but that is not the same thing as knowledge. Hume laid enormous stress on the distinction, already spelt out by Leibniz (see p.97) between what have since come to be called analytic and synthetic statements, and asserted that synthetic statements can never be known with certainty to be true. We should therefore not give house-room in our heads to Theories of Everything, whether in philosophy, politics, science, religion, or any other sphere; for if we cannot be certain of anything, how ridiculous it is to think we have the answer to everything! Vast, organized systems of belief are *out* for Hume. He believes

we should hold our opinions and expectations diffidently, knowing them to be fallible, and should respect those of others. The whole temper of his philosophy is in this way modest, moderate, and tolerant, like his own character and life.

Hume's views have exerted a large and continuing influence down to our own day. Some of the fundamental problems he posed are still regarded by certain philosophers as unsolved, above all the problem of induction – the apparent impossibility

**RULED BY THE HEART**

*...ume believed that our behaviour is determined by our ...notions – our desires and passions. Reason, the slave of the ...ssions, only comes into play in order to secure those*

*desires. In his painting* The Bolt *(c. 1777), the French Baroque artist Jean-Honoré Fragonard powerfully expresses one of the overriding human passions – that of desire.*

...f leaping from any finite number of individual ...stances, however large, to a general conclusion. ...is writing style has also rubbed off on others: he ...owed that it is possible to write with clarity and ...it about some of the deepest and most difficult of ...hilosophical problems. Not only subsequent writers ... the English language, such as Bertrand Russell and

A. J. Ayer, have attempted to follow him in this, but also French and German philosophers. Schopenhauer, for instance, disgusted by the obscurity that had characterized philosophy in German up to his time, made a conscious attempt to write German in the way Hume had written English – and produced some of the best German prose ever written.

> *"The Christian religion not only was at first attended with miracles, but even at this day cannot be believed by any reasonable person without one"*
> DAVID HUME

**HUME'S INFLUENCE**
*David Hume was one of the major figures of his century. On the continent of Europe, especially in France, Hume is seen as one of the most important philosophers that Britain has ever produced.*
*In Germany, Kant read Hume and claimed that the experience had awoken him from his "dogmatic slumber".*
*Hume's ideas on moral philosophy had a formative influence on the 19th-century Utilitarians Jeremy Bentham and John Stuart Mill. If a poll were taken today among professors of Philosophy on who has written the finest philosophy in the English language, the winner would certainly be Hume.*

# BURKE
## THE SUPREME CONSERVATIVE

*Because in a developed society tradition embodies the accumulated wisdom and experience of many generations it is likely to be a more reliable guide to action than any one person's opinion.*

**BURKE AS AN MP**
In 1765 Burke became private secretary to the Marquess of Rockingham, leader of one of the Whig groups (the liberal faction in Parliament), and entered the House of Commons. Among his colonial policies were a call for the easing of political and economic pressures on Ireland, a conciliatory attitude towards the American colonies, and a proposal that India be governed not by the British East India Company or the Crown, but by a board of independent commissioners.

EDMUND BURKE (1729–97) was born in Ireland, into a family of modest means, and brought up a Protestant. He was educated at Trinity College, Dublin, and then at the lawcourts in London, though he never became a practising lawyer. Instead he worked as an author and journalist, then entered the House of Commons at the age of 37. A speech he made to his electors in Bristol is the classic statement of the principle that a Member of Parliament is a representative but not a delegate – in other words, an MP's vote cannot be mandated, because his duty is to vote according to his own judgement. His best-known book, *Reflections on the Revolution in France*, was published in 1790, the French Revolution having broken out the previous year. Although he never held ministerial office, the

**EDMUND BURKE**
*The Whig politician and political theorist, Edmund Burke, was one of the finest political thinkers England has ever known. He remains an important figure in the history of political theory.*

sheer quality of the content of his public speeches and his journalism made him one of the most influential figures of his day. He has been regarded since as the classic expositor of the conservative position in politic

### PAST WISDOM
In Burke's view a developed society is so big and so complicated that a single mind cannot possibly contain it all and understand it. It has come into being over many generations through numberle acts of initiative and organizatic on the part of individuals and groups who have all had to cope with reality. Its institution and arrangements embody innumerable choices an decisions, balanced judgements arrived at through experience, preferences based on knowledge. The whole thing is like a vast and complex organism; and it changes organically, developing new capacities in response to need, and perpetuall adapting to ever-changing circumstances. It is not at all like a machine which can be built from scratch to a blueprint, and whose working parts can be removed and replaced at will. Neither in theory nor in practice could any one political thinker, or any small group of political leaders, wipe out a developed society and replace it with one that was adequate. (This was Burke's fundamental objection to what the French revolutionaries were trying to do.) The only acceptable mode of political change, he thought, and the only one consonant with reality, is organic, not revolutionary. Each generation needs to regard itself not as owning the assets of society but as taking care of them: it has inherited a treasure from the past which it is its duty to pass on, augmented if possible but at any rate not depleted, to future generations.

**THE CHANGING FACE OF SOCIETY**
*Burke believed that a society's institutions embody balanced judgments based on experience and knowledge. The Mansion House, completed in 1753, is the official residence of the Lord Mayor of London (also Chief Magistrate of the City), and is also used as a court.*

**A CLASS BORN TO RULE**

*Burke believed that the public are more likely to thrive under the administration of men who are used to taking responsibility for others – a combination most likely to be found, in Burke's opinion, among people born to wealth, such as the members of the aristocracy depicted in Thomas Gainsborough's* Mr and Mrs Andrews *(c. 1749).*

Human beings are imperfect creatures, and therefore the idea that any human society could be perfect is an idle fancy – another reason why the aims of idealists are unattainable. Governments have to deal with people as they are, extremely unequal in talent and ambition yet each a mixture of good and bad. The public are likely to prosper more under the administration of practical-minded men who are used to carrying responsibility for others in their day-to-day affairs than they are under the rule of theoreticians, even though the theoreticians may be clever as individuals. It is not intellectual brilliance that is called for in government but a sound understanding of people and the ways of the world, steadiness of character, and common sense – plus perhaps a dash of flair. This combination is more likely to be found among people born to wealth and responsibility than among clever people who have made their way up from humble backgrounds – though a few of the latter may with advantage be admitted into the governing class of each generation.

This whole attitude is woven from the coming together of particular leading strands: affection and respect for existing social reality, and for the past out of which it has developed; a cautious attitude to change, and a desire to see it take place gradually; acceptance of the mixed character of human beings and their motivations, and a firm disbelief in their perfectibility; rejection of egalitarianism; a dislike of intellectualism in politics, that is to say a scepticism about the applicability of grand ideas, ideologies and "isms", to the lives of flesh-and-blood human beings, and also about the motives of those who advocate them. There are different kinds of conservatism, even within a society so tradition-bound and continuous as that of Britain, but Burkean Toryism is one of the most civilized and most rationally arguable, and perhaps for that reason tends to be respected even by its opponents.

## THE SUBLIME

An important idea that Burke had which is altogether outside politics is worthy of mention. In his book *A Philosophical Enquiry into the Origin of our Ideas of the Sublime and Beautiful* (1756) he took issue with the 18th-century Enlightenment belief that clarity is an essential quality of great art. On the contrary, he maintained, great art strives after the infinite, and the infinite, having no bounds, can never be clear or distinct. That is why great art cannot be pinned down, and why we are capable of being so much more moved by suggestion than by any amount of clear-cut statement – and from this position Burke went on to write about the emotional pull of the unknown. In England, at least, it was this book that signalled the first turning away from the formal classicism of 18th-century thinking about art in favour of the romanticism that superseded it.

Philosophical Enquiry
INTO THE
ORIGIN of our IDEAS
OF THE
SUBLIME
AND
BEAUTIFUL.

LONDON:
Printed for R. and J. DODSLEY, in Pall-mall.
M DCC LVII.

**BURKEAN AESTHETICS**
Published in 1756, *A Philosophical Enquiry into the Origin of our Ideas of the Sublime and Beautiful* contributed to new trends in aesthetic theory. It gave Burke a reputation in England, and was noticed abroad by such figures as Kant and Diderot.

**KEY WORKS**

A Philosophical Enquiry into the Origin of our Ideas of the Sublime and Beautiful
*(1756)*

Reflections on the Revolution in France
*(1790)*

Présenté par le S⸍ cholat l'un des Vainqueurs de la Bastille.

# Revolutionary
# FRENCH THINKERS

IN 18TH-CENTURY FRANCE THE CONSEQUENCES OF THE NEW WAY OF THINKING BASED ON NEWTONIAN SCIENCE AND LOCKEAN PHILOSOPHY WERE PROPAGATED TO THE WHOLE READING POPULATION BY POPULARIZERS OF GENIUS. A NEW CLASS OF INTELLECTUALS CAME INTO EXISTENCE WHO WERE FREETHINKERS IN RELIGION AND RADICALS IN POLITICS. VOLTAIRE, THE NONPAREIL OF SATIRISTS, BLEW AWAY TRADITIONAL BELIEFS WITH GALES OF LAUGHTER. DIDEROT, COMPARABLY GIFTED, EDITED A MONUMENTAL 35-VOLUME ENCYCLOPEDIA WHOSE AIM WAS TO CHANGE THE COMMON WAY OF THINKING. THE TRADITIONAL BELIEFS ON WHICH CHURCH AND STATE RESTED WERE UNDERMINED, AND A BRAND OF REVOLUTIONARY RADICALISM WAS BORN THAT HAS BEEN CONTINUOUSLY ACTIVE TO THE PRESENT DAY.

THE ENCYCLOPEDIA
*There are 35 volumes of the Encyclopedia (1751–80).*
*These are first editions from the collection of Louis XVI.*

**VOLTAIRE DICTATES WHILE
GETTING DRESSED**
Voltaire had an
unusually long writing
career, during which he
wrote plays, novels,
pamphlets, letters,
biographies, historical
works, and critical
reviews. He is pictured
here dictating to his
secretary while dressing,
in order to make the best
use of his time.

**JEAN-PHILLIPPE RAMEAU**
*The late Baroque
composer Jean-
Phillippe Rameau
(1683–1764) was a
friend of many of the
leading intellectuals
of his day, including
Voltaire, and was
involved in several
theoretical disputes
with Diderot and
Rousseau. Best known
for his harpsichord
music, in his lifetime
he was famous as a
composer of operas
and as a musical
theorist. His works
include the operas
Hippolyte et Arcie
(1733) and
Pygmalion (1748).*

# VOLTAIRE
## THE SUPREME POPULARIZER

*Voltaire did more than any other writer to propagate the
revolutionary implications of the new science and the new
liberalism in Continental Europe.*

VOLTAIRE (1694–1778) came from a well-to-do
Parisian family: his invented pen-name was a part-
anagram of his real surname, Arouet. He received
a first-rate classical education at the hands of the
Jesuits, then took to satirical writing. At this he was
very brilliant very young – so much so that he was
banished from Paris several times while still a young
man, had to go into exile briefly in Holland at the
age of 19, and spent nearly a year in the Bastille
in his mid-twenties. But also while still young he
established himself as the best playwright in France.
He was to dominate the French stage for 50 years,
and from this position (strikingly similar to that
of Bernard Shaw in 20th-century Britain) he
bombarded the world non-stop with advanced
views on every subject under the sun, always
expressed with humour and freshness of intelligence.

### THE LIGHT OF REASON
After a second term of imprisonment in the Bastille
Voltaire was forced to spend more than two years
in exile in England. This experience proved to be
the intellectual turning point of his life. The high
level of freedom he found in the England of that

## "THE SUPERFLUOUS IS VERY NECESSARY"
VOLTAIRE

day, the respect for the individual and the law, gave
him the yardstick with which he was to beat the
French for the rest of his life. He mastered the
English language, and immersed himself in serious
study of the new science as represented by

**VOLTAIRE**
*A courageous crusader against tyranny, bigotry, and cruelt
Voltaire is still recognized as one of the greatest French autho
and the embodiment of 18th-century enlightenment.*

Newton, and the new liberal philosophy as
represented by Locke. He was never to contribute
to this body of ideas anything of great significance
that was original, but the ideas took him over, and
throughout the remainder of an uncommonly long
writing career they provided him with the staple
intellectual content of his work. He propagated the
through every medium available to him – plays,
novels, biographies, historical works, pamphlets, ope
letters, critical reviews – and with such wit and
brilliance that they became known to every seriou
reader in Western Europe. Seldom anywhere has
there been so gifted a popularizer, or one who mad
so substantial an impact on the society around him

Perhaps the most explosive principle he
propounded was Locke's idea that the confidence
we have in our beliefs needs to relate to the

idence that exists in their support. So many
stablished beliefs in the religious and social life
f that time were supported by little more
ibstantial than the authority of Church and
ate that they began to collapse when
ibjected to rational enquiry. This
isistence on viewing everything in
ie light of reason became known
s "enlightenment", and this period,
i which it took hold in Western
urope, has been known ever
nce as "the Enlightenment".

CUTTING EDGE
ith Voltaire, liberalism took
n a sharper edge on the
ontinent of Europe than
had in England, where
ie comparative freedom
nd decency of life gave
formers scant
citement to militancy.
he Church of England
as almost notoriously
isygoing: from Church
s well as State there was
rtle in the way of

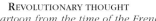

REVOLUTIONARY THOUGHT
*This cartoon from the time of the French
Revolution represents the peasant weighed down by
the nobility and the clergy. Voltaire, though not
a revolutionary himself, was considered, along with
Diderot and Rousseau, as one of the founders of
revolutionary thinking in France.*

ppression, and therefore little was aroused in the
ay of revolutionary feeling. In France, by contrast,
iere was despotic rule by individuals who flouted
ie law, hand in hand with an intolerant Catholic
hurch that used the political power thus conferred
n it for purposes of persecution. Most of the rest
f Continental Europe was more like France in
iese respects (some of it worse) than like England.
i such societies liberalism became a revolutionary
reed, dedicated to the overthrow of tyranny and
ierarchy and their replacement by social equality
nd the rule of law.

CHANGE WITHOUT VIOLENCE
i intellectual matters liberals advocated the use of
:ason and the right of individual dissent as against
informism and obedience to tradition and
ithority. Voltaire believed that these battles could
e fought and won with no greater accompaniment
f violence than the kind of imprisonment, exile,
id censorship that he himself had suffered so
xtensively; but many of his followers came to the
ew that revolutionary violence was necessary to
veep away the *ancien régime*. Thus Voltaire,
iough himself not a revolutionary, came to be
:en by almost everyone as the godfather of
:volutionary freethinking in 18th-century France,

the kind of thinking that did
so much to bring about the
French Revolution of 1789.
From then until almost the
end of the 20th century the
cause of radical reform in
Continental Europe showed more
of a tendency towards militancy,
a greater willingness to use
violence in order to promote the
values of the Enlightenment, than
its counterpart in the English-
speaking world. In Anglo-Saxon
countries this revolutionary
tradition never took firm root –
and therefore nor did the
counter-revolutionary
tradition represented
by Fascism. In the 20th
century the revolutionary
left and the counter-
revolutionary right were
between them to ravage
first Continental Europe
and then large parts of
the rest of the world,
but throughout that
period they left the English-speaking world
comparatively untouched. From there it seems
that liberalism is now once again invading the
rest of the world.

THE BASTILLE
*In 1380, at the order
of King Charles V, the
Bastille was built to
protect the wall
around Paris against
English attack. In the
17th and 18th
centuries it became a
state prison. Prisoners
were interned by*
lettre de cachet, *a
direct order of the
king, and prohibited
books were also
placed there. The
capture of the Bastille
took place on 14 July
1789, an event
commemorated in
France by Bastille
Day, a national
holiday. The Bastille
was subsequently
dismantled by the
revolutionary
government.*

THE STORMING OF THE BASTILLE
*On the morning of 14 July 1789 the Paris mob seized the Bastille in order to obtain arms.
They released seven prisoners: four counterfeiters, two madmen, and a young aristocrat.
This dramatic action came to symbolize the end of the* ancien régime.

# DIDEROT
## THE ENCYCLOPEDIST

*All-round genius – philosopher, satirist, novelist, playwright, art critic – Diderot was the leading editor of the French Encyclopedia, whose impact was international.*

**DENIS DIDEROT**
*The French philosopher and man of letters, Denis Diderot was one of the most prolific and versatile writers of the 18th century. He was the chief editor of the famous Encyclopedia, and also wrote novels, dramas, satires, philosophy, literary criticism, and brilliant letters.*

*"The first step towards philosophy is incredulity"*
DENIS DIDEROT'S
DYING WORDS

DENIS DIDEROT (1713-84), like Descartes and Voltaire before him, received an unusually good education from the Jesuits before turning against them. He refused to settle to any profession, but just went on being a brilliant student, long after his allowance had been cut off. He absorbed fundamental knowledge first in one field, then another, from mathematics and the sciences to ancient and modern languages. For many years, while doing this, he lived in poverty and obscurity. He first became known – and made money – by translating intellectually important books from English into French. His first original work, *Philosophical Thoughts*, appeared in 1746; and in the same year he became associated with the Encyclopedia.

This encyclopedia had begun in a modest way, as a straightforward commercial undertaking to translate the Chambers *Cyclopedia* of 1728 from English into French. But the project grew until it lost all connection with its original intentions.

Diderot became its editor, and it provided his chief occupation and source of income until 1772. Volume after volume was published under him as the years went by, until the complete work ran to 35 volumes. It was far and away the biggest publishing venture that had appeared in any language up to that time. What made it intellectually and historically important was that it embodied the new attitude to knowledge that Voltaire had imported into France from England – a scientific approach that looked to Francis Bacon and Isaac Newton as its great forebears, married to a philosophical approach that looked, above all, to John Locke. Diderot admitted that, as its editor, his aim was "to change the common way of thinking". And to a very considerable extent, he did.

### ANTI-AUTHORITY
The negative side of this was of crucial importance, and was to bring the Encyclopedia into trouble with the authorities. This whole huge work implicitly denied that religious teaching was a valid source of factual information about the world, and thus denied any intellectual authority to the Bible or the Church. It also refused to

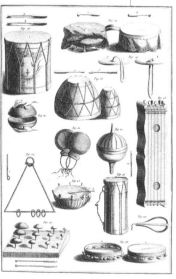

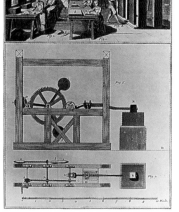

**PLATES FROM THE ENCYCLOPEDIA ON PERCUSSION INSTRUMENTS, MINING, AND PAPERMAKING**
*The first edition of the Encyclopedia (1751) was inspired by the success, in England, of Chambers* Cyclopedia. *Under Diderot's editorship it became a showcase for nearly all the important French writers of the time, including Rousseau, Montesquieu, and Voltaire. It also became the focus of artistic and religious controversy.*

recognize political power as a source of authority in intellectual or artistic questions. It went against nearly all the basic social, political, and religious orthodoxies of the day. One can say that, on a massive scale, the Encyclopedia put forward a conception of knowledge and learning, in both the sciences and the arts, that was to become one of the leading characteristics of the modern age.

## SHOWCASE OF IDEAS

Most of the outstanding writers and thinkers of France contributed to the Encyclopedia: Voltaire, Rousseau, Montesquieu, and of course many others. Unusually, for that time, a good many of these contributors were identified by name, including the best-known ones. Some of their articles have since acquired classic status as essays. Diderot himself wrote quite a few of them. Of the complete Encyclopedia in its original edition about 4,225 sets were sold. There was simply none to compare with it in any country, and its impact on the intellectual life of Europe was incalculable. It must

## "THE WORD FREEDOM HAS NO MEANING"

DENIS DIDEROT

be remembered that Paris was regarded internationally at this time as the intellectual and artistic as well as the social and political capital of the world. Educated people everywhere knew French. It was the language of international diplomacy. There were even several lands whose rulers spoke French in preference to the language of their own people. Understandably, it has not been easy for the people of France to accept that their language has been superseded by English in these respects during the course of the 20th century.

The Encyclopedia got into more and more trouble with official censorship as successive volumes appeared, and in 1759 it was suppressed by royal decree. However, Diderot and his contributors, and of course the printers, continued to work in secret, and made underground preparations for the remaining volumes, which eventually saw the light of day.

While all this was going on, Diderot was also writing personal works of his own. But these too, he knew, would not get past the official censor, because of their explicit materialism and atheism. Nevertheless, he continued to write them, confident

### THE ENCYCLOPEDISTS
*The authors of the Encyclopedia, known as the Encyclopedists, consisted of men dedicated to the advancement of rationalism, the new science, toleration, and humanitarianism.*

that posterity would one day recognize their merits. And so it has. The result is that, whereas during his lifetime he was thought of by everyone as the editor of the Encyclopedia, the Encyclopedia has now been very largely superseded by the onward march of science and scholarship, while the writings on which Diderot's fame now chiefly rests came out after his death. Perhaps the best known among these are two dialogues, *Rameau's Nephew* (1821) and *D'Alembert's Dream* (1830), and a novel, *The Nun* (1790): but several others are also noteworthy.

Diderot, then, was an encyclopedist in a double sense. He was himself an individual of encyclopedic knowledge and interests, able to write with effervescent style and authority in an astonishing variety of forms about subject matter across an exceptionally wide range. And he was the editor of the most influential encyclopedia ever.

MONTESQUIEU
*Although Charles-Louis de Secondat Montesquieu (1689–1755) is now remembered mainly as a liberal political philosopher, he was also well known in his own time as an acute satirist, a prominent social figure, and a brilliant stylist. When he was asked to write on democracy and despotism for the Encyclopedia he declined, saying that he had already had his say on those themes but that he would like to write on taste. This was his last work.*

### INTELLECTUALS GATHERING AT THE CAFÉ D'ALEXANDRE, PARIS
*The 100 years preceding the Revolution of 1789 constituted the ancien régime. Society was centred in Paris and, in contrast to the corruption that was rife at the court of Louis XV, the economy thrived, arts flourished, and her intellectuals were known throughout Europe.*

# ROUSSEAU
## CRITIC OF CIVILIZATION

*Rousseau was the first Western philosopher to insist that our judgements should be based on the requirements of feeling rather than reason.*

*"There is no original perversity in the human heart"*
JEAN-JACQUES ROUSSEAU

JEAN-JACQUES ROUSSEAU (1712–78) was born in Geneva when it was an independent state. That he was not French is an important fact about him, for unlike most writers in French he was never an admirer of French culture, or indeed of any culture. That he was Swiss had a profound effect on his attitude to democracy, the thing with which eventually he came to be most associated. Unlike most eminent philosophers he received very little in the way of formal education, and this too was important, in that it reinforced his espousal of spontaneous feeling as against conceptual thinking.

Rousseau's mother died a few days after he was born, so he was brought up by an aunt and an erratic father, who at least taught him to read. He was parcelled out, first to a country minister, then to an uncle. He was apprenticed, first to a notary, then to an engraver, who treated him brutally and from whom he ran away. His life was to continue like this, often full of violent emotions, always rootless, always wandering, from one job to another, one woman to another, one country to another. He experienced plenty of the harsher realities of life, working at a range of jobs from tutor to lackey, and having five illegitimate children by an ignorant servant girl. But he also met Diderot and other *philosophes*. (This word is still used of the writers associated with the Encyclopedia: it means little more than our present-day "literary intellectual".) He was even invited to contribute to the Encyclopedia himself.

**JEAN-JACQUES ROUSSEAU**
*Swiss-born Jean-Jacques Rousseau was one of the greatest European thinkers of the 18th century. His work inspired the leaders of the French Revolution and influenced what became known as the Romantic generation.*

Rousseau's Encyclopedia articles were about music indeed, when he first went to Paris with the hope of making his name there it had been through music, for he had invented a new system of musical notation. But there was to be no long-term follow-up to his hopes in this direction – though some years later he did have his opera *Le Devin du Village* (*The Cunning-Man*, 1766) performed, with great success, in front of Louis XV at Fontainebleau. Nevertheless it was his prose writings that brought him lasting reputation.

He began with two essays, *Discourse on Science and the Arts* (1750) and *Discourse on the Origins and Foundations of Inequality* (1754). Then, in the two years 1761–62, came three of his four most famous books: *La Nouvelle Héloïse*, *Emile*, and *The Social Contract* – the fourth being the autobiography

*"MAN WAS BORN FREE, AND EVERYWHERE HE IS IN CHAINS"*
JEAN-JACQUES ROUSSEAU

*Confessions*, which was not published until after his death. In the mid-1760s he decided to live in England, in response to an invitation from the British philosopher David Hume, who was personally known, loved, and revered by many of the leading *philosophes*. But in England he had

MADAME DE POMPADOUR
*Born Jeanne-Antoinette Poisson (1721–64), the future Madame de Pompadour became the mistress of Louis XV after she met him at a ball in 1745. She was installed at Versailles, made the officially recognized mistress to the king, and ennobled as Marquise de Pompadour. A great influence on the king's policies, she was also a great supporter of the arts. She founded the École Militaire, the porcelain factory at Sèvres, and became patron to Voltaire, Montesquieu, and Rousseau.*

THE NOBLE SAVAGE

*...e idealized concept of uncivilized man, who symbolizes ... innate goodness of natural man uncorrupted by ...ilization, was common in literature long before Rousseau. ...his Romantic epic* Atala *(1801), the French writer*

*Chateaubriand sentimentalized the North American Indian. Mussini's painting of* The Death of Atala *(1830) shows the hero, Chactas, at the death-bed of Atala, who has poisoned herself to escape temptation and keep her vow of virginity.*

...me sort of paranoid breakdown, denounced ...me as seeking his undoing, and fled in panic ...ck to France – where eventually he died in 1778.

Rousseau introduced three revolutionary ideas ...o the mainstream of Western philosophical ...ought which have played a role of immense ...portance ever since. The first is that civilization ...not a good thing, as everyone had always ...sumed; and not even a value-neutral thing; but ...sitively a bad thing. The second is that we should ...k of everything in our lives, whether our private ...public lives, that it meet the requirements not of ...ason but of feeling and natural instincts: in other ...rds, feeling should replace reason as our guide to ...e and our judge. The third is that a human society ...a collective being with a will of its own that is ...fferent from the sum of the wills of its individual ...embers, and that the citizen should be entirely ...bordinate to this "general will".

On the first point, Rousseau believed that ...man beings were born good but were corrupted

by the experience of growing up in society. Because he believed that our natural instincts are good, his view of the state of nature was the direct opposite of Hobbes': man in a state of nature is a "noble savage", according to Rousseau. But a child growing up in a so-called civilized society is taught to curb and frustrate his natural instincts, repress his true feelings, impose the artificial categories of conceptual thinking on his emotions, and pretend not to think and feel all sorts of things that he does think and feel, while pretending to think and feel all sorts of things that he does not think or feel. The result is alienation from his true self (the term "alienation" was not coined until later, by Hegel), and all-pervading falsehood and hypocrisy. Thus civilization is the corrupter and destroyer of true values – not, as people seem always to assume, their creator and propagator.

However, once having taken the step into civilization, man no longer has the option of returning to the primitive state. So what we must do is, as it

PERSECUTED ROUSSEAU
Rousseau's *Emile* and *The Social Contract* were condemned by the Parlement of Paris in June 1762 as contrary to the government and religion. Rousseau had to flee to Switzerland, but there, too, he and his works were banned. He defended himself in his *Letters Written from the Mountain* (1764). After further persecution he fled to England at the invitation of David Hume.

> "*Social man lives constantly outside himself*"
>
> JEAN-JACQUES ROUSSEAU

**EMILE**
Completed in 1762, *Emile: Ou de l'éducation* was one of Rousseau's greatest projects. It tells the story, in novel form, of a child reared apart from other children. Through this tale Rousseau attempts to advise parents how to rear their children, by "following nature".

ROUSSEAU'S FAMILY LIFE
*From the time his father went into exile, in 1722, Rousseau had an itinerant lifestyle. Although he had had little early family life himself his mother having died soon after his birth, and despite his later proclamations about "the innocence of childhood", all five of his children, the result of an association with an illiterate maidservant, were abandoned to foundling hospitals.*

were, to civilize civilization – we must change it in ways that allow our natural instincts and our feelings fuller and freer expression. The outstanding novel in which Rousseau elevated and glorified the claims of sentiment and emotion above those of reason and self-restraint was *La Nouvelle Héloïse*.

Rousseau advocated fundamental changes in education to free the individual from the psychological shackles of civilization. His central point here is that education should not aim, as it did in his day, to repress and discipline a child's natural tendencies, but, on the contrary, to encourage their expression and development. The main vehicle of instruction should not be verbal instruction, still less books, but practice and example, in other words direct experience of people and of things. The natural environment for this to take place in is the family, not school; and its natural incentives are sympathy and love, not rules and punishments. The book in which Rousseau put

all this forward was *Emile* – and it is probable that this book had more influence on educational developments in Europe than any other has ever had.

Rousseau's attitude to religion was in keeping with his other view. He was not, like so many of the *philosophes*, an atheist, but he was entirely against religion being seen as a matter of intellectually formulated beliefs, and thus of creeds, dogmas, and catechisms. It should be recognized, he though that God is beyond all the formulations of reason. Emotions of awe and reverence should be allowed to dominate, acknowledgir that religion is above all a matter of the heart, not the head.

## THE GENERAL WILL

When it came to law-making or law-changing, Rousseau believed that it should be carried out by all the people coming together and deliberating, then voting, as in a Greek city state or a Swiss canton. What was thus expressed was the "general will", a perception of wha was best for the society as a whole although this might not be what w actually desired by any individual (as, for example, when the society demanded painful and dangerous sacrifices from everyone). The sovereign people were then free to give the task of putting these laws into effect to whoever they chose – a monarch, perhaps; or perhaps a group of politicians or officials – it mad no difference in principle, because the law, having been made by all the people acting together, was now absolutely binding on everyone. No defalcatio was to be allowed. Rousseau acknowledged that a population at large might constitute an ill-informe undisciplined and short-sighted legislative body: h solution to this problem lay in special individuals whom he referred to as "Legislators", charismatic leaders who instinctively understood the general will and drafted legislation themselves, and then persuaded the people to accept it.

Rousseau's political philosophy has had an enormous influence. It provided the movements leading up to the French Revolution with significant quantities of their emotional and

tellectual fuel. And it offered a fundamentally
different conception of democracy from Locke's,
one which flourished and was actively followed as
a living alternative until the late 20th century. The
mainspring of the Rousseau idea of democracy is
the forcible imposition of the general will, whereas

## "LIBERTY, EQUALITY, FRATERNITY"

JEAN-JACQUES ROUSSEAU

the mainspring of the Locke model is the
protection and preservation of individual freedom.
The two are very different, in fact they
are potentially opposite.

With Rousseau the individual has no
right at all to deviate from the
general will, so this concept of
democracy is compatible with a
complete absence of personal
freedom. Here was the first
formulation in Western philosophy
of some of the basic ideas
underlying the great totalitarian
movements of the 20th century,
Communism and Fascism –
which likewise claimed to
represent the people, and to have
mass support, and even to be
democratic, while denying
individual rights; and which also
allotted a key role to charismatic
leaders; and which waged both hot
war and cold war against the Anglo-
Saxon democracies who based
themselves on Lockean principles.

### PASSION RULES

Rousseau's work was the first
onslaught from a major
philosopher on the values of the
Enlightenment, above all on its
appeal to the sovereignty of
reason. His hostility to civilization
as such was to reappear in the
philosophical anarchists of the
20th century, such as Proudhon,
and in the philosophy of

Nietzsche. Acknowledgement of the importance
of the role played by this hostility in the psyche of
every one of us was to be an important element in
the psychology of Sigmund Freud. In all these
respects, and above all in his glorification of
emotion, Rousseau was the acknowledged
forerunner of the Romantic movement, which soon
after him was to supersede the classicism of the
18th century. Even more than that, he launched a
tendency in Western thought and art that has
remained powerful ever since, the longing to throw
off the constraints of reason and give untrammelled
expression to feeling and instinct. This way of
looking at things often has powerful appeal for the
young. Now that it has become centrally established
as a part of Western sensibility it is unlikely to
disappear in the foreseeable future. Its dangers are
obvious, but we must find ways of living with them.

**MAXIMILIEN ROBESPIERRE**
Known to his peers as
"the Incorruptible",
Robespierre (1758–94)
played a leading part in
the French Revolution.
He thought, like
Rousseau, that moral
virtue was inseparable
from the exercise of
sovereignty. Although his
adherence to this won
the approval of the
French people, his belief
in coercion in order to
save the republic cost
him his life.

**DECLARATION OF THE RIGHTS OF MAN**
*One of the basic charters of human liberties, this Declaration, written in 1789,
stated that "all men are born free and equal in rights." Based on the theories of
Rousseau and the American Declaration of Independence, it aimed to embody the
freedoms denied to the French under the pre-Revolutionary absolute monarchy.*

*"Man is
naturally good,
loving justice
and order"*
JEAN-JACQUES ROUSSEAU

**EUROPE'S CITIES**
*During the 18th
century the great
cities of Europe were
expanding as never
before. By the 1750s
London and Paris
had developed into
urban centres each
with a population of
half a million people.
The cities reflected the
rise of the middle
class whose lives were
based not on land-
owning but on trade.
While the rich built
fine new houses, the
poor lived in squalor,
in crowded and
insanitary conditions.*

# Golden Century
# of
# German
# Philosophy

Between the 1780s and the 1880s a
flowering of philosophy occurred in the
German-speaking world such as had not
been seen since the time of the ancient
Greeks. It began with Kant. His work was
enriched and extended by Schopenhauer.
Fichte and Schelling also took off from
Kant as their point of departure.
Hegel produced a philosophy of absolute
idealism. Marx took over the framework
and vocabulary of Hegel's philosophy but
substituted materialist for idealist values.
Nietzsche mounted an onslaught on the
whole of existing morality. The wealth of
ideas produced by these philosophers
nourishes some of today's
newest developments.

ARMS OF THE KING OF PRUSSIA
*This late 19th-century coat of arms was designed for Wilhelm I, king
of Prussia from 1861. Wilhelm was German emperor from 1871–88.*

# KANT

## RATIONALISM AND EMPIRICISM COME TOGETHER

*Our experience is in forms determined by our bodily apparatus, and only in those forms can we imagine anything's specific existence.*

**JOHANN SCHILLER**
One of the great German poets and dramatists, Johann Schiller (1759–1805) studied the philosophy of Kant between 1793 and 1801. In his essays he sought to define the character of aesthetic activity, its function in society, and its relation to moral experience. His early tragedies were attacks upon political oppression and his later plays were concerned with the freedom of the soul – allowing man to rise above his physical conditions.

IMMANUEL KANT (1724–1804) is commonly regarded by devotees of philosophy as the outstanding figure to have emerged in the subject since the ancient Greeks. He was born in the provincial town of Königsberg, East Prussia, and never went outside his native province in the whole of his life. He never married, and outwardly his life was uneventful and routine – the people of Königsberg could correct their watches by him as he passed their windows on his daily walk. But he was not the dull dog that this suggests. He was bright and dapper in person, and amusing in conversation; he relished company, and never dined alone. The brilliance of his lectures became legendary. Although he never left Königsberg he became internationally famous in his lifetime.

### AN ACADEMIC OF GENIUS

Kant was the first great philosopher since the Middle Ages to be a professional academic. After him it was unsurprising for a major philosopher to be a university professor, but none had been before him, and many of those after him were not either. It was not until the 20th century that nearly all outstanding philosophers were academics. This professionalization of philosophy was sharply criticized early on by Schopenhauer as being bad for the subject, and has always been controversial, but it is now institutionally entrenched, and seems unlikely to be reversed.

Until he became elderly, Kant's reputation was much like that of other first-rate academics, that is to say outstanding at the time but not built to last. However, at the age of 57, after a 10-year silence, he published one of the great books of all time,

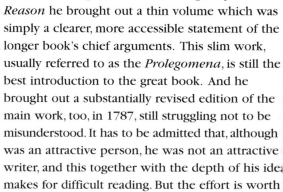

**IMMANUEL KANT**
*The German philosopher Immanuel Kant – one of the greatest philosophers of all time – argued that we gain knowledge through both experience and understanding.*

*Critique of Pure Reason* (1781). There followed the *Critique of Practical Reason* in 1788, and t[?] *Critique of Judgment* in 1790. Meanwhile, in 1785, he broug[?] out an unusually short book with an unusually long title, *The Fundamental Principle[?] of the Metaphysics of Ethics* which has been influential ever since. He was in the middle of writing another of his large-scale works when he died at the age of nearly 80.

This late harvest of his thought was so profoundly original in content that it was n[?] at all easy to understand. In fact Kant felt it to be generally misunderstood at first, so two years after the publication of *Critique of Pure Reason* he brought out a thin volume which was simply a clearer, more accessible statement of the longer book's chief arguments. This slim work, usually referred to as the *Prolegomena*, is still the best introduction to the great book. And he brought out a substantially revised edition of the main work, too, in 1787, still struggling not to be misunderstood. It has to be admitted that, although [?] was an attractive person, he was not an attractive writer, and this together with the depth of his ide[?] makes for difficult reading. But the effort is worth [?] His work is the gateway to the most significant developments in philosophy beyond Hume.

### HOW DO WE KNOW?

Before Kant, many if not most thinkers, including scientists, took it for granted that the ultimately significant limit imposed on what human beings can know is set by what there is: we can, in principle, go on finding out more and more, until in the end there is nothing left to find out. Kant, veloping a line of thought inaugurated by Locke, sisted that in addition to this our knowledge is o subject to another limitation of an entirely fferent sort. Everything we apprehend in any way all – whether it is a perception, a feeling, a memory, hought, or whatever it may be – is apprehended us through our bodily apparatus, namely our five nses, our brains, and our central nervous systems. erefore anything that this apparatus can deal with capable of being experience for us. But anything cannot deal with can never be experience for us, we have no way of apprehending it.

## EING AND SEEMING

e point here is that all apparatus, our own or any her, is good for some purposes but not for others, its own nature sets limitations to what it can do. u cannot take a photograph with a can-opener, or ke sausages with a car engine. A camera will make hotograph of a scene, but not a sound recording it. Sound equipment will make a recording of the me scene, but not a photograph of it. If there is mething that is neither visible nor audible – let us a motionless body of colourless gas – it can be

> ## "THE TERM 'WHOLE' IS ALWAYS ONLY COMPARATIVE"
>
> IMMANUEL KANT

ither photographed nor sound-recorded: nothing ll appear on a negative, and nothing on a sound e. But this is not to say that the gas does not ist: on the contrary, it does, and its existence may crucially important to you – it may even kill you. t it can be neither seen nor heard, and its istence will be undetectable to any camera or e recorder. So if you do not have the means of tecting it with a completely different sort of uipment its existence will remain unknown to you.

All these considerations, Kant says, apply to our dily apparatus. Our eyes can do certain very portant things, but not anything else. Ears can do ite other things, which eyes cannot do. Our taste ds can register things that neither eyes nor ears n detect. Our brains can do innumerable different rts of things from any of these. And so on and so th. When all our faculties have been enumerated,

the sum total of what they are able to deal with is the sum total of what we can apprehend. This is not to say that nothing else can exist. As far as our knowledge goes, *anything* else may exist. But if anything else exists, whatever it may be, we have no way of apprehending it.

So there are two different sorts of limitation on what we can know, and not just one. The first is what exists. The sum of everything there is – whether or not it includes a God or immortal souls or anything else – makes up total reality. But we

### THE NATURE OF EXPERIENCE
*Kant believed that anything that cannot be apprehended by our bodily apparatus can never be experience for us. The woman depicted in John Everett Millais' The Blind Girl (1856) can enjoy the sound of music from her concertina, the touch of her daughters' hand and the smell of her hair, but can never "experience" the rainbow in the sky behind her.*

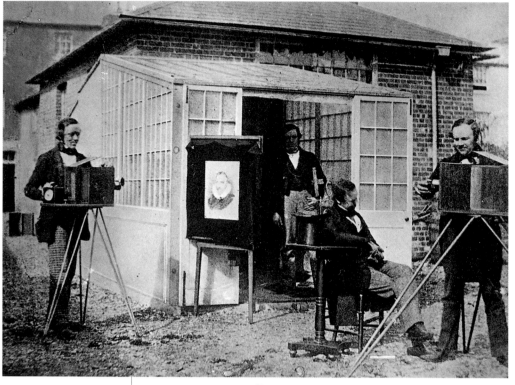

REPRESENTATION AND REALITY
*The nature of a particular piece of apparatus sets limits to what it can do. A photograph is a representation of a scene in a particular form – not the scene itself. Kant says that these considerations also apply to human experience.*

on it; and the sound recording is a coil of electro-magnetic tape. It is a fundamental mistake, the sort of mistake we associate with children and primitive man, to confuse the representation of a thing with the thing itself.

Again, these considerations apply to human experience, says Kant. What is delivered to our consciousness is the product of our bodily apparatus, and takes the forms it does because of the nature of that apparatus: there cannot be visual representations without eyes, or aural representations without ears; there cannot be thoughts or ideas without brains. But sights, sounds, ideas and so on, are not the objects external to us, they are our representations of those objects. They exist only in the human apparatus that produces them. And there is no intelligible sense in which they can be "like" objects that exist independently of experience: a sound can only be like, or for that matter not like, another sound, and a sight can only be like, or not like, another sight; and sounds *as such*, and sights *as such*, are subject-dependent. They give us information, often of minute accuracy, but they do so as gauges, not pictures. To *mis*take them as pictures is like mistaking a patient's temperature for his portrait.

human beings can know only such of it, or such aspects of it, as our bodily apparatus is able to deal with. So on the one hand there is what exists, independently of us and our capacity for experience, and on the other hand there is what we have the means of experiencing; and there could never be good reason for believing that these are the same. The latter is almost certainly narrower than the former, and likely to be very meagre indeed compared to it.

The two are more radically different than our investigation up to this point has made explicit. When we were talking just now about the differing purposes that different sorts of apparatus can serve we made the point that each piece of apparatus delivers its end-product in terms that are dictated by its own structure: a camera gives us a photograph, a tape-recorder a sound recording, and so on. But a photograph is not itself the scene photographed: it is a representation of that scene in a particular form. A sound recording that was being made when the photograph was taken is a representation of the same scene in a totally different form. The scene itself may have consisted of a panoramic vista containing mountains, villages, human beings, animals, and all sorts of other things, but the photograph is just a piece of paper that you can hold in your hand, a piece of paper with markings

## "IT IS PRECISELY IN KNOWING ITS LIMITS THAT PHILOSOPHY EXISTS"

IMMANUEL KANT

this means that what things *are* independently of our modes of perception and thought is something of which we cannot form any conception. On the one side we have the world of things as they appear to us – what Kant calls the world of phenomena. This is the world of possible knowledge for us. But all the forms this knowledge takes are subject-dependent. On the other side there is the world of things as they are in themselves, what Kant calls the noumenal world. Its mode of existence has nothing to do with the particular ways in which we register things. But to this realm, for that very reason, we have no means of access. Everything about this noumenal world is what Kant calls "transcendental", by which he means that it exists but cannot be registered in experience.

## ORDER OUT OF CHAOS

The world as it appears to us is not a chaos or a jumble, it is pervaded with order of many different kinds. Objects exist side by side in three-dimensional space, all of them attracting one another in accordance with the inverse-square law of gravity; movements and processes go on alongside one another in a fourth dimension of time. Large numbers of these processes are causally interconnected, and interact in orderly and predictable ways that can be expressed in mathematical equations. What appear to be the fundamental constituents of this whole order of things are precisely those mentioned: material objects existing in a space-time framework, moving in ways that causally interconnect. It is to be stressed as of the utmost importance that what these fundamentals characterize is the world of *experience*. They are characteristics of the way we human beings perceive and understand. We cannot conceive of anything specific as existing without its being *something*, without its having a real identity. We cannot conceive of effects without causes. These are categories of our understanding, without which we would not be able to grasp anything at all about the world around us.

Similarly we cannot conceive of any actual object as existing other than in a space – or as moving, if not in time. Space and time are forms of our sensibility, without which we would not be able to perceive or apprehend anything in the world. These forms of sensibility are the nets within which we catch whatever we

perceive, and those categories of understanding are the frameworks within which we make intelligible to ourselves whatever it is that our senses pick up. All these things are features of how we function as experiencing subjects, beings in the world. But they are characteristics of experience, not characteristics of things as they exist in themselves independently of being experienced.

## FAMILIAR IDEA

These ideas would be much more difficult for us to grasp than they are if they were not already familiar to us in a different context, namely a religious context. Adherents of most of the world's great religions believe that this world of material objects in space and time is not the whole of reality, that there is also another level of reality that is not material, and is outside space and time; but that human beings are able to experience only the first of these levels, not the second. What Kant is doing is grounding that whole view of things in philosophical argument, rational argument, without positing a God, or a soul, or any appeal to faith; so that an entirely non-religious person with no belief in God or the soul could regard himself as having good reasons for believing it. Kant believes that the crucial non-religious aspects of it can be shown to

**ABOVE AND BEYOND**
*Most followers of the world's religions believe that the world of material objects does not comprise the whole of reality. Caspar David Friedrich's brooding painting,* Two Men by the Sea looking at the Moon rising *(c. 1817), suggests another level of reality outside the confines of space and time. Kant called this world the "transcendental" world – that is, one that cannot be registered in experience.*

be true by rational argument alone. His actual arguments, and his detailed analyses of the issues involved, are complicated and profound, and for that reason sometimes difficult to follow; but his main conclusions are such as are already familiar to anyone who is acquainted with, shall we say, Christianity

## THE PROBLEM OF FREE WILL

Kant believed that the key to knowledge and understanding of the world of experience, the world of material objects in space and time, had now been placed into our hands by science. The inner constitution of every material object, and all its movements in space and time, seemed to him to accord with principles that science was now able, at least in principle, to uncover; and he could see no reason why, by pursuing the path we were on, we should not be able to arrive eventually at a complete knowledge of them.

But there was a serious problem here concerning human beings. Our bodies are material objects existing in space, and moving in space and time. If their movements are entirely subject to scientific laws, we can have no such thing as free will. Yet Kant believed that we *do* have free will – and, what is more, that this is demonstrable. His solution to this problem was to say that our free acts of will take place not in the phenomenal world, which is to say that part of reality to which scientific laws apply, but in the other part, the part to which scientific understanding cannot reach, the noumenal world.

His actual demonstration was not so much that we have free will as that we find it impossible to believe that we do not. It is an empirical fact that we have moral concepts such as *good* and *ought* and *right*, and it is an empirical fact that we have moral convictions about what is good (or not), what we ought or ought not to do, and so on. It is also an empirical fact that nearly all of us are not able wholly to disregard these convictions of ours even when we try to, or wish that we could. Now, says Kant, for these concepts to have any content at all, and for our moral convictions to have any meaning or application at all, it must at least sometimes be the case that we have a choice whether to do or not do something. If we *never* have that choice, then

**MOSES MENDELSSOHN**
The Jewish philosopher and biblical scholar Moses Mendelssohn (1729–86) argued for rationality of belief in the existence of God. Typical of his thinking is the *Phaedon* of 1767, which is a philosophical exposition on the doctrine of immortality of the soul – which he believed, like Kant, to be based not on dogma but on the demands of reason.

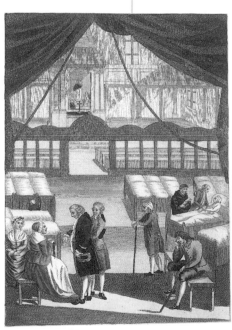

**MORAL CONVICTIONS**
*Kant argued that in order for moral concepts such as whether we ought to care for the sick, to have meaning, we must have free will. We must have the choice to do or not do something.*

**WILFUL INTENT**
*Kant believed that human beings have free will. If we did not, then there would be no point complaining when others treated us badly or illegally, because it would have been impossible for them ever to do anything else.*

it is simply false ever to say that I ought to do, or not do, anything, because I never have any choice in the matter. The whole of so-called morality is then an empty illusion, and all so-called moral utterances are meaningless. Words like *duty*, *right*, *ought*, and all the rest of them, never apply. For us to recommend one course of action rather than another to anyone is pointless. The whole vocabulary of praise and blame, admiration and condemnation, approval and disapproval, needs to be expunged from our language and our thoughts, for neither in our private lives nor our social lives does any space exist for such notions to occupy. There would be no point in our complaining if others treated us with vicious brutality, because it would have been impossible for them ever to do anything else. It would be wrong of us to say that they ought not have done it, because they would have had no choice

## THE BASIS OF ETHICS

Anyone who genuinely believes in determinism as applied to human beings is committed to these consequences. However, there seem to be no such people. It appears to be a fact that for us to think like that is impossible. Even those of us who are rascals and criminals, and even those of us who are psychopaths, even those who believe themselves to be determinists, seem to object and be outraged when they are treated brutally, and to think that whoever did it ought not to have done it. So it ppears that we cannot but believe that there is such a thing as free choice, at least sometimes. ut the fact that we believe this means that we annot help believing that some of the movements f material objects in space are not determined holly by the laws of science: some of them are ecided by the free operations of our will – and ree" in this context means not impersonally etermined, not governed by scientific laws.

So, says Kant – and whether we like to admit it or ot – we do in fact believe that it is not the empirical orld alone that exists. We believe that there is a on-empirical realm in which decisions are made at affect the movements of our bodies; and also at to the choices thus taken the vocabulary of

# "PLATO THE DIVINE, AND THE ASTOUNDING KANT"

### THE OPENING WORDS OF SCHOPENHAUER'S FIRST BOOK

raise and blame can be applied. The whole of Kant's hilosophy can be seen as an attempt to understand ow this is possible – how morality and ree will can exist in a world that is evertheless amenable to scientific xplanation.

Kant believed that only a creature apable of understanding reasons for and gainst doing something could be said to e behaving morally or immorally, and herefore that morality was a possibility or rational creatures only. A poisonous nake cannot be condemned for nmorality. But the validity of such easons is not just a matter of individual aste. We may differ in our judgments bout whether or not a particular reason a good one, but the very fact that we rgue about it and try to persuade one nother shows that we believe that a eally good reason commands assent. valid reason is *universally* valid, not omething just to take or leave. It is ndefensible to maintain that something ould be the right thing to do for me and et wrong for somebody else in identical ircumstances: if it is right for me it must

be right for anyone else in the same position. This means that, just as the empirical world is governed by scientific laws that have universal application, so the moral world is governed by moral laws that have universal application. And it means that morality is founded on reason, as science is founded on reason.

These considerations led Kant to formulate his famous Categorical Imperative as the fundamental rule of morality: "Act only according to maxims which you can will also to be universal laws."

## NO "PROOF" FOR GOD

What a philosophy rules out is always a matter of importance. Kant's doctrine that we can never know for certain that anything exists of which our bodily apparatus can give us no apprehension rules out knowledge of the existence of God, and of immortal souls. It is important to realize that it does not rule out the existence of God, only *knowledge* of the existence of God. As Kant himself famously put it, he had ruled out knowledge in order to make room for faith. This aspect of his philosophy has been of historic importance: he demolished so-called "proofs" of the existence of God, and in doing so reduced to rubble much of the philosophizing of centuries, if not of millennia. Since Kant it has been accepted almost universally by serious thinkers that the existence of God is not something that can be proved – or, for that matter, disproved.

### SOUND ARGUMENT

*In this scene at the House of Lords, at the Palace of Westminster, members debate the validity of their arguments. The very fact that we argue about whether a particular reason is a good one means that we believe that a good reason deserves universal sanction. If a reason is valid, it is universally valid.*

# SCHOPENHAUER

## WESTERN PHILOSOPHY LINKS UP WITH EASTERN PHILOSOPHY

*Schopenhauer believed he had corrected and completed the work of Kant, leaving not a Kantian philosophy and then, separately, a Schopenhauerian philosophy, but a single Kantian-Schopenhauerian philosophy.*

**AN EARLY MANUSCRIPT**
Schopenhauer's metaphysical theory is summarized in the title of his major work, *The World as Will and Representation*, which he first published in 1818 and expanded upon in 1844. Within its two volumes he argued that the empirical world exists, for the experiencing subject, only as representation. The search for the "thing-in-itself" behind the representation is futile- if we turn our thoughts to the natural world. But we, too, are the "thing-in-itself", and it is this dual nature that gives us the key to the nature of all reality.

**JOHANN GOETHE**
*The German writer Johann Wolfgang von Goethe (1749–1832) was a polymath whose interests included science, journalism, drama, poetry, and natural philosophy. Goethe was influenced by Herder, the pioneer of German Romanticism, and was friends with Schiller with whom he worked on a literary magazine. One of Goethe's many admirers was Schopenhauer, who added to Goethe's work on the* Theory of Colour *(1810).*

ARTHUR SCHOPENHAUER (1788–1860) was born in what was then the free German-speaking city of Danzig but is now Gdansk, in Poland. His family were rich merchants. They intended that Arthur should go into the family business, but he rebelled, and instead he used his private income to finance a lifetime of private study and writing. His doctorate thesis, which had the off-putting title *On the Fourfold Root of the Principle of Sufficient Reason* (1813), has become a minor classic. While still in his twenties he wrote his masterpiece, *The World as Will and Representation*, which was published in 1818. He believed that this book solved the enigma of the universe, and he was greatly taken aback when no-one took much notice of it. It left him not knowing what to do. After a long silence he produced a little book, *On the Will in Nature* (1836), designed to show that the on-going progress of science was supporting the arguments of his main work. Then he produced two short and excellent books on ethics, *The Freedom of the Will* (1841), and *The Foundations of Morality* (1841).

### FAME AT LAST
In 1844 came a revised edition of *The World as Will and Representation*. By this time the amount of new material he had accumulated for it exceeded in length the entire first edition, so instead of trying to incorporate this material into the original book he left that pretty much as it was and added an even bigger volume of commentary on it. The work has ever since taken this unusual form: a two-volume book whose second volume is a commentary on the first. After this there was only one new publication, a two-volume collection of essays. With his flair for unattractive titles Schopenhauer called it *Parerga and Paralipomena*, from the ancient Greek words meaning additions and omissions (the reference being to his main work). These essays were published in 1851, when he was 63 – and they made his reputation. After a lifetime of neglect he tasted the delights of international fame during his last few years, before his death at the age of 72.

### THE LEGACY OF KANT
Schopenhauer believed that Kant had either made or greatly reinforced the most important breakthroughs there had ever been in human understanding. Among these were the division of total reality into what was susceptible of being

**ARTHUR SCHOPENHAUER**
*The German philosopher Arthur Schopenhauer – the "philosopher of pessimism" – emphasized the role of the will as the irrational force in human nature. He argued that art represented the only kind of knowledge that was not subservient to the will, and saw art as the only escape from a world without reason.*

experienced and what was not; the insistence that the forms and frameworks of all possible experience were dependent on the contingent nature of our bodily apparatus, and would have been so whatever that apparatus had been (this point is extremely important to the understanding of Kant); the inference from this that we were unable to envisage what anything was like independently of being experienced, and therefore that the nature of independent reality must remain a permanently closed book to us, being

> ## "...SO LONG AS WE ARE GIVEN UP TO THE THRONG OF DESIRES WITH ITS CONSTANT HOPES AND FEARS...WE NEVER OBTAIN LASTING HAPPINESS OR PEACE"
>
> ARTHUR SCHOPENHAUER

inconceptualizably and unimaginably different from anything we could apprehend; that time, space, and causally interconnected material objects were features of this world of experience only, the empirical world, and could have no being outside it; that the key to the understanding of this world was science, but that science too could have no purchase outside the empirical world. These doctrines, propounded by Kant, were seen by Schopenhauer as being basically right, and so fundamental that "the effect his words produce in the mind to which they really speak is very like that of an operation for cataract on a blind man".

**DIFFERENTIATION**
*Apparently identical objects can be reproduced many times, but each one is different because it exists separately in space. Schopenhauer said that for one object to be different from another object they have to be distinct in either space or time and belong to the phenomenal world.*

Schopenhauer believed that only people who had taken all these things on board from Kant would be able to understand his own philosophy. He saw no point in arguing them through from the beginning all over again, for that would be to reinvent the wheel, but he presupposed them at his starting point. However, he did not believe that Kant had been right about everything, so as well as adding to Kant's arguments, and extending them into new fields, he corrected what he thought to be Kant's errors, some of them major. The logical starting point of Schopenhauer's philosophy is therefore his critique of Kant.

## IMPERSONAL REALITY
Schopenhauer believed that Kant was right to divide total reality into the phenomenal and the noumenal, but that the noumenal could not possibly consist of things (in the plural) as they are in themselves. This is because for different things to exist, differentiation has to be possible, and it is possible only in a realm in which there are time and space. If one object is to be different from another they have to be distinct in either time or space, otherwise they are the same object. Even for one abstract object such as a natural number or an alphabetical letter to differ from another the notion of sequence has to have some content, and again

> *"Man is a wolf to man"*
>
> ARTHUR SCHOPENHAUER

**A MINOR CLASSIC**
It was Schopenhauer's thesis *On the Fourfold Root of the Principle of Sufficient Reason* (1813) which earned him his doctor of philosophy degree from the University of Jena. He paid to have it published and the work has become a minor classic. His first book, it considers the nature of explanation and the structure of our experience as a whole.

this is so, ultimately, only with reference to time or space. So, says Schopenhauer, outside a realm in which space and time obtain there can be no differentiation: all must be one and undifferentiated. (We recall a distant connection here with Parmenides and his doctrine that "All is One" – see p. 17.)

Furthermore, said Schopenhauer, it is not possible for the noumenal to be the cause of phenomena, for Kant himself had shown that causal connection, like space and time, could obtain only within the phenomenal realm: therefore causality cannot be what connects that realm to what is outside itself. For example, Kant had taught that acts of will, which inhabit the noumenal realm, are the causes of our "free" bodily movements; but Schopenhauer said this was impossible. The truth of the matter, he said, is that an act of will and the bodily movements associated with it are one and the same event apprehended in two different ways, in one case experienced from inside, in the other observed from outside. "Motives are causes experienced from within." The phenomenal is not a different reality from the noumenal but the same reality known in a different way.

The whole noumenal realm, thought Schopenhauer, has the character of will, though not as this word is usually understood. The entire

**JOHANNA SCHOPENHAUER**
Following her husband's death, Schopenhauer's mother, Johanna moved to Weimar, where she kept a literary salon at which she entertained such figures as Goethe and the Brothers Grimm. She herself achieved fame as a romantic novelist, and one of her poems was set to music by Schubert.

**SCHOPENHAUER AND WAGNER**

*In 1854 Richard Wagner (1813–83) sent Schopenhauer the libretto of his opera cycle,* The Ring of the Nibelung, *inscribed "With reverence and gratitude". Wagner's discovery of Schopenhauer's book* The World as Will and Representation *in 1854 was one of the most important events of the composer's life, and greatly influenced his subsequent works. His opera* Tristan and Isolde *(1859) contains many Schopenhauerian notions – such as the unsatisfiability of the will in the phenomenal world.*

**FIELD OF FORCE**
*For Schopenhauer, the vast scale and the phenomenal energy of the universe has no connection with the mind or consciousness – it is an utterly impersonal force, without any purposes or goals.*

**THE WILL TO WIN**
*Schopenhauer believed that the act of will and the bodily movement associated with it are one and the same event apprehended in two different ways – in one case experienced from the inside, in the other, observed from the outside. The straining oarsmen in Thomas Eakins' painting* The Biglin Brothers Racing *(c. 1873) illustrate Schopenhauer's point.*

osmos instantiates energy in quantities that numb
he imagination – whole galaxies of stars and suns
urtling through space, expanding, exploding,
eating, cooling, rotating on their axes... All this
henomenal energy, drive, go, on a scale so vast as
> be inconceivable by us, has nothing whatsoever

> ## " MOTIVES ARE CAUSES EXPERIENCED FROM WITHIN "

ARTHUR SCHOPENHAUER

> do with mind or consciousness. It is a wholly
indless phenomenon, blind, without personality
r intelligence, and therefore without purposes
r aims or goals, an utterly impersonal force. This
rce is the manifestation in the phenomenal world
f whatever it is that is noumenal. Schopenhauer,
oking for a word for the noumenal, considered

first of all calling it "force", but then reflected that
this word has special associations with science,
and science can apply only within the world of
phenomena. So, as a second thought, he decided
to call it "will", on the ground that the nearest
we can ever come to having direct experience
of one of its manifestations is our own acts of will,
in which we experience from within the otherwise
inexplicable go, drive, force, energy, instantiated
in physical movements.

This use of the term "will" has led to much
misunderstanding, because people find it difficult to
think of a will that has no personality, no kind of
mind or intelligence, and no aims or goals: but this
is what Schopenhauer says quite clearly that he
means. He would have regarded the discovery by
physics in the 20th century that the entire contents
of the empirical world, including all material
objects, are reducible to energy and fields of force,
operating in a space-time framework, as fitting in
perfectly with his philosophy.

### THE ETHICS OF COMPASSION

As physical objects in space and time, our human
bodies are manifestations of the undifferentiated
One that is the noumenal. This fact, if it is a fact, is
taken by Schopenhauer to be the basis of morality –
an outstanding example of metaphysics being made
the foundation of ethics. It is only in this world of
phenomena, says Schopenhauer, that we appear to

**THE BROTHERS GRIMM**
The works of Jacob and
Wilhelm Grimm are
among the greatest
examples of German
literature. Described as
the earliest "scientific"
collection of folktales,
their famous book
*Grimm's Fairytales*
(1812–14) was firmly
rooted in the oral
tradition of folklore.
Jacob (1785–1863) also
produced books on
linguistics and grammar,
and worked together with
Wilhelm (1786–1859) on
a huge German dictionary.

**1848:** THE YEAR
OF REVOLUTIONS
*Throughout Europe
economic and social
problems caused
by the Napoleonic
wars had led to
general discontent.
In 1848 a rise in
national liberalism
and socialism
culminated in
uprisings in many
cities, all of which
were quelled.
Schopenhauer, who
had been living in
Frankfurt since 1833,
condemned the
uprising as primitive.*

FRIEDRICH MAJER
The orientalist Friedrich
Majer (1772–1818), a
disciple of Herder,
introduced Schopenhauer
to Hinduism and
Buddhism. The image
above is of Krishna, from
Majer's *Mythological
Lexicon* (1804). Majer's
work was to have a
lifelong influence on
the thought of
Schopenhauer, whom he
knew personally.

be separate individuals.
In the ultimate ground
of our being, the
noumenal, we are one
and undifferentiated.
This explains compassion,
the ability of human beings
to identify with one
another, and feel for one
another, sharing one
another's sufferings and
joys. If I hurt you I am
damaging my own ultimate
being. It is this, said
Schopenhauer, this
compassion – and not, as
Kant mistakenly believed,
rationality – that is the
foundation of ethics. It is
also the foundation of
interpersonal relationships
and communication, to
which the decoding by
eye and ear of messages
transmitted between our material bodies makes
a lesser contribution. Compassion is the true
foundation both of ethics and of love.

THE QUALITY OF COMPASSION
*In Schopenhauer's noumenal world we are all
one – this is why we can identify with one another
and share each other's feelings. Schopenhauer believed
that this compassion is the basis of our relationships
and the foundation of ethics and love.*

### EAST MEETS WEST

Schopenhauer tells us that it was only after he had
worked out these ideas that he discovered Eastern
philosophy. Before his time the classic texts of
Hinduism and Buddhism were virtually unknown
in Europe, so Western philosophy had developed
up to that point in ignorance of them. Not until
the 19th century did they begin to be translated
in any significant number into European languages.
The pioneer of this development as far as the
German language was concerned was someone
whom Schopenhauer got to know in his middle
and late twenties, an orientalist called Friedrich
Majer. By this time Schopenhauer had already
published his first book and was deep into the
writing of his masterpiece. It was Majer who, in
the second decade of the 19th century, introduced
Schopenhauer to Hinduism and Buddhism.
Schopenhauer was astounded to discover that some
of the central doctrines of these religions coincided
with conclusions that he and Kant had reached
through an entirely different route.

Kant and Schopenhauer had been working
within the central tradition of Western philosophy,
going back to the ancient Greeks. They had studied
Plato and Aristotle, and were familiar with the

history of Western
philosophy since that time.
In particular they felt
themselves engaged in an
enterprise that had been
launched by Locke and
developed by Hume, an
enquiry into what the
limits were of the ability
of human beings to get to
know and understand the
human situation. Most of
the outstanding figures in
this tradition, from Plato
onwards, had believed that
a mathematically based
physics was the key to
understanding the
empirical world, but had
not believed that the
empirical world was all
there is. However, they had
kept their religion, if they
had any, out of their
philosophy, and tried to pursue their philosophical
investigations on the basis of rational argument alone.
Eastern philosophy, as Schopenhauer discovered,
was unlike this. It was not science-based but
religion-based – so much so that religion dominated
philosophy. Yet in this entirely different intellectual
context, and in societies completely different from
Europe's, with different languages and cultures
altogether – and in different historical ages,
sometimes thousands of years apart – serious
thinkers had arrived at many of the same conclusions
as the most advanced and recent Western
philosophers. This is a subject of such interest that
the next section of this book will be devoted to it.

### LONE ORIENTALIST

Schopenhauer at once began to read Hindu and
Buddhist texts in translation, and to refer to them
in his writings, drawing parallels between his own
arguments and theirs. This has caused it to be said
that he got many of his ideas from them, but that is
not the case. In fact, what seemed to him the most
significant point of all was that Western and Eastern
philosophy had travelled in complete independence
of one another along entirely different paths and
yet arrived at substantially the same conclusions
about the most important matters. But by writing
in this way, although his ideas were not materially
shaped by those of Hinduism and Buddhism, he
became the first well-known European writer to

ng an awareness of the serious intellectual
ntent of those religions to his readers. And to this
y he remains the only major Western philosopher
 have had a genuinely deep knowledge and
derstanding of Eastern philosophy.

 Besides being the first great Western
ilosopher to draw connections between Western
d Eastern thought, Schopenhauer was also the
st to be openly and explicitly atheist. Hobbes and

# "THE WORLD IS MY EPRESENTATION"

ARTHUR SCHOPENHAUER

me may well have been atheists in fact, but they
ed at times when to publish in print a denial of
d's existence was a criminal offence; so they
ided the issue. Schopenhauer regarded the
a of a personal God as conceptually muddled,
cause nearly all our conceptions about the nature
 personality are derived from human beings,
d perhaps the higher animals, so that the
tion of a personal God is little more than
thropomorphism. Similarly with the
a of a soul: because Schopenhauer
ught there could no more be
owing without a brain than there
uld be seeing without eyes, or
gestion without a stomach, he
ote: "Since the concept of 'soul'
pposes knowing and willing to
 inseparably connected and yet
dependent of the animal organism
s unjustifiable, and therefore not
 be used."

## HE NOTHINGNESS
 THE WORLD
hopenhauer believed that the
pirical world was without
aning or purpose, and was
imately, in itself, nothing at all.
cause it was all subject-dependent,
d yet we had this built-in tendency
 think of it as existing independently
 ourselves, there was a sense in which
was all illusion. He believed that we
ould not be taken in by it, that we
ould hold it of no concern, and not

let ourselves become involved in its ways – that we
should repudiate it. He called this the turning away
of the human will from the world, and he saw it
as the end result of philosophical understanding.
All this, again, is astonishingly similar to certain
Buddhist teachings – but these ideas were, again,
arrived at independently of any knowledge of
Buddhism on his part.

## THE HORROR OF EXISTENCE
In Schopenhauer's case there was an active dislike
of the world. The realm of animal nature seemed
to him unspeakably appalling: most of the creatures
in it lived by hunting down and devouring other
creatures, so that in every second of every day
thousands of animals were being torn to pieces
or eaten alive – the cliché about "nature red in
tooth and claw" is literal bloody reality. His view of
the human world was very much the same. Violence
and injustice are rife on every side. Each individual
life is a meaningless tragedy ending in inevitable
death. Throughout the whole of the time we are
alive in this world we are the slaves of our desires,
no sooner satisfying one than another takes its

**NATURE RED IN TOOTH AND CLAW**
*For Schopenhauer, the natural world was a cruel and savage place – a world brilliantly evoked
in George Stubbs'* Horse Attacked by a Lion *(1769). This was also Schopenhauer's view of the
human condition – a world of violence and injustice, ending in death.*

**LEO TOLSTOY**
The great Russian novelist Leo Tolstoy (1828–1910), the son of a family of the landed aristocracy, is famous for his epic novels such as *War and Peace* (1869), set during the Napoleonic wars, and *Anna Karenina* (1877). As soon as Tolstoy had finished *War and Peace* he started to read Schopenhauer, and he came to the conclusion that Schopenhauer takes us as far as philosophy can.

place, so that we are perpetually in an unsatisfied state, and our very existence itself is a source of suffering to us. Schopenhauer has come to be thought of as the supreme pessimist among philosophers, in the same way as Spinoza is thought of as the supreme pantheist, or Locke as the supreme liberal. He took the blackest view of our existence it seems possible for anyone to take and still remain sane. Indeed, as one might expect, he derived a certain grim pleasure from it.

## THE VALUE OF ART

However, in Schopenhauer's view there is one way in which we can find momentary release from our imprisonment in the dark dungeon of this world, and that is through the arts. In painting, sculpture, poetry, drama, and above all music, the otherwise relentless rack of willing on which we are stretched out throughout life is relaxed, and suddenly we find ourselves free from the tortures of our existence. For a moment we are in touch with something outside the empirical realm, a different order of being: we literally have the experience of being taken out of time and space altogether, and also out of ourselves, even out of the material object that is our body. Schopenhauer goes at great length into how this occurs, and why it is so. In the course of

doing this he deals with the individual arts more extensively, and more insightfully, than any other major philosopher. He also accords the arts in general a more important place in the overall scheme of things than any other major philosophe (The only one who vies with him in this respect is Schelling.) He regarded music as a sort of super-ar transcending all the others in metaphysical significance. Some of the greatest composers since his day, for instance Wagner and Mahler, have regarded his writings on music as being the profoundest that there are.

Schopenhauer has had a greater influence on creative artists of the front rank than any other philosopher of recent centuries – more even than Marx. Novelists in particular have come under his spell: Tolstoy and Turgenev, Maupassant, Zola, Proust, Hardy and Conrad, Thomas Mann – all of these absorbed his work into their own. He was the most important non-musical influence in Wagner's life. And aside from the arts, he was a formative influence on some of the outstanding philosophers since his time, in particular Nietzsche, Wittgenstein, and Popper – Nietzsche wrote a short book called *Schopenhauer as Educator* (1874). Freud acknowledged that the mechanism of repression had been fully explained before him by Schopenhauer, and described this as the cornerstone psychoanalytic theory, but claimed to have arrived at it independently Altogether, the influence of Schopenhauer on the culture of the age is something of a phenomeno

## STYLISH

The interest of all this is greatly added to, in reading Schopenhauer by the quality of his prose. He is one of that small company of great philosophers who are also great literary artists, a company that includes Plato, St Augustine, Descartes, Rousseau, and Nietzsch but not many others. His sentence are often so sparkling that many have been plucked out and published in little collections, presented as if they were epigrams. This gives a completely false idea of him as a thinker, for along with Kant he is one of the greatest of all system-builders among philosophers.

**PROFOUND PLEASURES**
*Schopenhauer believed that it was through the arts, particularly through music, that human beings find release from the pain of existence. For Schopenhauer, music is abstract and does not represent the phenomenal world, and through it we can enjoy the experience of being out of space and time. The subjects of* A Musical Soirée, *by Etienne Jeaurat (1699–1789), appear to be experiencing music's liberating power.*

# The LEGACY of SCHOPENHAUER

An unusual thing about Schopenhauer is the scale and quality of the influence he had on people who were themselves famous, or about to become famous, in most cases outside philosophy. The composer Richard Wagner said that he wrote what many regard as his greatest opera, *Tristan and Isolde,* partly in response to his reading of Schopenhauer. The score was published in 1859, and therefore before Schopenhauer's death in 1860; but it is almost certain that the philosopher never knew of its existence. Sigmund Freud acknowledged that the analysis of repression that is the cornerstone of psychoanalytic theory had been spelt out before him by Schopenhauer. Later, references to Schopenhauer were frequent in the work of Freud's best-known successor, Jung.

Perhaps the most extensive field in which Schopenhauer's influence made itself felt was that of the novel. The supreme Russian novelists Tolstoy and Turgenev; the great French writers Proust and Zola; perhaps the greatest of all German novelists, Thomas Mann; and in English, the novelists Hardy and Conrad; all acknowledged that their own books had been actively nourished by their reading of Schopenhauer. The philosopher is even mentioned by name in some of their novels, for instance in Tolstoy's *Anna Karenina* (1877), and in Hardy's

## AN UNPARALLELED DEPTH OF INSIGHT INTO THE HUMAN CONDITION

*Tess of the D'Urbervilles* (1891). What may be claimed as the best of all short-story writers – Maupassant, Chekhov, Maugham, and Borges – reveal similar influence. And this extraordinary effect of Schopenhauer's on creative writers was to continue well into the 20th century. He is mentioned by name

in more than one of Chekhov's plays, and after Chekhov his influence is felt in the plays of Bernard Shaw, Pirandello, and Samuel Beckett. It brushed the wings of even the greatest of 20th-century poets, Rilke and T. S. Eliot.

There is no other philosopher, at least since Locke, of whom anything like this can be said. Not even Marx, whose effect on art and artists was very great, can count so many stars of such magnitude among those whose works he influenced. And of course the influence was felt by philosophers too. Nietzsche, the outstanding philosopher of the 19th century after Schopenhauer's death, said that it was the reading of Schopenhauer that had turned him into a philosopher. And in the first part of the 20th century Wittgenstein began his philosophizing from a starting point provided to him by Schopenhauer.

The reasons for his unique range of influence are many and complex, but perhaps chief among them are Schopenhauer's combination of an unparalleled depth of insight into the human condition with a literary style of exceptional quality.

# SOME COMPARISONS OF EAST AND WEST

## A CONVERGENCE OF TWO GREAT TRADITION

*Eastern philosophy has been in some ways profounder than Western philosophy for much of the past, but in the last two hundred years the balance has been redressed.*

*"The man who, casting off all desires, lives free from attachment... obtains tranquillity "*
THE *BHAGAVAD GITA*

ALMOST THE FIRST THING a Christian has to believe if he is to be a Christian at all is that certain historical events took place in the Middle East about two thousand years ago – that God came and lived on earth as a man, was crucified, and after three days rose again from the dead, and so on. In this important sense Christianity is a history-based religion: it centrally involves believing that certain things happened. The great religions of the East, such as Hinduism and Buddhism, do not share this characteristic to anything like the same extent. They too have their stories to tell about the lives of their founders or their important early figures, but the defining characteristic of belonging to those religions is not believing in the truth of these stories, it is believing in the validity of the religion's philosophical or quasi-philosophical

doctrines, and trying to live in accordance with its moral precepts. This gives them a character which is altogether more "philosophical", and less "historical", than Christianity.

Perhaps partly for this reason, philosophy has developed in a more consistently symbiotic relationship with religion in the East than in the West. And, since the religions themselves are more

*" IT IS INEFFABLE AND BEYOND THOUGHT...IT IS KNOWN ONLY THROUGH BECOMING IT "*
FROM THE *UPANISHADS*

philosophical, philosophy has been able to develop more freely in the East than it was able to do in the West during the period when it was treated as little more than a handmaiden to religion: it was allowed to have more independently interesting philosophical content. However, even the most learned scholars in the West were scarcely aware of any of this until the early years of the 19th century. It is only in the last two hundred years that there has been any sustained contact between Western and Eastern philosophical thought.

When deeply reflective and intelligent people confront the same problems it is not surprising if they arrive at many of the same conclusions. There are obvious similarities between many of the doctrines of Hinduism and Buddhism, on the one

**SCENES OF THE STORY OF CHRIST**
*Christianity is a history-based religion. Its followers, if they are to call themselves Christians, must believe that certain events in the life of Christ – such as those depicted on this 14th-century altarpiece – really took place.*

...nd, and Kantian-Schopenhauerian philosophy ...n the other. The chief difficulty in making ...mparisons is due to the fact that there are so ...any different schools of thought within the ...astern religions, especially within Buddhism, that ...xceptions can be registered against almost any ...eneralization. Nevertheless, certain broad ...milarities are unmistakable.

The *Upanishads*, the most metaphysical of the ...rthodox Hindu scriptural texts, were written in ...dia in the period between the 8th and 5th ...enturies BC. Their language is Sanskrit. Their ...entral concern is with the nature of total reality, ...d they present a picture of it as divided into two ...alms of unequal significance. There is the world ...presented to our senses, the world of experience; ...d then, "behind" this, there is another world ...at is not directly accessible to us because the ...rst one is screening it off from us.

## ...HE VEIL OF ILLUSION

...verything about the first world, the ...e we experience, is dependent in ...e form it takes for us on the bodily ...oparatus we have for experiencing it, ...d it exists in that form only for as ...ng as we are experiencing it. But in ...y case both our senses and our ...ental operations constantly mislead ...s in all sorts of different ways; so ...together the world as thus ...oprehended is ephemeral and ...nstable – nothing in it stays the ...me, and nothing lasts. Sooner ...r later it all vanishes as if it ...ere a dream. The whole ...ing is, as it were, a veil of ...usion. But behind it is ...ermanent reality, not ...eparated into all sorts of ...fferent objects like the ...ohemera of this world, ...ut integrated, single – ...r, as writers often like ...express it, One. The ...oparent separateness ...f individual objects in ...e world of experience, ...cluding people, is ...erely part of the ...usoriness of their ...orld. They are fleeting ...anifestations of the ...me ultimate thing, the

same One. When a person dies he is like a raindrop falling into the ocean: his brief individual existence ceases, and he becomes one again with the great ocean of being.

## NOBLE TRUTHS

Buddhism, unlike Hinduism, derives very much from the teachings of a single historical individual, an Indian prince who lived mostly in the 6th century BC and died at the age of about 80. His original name was Siddhartha Gautama, but as a comparatively young man he experienced a

**TIBETAN BUDDHISM**
The form of Buddhism that developed in Tibet is a combination of Mahayana and Vajrayana thought. It was first given recognition in the 7th century AD and continued to develop in the 11th century when many Tibetans travelled to India to bring back translated texts. By the 14th century separate orders of monks were established, and rivalries arose culminating in the defeat of the Gtsangs by Mongol forces who were supporting the Dalai Lama. The Dalai Lama and the Dge-lugs-pa sect ruled Tibet from 1642 until the Chinese communist invasion in 1951. The photograph above is of a Tibetan "rock" Buddha.

**PHILOSOPHY IN INDIA**
*Since very early times nearly all philosophy in India has taken the form of commentary on already-existing texts, so to be a philosopher meant to interpret a text. The texts themselves fell into certain recognizable traditions, so these have defined the schools to which the philosophers have been seen as belonging. In the classical period the main broad division was laid down between Hindus, Buddhists, and Jainas.*

**HINDU WORSHIP**
*The Basavanagudi Temple is one of the oldest temples in Bangalore, India. Built by Kempe Gowda in the mid-16th century, it is famous for its vast carving of Nandi the Bull, vehicle of the god Shiva. Each year a festival is held here at which farmers offer crops to Nandi.*

revelation concerning the true nature of things, and after this he was known as "the awakened one" or "the enlightened one", this being what "the Buddha" means. He spent the rest of his long life trying to share his enlightenment through teaching. But – like Socrates and Jesus after him – he never wrote anything. His teachings were transmitted orally by his disciples.

After his death this led almost inevitably to disputes about whose version of the teaching was the authentic one. These disputes went on over literally centuries, and no fewer than three councils were held to try to settle the question. It was not until the 1st century BC that an agreed version of the Buddha's doctrines was reduced to writing, the language of those writings being Pali. They constitute what is known as Theravada Buddhism, and claim to represent the Buddha's original teaching in its purest form.

The Buddha summed up his doctrines in what he called the Four Noble Truths. These are: one, that life is inherently

unsatisfactory and a burden, an experience of inevitable suffering; two, that at bottom this suffering is caused by our endlessly grabbing at things, grasping, wanting, craving; three, that a cessation can be found of this suffering through ceasing to crave or want; and four, that this cessation of craving or wanting can be achieved by what the Buddha spelled out as the Noble Eightfold Path. There then follows an eightfold set of precepts

Although the Buddha believed that human beings lived through a series of lives he did not believe that they possessed immortal souls. On the contrary, because he regarded life as inherently unsatisfactory and burdensome he thought that

> " HAPPY IS HE WHO HAS OVERCOME HIS EGO...WHO HAS ATTAINED PEACE...WHO HAS FOUND THE TRUTH "
>
> GAUTAMA BUDDHA

the highest state to which individuals could aspire was release from any need to be born into this life again. Such a state is known as nirvana. It is a condition of ultimate insight and bliss, and, after it, all separate existence ceases.

The Buddha no more believed in the existence of a permanent cosmic self than he did in the existence of a permanent human self: in other words he did not believe in the existence of a creator God. He seems to have found the widespread prevalence of evil and suffering an insuperable obstacle to any such belief. There were certain other fundamental questions about the universe which he regarded as inherently unanswerable, such as whether space and time were infinitely extended or not. And because he saw these questions as inherently unanswerable he discouraged his disciples from getting bogged down in them.

THE BODHISATTVAS
*An advanced spiritual being who has chosen not to pass into nirvana, but to continue in the cycle of rebirth to help others is known as a bodhisattva. The career of a bodhisattva will last 3, 7, or 33 eons, during which time he traverses 10 stages (spiritual levels) and perfects his generosity, morality, patience, vigour, meditation, and wisdom. Once a bodhisattva has reached the final stage he will become a buddha.*

THE BUDDHA
*Buddhism began historically in North India in the 6th or 5th century BC when a man called Siddhartha Gautama attained "enlightenment", the ultimate truth by which people are freed from the cycle of rebirth. This Nepalese Buddha is made of gilt-copper.*

ll the doctrines of Hinduism and
Buddhism that have been cited here are
among those which are central to those
religions, and they also have obvious
counterparts in Kantian-Schopenhauerian
philosophy. The starting point of Kant's
*Critique of Pure Reason* is the antinomies
of space and time, together with Kant's
assertion that these antinomies are
insoluble by the use of reason alone.
Both Kant and Schopenhauer regard the
empirical world as something in whose
formation the experiencing subject is
actively involved, and therefore as something
that does not exist in that form at all
independently of being experienced. Being
so, it must, of its nature, be less permanent
than us, or so both philosophers believed.

## BELIEFS IN COMMON

Both also believed that permanent reality,
"real" reality, lies somehow behind the
world of appearances, but is inaccessible
to us. Schopenhauer – like the Hindus, but
unlike Kant – believed that it must be one
and undifferentiated. Like the Buddhists, he
believed that life is full of suffering, that the
suffering is due to our unsatisfiable willing,
and that the way to escape from this
suffering is to repudiate desire as such, to
abjure willing. Again like the Buddhists, he
does not believe that we have permanent
selves, and he does not believe in the
existence of a personal God.

This absence of a belief in the existence
of God or an immortal soul has led many
commentators to assert that Buddhism
is not a religion at all but an atheistic
or agnostic world-view. Looked at in
this light it can be viewed more or less
as a philosophy, and one that shares most
of its central doctrines with the Kantian-
Schopenhauerian philosophy of the West.
Even so, and indeed even when this is
done, there remains one radical difference
between the two sets of ideas, and
implications of this difference go deep.

## A SERIES OF LIVES

Both the Hindus and the Buddhists believe that we
have a series of lives, and not only one life. Because
of this, all their philosophical doctrines have to be
understood as applying, or as working themselves
out, over a series of lives, and not as necessarily

### BUDDHIST COSMOLOGY
*In this temple hanging from the 19th or 20th century, Yama, Lord of
the Dead, turns the Wheel of Life. These hangings (thang-kas) are used
in meditation as a means of visualization. Inside the Wheel of Life
lie the six spheres of existence in which beings can be reborn. At the
very centre are the three symbols of humanity's cardinal faults:
the pig (greed), the snake (hatred), and the cock (delusion).*

characterizing the experience of one-off individuals.
In most Western eyes this is a difference of a
markedly religious character, because belief in a
succession of lives is a belief about the way reality
is, yet it is almost entirely unsupported by empirical
evidence. So to most Westerners it gives the

*" When one
attains the
release called
the Beautiful,
at such a time
he knows in
truth what
Beauty is "*
GAUTAMA BUDDHA

TIBETAN BURIAL GROUND

*After a traditional sky burial, when a body is left to the vultures, stones are carved
with memorial prayers, and people write of their troubles on prayer flags, believing that
as the wind blows the flags, so their problems are blown away. Originating in Indian
and Chinese folklore, the practice has become common among Tibetan Buddhists.*

HINDU GODS

The three main Hindu
gods are Brahma (who
creates the universe at
the beginning of each
cycle of time), Vishnu
(who preserves it), and
Shiva (who destroys it).
Devotees of Vishnu as
Ishvara, the supreme
being, are known as
Vaishnavites and images
of the god are found
on many temple wall
carvings. Vishnu's
preserving and
protecting powers are
represented in ten earthly
incarnations, known as
*avatars*. The image
above shows Shiva the
destroyer riding on the
back of Nandi the Bull.
The bull is said to
embody sexual energy.

the development of early
Greek philosophy – and
indeed on early Christianity
too. As possible recipients of
this influence the outstanding
candidates are Pythagoras and
Plato. But influence, of its
nature, is difficult to specify
and pin down. In this case it
seems quite possible that there
may have been some, but it
has never been proved.

## CONVERGENCE

After Plato the development of
Western thought was impelled
forward for a long time by
intellectual drives internal to
the Western tradition – first of
all Greek thought itself, then
Christianity, then the rise of
modern science. The only important fructification
from outside during this very long period came
from the Arab world, and occurred during the
Middle Ages (see p.54). After Platonism had worked
itself out in neo-Platonism it was not until Kant that

> ## " FOR CERTAIN IS DEATH FOR THE BORN, AND CERTAIN IS BIRTH FOR THE DEAD "

THE *BHAGAVAD GITA*

appearance of unsupported faith; and this is what
makes Buddhism seem to them unquestionably
a religion in spite of its lack of assertion of a belief
in God or of a soul.

There have, of course, been great philosophers
in the West also who believed that human beings
live a succession of lives. Pythagoras and Plato are
obvious examples. In Plato's case this belief played
a significant role in his epistemology. But he has
had no notable successors in this respect among
Western philosophers – even his pupil Aristotle
gave no credence to the idea. Schopenhauer toyed
with it, and was ambivalent, but never plumped
firmly for it, and at most he says contradictory
things on the subject. Apart from him, there has
been no Western philosopher of name since the
ancient world of whom it could even plausibly be
claimed that he believed it.

Because of all these considerations, if the
question is raised: "To what extent has Eastern
philosophy influenced Western philosophy?" the
answer has to be either "Very little" or "Not at all",
depending on whether it can be said to have done
so during the very earliest stages of the latter's
development. The *Upanishads* were mostly written
before Western philosophy was born. Throughout
the centuries during which ancient Greek
philosophy was forming, Hinduism and Buddhism
were intellectually lively and were spreading across
vast areas of Asia. This being so, there have for a
long time now been scholars to whom it seemed
self-evident that influences from east of the Middle
East must inevitably have made themselves felt on

mainstream Western philosophy was to find itself
once more close in fundamentals to Eastern
philosophy. And it is almost certain that Kant
himself was unaware of this. For it was not until the
years immediately after his death that important

translations of basic Hindu and Buddhist texts began to appear in European languages in any significant numbers. Even then these translations were often at one or even two removes. For instance, the edition of the *Upanishads* that Schopenhauer dipped into every night before going to sleep was a Latin translation of a Persian translation of the original. This sort of thing came about because Europe at that time contained so few scholars in Sanskrit or Pali. In any case, translations at two removes may not be as odd or rare as might be supposed: later in the 19th century the first performances of Ibsen's plays in London were of English translations of German translations of the original Norwegian.

After Plato, then, there is only one great Western philosopher of whom it could even plausibly be claimed that he was materially influenced by Hinduism or Buddhism, and that is Schopenhauer. Characteristically, Schopenhauer himself says contradictory things on the subject: usually he claims that he worked out all his ideas on the basis of Kant's philosophy before discovering Hinduism and Buddhism; but he did once remark that his work had become possible only now that Plato, Kant, and the *Upanishads* were all accessible

to a single mind. When he differs from Kant on essential points it is usually in the direction of Buddhism. It is possible to see his philosophy as a more or less seamless fusion of Kantianism and Buddhism expressed in the vocabulary of mainstream Western philosophy. To someone who looks at it in this light Eastern philosophy might appear to have been metaphysically more profound and philosophically more advanced than Western philosophy until the Kantian revolution, but to have lost its advantage at that point, when Western philosophy caught up with it in metaphysics, and had itself then the immense advantage of having got there independently of religion, and with a tradition of tighter logical rigour behind it, and also a symbiotic relationship with both mathematical physics and (newly with Schopenhauer) the arts.

## FROM WEST TO EAST

Some other important advances that had by that time become incorporated into Western philosophy had never been made in the East - for example the distinction between the roles played by reason and experience in the acquisition of knowledge, and the distinction between contingent and necessary truths. Since the middle of the 19th century the

MYTHOLOGICAL LEXICON
It was not until the early 19th century that many German translations of classic Hindu and Buddhist sacred texts began to appear. Friedrich Majer's *Mythological Lexicon* was published in 1804.

ARJUNA AND KRISHNA

The Bhagavad Gita, "the Song of the Lord", is famous for the religious and philosophical dialogue between Krishna, an avatar (manifestation) of Vishnu, and Arjuna. In this drama of two warring factions, Arjuna, hero of the favoured party, is racked with doubts about his moral position as he enters battle, and is guided by Krishna, his charioteer, friend, and adviser.

learning process between East and West has taken more the form of East learning from West than the other way round, in philosophy as in so many other respects. But of course this process has at least as much to do with the realities of political power as it does with intellectual considerations.

## IMPERIALISM IN IDEAS

Throughout the 19th century, and for the first half of the 20th, the entire Indian sub-continent was governed by Britain. Britain and other imperialist Western powers – the Americans, the French, the Dutch – were also aggressively active in many other parts of Asia. Inevitably, one consequence of this was an enormous impact of Western culture and ideas on the East generally – an impact that in many respects continues to this day. In India the entire educated class became English-speaking, and English became the language of their own common culture, all-pervading in Indian intellectual life. In the late 19th century the first English-type universities were founded in India. Not only was their teaching in English, their syllabuses were modelled on those taught in England. This was true of philosophy; and by the end of the century large numbers of Indian undergraduates were studying the utilitarian philosophies of Jeremy Bentham and John Stuart Mill (see pp.182–85). By that time the

**SUN YAT-SEN**
The leader of China's Nationalist party, Sun Yat-sen (1866–1925) played a leading role in the overthrow of the Ch'ing dynasty and became the first provincial President of the Republic of China. His political doctrines are summarized in his Three Principles of the People – these being nationalism, democracy, and the equalizing of land rights.

**LORD CURZON**
*In 1898 George Nathaniel Curzon (1859–1925) became the youngest ever Viceroy of India. During his early years in India he introduced many reforms, including the partition of Bengal. His appointment of Lord Kitchener as commander-in-chief of the Indian army led to a terrible personality clash and the British government manipulated the crisis to encourage Curzon's resignation.*

> ## "VICTORY BREEDS HATRED, FOR THE CONQUERED IS UNHAPPY"
>
> GAUTAMA BUDDHA

philosophy most fashionable in Britain itself was a form of Hegelianism; but it was usual for colonies to be a generation or two behind the mother country in anything that was a question of fashion. Kant, Schopenhauer, and Hegel became known in India at this time, but their heyday was yet to come, in the early years of the 20th century.

It was in the early 20th century that the teaching of philosophy at post-graduate level

**THE BRITISH IN INDIA**
*Following the 1857–58 Indian mutiny – the last effort of traditional India to oppose British rule – the old East Indian Company was wound up and the British government took control of India. From 1899–1905, Lord Curzon (centre) reigned as viceroy, a period that marked the peak of imperial centralization of authority by the government of India.*

gan in Indian universities. The combination of a more advanced level of teaching with the catching up on developments at Oxford and Cambridge resulted in a major breakthrough taking place in the study of German philosophy in India. The Western philosophers who were studied most were Kant and Hegel. The large-scale similarities between their philosophies and those of the major Indian religions were fully revealed to Indian scholars. An approach to post-Kantian philosophy developed in India that has flourished there ever since, the study and teaching of it by scholars whose frame of reference is as much, if not more, to Eastern as to Western thought.

**INDIAN PHILOSOPHY STUDENTS**
*This photograph shows a co-educational philosophy class at Baroda State University, India, in 1947. Western philosophy first began to be studied seriously in India in the early 20th century.*

## WESTERN IDEAS COME TO POWER

But it was with Marxism that a truly apocalyptic impact of Western on Eastern thought occurred. If one separates philosophic-type thought from politics and administration, science, technology, trade, and fighting, it was the greatest influence of West on East that there has ever been, greater even than Christianity. Again, the decisive causal factors were political, above all the Russian Revolution of 1917, which aimed to transform society in accordance with the ideas of Karl Marx. The leaders of this revolution believed at the time that it was the vanguard of a global revolution. They also believed that the more quickly neighbouring countries came under Communist rule the sooner their own position would be secured. So while the revolution was still going on in Russia the Marxist leaders there began promoting Communist movements in neighbouring Asian countries, particularly China.

In 1921 they gave large sums of money to Sun Yat-sen, the leader of the parliamentary opposition both to the Chinese emperors and to the Japanese invaders, getting him to reorganize his party, the Kuomintang, along Communist Party lines. But in the same year they also promoted the foundation of an independent Chinese Communist Party. Each of these in turn became the government of China, ending with the Communists in 1949. They remain in power to this day. Other Marxist parties led armed insurgencies in several other parts of Asia in the years after World War II, and came to power in some countries: North Korea, Viet Nam, Cambodia. At the time of writing, Asia is the only continent left in which large-scale Communist Party rule survives, and it governs the lives of something approaching one and a half billion human beings.

## IDEAS OF MARX STILL RULE IN CHINA

This is a simply gigantic phenomenon. Wherever its influence has been felt, the traditional patterns of thought and custom have inevitably been brought into question, especially in its earlier and more idealistic phases. At a purely intellectual level it is far and away the biggest single instance of cross-fertilization between Western and Eastern thought. Belief in the validity of Marxist intellectual and ideational content has withered away in recent years, not least within the Marxist parties themselves, yet they continue to govern where they have achieved power, and to pay lip-service to many of Marx's ideas. It is an astounding influence for an individual European thinker to have had in Asia.

**MAO ZEDONG**
*As the principal revolutionary thinker in the Chinese Communist Party, Mao Zedong (1893–1976) sought to adapt Communism to Chinese conditions, using a rural-based revolution. Mao set about creating a Communist philosophy based on re-education and "rectification". His Little Red Book dominated the People's Republic between 1949 and 1976, arguing the need for "perpetual revolution". In the mid-1960s a Cultural Revolution was directed against bureaucracy and intellectuals with the intention of purifying Chinese Communism.*

**REVOLUTION IN CHINA**
*After years of civil war, Mao's Communists defeated the Nationalist régime of Chiang Kai-shek and proclaimed a People's Republic in Beijing on 1 October 1949. The photograph above shows starving rioters in the streets of Shanghai in 1948.*

**JENA UNIVERSITY**
The University of Jena, situated in east Germany, was founded in 1548 as an academy and raised to university status in 1577. Perhaps its most brilliant period was from 1787–1806 when the philosophers Fichte, Hegel, and Schelling, and the writers Schlegel and Schiller were all on its teaching staff.

# FICHTE

## THE OUT-AND-OUT IDEALIST

*Far from human knowledge being derived from empirical reality, Fichte taught the opposite, namely that the empirical world is the creation of the knowing mind.*

**JOHANN GOTTLIEB FICHTE**
*Fichte, the son of a ribbon weaver, was educated at the universities of Jena and Leipzig, where he came into contact with the rising first wave of German Romanticism. Fichte went on to formulate a philosophy of absolute idealism based on Kant's ethical concepts.*

> *"I am a living seeing"*
>
> JOHANN GOTTLIEB FICHTE

JOHANN GOTTLIEB FICHTE (1762-1814) was born in humble circumstances in rural Germany. As a small boy he tended geese. One Sunday a local nobleman who had missed the sermon was advised that little Fichte would be able to repeat it to him more or less word for word, which he did. The nobleman took the boy under his wing and secured him a good education, first privately from a Lutheran pastor, then at a famous school, Pforta, followed by a famous university, Jena. After finishing his university studies, Fichte experienced great poverty, his patron having died. His first philosophical work, *Critique of All Revelation*, was published anonymously in 1792, and was mistakenly supposed by the reading public to be a fourth *Critique* by Kant – and was acclaimed accordingly. Opinions differ as to whether Fichte

intended this to happen. In any case, it made his name, and in 1794 he became Professor of Philosophy at Jena. One of his colleagues there, a Professor of History, was the poet Schiller, who became a friend. So did Goethe.

Fichte was a brilliant lecturer, and at first had great success. But he was afflicted with a troublesome personality – stern and unbending, he was a harsh teacher and a difficult colleague – and over time he alienated the people around him. His career became a patchwork of quarrels and resignations. Most of his writings were extremely obscure; but at one point, when he thought he was going to have to earn his living as a freelance writer outside the university, he wrote a short, clear, and attractive book for the general reader called *The Vocation of Man* (1800), which remains the best introduction to his philosophy. He died of typhus – contracted from his wife, who caught it as a nurse – at the age of 52.

### TO BE IS TO ACT

Fichte had learnt from Kant, who in turn had got it from Hume, that our scientific knowledge of the world cannot be accounted for by a combination of observation and logic: from no number of observations can a scientific law be logically derived. What struck Fichte, though, was that there is a deductive logical relationship running in the opposite direction: although scientific laws cannot

**EMPIRICAL OBSERVATIONS VERSUS SCIENTIFIC LAWS**
*Fichte had learnt from Kant that scientific laws cannot be deduced from empirical observations. However, based on a belief that Newtonian physics was timelessly true, Fichte thought that empirical observations could be deduced from scientific laws.*

deduced from empirical observations, empirical
servations can be deduced from scientific laws.
hte believed, as had everyone else since Newton,
at the laws of classical physics were completely
jective and timelessly true: given a scientific law,
follows with absolute logical necessity that
ecific events in the empirical world must be such
d so; and they invariably are. From this starting
int Fichte evolved the doctrine that the universe
the creation of the subject; that we carry within
rselves an ordered conception of the universe,
d that the universe is derived from this in
cordance with logical necessity.

This teaching of Fichte's was sustained by two
her important doctrines. He accepted Hume's
gument that we find it impossible to locate the
f as an object of knowledge, but he claimed that
e nevertheless have direct experience of the
istence of our selves, not in our capacity as
owing subjects but in our capacity as moral
ents. We act, and in doing so we make choices
d decisions; and in doing these things we have
rect experience of our own existence – not as
jects in the empirical world but as moral agents.
d because we know ourselves to bear moral
sponsibility for our actions we know our selves
persist over time.

MORALITY IS ULTIMATE REALITY
chte believed that the primary and fundamental
ture of all reality consists in its moral character.
accordance with this, he believed that the
imary and fundamental nature of human beings
s not in their being consciously in receipt of
perience, and therefore "knowing beings", but
their being conscious
ents, and therefore "moral
ings". It is the moral will,
t the knowing mind, that is
e basic constituent of our
man existence.

But for me to exist as a
oral agent I need to be able
act and make choices.
d for this to be a possibility
me there needs to be a
ld of reality that is not me,
hich in a sense opposes
elf to me, but in which I
n nevertheless active, and
which I can make myself
t. This is the empirical
orld; and the fact that
ality is fundamentally

moral in its nature makes it possible for the empirical
world to be a creation of moral factors – indeed
would make it impossible for it to be ultimately
anything else. So the ego, which is the willing self,
creates the empirical world, which is the realm of

> ## "WHAT SORT OF PHILOSOPHY ONE CHOOSES DEPENDS ON WHAT SORT OF PERSON ONE IS"
>
> JOHANN GOTTLIEB FICHTE

possible knowledge for that self, in order that there
should also exist the possibility of moral self-
fulfilment for what is essentially a moral being.

This philosophy has always held a quasi-religious
attraction for certain people. Some have combined
it with a belief in God, others have found in it a
way of being thoroughgoing moral idealists without
believing in God. Quite apart from this side of it,
Fichte was the first philosopher to account for
scientific knowledge as a free creation on the part
of human beings, and this view of the nature of
science was to acquire widespread support in the
late 20th century.

### KEY WORKS
Critique of
All Revelation
(1792)

The Vocation
of the Scholar
(1794)

The Science of Rights
(1796)

The Science of Ethics
as Based on the
Science of Knowledge
(1798)

The Vocation of Man
(1800)

The Way Towards
the Blessed Life
(1806)

FICHTE ADDRESSES THE GERMAN NATION
*Fichte became famous as an orator in 1808 when he delivered at Berlin his* Addresses to the German Nation, *reprimanding Germany for the disunity which had caused them to submit to Napoleon's armies, and giving practical views for national recovery and glory. Fichte is remembered as one of the founding fathers of German nationalism.*

# SCHELLING

## PHILOSOPHER OF NATURE

*Man is part of Nature. Therefore human creativity is part of Nature's productivity. In man, Nature has arrived at self-awareness.*

*"It is a poor objection to a philosopher that he is unintelligible"*

FRIEDRICH SCHELLING

FRIEDRICH SCHELLING (1775–1854) was born in Germany, the son of a Lutheran minister who, two years after his birth, became a professor of Oriental languages. The boy received an outstanding education, and was academically brilliant even as a child. In his teens he became interested in philosophy, under the influence of Kant and Fichte, and to some extent also Spinoza. At the age of 23 he was appointed Professor of Philosophy at Jena, which was then the academic centre of Germany. He became immensely celebrated while still young – at the age of 31 he was ennobled by having a "von" inserted in his name, thus becoming Friedrich von Schelling. Unlike most well-known philosophers he did not produce a single body of thought but kept going back to fundamentals and beginning again. The result was that over the years, he produced a series of what must be called different philosophies. He may have become self-conscious about this, but in any case, for a variety of reasons, he stopped publishing altogether when he was 35. Even so, he continued for many years to write and lecture; and, like Kant, he went on working until not far short of his death at an age of nearly 80.

FRIEDRICH SCHELLING
*Schelling argued that consciousness itself is the only immediate object of knowledge and that only in art can the mind become fully aware of itself. He thus became an important influence on the Romantic Movement.*

### SPIRIT FROM MATTER

Of Schelling's various philosophies, the best known and most influential was his so-called Philosophy of Nature. It was partly a reaction against Fichte. Fichte had posited a universe of lifeless matter as the separate creation of a living self; but Schelling said that on the contrary, all life was a creation of Nature, which had at one time been a world of lifeless matter. Schelling put forward a picture in which Nature was total reality, perpetually evolving. At first it had been nothing but dead matter; but then life had emerged within it and begun to develop, first of all as plants, then as animals too, and finally in human form. There are several points to stress about this picture. First, Nature is a unity. Second, Nature is not a state of affairs but a process, always on-going. Third, human beings have emerged within this process as an integral part of it. Life is not separate from matter, expressive of some principle that is in opposition to it: the two are continuous with one another, different aspects of a single process. Thus man does not exist outside the world, as if somehow standing against Nature, which is how the Enlightenment had tended to see him: he is simply a part of Nature. Man is matter spiritualized. But to say this is to say that matter by itself is potential spirit, latent spirit, and this is how Schelling saw it.

Given all this, Schelling believed that Nature, in other words total reality, can be understood only in terms of the direction taken by its on-going development. Its most impressive characteristic is

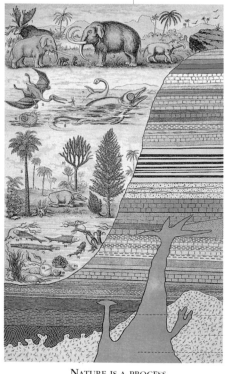

NATURE IS A PROCESS
*This print, published in 1880, illustrates the formation of rocks and the evolution of life on earth. Before Darwin had even begun to write about evolution, Schelling had proposed his Philosophy of Nature in which he explained nature as an on-going process.*

profligate creativity. In every second millions new living things are coming into existence – what Spinoza had called *Natura naturans*, Nature creating Nature. Nature's highest creation of all, human beings, are themselves creative too, in all sorts of ways. The most spiritually advanced and significant of these ways are the creative arts. However, there is a crucial difference between this creativity in man and creativity in the rest of Nature in that in man the process is self-aware. At the best of his art man is exploring and getting to understand the innermost depths of his own being. But since man is an integral part of Nature this means that in creative art Nature is attaining profound self-awareness. Schelling believes that this is what the whole process has been working up towards: that the whole vast on-going phenomenon of Nature has been a development towards self-awareness; and therefore that the very *raison d'être* of reality is achieved in creative art. This means that the creative artist is the very summit of existence, the embodiment of the reason why anything exists at all.

## WHY IS THERE ANYTHING?

The Romantic Movement, which was contemporary with Schelling, found in his writings several of its own deepest convictions expressed in philosophical terms: the all-importance of Nature, man's one-ness with Nature, the glorification of art, and the near-deification of great creative artists. Many of the leading Romantic artists in the Germany of his time were personal friends of his, including Goethe, the composer Weber, and the poets Hölderlin and Novalis. For all these reasons taken together they welcomed his philosophy of Nature with an overflowing enthusiasm and he became, if one may so put it, the house philosopher of the Romantic Movement. In England, the leading theorist among the Romantic poets, Coleridge, recycled Schelling's ideas in his own prose writings.

In the later part of Schelling's career, when he was lecturing in Berlin to an audience of the highest distinction – it included Marx's collaborator Friedrich Engels, the anarchist Bakunin, the great historian Burckhardt, and the Danish philosopher Kierkegaard – he posed what he himself described as "the final desperate question: why is there anything at all? Why not nothing?" This can be thought of as the ultimate question for anyone who does not believe in God. The way that Schelling explained what he was now doing was to say that in his youth he had opened a new page in the history of philosophy, and now in his maturity he wanted to turn that page and begin on another new one. In the late 20th century those Berlin lectures were still being treated as an important source of active stimulation by existentialist philosophers. The question "Why does anything exist at all?" is one that fascinates many non-religious philosophers today.

**PHILOSOPHY OF NATURE**
Whilst a professor at the University of Jena, Schelling wrote a number of books through which he developed his Philosophy of Nature. His aim was to show that Nature displays an active development towards the spirit, a notion popular within the circles of the Romantics.

*"Architecture is frozen music"*
FRIEDRICH SCHELLING

**SAMUEL TAYLOR COLERIDGE**
The English poet and critic Samuel Taylor Coleridge (1772–1834) was one of the founders of the English Romantic Movement. His poems include *Kubla Khan* and *The Rime of the Ancient Mariner*. In *Biographia Literaria* (1817) and other writings, he revealed to English readers the thought of contemporary German philosophers, particularly Schelling.

**MAN'S ONENESS WITH NATURE**
*Schelling maintained that human beings have emerged from Nature and continue to be a part of the on-going processes that occur within it. The figure in Samuel Palmer's (1805–81) painting* The Magic Apple Tree *blends in with her surroundings as harmoniously as the animals and plants around her.*

# HEGEL
## EVANGELIST OF THE ABSOLUTE

*Hegel regarded everything about the world and its history as the development of something non-material, a historical process that culminated in the self-awareness provided by his philosophy.*

**THE PHILOSOPHY OF HISTORY**
Hegel looked at human nature in historical terms. He saw that reality was a process, always moving forward, never static. He called this the "dialectical process". He regarded Greek society as one in which there was a balance between harmony and desire.

*"There soon creeps in the misconception of already knowing before you know"*
GEORG WILHELM FRIEDRICH HEGEL

**KEY WORKS**
The Phenomenology of Mind
*(1806)*
The Science of Logic
*(1812)*
Encyclopaedia of the Philosophical Sciences in Outline
*(1817)*
The Philosophy of History
*(1818)*
The Philosophy of Right
*(1821)*

GEORG WILHELM FRIEDRICH HEGEL (1770–1831) was born in Stuttgart. One of his fellow students at the University of Tübingen was Schelling; but whereas Schelling was intellectually precocious, Hegel was a late developer, so his philosophy came half a generation after Schelling's, and was greatly influenced by it. Hegel's career took him from being a private tutor to being a newspaper editor, then a headmaster, and finally a professor of philosophy, first at Heidelberg, then at Berlin. He was extremely productive, and by the time of his death he was the dominating intellectual figure in Germany. Among his most influential works are *The Phenomenology of Mind* (1806), *The Science of Logic* (1812), *The Philosophy of History* (1818), and *The Philosophy of Right* (1821).

**GEORG WILHELM FRIEDRICH HEGEL**
*Hegel's academic career was interrupted in 1806 when the university at Jena was shut down after Napoleon's victory. He worked as a newspaper editor and a headmaster before he resumed his university work at Heidelberg in 1816.*

Hegel's first published book was about the difference between Fichte's philosophy and Schelling's, and his own philosophy can be seen as being to some extent a conflation of these two. Like Schelling, Hegel saw reality as an organic unity, and one that was not in a stable condition but in an ongoing process of development. Also like Schelling he saw the ultimate goal of this development as being the achievement of self-recognition and self-

## "THE FINITE HAS NO GENUINE BEING"

GEORG WILHELM FRIEDRICH HEGEL

understanding. However, he did not, as Schelling did, identify the whole process with Nature. He saw it all as happening to something that was more moral than material. In this respect he was more like Fichte. Hegel did not think of mind or spirit as having emerged out of inanimate Nature, but as being themselves what existence primarily consists of – and therefore as being themselves the subject of the historical process that constituted reality.

On this point, Hegel presents his non-German readers with a difficulty in translation. What this whole process of historical change is seen as ppening to is something that Hegel lls, in German, *Geist*. What *Geist* eans is midway between irit and mind – its nnotations are more ental than the English ord "spirit", and more iritual than the English ord "mind". For Hegel *eist* is the very stuff of istence, the ultimate sence of being; and the tire historical process at constitutes reality is e development of *Geist* wards self-awareness d self-knowledge. When is state is reached, all at exists will be rmoniously at one with elf. Hegel called this lf-aware one-ness of erything "the Absolute". cause he viewed the sential stuff of what ists as something non-aterial his philosophy came known as bsolute Idealism". Hegel mself combined this ilosophy with belief in ristianity, but some of s followers embraced it a kind of pantheism, d others as a sort of ligion-without-God. The ost radical of them all, Karl Marx, took over most Hegel's ideas but claimed that the subject of the hole historical process was nothing mental or iritual at all but was material.

## HE LAW OF CHANGE

egel's central insight was very like that of eraclitus (see p.14). He saw everything as ving developed. Everything that exists is the tcome of a process; and therefore, he thought, nderstanding in any broad area of reality always volves understanding a process of change. He ent on to claim that change is always intelligible, ver merely arbitrary. Every complex situation ntains within itself conflicting elements, he lieved, and these are destabilizing. Therefore no ch situation can just continue indefinitely. The nflicts have to work themselves out, until they

achieve resolution, and this will then constitute a new situation – and of course a situation that contains new conflicts.

This, in Hegel's view, is the rationale of change; and he produced a vocabulary to describe it. The process as a whole he called the dialectical process, or just the dialectic, and he analysed it as made up of three main stages. The description of the first stage, the initial state of affairs, whatever it is, is the thesis. The reaction that this always provokes, the countervailing forces, the conflicting elements, are described by him as the antithesis of the thesis. The conflict between the two eventually resolves itself into a new situation which sheds elements of both but also retains elements of both, and this is called the synthesis. But because the synthesis is a new situation it contains new conflicts, and therefore becomes the beginning of a new triad of thesis, antithesis, synthesis. And so the process of change goes on being seamlessly woven, always evolving further change out of itself. This, says Hegel, is why nothing ever stays the same. It is why everything – ideas, religion, the arts, the sciences, the economy, institutions, society itself – is always changing, and why in each case the pattern of change is dialectical. (After Hegel's time the dialectic came often to be referred to as "the law of change".)

## THE TIDE OF HISTORY

Because change is a product of the operation of historical forces, the individual caught up in it has no real power to direct it. He is swept along in it. Even in matters of individual creativity a person is enveloped in the spirit of his time (what Hegel called the *Zeitgeist*, *Zeit* being the German word for time). If a great genius in the year 2000 tried to

**TOWARDS SELF-AWARENESS**
*The historical process that constitutes reality is the development of Geist – the ultimate essence of being – towards self-awareness. Hegel compares this development to the agony, death, and resurrection of Christ; redemption comes when the process is understood.*

SAMUEL HIRSCH
*The German Jewish theologian Samuel Hirsch (1815–89) was the leader of the modern revival of orthodox Judaism. His work was strongly influenced by Hegel, most evidently in his method and in the task he assigned to the philosophy of religion – the transformation of religious consciousness into conceptual truth. Contrary to Hegel, however, he did not consider religious truth inadequate to philosophical truth.*

**GERMAN ROMANTIC LITERATURE**
*The first German Romantic school was founded in Jena in 1798. Important work of the period includes the poetry of Novalis (1772–1801) and Friedrich Hölderlin (1770–1843), and the stories and plays of Heinrich von Kleist (1777–1811). Romantic scholars also developed German philology, translated Shakespeare, and collected the nation's folk-tales.*

rite plays like Shakespeare's, or compose
mphonies like Beethoven's, his work would be
authentic, imitation, pastiche, no matter how
illiantly gifted he was. You cannot just jump out
history; that is to say, you cannot make yourself
dependent of the dialectical process.

In any given process of development the only
ing that could put an end to this pattern of
ange, and in doing so give the individual his
eedom, would be the emergence of a conflict-free
uation: if there were no further conflict there
ould be no further change. If what we are talking
out is the historical development of society as

# "MAN OWES HIS ENTIRE EXISTENCE TO THE STATE"

GEORG WILHELM FRIEDRICH HEGEL

whole, this will happen when a conflict-free
ciety is achieved. The ideal state of affairs will
en have been reached, and further change will be
either necessary nor desirable. Hegel conceives of
is situation as an organic society in which every
dividual is a harmoniously functioning part of the
hole, freely serving the interests of a totality very
uch greater than himself. He believed that such a
ciety altogether transcended the values of liberal
dividualism. If, however, what we are talking
out is the development of ideas, a conflict-free

THE CONCEPT OF ALIENATION
*By alienation Hegel meant the idea that something which
is in fact part of ourselves seems to us foreign and hostile.
In both the spiritual and the material world (such as the
world of work), this state of alienation provides the motive
force for dialectical change.*

situation will be reached when the *Geist* comes to
know itself as the ultimate reality, and realizes that
everything that it had hitherto regarded as alien
to itself is in fact a part of itself, not in conflict with
it. But until this situation is reached, *Geist* will
continue to be alienated from itself. The individual
will still be enmeshed in conflict, will not know
himself, and will not be free. This state of alienation
will continue to provide the motive force for
further dialectical change.

If one asks oneself the question, "At what point
in the actual history of ideas does *Geist* achieve
the realization that it itself is the ultimate reality?"
the answer can only be, "With Hegel's philosophy".
Thus Hegel is unique among the great philosophers
in that he regarded himself as not just supplying
the rest of us with the key to understanding reality –
many philosophers have done that – but as being
himself the culmination of the world-historical
process, the embodiment of reality's purposes
as regards understanding, the very incarnation
of our enlightenment.

## THE WORSHIP OF THE STATE

If one considers Hegel's thought at the political
and social level and asks, "At what point in the
development of society is a conflict-free situation
achieved?" the answer is less obvious. Hegel himself
seemed to think it was already embodied in the
constitutional monarchy of the Prussia of his day.

*"No-one
knows, or even
feels, that
anything is a
limit, or defect,
until he is at
the same time
above and
beyond it"*

GEORG WILHELM
FRIEDRICH HEGEL

NAPOLEONIC EMPIRE
*Napoleon Bonaparte
(1769–1821)
declared himself
emperor of the French
in 1804. By 1810 he
had succeeded in
consolidating most of
Europe as his empire.
His downfall began
with his disastrous
invasion of Russia in
1812. In 1815 he was
finally beaten by the
British (under the
Duke of Wellington)
and the Prussians at
Waterloo and was
exiled to St Helena.*

FREDERICK WILLIAM III, KING OF PRUSSIA, GIVING UNIFORMS AS PRESENTS TO HIS SONS, CHRISTMAS EVE, 1803

*Hegel's thought was very influential in a number of fields, not just in philosophy, but also in history and politics. After Hegel's death the conservative Right Hegelians took his*

*political philosophy to mean that a state based on Prussian lines, with a constitutional monarchy, was the type of state to be desired, and that there was no need for further change*

**CHARLES DARWIN**
The English naturalist Charles Darwin (1809–82) is best known for his documentation of evolution and for a theory of its operation called natural selection. He began to formulate his ideas while working as a naturalist aboard the HMS *Beagle*, on a five-year voyage around South America and the Pacific islands. It was, however, a further 20 years before he actually began to write about evolution.

Devotees of that state seized on this aspect of his thought and made it the philosophical basis of a recognizably German form of state-worship which had a long subsequent history. For some time these people were known as Right Hegelians, and through them Hegel came to be seen as the founding philosopher of the sort of right-wing German nationalism that culminated in Hitler. However, there were other followers of Hegel, known as Left Hegelians, who saw the Prussia of 1830 as self-evidently far from ideal, and believed that radical if not revolutionary further change was necessary before the ideal society could be achieved. The most important of the Left Hegelians was Karl Marx. The split between Right and Left Hegelians explains a fact which has puzzled many people, namely that the same philosopher, Hegel, was the intellectual grandfather of both Nazism and Communism.

## THREE KEY IDEAS

Certain ideas are associated with Hegel which have played an important role in Western thinking ever since. One is that reality is a historical process, which therefore can be understood only in terms of how it came to be what it is, and also how, at this very moment, it is becoming something else – in

other words, can be understood only in the categories of historical explanation. It may seem incredible now, but this historical dimension had been absent from previous philosophy. Before Hegel philosophers had thought of reality as a highly complex but given state of affairs which they were called on to explain. Since Hegel, however, historical awareness has entered into the way we look at almost everything. Two figures emerged after him who were destined to be the most influential thinkers of the 19th century, Marx and Darwin, and both of them made this concept of perpetually on-going development central to their thinking. In the case of Marx it was taken directly from Hegel. Another idea introduced by Hegel was that the history of the world has a rational structure, and that the key to understanding the structure is the law of change, in other words the dialectic. This also was taken over by Marx: we shall have more to say about it when we come to consider Marx directly.

A third idea of Hegel's that has been highly influential is that of alienation. The point here is that man, in the process of building his own civilization, creates all sorts of institutions and rules and ideas that then become constraints on him, external to himself, despite the fact that they are

nd articles, but there was one full-length book, is masterpiece, *Das Kapital*, (which means simply apital), published in 1867. It is, beyond any uestion, one of the most influential books in the istory of the world. Marx died in London in 1883, nd lies buried in Highgate Cemetery.

## CHILD OF HEGEL

ne reason why Marxism was to prove such a rich ystem of thought was that it fused together three ntellectual traditions that were each already highly eveloped: German philosophy, French political heory, and British economics. It can therefore ot be categorized simply as "philosophy" in the ormal sense. Nevertheless it contained a major hilosophical dimension, and was to exercise an mmense influence on a great deal of subsequent hilosophical thinking. So no history of philosophy a the modern era could possibly disregard it.

The philosophical element in Marxism was nearly all taken from egel, and has continued from that ay to this to be expressed by Marxists in Hegel's terminology. is worth giving a check-list of leas that are at the heart of egelianism and are also central Marxism: one, that reality is not state of affairs but an on-going istorical process; two, that because f this, the key to understanding eality is to understand the nature f historical change; three, that istorical change is not random but beys a discoverable law; four, that he discoverable law of change is he dialectic, with its repeated triadic novement of thesis, antithesis, and ynthesis; five, that what keeps this aw perpetually in operation is lienation, which ensures that ach successive state of affairs is ventually brought to an end by its wn internal contradictions; six, that he process is not under the control f human beings, but is driven orward by its own internal laws, nd human beings are swept along y it; seven, that the process as hus described will continue until situation is reached in which all nternal contradictions have been esolved: there will then be no lienation, and therefore no longer

any force at work promoting change; eight, that when this conflict-free situation is reached, human beings will no longer be swept along by forces outside their control, but will be able for the first time to take their destiny into their own hands, and will become themselves the arbiters of change; nine, that this will for the first time make human freedom and self-fulfilment possible for human beings; ten, that the form of society within which this freedom will be exercised, and self-fulfilment achieved, will not be the atomized society of independently functioning individuals that is envisaged by liberals, but an organic society in which individuals are absorbed into a whole that is much bigger, and therefore more fulfilling, than their own separate lives.

But after these ten great similarities with Hegel comes the big difference, which is something Marx took from his near-contemporary, another German

### REVOLUTION IN EUROPE
*During the 19th century the nationalist sentiment that sprang up throughout Europe provided the ideological impetus for several rebellions against existing imperial powers. This plate depicts a scene from the 1848 revolution in Berlin.*

---

## Das Kapital.

Kritik der politischen Oekonomie.

Karl Marx.

Erster Band.

Hamburg
Verlag von Otto Meissner.
1867.

*DAS KAPITAL*
Described as the "Bible of the working class" in a resolution of the International Working Men's Association, *Das Kapital* was published in Berlin in 1867. In what was one of the most influential works of the 19th century, Marx predicted the supersession of capitalism by socialism. Only the first volume was completed and published in Marx's lifetime, the second and third volumes, edited by Engels, were published after his death.

*"From each according to his abilities, to each according to his needs"*
KARL MARX AND
FRIEDRICH ENGELS

### THE INDUSTRIAL REVOLUTION
*During the 18th and 19th centuries the advent of mass production brought about revolutions in the production of textiles, iron, steel, and coal. Agricultural nations in Europe and North America became industrialized, and populations began to migrate into cities. Britain led this revolution and by the 18th century it had become the dominant international trading power.*

philosopher called Ludwig Feuerbach – who, like himself, had been a Left Hegelian. Whatever it is of which reality basically consists is believed by Marx to be not something spiritual but something material. He is, he insists, a materialist, not an idealist. So this whole vast historical and dialectical process that we have just followed through in ten theses is seen by Marx as happening to the material forces of which he believes the world to consist. This is why he called his system "historical materialism" or, alternatively, "dialectical materialism", two names which describe it appropriately. The two terms are interchangeable, but "historical materialism" seems the more apt when talking about human affairs, "dialectical materialism" when talking about non-human aspects of the universe. Engels was to write a good deal more than Marx did about the latter.

## ECONOMICS AS FUNDAMENTAL

With regard to human affairs, the way Marx believed that the dialectic operated was something like this. The irreducible thing that human beings have to do if they are to live at all is to get the means of subsistence: they must have the wherewithal to feed, clothe, and house themselves, and to meet other basic wants. Producing these things is the one task that cannot be avoided. But as soon as the means of production have developed beyond the most primitive stage it becomes in the interest of individuals to specialize, because they find they are all better off if they do. And this makes them dependent on one another. Production of the means of life becomes a social activity and is no longer an individual one. Within this mutual dependence, which is of course society itself, the defining characteristic of each individual is his relationship to the means of production: what he does to get a living determines most of the basic things about his way of life, and is also his contribution to society as a whole. It determines who else's interest in the division of the social product is the same as his own, and whose is in conflict with it. This gives rise to the existence of socio-economic classes, and also to the conflict between classes.

**MARX'S DAUGHTERS**
Marx was an affectionate father. Unfortunately, of his seven children, only three grew to maturity. This photograph taken in 1864 shows Marx with his daughters Laura, Eleanor, and Jenny, together with Engels. Marx's daughters were almost the only people who could read his writing and were therefore responsible for transcribing his manuscripts.

**THE MEANS OF SUBSISTENCE**
*In order to achieve a level of subsistence, human beings must meet their most basic needs. Marx's theories describe how the means of production develop that meet these needs. This illustration shows a slum dwelling in London's East End in 1872.*

**POLARIZATION OF THE CLASSES**
*Marx's theory defines social classes economically. He believed that technological advance would concentrate ownership and control into fewer and fewer hands, so that the capitalist class would get ever smaller while the working class grew larger.*

However, the means of production are in a continuous process of change. So the relationship of people to them, and therefore to one another, has to keep changing. With each major change in the means of production the composition of social classes is changed, and with it the character of the class conflict. Marx sees each of these different levels as developing dialectically. At the ground-floor level, the fundamental determinant of all social change is the development of the means of production. Riding forward on the back of this, and being both made and unmade by it, comes the development of social classes and the conflict between classes. Then above this comes what Marx calls "the superstructure": social and political institutions, religions, philosophies, the arts, ideas; all such things, he says, grow up on the basis of the economic substructure, and are ultimately determined by it.

# "THE PHILOSOPHERS HAVE ONLY INTERPRETED THE WORLD IN VARIOUS WAYS; THE POINT IS TO CHANGE IT"

KARL MARX

**THE LOWER MIDDLE CLASS**
European society was radically changed by industrialization. The gradual shift of the population away from the countryside and towards the industrial centres led to the development of cities and to a more complex society. In the picture above, a typical English lower middle class family of the 1890s pose for a photograph outside their cottage.

A Marxist historian of philosophy could also point out that it was with the beginnings of the Industrial Revolution, towards the end of the 18th century, that we get the first philosopher who sees knowledge as a product, namely Kant. That would be typical of the way Marxists analyze intellectual

examples will help to illustrate some of these points. Marx drew attention to the fact that in the earliest stage of industrialization, when transport of heavy raw materials was still done chiefly by boat, and when mills and factories were still dependent on water power, industrial towns grew up along river banks and sea coasts, and on the shores of lakes. But the development of steam power, including steam-powered trains, freed the development of industrial towns from this constraint, and then they began to grow up closer to their sources of raw material, or their chief markets. Here is an outstanding example of a change in the means of production bringing about changes in the substructure. It came as a great illumination when Marx pointed out these things, because no one had consciously perceived them before: it permanently changed the way historical development was viewed. Like so many good ideas, it seems obvious once somebody has actually had the idea, and then it becomes difficult to understand how people previously failed to think of it.

**THE DEVELOPMENT OF TRANSPORT DURING THE INDUSTRIAL REVOLUTION**
*Demand for reliable and cheap access to raw materials and markets resulted in major improvements to Britain's transport facilities. Initially, this development took the form of improved roads and canals. Later on, the railways became the preferred means of transport: seen here is an early steam train at Hetton Colliery, County Durham, in the early 1820s.*

A DISPLAY OF WEALTH AND POWER

*Photographed in 1890, this drawing room is a typical example of the opulent taste of the British ruling classes. The crowded, ostentatious display of arts and crafts was popular with the bourgeoisie, who, according to Marxists, used the arts to serve their own interests – to glamorize their achievements in an overt display of their wealth and power*

COMMUNIST MANIFESTO
Published in 1848, the *Communist Manifesto* became the most celebrated work in the history of the Socialist movement. Written by Marx and Engels, it argued that all history had hitherto been a history of class struggles. The manifesto ends with its famous call to the workers of all lands to unite.

developments. The arts are seen by them as serving the interests of the ruling class, by putting across ideas and values that promote those interests, or display their wealth and power, or glamorize their achievements, or divert the attention of other classes from politics. Similar functions are served by religion, "the opium of the people". A whole analysis of society and its history has grown up on the basis of this way of seeing things. And although scarcely any serious thinkers nowadays would accept the validity of the analysis as a whole, there can be no doubt that much of it is insightful, and has made a major contribution to what might be called the modern outlook.

## THE REVOLUTION

Marx saw the Industrialist Capitalist society of his day as the last-but-one stage of historical development before the advent of the conflict-free society. He thought that the relentless development of modern technology was bound to go on putting more and more people out of work, with the result that the masses would become more numerous, more alienated from the means of production, and more impoverished, while ownership and control of the means of production would become concentrated into fewer and fewer hands. This would increasingly polarize society into two classes, the capitalists and the workers. The conflict between them was bound to grow ever more bitter until the workers, in their overwhelming superiority of numbers, would rise up against the capitalists and overthrow them, taking the means of production into their own

> "WHAT THE BOURGEOISIE PRODUCES...IS ITS OWN GRAVEDIGGERS. ITS FALL AND THE VICTORY OF THE PROLETARIAT ARE EQUALLY INEVITABLE"
>
> KARL MARX

nds. This revolution would be, in a double sense,
e end of history, because it was the climax towards
hich events were inevitably moving, and after it
ere would be no more dialectical change. The
vision of society into classes would have ended.
e means of production would be owned by all
d operated in the interests of all. Society, being
ass-free, would be conflict-free. As Engels once
xpressed it, there would be no more need for the
overnment of people, but only the administration
things. And being no longer coerced by
ncontrollable historical forces, or by government,
man beings would be free to fulfil themselves.

## ALSE PROPHET

ne future that lay immediately ahead of the time
hen Marx was writing did not at all develop in the
ay he said it was bound to. This is partly because
e was mistaken as to the nature of his theory. He
elieved it to be scientific, in the same sort of way
Newton's physics is scientific. If we have the
ght information about the current state of any

**RUSSIAN DISSIDENTS**
*Marxists were intolerant of alternative views. Some
dissidents were imprisoned and others were executed. This
c. 1932 photograph of a Russian labour camp shows
detainees being forced to work on the construction of a canal.*

**CAPITALIST OPPRESSION**
*This Russian poster of 1918 shows the Tsar, the priest, and
the rich man carried by the working people. Marx believed
that capitalism would collapse from its own contradictions,
to be followed by a dictatorship of the proletariat. As the
capitalists increased their oppression of the workers, so
conflict between the classes would lead to a revolution,
and the workers would overthrow their oppressors.*

physical system of objects in motion, then with
the aid of Newton's laws we can predict accurately
what the state of that system will be at any future
time. Marx believed that he had uncovered the
economic laws of motion of society in precisely
the same sense – he says so in the Preface to *Das
Kapital*. With this knowledge he thinks he is able
to predict the inevitable future development of
society. It was of enormous importance to him
that Marxism should be seen as "scientific", and he
called his brand of socialism "scientific socialism"
to distinguish it from the others. Indeed, he
despised the others. He thought they were based
on mere Utopian dreams, or moral uplift, or wishful
thinking; whereas he, by contrast, had carried out
a scientific study of society to discover what
forces were actually at work within it, and what
the laws were that governed the operation of
those forces, and then had based his political
teachings on these realities.

The notion that Marxism was scientific was
to account for an important part of its appeal until
quite late in the 20th century. Marxists tended to
regard their beliefs not just as personal opinions
but as scientific knowledge, and therefore as
"known" with absolute certainty. This gave them
enormous confidence and made them famously
intolerant of all alternative views and opinions;
and whenever they got into power they forbade
the publication or teaching of any ideas that were
incompatible with theirs. Another source of
Marxism's appeal was the fact that, since it claimed
to predict the future developments of society with

*"Religion is
the opium of
the people"*
KARL MARX

**READING ROOM OF THE
OLD BRITISH LIBRARY**
The vast round Reading
Room of the British
Library was designed by
Robert Smirke, architect
of the British Museum.
Completed in 1857, it was
built to give "all studious
and curious persons"
access to the collections.
Many great intellectuals
have used the room,
including George Bernard
Shaw, Mahatma Gandhi,
and Marx himself.

scientific accuracy, socialism was believed to be "inevitable", and this meant that socialists were, so to speak, on the side of the future. What they believed in and wanted was going to happen regardless of what everybody else did or said. The whole world was going their way. As they liked to put it, "history is on our side", and their opponents were going to be consigned, as Trotsky expressed it, to the dustbin of history. This made them even more modern than "modern", for they were living not just in the present but in the future too, and before anyone else had got there.

## POWERFUL APPEAL

This combination of ideas – "science", "modernization", "being on the side of the future" – had almost hypnotic appeal for large numbers of intellectuals in underdeveloped countries. So did the economic side of Marxism, which called for the centralized planning and control of the economy – "the planned solution" seemed to be just what rationality itself called for. Just as in the 18th century Locke's theories had played a crucial role in helping to bring about the American and French revolutions, so in the 20th

RUSSIAN FUTURIST ARCHITECTURE
*The poverty and social chaos of the early revolutionary years propelled artists and architects towards ever-more radical solutions – such as Georgy Tikhonovich Krutikov's vision of a flying city (1928).*

# "THE PROLETARIANS HAVE NOTHING TO LOSE BUT THEIR CHAINS"

KARL MARX

century Marx's theories played a significant role in helping to bring about the largest-scale revolutions of all time, the Communist revolutions in Russia (1917) and China (1948–49). Throughout the period following World War II, Communist movements declaring their allegiance to Marx's

**THE RUSSIAN REVOLUTION**
In March 1917 revolution broke out in Petrograd (now St Petersburg) and revolutionary councils (soviets) of soldiers, workers, and peasants were set up all over Russia. The Tsar abdicated and a provisional government was set up. In the summer of that year Aleksandr Fydorovich Kerensky (1881–1970) became the chief minister, but the Petrograd Soviet was controlled by Lenin's Bolsheviks. On 7–8 November Kerensky was ousted in a coup led by Lenin.

**LEON TROTSKY**
A leader in Russia's Revolution of 1917 and the raising of the Red Army, Leon Trotsky (1879–1940) was also Stalin's chief rival for power following Lenin's death in 1924. Stalin defeated him, and in 1929 Trotsky was deported. He settled in Mexico, where he was assassinated in 1940 by a Stalinist agent.

ideas were significant throughout the Third World. In several Third World countries they came to power. At the time these words are written there are still some that govern. It is a spectacular demonstration of the practical importance that ideas do in fact have in the real world.

## DECLINE AND FALL

The central emphasis that Marx placed on the claim of his ideas to be "scientific" exposed them nakedly to refutation by events, as all genuinely scientific ideas have to be – that, after all, is the point of experiments. And by the end of the 19th century it was becoming evident that events were not turning out as Marx's theories said they must. Nowhere in the world, in fact, was there a society where changes were happening in accordance with Marx's so-called "scientific laws of historical development".

This gave rise to something that became known as "revisionism". Various Marxist thinkers started trying to revise Marx's theories so as to fit in with the contrary evidence – and also started to reinterpret the evidence to fit in with Marx's theories. Out of this grew a plurality of differing Marxist schools of thought, at odds with one another, sometimes violently so. What led in the end to the withering away of most of them was the fact that wherever Marxist political movements came to power the result was, invariably and without exception, a bureaucratic dictatorship, a society not in the least like the one the theory had claimed was inevitable. Also without exception the economies of such societies failed, so instead of prospering they became impoverished. Marxist government, then, gave people both poverty and tyranny. In the long run this caused all but a handful of people to conclude that there must be something wrong with Marxist theory. But by this time the indirect influence of Marx's ideas had spread throughout modern culture; so although Marxism now retains few wholehearted adherents it nevertheless remains a significant element in the worlds of what are generally thought to be "modern" ideas, including not least literature and the arts.

# The POWER of IDEAS

It can seriously be claimed for Karl Marx that his ideas had a greater influence in a shorter time than those of any other thinker in history. During his lifetime he was a little-known, impoverished intellectual, living on the charity of friends and spending his days reading and writing, often in the British Museum. Yet within 70 years of his death in 1883 something like a third of the entire human race was living under governments that called themselves by his name – called themselves "Marxist".

This included all the countries of Eastern Europe, the whole of Russia, and the former Tsarist land empire, and the whole of China. Nothing like this had ever occurred before, nor (dare one say it?) is likely to happen again. Even the spread of early Christianity or Islam could not match it, nor could the spread of Buddhism during its expansionist phase. It is an utterly amazing phenomenon, more so in view of the fact that on a practical level the record of Marxism was one of persistent failure: the ideas conquered, yet the societies to which they gave rise either collapsed or detached themselves from Marxist policies.

Many leading figures on the stage of recent history have been guided by Marxism. In Russia there was Lenin, followed by Trotsky and Stalin. In Yugoslavia there was Tito; and there was Mao Zedong in

## THE TRUE FUNCTION OF ART IS SOCIAL CRITICISM

China, Ho Chi-minh in Viet Nam, Fidel Castro in Cuba. These were people who changed the world.

During its period of ideological triumph Marxism had a global influence on the arts as well as on politics. World-famous figures in the arts such as the playwrights Jean-Paul Sartre (who was also a leading novelist and philosopher) and Bertolt Brecht (who was also a major poet) – or among poets, Pablo Neruda; or, among painters, Pablo Picasso – regarded themselves as Marxists or Communists; and some of their work is almost bound to survive.

More generally, there is a specifically Marxist view of the role of art in society that remains widely held and is powerfully operative in the world of today. It is that the true function of art is social criticism. According to this view, art should get people to understand in a deeper way than they do what is wrong with the society they live in, and with their own relationship to that society, and therefore with their own lives; and it should make them want to change society. Thus Marxists view art as a revolutionary instrument. Bad art is art which upholds the values of existing society, and tries to lull or deceive people into accepting those values. This view of the role of art, which was not at all widely held before Marx, comes close to being the prevailing orthodoxy in today's world. It may be the last bastion of Marxism to fall.

# NIETZSCHE
## "GOD IS DEAD"

*The morals and values of Western man derive from religious beliefs that he is ceasing to hold. He therefore needs to re-evaluate his values*

*"There are
no facts, only
interpretations"*

FRIEDRICH NIETZSCHE

**RICHARD WAGNER**
After beginning his career
as a conductor in Riga,
Wagner travelled
throughout Europe but
did not meet with much
success until he came
under the patronage of
Ludwig II of Bavaria.
After an affair with
Cosima von Bülow
Wagner was forced to
flee Munich, and settled
in Switzerland. It was
here that he wrote his
most famous works,
including *The Ring*,
which was not
performed until 1876.

FRIEDRICH NIETZSCHE (1844–1900) came from a line of Protestant churchmen: his father and both his grandfathers were Lutheran ministers. His school and university studies were based on the classics: so brilliant was he academically that he became a full professor in his middle twenties – an almost unheard of thing. But he never formally studied philosophy. What turned him into a philosopher was the reading of Schopenhauer. In imitation of Schopenhauer he gave up an academic career and lived a life of solitude and simplicity, much of it spent wandering in Switzerland and Italy. Over a 16-year period he poured out his writings in comparative obscurity. Among those of his books that are now best known are *The Birth of Tragedy* (1872), *Human All Too Human* (1878), *Beyond Good and Evil* (1886), *The Gay Science* (1887), *The Genealogy of Morals* (1887), and *Thus Spake Zarathustra* (1891).

### LIVING TO THE FULL

As a young man, in addition to being a disciple of Schopenhauer, Nietzsche fell deeply under the spell of the composer Wagner. The two men became personal friends, in spite of the fact that Wagner was old enough to be Nietzsche's father. However, Nietzsche eventually established his independence by rebelling against both Wagner and Schopenhauer, and he produced some famous anti-Wagner polemics in two books, *The Case of Wagner* (1888), and *Nietzsche versus Wagner* (1895). Tragically, when he was still only in his middle forties he collapsed into mental illness, an illness almost certainly brought on by tertiary syphilis. He was to remain hopelessly insane until his death in 1900; so although his reputation became international during the course of the 1890s he himself was oblivious of the fact.

Nietzsche agreed with Schopenhauer that there is no God, and that we do not have immortal souls. He also agreed that this life of ours is a largely meaningless business of suffering and striving, driven along by an irrational force that we can call will. But he rejected Schopenhauer's view that this world is only a part, and what is more an unimportant part, of total reality: he believed it

FRIEDRICH NIETZSCHE
*The philosopher Friedrich Nietzsche, a masterly writer of German prose, was devoted to his craft, working in utter solitude and living frugally. In 1889, he suffered a mental collapse and wrote nothing in his last 11 years.*

to be the whole. Above all, Nietzsche rejected Schopenhauer's conclusion that we should turn away in disgust from such a world, reject it, and withdraw from it. On the contrary, he believed that we should live our lives to the full in it, and get everything we can out of it. The central question posed by Nietzsche's philosophy is how best to do this in a godless, meaningless world.

### THE NEED FOR NEW VALUES

Nietzsche begins by mounting an onslaught on our attachment to existing morals and values. These derive very largely from ancient Greece plus the Judaeo-Christian tradition, he says, which means they come from societies quite unlike any that exist today and from religions in which many

not most of us do not believe. This
[an] indefensible state of affairs, says
[Ni]etzsche: we cannot base our lives on
[val]ue systems whose foundations we
[re]pudiate. It makes our lives, and us,
[bo]gus. We must either find a basis that
[w]e really do believe in to support our
[val]ues, or else abandon these values and
[fin]d others that we can honestly espouse.

## [FU]LFILMENT

[Ni]etzsche's next step is to attack our
[ex]isting values, and to assert that we
[ou]ght not to want to preserve them
[in] any case. What enabled human beings
[to] emerge from the animal state, he says,
[an]d to develop civilization, including
[ev]erything we mean by the word culture,
[wa]s the perpetual elimination of the
[we]ak by the strong, the incompetent by
[th]e competent, the stupid by the clever.
[On]ly because these processes carried on
[ov]er countless ages did the things that we most
[val]ue about our human existence come into being.
[Bu]t then along came the so-called moralists like
[So]crates and Jesus and said that these values were
[all] wrong – that there should be laws to protect
[th]e weak against the strong, and that justice should
[re]ign, not strength; and that the meek, not the

**MOUNT OLYMPUS, HOME OF THE GREEK GODS**
*According to Nietzsche, our existing morals derive largely from ancient
Greece and the Judaeo-Christian tradition. He argued, however, that
in a godless world we cannot base our lives on societies that no longer
exist and on religions that many no longer believe in.*

that has produced culture and civilization. If it is
allowed to go on, it will put an end to everything
that we value most in our world. We must on no
account continue with these slave-moralities.

# "ART RAISES ITS HEAD WHEN [R]ELIGIONS RELAX THEIR HOLD"

### FRIEDRICH NIETZSCHE

[en]terprising should inherit the earth. The very
[pr]ocesses by which man had been raised above
[th]e animals, and civilization brought into being,
[we]re then put into reverse. Natural leaders – the
[co]nfident, the courageous, the innovators – were
[sh]ackled by value systems that set them on equal
[te]rms with the mediocre mass of mankind.
[Th]e typical characteristics of slaves were hailed
[as] virtues: a life of service to others, self-denial,
[sel]f-sacrifice. Even gifted individuals were what
[Ni]etzsche calls "un-selfed" by this. And it was all
[do]ne in the name of morality! It is all, says Nietzsche,
[th]e worst possible decadence, a denial of everything

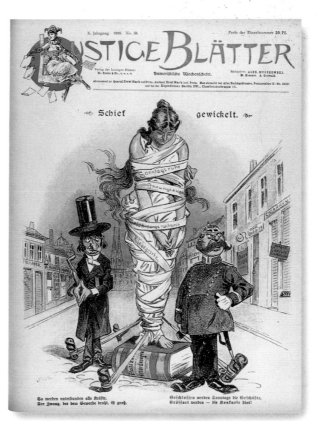

**SHACKLED BY VALUE SYSTEMS**
*Nietzsche believed that innovators were constrained – in the
name of morality – by values that set them on equal terms
with the mass of mankind. This German illustration of 1895
shows Sunday tied by the value systems of Church and State.*

**OTTO VON BISMARCK**
*The Prussian statesman
Otto von Bismarck
(1815–98), the first
chancellor of the
German Empire
(1871–90), was in
agreement with
Nietzsche in several
areas, stating that "It is
the destiny of the weak
to be devoured by the
strong." Successful
though Bismark was at
keeping Europe stable
for 26 years after the
Congress of Berlin in
1878, William
Gladstone said of him
"He made Germany
great and Germans
small." He was a
genius, but also an
opportunist.*

### SIR RICHARD BURTON
The superman characteristics defined by Nietzsche were embodied in Sir Richard Burton (1821–90), an English explorer, soldier, botanist, geologist, and translator. His travels included trips to the Middle East – he was one of the first Europeans to enter the sacred cities of Mecca and Medina – and to East Africa, where he and fellow traveller John Speke discovered Lake Tanganyika. Burton wrote a wide range of books, including a translation of the *Arabian Nights* (1885–88), but his unexpurgated translations of Eastern erotica led him to be condemned for promoting vice.

### NATURE'S LEADERS
*All men should be free to realize their potential – their "will to power", said Nietzsche, by which he meant in cultural and political activities as well as in conquests. Napoleon, shown here studying at the Royal Military Academy, Brienne, in 1779, was a man who unarguably realized his "will to power".*

and created civilization: the elimination of the inferior by the superior in every aspect of life. The imaginative, the daring, the creative, the bold, the courageous the curious and brave, nature's leaders of all kinds, should be free untrammelled by slave moralities free to live life to the full, and to fulfil themselves. Nietzsche called their drive to do this their "will to power", by which he was thinking not only of politics or conquests but of cultural activities as well.

A human being who thus develops his maximum potential becomes a sort of super-human-being, and for that reason Nietzsche coined the term "superman", which has now entered into most European languages, including English. By this term Nietzsche meant not only people like Napoleon but also people like Luther and Goethe – even Socrates, who, although Nietzsche so powerfully disapproved of what he did, undeniably carried out his life-project with immense personal strength and bravery. Acceptance of these values will bring a double benefit. First, the creative potential of the human race will be given a free rein, so that in every area of life the highest achievable goals will be attained, and civilization will develop at the fastest possible rate – something which is self-evidently in the interests of mankind as a whole. Second, the most gifted individuals will be able to live fulfilled lives, and thus experience personal happiness instead of frustration – happiness being understood by Nietzsche very much to mean self-fulfilment, not merely the enjoyment of transitory pleasures.

## SAY YES TO LIFE
So the central values that we should embrace, says Nietzsche, are those of life-assertion. Each one of us should be himself to the full, and live his life to the full, say yes to life, live all out, to the very top of his bent. One of the words he uses most frequently is "dare"; and perhaps his first commandment is: "Dare to become what you are." This is how all living creatures behave spontaneously in nature,

But when we reject them, how shall we then go about finding new morals and values to take their place, more genuine ones that we can authentically live by? Well, says Nietzsche, since there is no God, and no world other than this one, then morals, ethics, and values cannot be what is called transcendental: they cannot come to us from anywhere outside this world, for there is nowhere "else". They must be human creations. The slave-moralities that we abase ourselves before are not handed down to us from some divine source, they are put over on us by, among others, the slaves themselves, the herd, the rabble, in whose interests such systems operate. And it is, of course, only too easy to see why they want us to accept them.

Once we grasp the fact that we human beings are the creators of our own values we realize that we are free to choose whatever values it is most in our interests to have. And these are surely the values that have led us out of the animal kingdom

er all. Of course it will bring us into conflict with
e another, but what is wrong with that? The bold
d adventurous find conflict exciting, they relish it,
d it helps to stretch them to their utmost, which
ey also enjoy, and which develops their abilities.
course the weak will go under, but that is to be
lcomed. To want to abolish strife, suffering, and
feat is just as uncomprehending and futile as it
uld be to want to abolish bad weather.

LIVE CHALLENGE
etzsche judges all other values by this yardstick
life-assertion. "Good" is that which asserts life or
sists life-assertion. Even "true" is that which is on
e side of life, and not against life. A critic might
y to Nietzsche: "But what is the point of it all?
u say there is no life other than this, and no
orld other than this. What then does it matter
hat anyone does? The most triumphant and self-
lfilling of lives are still going to end quite soon in
ath, and then those individuals will exist no more,
d all will be forgotten in the end. Everything goes
wn into eternal annihilation. So what does any
it matter?" To this Nietzsche gives a twofold reply.
rst, his prescription is for a life which is fulfilling

## "THE BITE OF CONSCIENCE IS INDECENT"

FRIEDRICH NIETZSCHE

its own terms, and therefore worth living for its
wn sake. Such a life does not seek to derive any
its meaning or significance from outside itself,
d is not to be understood in terms of anything else.
this respect it is like a work of art, you might say.
his fact has caused both Nietzsche and others to
eak of him as having an aesthetic understanding
life – an unfortunate term that can be very
isleading, for there is nothing arty about
ietzsche's attitude to life. The second part of
s twofold reply is that everything, far from going
wn into eternal annihilation, is going to come
ck eternally: the passage of time moves in vast,
smic epicycles, so that everything that has

happened before will eventually come round again –
and then again after that at another huge distance
of time. By living to the utmost of our being we
are living as we would wish to live eternally; and
the eternal recurrence of time will bring us as near
to eternal life as it is possible to get in a world that
is finite and bounded.

In evaluating Nietzsche's philosophy a
distinction has to be made between the challenge
it presents and Nietzsche's own answer to that
challenge. Most people have found the challenge
legitimate and exceedingly powerful while rejecting

### THE CHALLENGE OF CONFLICT
*If one lives one's life to the full it brings one into conflict with others, yet Nietzsche believed that the thrill of conflict stretches leaders and helps them to develop their abilities. This French soldier celebrates the capture of the Prussian flag during the Battle of Jena in 1806.*

### ZOROASTER

Also known as Zarathustra, Zoroaster was the founder in the sixth century BC of a pre-Islamic Persian religion. He modified the Aryan folk religion with his idea of eternal punishment according to the balance between good and evil deeds on earth. Nietzsche used Zarathustra as a mouthpiece for his own theories on Christianity – which he despised – and to expound on other areas including the death of God and the necessity for conflict in society.

### THUS SPAKE ZARATHUSTRA

Completed when Nietzsche was 40, *Thus Spake Zarathustra* (1891) was not very successful when it was first published, but is now generally considered to be a masterpiece of world literature. Within its four volumes Nietzsche presents an overall view of his philosophical thoughts. Daring in its form and ideas – especially about morals and psychology – the book introduces Nietzsche's concept of the "superman".

### ART FOR ART'S SAKE

*The Austrian painter Gustav Klimt (1862–1918), who was familiar with Nietzsche's writings, challenged the prudish conventions of turn-of-the-century Vienna, where a social epoch was coming to an end, and with it certain artistic conventions. The sensual, erotic quality of his work, as seen in The Kiss (1907–08), was deemed by some to be pornographic but it was a perfect expression of Nietzsche's belief that we are under an obligation to reappraise our morals and value*

Nietzsche's own response to it. The challenge is that if we no longer hold traditional religious beliefs it is illegitimate for us to go on embracing a morality and values that derive their justification from those beliefs. Our whole position, if we do that, is phoney, false. We are under an obligation to, as Nietzsche puts it, re-evaluate our values. In other words we need, from the bottom up, to carry out a radical reappraisal of our morals and our values on the basis of beliefs that we do really genuinely hold. This is a hair-raising challenge, and one of fundamental urgency in an increasingly irreligious world. Ever since Nietzsche put it before us, it has remained the supreme ethical challenge confronting not only the West but people everywhere who no longer have faith in a religion. It set the moral agenda for the existentialist philosophies of the 20th century. And it remains unanswered in the minds of most people who have given it their serious consideration. Indeed,

> ## "MAN IS A ROPE, TIED BETWEEN BEAST AND SUPERMAN – A ROPE OVER AN ABYSS"
>
> FRIEDRICH NIETZSCHE

in the opinion of many it is the most important philosophical question that confronts us today. For this alone, Nietzsche stands at or near the head of those philosophers whom we ourselves have to come to terms with.

He does not hold that position because of his positive views, the doctrines he put forward in answer to his own challenge. Nevertheless, these did have a considerable influence for something like half a century. Mussolini, the founder of Fascism, read Nietzsche extensively: Hitler gave

Mussolini a present of the collected works of Nietzsche at their historic meeting on the Brenner Pass in 1938. The Nazis themselves, in their propaganda, made repeated use of Nietzsche's words, such as "superman" and "the will to power". His came to be regarded as the representative voice of Fascist philosophy by both Fascists and their opponents. For several generations, subsequently, this got in the way of his philosophy being taken at its true value by those people who hated Fascism.

## INFLUENCE OF THE ARTS

In the late 19th and early 20th centuries Nietzsche exerted a widespread influence on creative artists. The internationally acclaimed playwrights August Strindberg and Luigi Pirandello came noticeably under that influence. Bernard Shaw called one of his best plays *Man and Superman* (1905), and said of himself later: "My reputation has been gained by my persistent struggle to force the public to reconsider its morals." He observed appreciatively that the

**LOU SALOMÉ**
In 1873 Nietzsche met Paul Rée, a fellow philosopher, and the two became close friends. Rée then introduced Nietzsche to Lou Salomé (1861–1937) and a complicated three-way relationship developed. However, Paul's feelings for Lou began to undermine his friendship with Nietzsche, whose sister exacerbated the situation with her insane jealousy of Lou.

THE TRIUMPH OF THE WILL
*Phrases from Nietzsche's work, such as "the will to power", were used in the Fascist propaganda of both Mussolini and Hitler. But Nietzsche was neither a nationalist nor an anti-Semite, and the association of Nietzsche's Superman with the Nazi conception of the pure Aryan is mistaken. The photograph above shows a rally held by the Nazis in September 1934 at Nuremberg, Germany.*

**CESARE LOMBROSO**
*Nietzsche's idea of the "superman", and of an aristocracy of superior individuals, was reinforced by other theories circulating at the time. Cesare Lombroso (1836–1909), an Italian professor of medicine, psychiatry and criminal anthropology, postulated one such theory: he believed that members of the criminal underclass were distinguishable by their physical appearance – including the shape of the skull, nose, and brow ridges.*

**WILLIAM BUTLER YEATS**
The Anglo-Irish poet and dramatist William Butler Yeats (1865–1939) had a complex relationship with his country. After falling in love with the political activist Maud Gonne, Yeats became passionate about Irish nationalism. Yeats first read Nietzsche in 1902, and after this date his work was strongly influenced by him.

**FASCISM**
*Many elements of Nietzsche's philosophy were misappropriated by the Fascists and Nazis before World War II. The Fascists' rise to power in Italy was due mainly to extreme poverty, and in Germany the Nazis preyed upon people's fears caused by a weak civilian democracy. There were many aspects of Fascism that Nietzsche despised including nationalism and state authority, but his name is inextricably linked with Fascism in people's minds.*

whole of Nietzsche was expressed in three lines that Shakespeare puts into the mouth of Richard III:

> *Conscience is but a word that cowards use*
> *Devised at first to keep the strong in awe.*
> *Our strong arms be our conscience, swords*
> *our law!*

The leading poet in English of the period, W. B. Yeats, shifted direction in his own poetic development in response to his reading of Nietzsche. Among German poets Rainer Maria Rilke and Stefan George were influenced by Nietzsche, as were Thomas Mann and Hermann Hesse among novelists. As for French writers, the names range from André Gide and André Malraux to Albert Camus and Jean-Paul Sartre. In the light of all this it can confidently be claimed for Nietzsche that he had more influence on European writers of the front rank than any other philosopher after Karl Marx – if indeed Marx can be satisfactorily thought of as a philosopher.

More surprisingly, since one does not easily expect a philosopher to be taken up by composers, Mahler, Delius, and Schoenberg all set Nietzsche's words to music, and Richard Strauss wrote an orchestral tone-poem called *Also Sprach Zarathustra* (1896) which is still frequently performed and recorded. So Nietzsche penetrated widely as well as deeply into the culture of the late 19th and early 20th centuries.

## FACING UNPALATABLE TRUTHS

What appealed most about his positive doctrines is what might be called their stoic heroism, the idea that we must confront the most difficult and unpalatable truths about ourselves without flinching, go on looking them clean in the eye, and live in the light of this knowledge without any reward other than the living of such a life for its own sake. Many large-hearted people for whom the absence of religious belief was a consciously felt loss were grateful to Nietzsche for giving them this lead. His own heroism in pursuit of this path was beyond question. Sigmund Freud, the founder of psychoanalysis, said of him: "In my youth he signified a nobility which I could not attain." Freud also, according to his leading biographer, "several times said of Nietzsche that he had a more penetrating knowledge of himself than any other man who ever lived or was ever likely to live

**NIETZSCHE AND WAGNER**
*In 1868 Nietzsche met the composer Richard Wagner, and through their shared veneration for Schopenhauer the two became close friends. In the year before he went insane Nietzsche published* The Case of Wagner *(1888) and wrote* Nietzsche versus Wagner *(1895). This scenery design for Wagner's opera* Parsifal *(1882) was created by Max Brückner.*

# The PHILOSOPHER ARTIST

Nietzsche is one of the supreme literary artists among philosophers. Many Germans regard him as the greatest of all writers of German prose. One reason why Nietzsche has been able to speak to so many creative artists is that he was himself something of an artist among philosophers. He wrote good poetry, composed music (which was perhaps not so good), and the most significant friendship in his life was with the composer Wagner. But more important than any of this, his literary style was one of extraordinary brilliance; and this was almost bound to be attractive to other writers. Most of his books are not written in the same sort of extended prose as other philosophy, with arguments and counter-arguments, laid out at length, but are presented in broken-up forms: aphorisms, or biblical verses, or separately numbered paragraphs.

His typical method of trying to get his readers to look at things in a new way is to present them not with a persuasive argument but with a memorable image – the arguments are there by implication, but have to be inferred from the metaphors. Primarily, this mode of presentation is designed to put forward not arguments but insights, which often come at the reader like flashes of lightning followed by thunderbolts.

Sometimes they take the familiar form of epigrams, such as: "If married couples did not live

## FLASHES OF LIGHTNING FOLLOWED BY THUNDERBOLTS

together, happy marriages would be more frequent", or "Vanity is the involuntary inclination to set oneself up as an individual without really being one", or "A stubborn avoidance of convention means a desire not to be understood." But usually they are more philosophically deep than that. More characteristic are: "A thinker finds it a drawback always to be tied to one person", and "If you look for too long into the abyss, the abyss will look into you"; and "The day after tomorrow belongs to me. Some are born posthumously."

In view of the fact that Nietzsche was claimed by the Nazis as the philosopher who spoke for them it should be stressed that he was derisive of German nationalism and contemptuous of anti-Semitism. Although a German himself, he was constantly making rude generalizations about the Germans. For instance: "The German possesses the secret of knowing how to be tedious in spite of wit, knowledge, and feeling", and "The depth of a great German is generally closed up in an ugly-shaped box." As for anti-Semitism, he considered it beyond the pale. "The anti-Semites", he said, "do not forgive the Jews for having both intellect and money. Anti-Semite – another name for 'bungled and botched'." He was specifically critical of the German people for their tendency towards anti-Semitism. His final words on the subject were: "I am just having all anti-Semites shot." He was no Nazi.

# DEMOCRACY & PHILOSOPHY

AFTER THE FALL OF THE CITY STATES OF ANCIENT GREECE, IT WAS NOT UNTIL THE 18TH CENTURY THAT SOCIETIES THAT COULD BE CALLED DEMOCRATIC MADE THEIR REAPPEARANCE — A PERIOD OF MORE THAN TWO THOUSAND YEARS. THE FIRST WAS THE UNITED STATES OF AMERICA, FOUNDED IN 1776. ONLY 13 YEARS LATER THE FRENCH REVOLUTION OF 1789 GAVE A WHOLLY NEW IMPETUS TO THE PROPAGATION OF SIMILAR IDEALS THROUGHOUT EUROPE. DEMOCRATIZATION IN THE MODERN SENSE HAD BEGUN. IDEAS PLAYED A LEADING ROLE IN THESE DEVELOPMENTS, ABOVE ALL THE IDEA OF COMBINING FREEDOM OF THE INDIVIDUAL WITH SOCIAL EQUALITY. THE FURTHER PROBLEMS OF HOW TO RECONCILE THESE WITH SOCIAL ORDER AND ECONOMIC PROSPERITY HAVE COME TO DOMINATE POLITICAL PHILOSOPHY.

UNITED NATIONS
*The association of states for international peace, security, and cooperation has its headquarters in New York.*

# THE UTILITARIANS

## THE EMPIRICISTS CONCENTRATE ON MORALS AND POLITICS

*"Everybody to count for one, and nobody for more than one" and "The greatest good of the greatest number" are adopted as guiding principles.*

### PANOPTICON
One of Bentham's main objectives was prison reform and he believed that such reforms would result in "morals reformed, health preserved, industry invigorated and instruction diffused". To explain his vision he designed a model prison, the Panopticon, which unfortunately was never adopted. However, he was rewarded financially for his efforts and the money was put towards the establishment of University College.

### JEREMY BENTHAM'S KEY WORKS

A Fragment on Government *(1776)*

Defence of Usury *(1787)*

An Introduction to the Principles and Morals of Legislation *(1789)*

Constitutional Code *(1830)*

DURING THE FIRST HALF of the 19th century, philosophy in the English-speaking world proceeded in almost complete ignorance of Kant. His masterpiece, *Critique of Pure Reason* (1781), was not even translated into English until 1854, a full half-century after his death; and few educated English people, then as now, were able to read German. Consequently, little progress beyond Hume was made in metaphysics and theory of knowledge. The great advances came in moral and political philosophy. The application of these to public policy at a time when Britain governed something like a quarter of the human race had world-wide impact.

### LEFT AGENDA
The first lastingly influential philosopher in the English language, after Hume, was Jeremy Bentham (1748–1832). He was born in London and educated at Oxford, and then in London's law courts, where he qualified as a barrister. It was the widespread social injustice that he saw at work as a student of law that made him actively interested in questions of public morality. Although he was to write voluminously about ethical, political, and legal questions throughout a long life, he was always vigorously involved in the practical application of his ideas. He became the leader of a group known as the Philosophical Radicals who spearheaded the movement for liberal reform of prisons, censorship, education, the laws governing sexual activity,

**JEREMY BENTHAM**
*The English philosopher and social reformer Jeremy Bentham was the founder of Utilitarianism. He believed that the interests of the individual are at one with society.*

corruption in public institutions – in short, what has since become a familiar left-liberal agenda for social policy.

### NEW UNIVERSITY
The chief philosophical influences on Bentham were the pre-revolutionary French thinkers; and their further development through him was to lead on after him to the emergence of British socialism later in the 19th century. Bentham and his main followers were freethinkers; and since at that time freethinkers were still not allowed to study at Oxford or Cambridge they created England's first new university since the middle ages, University College London, founded in 1826 Jeremy Bentham remains a presence there in the most literal sense. In the entrance hall, in a glass case, sits his embalmed body wearing his usual clothes, with only his head replaced by a wax model. And until not long ago he was always described in the minute of the governing body as "present but not voting".

Perhaps in part because of his many practical involvements, Bentham took a curiously slap-happy attitude towards publication. Before completing one work he would start another, often leaving the first unfinished – or, if he finished it, he did nothing to get it published. It was mostly through the intervention of friends that his writings were published at all, many of them after his death. In fact what made his name most widely known

UTOPIA IN NEW LANARK, SCOTLAND

*he influence of Utilitarianism is to be found in the work of
*obert Owen (1771–1858), one of the most active utopian
*ocialists of the early 19th century. The owner of the New*
*Lanark mills in Scotland, Owen was concerned with the
social and economic conditions of the workers and made
many improvements in housing, sanitation, and child care.*

*vas a French translation by an admirer, published in
*aris in 1802. And by this time he had already been
*nade a citizen of the new French republic, in 1792,
*nd had acquired some influence in Continental
*europe and the United States. Bentham was a late
*eveloper, and unlike most people he became more
*adical as he grew older. In 1824, only a few years
*efore his death at the age of 84, he founded, at
*is own expense, the *Westminster Review*, which
*vas to be for many years an exceedingly effective
*orum for "advanced" ideas. It was, for instance, the
*Westminster Review*, nearly three decades later,
*hat drew the world's attention to Schopenhauer's
*hilosophy after it had lain unknown in almost
*omplete disregard for nearly 35 years.

## THE GREATEST GOOD

*As the guiding principle for public policy Bentham
*ook a maxim that had been enunciated early in the
*18th century by a Scots-Irish philosopher called
*Francis Hutcheson: "That action is best which
*rocures the greatest happiness for the greatest
*umbers." Bentham evolved this into a moral

philosophy, which held that the rightness or
wrongness of an action was to be judged entirely
in terms of its consequences (so that motives, for
instance, were irrelevant); that good consequences
were those that gave pleasure to someone, while
bad consequences were those that gave pain to
someone; and therefore that in any situation the
right course of action to pursue was the one that
would maximize the excess of pleasure over pain,
or else minimize the excess of pain over pleasure.

This philosophy became known as
Utilitarianism, because it meant judging each
action by its utility, that is to say its usefulness
in bringing about consequences of a certain kind.
Its proponents applied these principles to private
morality as well as to political, legal, and social
policy. It had a permanent influence on the way
Britain is governed. "The greatest good of the
greatest number" entered the English language
as a catchphrase familiar to everyone.

Once this principle was accepted, the only
difficulty involved in making decisions was the
difficulty of calculating consequences. In making

***THE WESTMINSTER REVIEW***
Much of Jeremy
Bentham's work was
aimed at securing
parliamentary reform,
and in order to spread
his ideas of philosophical
radicalism he established
a periodical called
*The Westminster Review*
with James Mill in 1823.
The magazine, which
was published from
1824 to 1914, also
covered education, art,
and science and was
generally well received.

#### THE "ABODE OF LOVE"
*Sexual activity which brought no suffering to anyone was unobjectionable to Utilitarians. It was in this spirit that the Rev. Henry James Prince founded the Agapemone cult (from the Greek word* agape, *meaning love of a spiritual kind) in the 1840s. Based at a spacious Somerset mansion (above), the cult soon acquired a reputation for practising free love.*

any such calculation another important principle was brought into play: "Everybody is to count for one, and nobody for more than one." The attitudes to which these principles gave rise were very different from traditional ones. For instance, forms of sexual activity which brought no suffering to

anyone were unobjectionable to Utilitarians, yet some such activities were savagely punished by the laws of their day. On the other hand there were then quite a few business methods that brought unnecessary suffering to people, even ruin, and were entirely legal. So the spread of Utilitarian ideas helped to bring about important practical changes in society. The Utilitarian attitude to punishment was that penalties should be harsh enough to deter, but no harsher, since that was to create useless suffering. During the second half of the 19th century Utilitarian principles came to pervade the

> "OVER HIMSELF, OVER HIS OWN BODY AND MIND, THE INDIVIDUAL IS SOVEREIGN"
>
> JOHN STUART MILL

institutions of government and administration in Britain, where they have retained a powerful influence ever since. To some extent this marks a difference between Britain and the United States, where the emphasis has always been more heavily on individual rights, with a correspondingly greater reluctance to sacrifice the individual to the welfare of the majority, and a lower readiness to accept government intervention.

### INFANT PRODIGY
The man who did more than anyone else to organize and lead the Philosophical Radicals on Bentham's behalf was called James Mill, and it was largely through his efforts that Bentham was able to achieve such a powerful influence on British politics. Mill's other claim to fame was that he was the father of John Stuart Mill, who was to become, and indeed remains, the best-known of all English-speaking philosophers of the 19th century.

John Stuart Mill (1806–1873) was educated entirely by his father: he went to neither school nor university. His father force-fed him educationally from the earliest age: Greek at three, Latin, arithmetic, and huge quantities of history from seven onwards, several branches of higher

#### PENALTIES FOR CRIMES
*Bentham was a highly influential reformer of the British legal, judicial, and prison systems. His attitude towards suffering led him to advocate that the penalties imposed for crimes should be sufficient to deter but not cause unnecessary suffering.*

athematics before the age of 12.
e was also brought up to believe
 Utilitarianism, and it was John
uart Mill who put that term into
eneral circulation.

At the age of 17 he started work
ith the East India Company, in which
s father was one of the most senior
fficials, and he remained with them
ntil the Company ceased to exist
5 years later, in 1858. This
verwhelming domination by
s father in everything to do
ith his life up to the age of
0 precipitated a breakdown
to serious depression at that
ge, which caused him to feel
e need for more personal
utlets. He came out of the
epression, however, and at
5 met a married woman,
arriet Taylor, with whom he
ormed a passionate attachment that came
ventually to be accepted by her husband, though
 shocked conventional society. After John Taylor
ied in 1851 Mill married Harriet, but she died in
858. During the years 1865–1868 Mill was a
Member of Parliament, where he distinguished
imself by proposing votes for women.

## EQUALITY FOR WOMEN

Mill's first book made him famous: it was *A System
of Logic*, a two-volume work published in 1843.
In spite of its title it was a general system of
philosophy as a whole, bringing
together and up to date the
empiricist philosophy developed by
ocke, Berkeley, Hume, and Bentham –
hough without Berkeley's theology
r Hume's scepticism. For many years
: was the best systematic exposition
vailable of that sort of philosophy,
nd this brought it worldwide
eputation and influence in spite of
he fact that it was not particularly
riginal except in detail. More
istinguished, and lastingly influential
own to the present day, were his
ooks *On Liberty* (1859) and *The
ubjection of Women* (1869).

The central thesis of *On Liberty*
s that "the sole end for which
nankind are warranted, individually
r collectively, in interfering with the

**ON LIBERTY**
The most popular of all
John Stuart Mill's works,
*On Liberty* was written
with help from his wife,
Harriet, and published
after her death. The book
defines and defends the
freedom of the individual
against social and
political control.

**JOHN STUART MILL'S
KEY WORKS**

A System of Logic
(1843)

On Liberty (1859)

The Subjection of
Women (1869)

Principles of Political
Economy (1848)

Utilitarianism (1863)

Three Essays on
Religion (1874)

**JOHN STUART MILL**
*The British philosopher and economist John
Stuart Mill wrote what is probably the most
influential defence of the freedom of the
individual that has ever been published.*

liberty of action of any of their
number, is self-protection". In other
words, the individual should be
free to do whatever he likes so
long as he does not bring any
significant harm to anyone else – for
at that point, as a judge once remarked
to a defendant: "Your liberty to swing
your arm ends where my nose
begins." Mill's book remains
the classic exposition of
the case for this conception
of the freedom of the
individual, and is still widely
read as such.

*The Subjection of Women*
is even more remarkable.
After Plato, who advocated
that girls should be brought
up on equal terms with boys,
the only figure of name and
note to demand equality for
women was Epicurus – and then, after him, no one
until the 18th century and the ferment of liberal
ideas surrounding the French Revolution. Why this
is so it is difficult to explain satisfactorily, especially
in view of Plato's incomparable prestige for long
periods during those two thousand years. *The
Subjection of Women* was the first book devoted
by any well known thinker to arguing the case
for sexual equality – and this it did with all of Mill's
characteristic cogency and attractiveness. For this
reason, as one might expect, it continues to be held
in high esteem by feminists everywhere.

**VOTES FOR WOMEN**
*The British suffragette movement began in 1866 when Mill presented the first
female suffrage petition to parliament. It was not until 1918, after years of
campaigning, that women over the age of 30 won the right to vote.*

**HARRIET TAYLOR**
Late in 1830 John Stuart
Mill met Harriet Taylor
and a close intimacy
developed, despite
Harriet being married
to someone else.
She introduced Mill to
a bohemian circle of
friends and soon moved
from being his disciple
to being his foremost
critic and consultant.

# THE AMERICAN PRAGMATISTS

## KNOWLEDGE AS A FORM OF PRACTICAL INVOLVEMENT

*Knowing is something we do, and is best seen as a practical activity. Questions of meaning and truth are also best understood in this context*

*"Everything real must be experienceable somewhere, and every kind of thing experienced must somewhere be real"*

WILLIAM JAMES

WHEN THE UNITED STATES established itself as an independent nation towards the end of the 18th century this gave new impetus to the development of a specifically American culture and approach to ideas. But it took another hundred years or so for American philosophy to develop to the point where it commanded international attention; and then there came a time at the end of the 19th century and the beginning of the 20th when the best university department of philosophy in the world was considered by many a good judge to be that of Harvard. Three outstanding American philosophers of that time have since acquired classic status and become known as "The American Pragmatists". Of these the most original was Charles Sanders Peirce; the most enjoyable to read was William James; and the most widely influential was John Dewey.

**CHARLES SANDERS PEIRCE**
*The American mathematician and physicist C. S. Peirce was the founder of Pragmatism. Peirce regarded logic as the basis of philosophy. In his final years he was ill with cancer and in abject poverty, relieved only by aid from friends such as William James.*

### KNOWING IS DOING
According to the *Encyclopaedia Britannica*, C. S. Peirce (1839–1914) is "now recognized as the most original and the most versatile intellect that the Americas have so far produced". His father was Professor of Mathematics at Harvard, and was the leading American mathematician of his day. C. S. Peirce himself graduated in mathematics and the sciences, and for a long time earned his living as a scientist, his philosophical activity being something he pursued in his spare time. But from the age of 48 he devoted himself entirely to

**KNOWLEDGE IS AN ACTIVITY**
*Peirce maintained that in order to gain knowledge we evaluate situations and learn from our mistakes. For example, much was learnt about the construction and design of bridges after the collapse of the Tay Bridge in Scotland in 1880; the picture above shows divers preparing to inspect the submerged remains.*

philosophy. He never wrote a book, and much of his work came out only after his death, when his *Collected Papers* were published in eight volumes.

Perhaps Peirce's central contention is that knowledge is an activity. We are moved to enquire, to want to know, by some need or lack or doubt. This leads us to evaluate our problem-situation, to try to see what it is in the situation that is wrong, or missing, and ways in which that might be put right. This scheme applies even when our problem is a purely theoretical one; and it applies both in everyday life and the sciences. The application of intelligence is primarily evaluative, and is aimed at achieving understanding. Knowledge consists of valid explanations. Peirce's first important paper was called "How to Make Our Ideas Clear" (1878), and in it he argued that to understand a term clearly we should ask ourselves what difference its application would make to our evaluation of our problem-situation, or of a proposed solution to it

at difference constitutes the
rm's meaning. A term whose
plication makes no noticeable
fference to anything has no
certainable meaning. Thus
ragmatism" – a term that Peirce
mself appropriated for use in this
ntext – was put forward by him
a method for ascertaining the
eanings of terms; and thus, we
n say, as a theory of meaning.

ALLIBILISM
great deal of originality is
ontained in these ideas. They
jected a view of knowledge that
d been accepted by scientists
r something like two and a half
nturies, a view of knowledge as
mpersonal fact. Without necessarily
alizing they were doing it,
ientists had accepted what
e might call a spectator view
knowledge, as if man were
mehow observing the world
om outside it, and reading off
nowledge from his observations.
e do not do this, said Peirce:
e acquire our knowledge as

**TO DO IS TO KNOW**
*Peirce argued that we acquire knowledge by participating and not spectating;
for example, when we learn to drive, we gain knowledge from our action as
a participant. This contradicted the view that scientists had held for almost
250 years, that knowledge is impersonal and is read from observations.*

articipants, not as spectators. We are part of the
rorld, living in amongst it all; and it is chiefly in
ursuit of survival in it that we strive for knowledge
d understanding of it. So we are interested
arties. Knowledge is an instrument, perhaps the

# THE REAL, THEN,
IS THAT WHICH,
SOONER OR
LATER,
INFORMATION
AND REASONING
WOULD FINALLY
RESULT IN "

CHARLES SANDERS PEIRCE

most important instrument for survival that we
have: we use our knowledge. And because the most
useful thing about it is its explanatory power we
will rely on it, as on any explanation, for only so
long as it works, so long as it yields accurate results;
if we start running up against serious difficulties
with it we try to improve it, or perhaps even
replace it. This means that scientific knowledge is
not a body of certainties but a body of explanations.
And the growth of our scientific knowledge does
not consist in adding new certainties to a body of
existing ones, it consists in replacing existing
explanations with better explanations.

A little earlier in the century a philosopher in
Cambridge, England, called William Whewell had
had some of these insights; but Peirce developed
them more extensively. From these beginnings there
grew a view of science and of knowledge generally
that was eventually to oust the prevailing 19th-
century view. In the 19th century people thought
of science as certain, incorrigible knowledge,
copper-bottomed fact, unchangeable; indeed, all
knowledge genuinely worthy of the name was
thought to have this characteristic of certainty.
Something could not be knowledge and

**HARVARD UNIVERSITY**
*The oldest university
in the United States,
Harvard was
established in 1636
in New Towne (later
renamed Cambridge),
Massachusetts.
The institution was
named after John
Harvard, a Puritan
minister, and was
initially under church
sponsorship.
Two centuries later
it was liberated from
clerical and political
control and earned
a reputation as a
hotbed of intellectual
development. As well
as many scientists
and philosophers,
Harvard has educated
six past presidents
of the United States.*

## WILHELM RÖNTGEN

One of the most amazing scientific advances of the late 19th century was the discovery by Wilhelm Röntgen (1845–1923) of X-rays. These electromagnetic rays enabled doctors to see inside the human body without recourse to surgery and had an enormous effect on people's perception of science.

## WILLIAM JAMES' KEY WORKS

The Principles of Psychology *(1890)*

The Varieties of Religious Experience *(1902)*

Pragmatism: A New Name for Old Ways of Thinking *(1907)*

The Meaning of Truth *(1909)*

### NONE OF OUR KNOWLEDGE IS CERTAIN
*Peirce thought that little that is "known" in one age continues to be thought of as unquestionable by later generations. The Wright brothers pioneered powered flight when previous generations had considered it an impossibility. Their first flight was near Kitty Hawk, North Carolina, on 17 December 1903.*

corrigible. In the course of the 20th century, however, people came to realize that none of our knowledge is certain, not even our science; that all of it is fallible, and in principle improvable, even replaceable. The history of knowledge so obviously bears this out that it may be considered surprising that no one had realized that before. Comparatively little that is "known" in any one age continues to be regarded as unquestionable by later generations. It is virtually certain that our own age will be no exception to this.

Another general characteristic of 20th-century thought that was prefigured by Peirce concerns man's existential relationship to his knowledge, the fact that he is not outside the world looking at it but is a part of it, a participant in it whose knowledge and understanding of it have above all else to meet urgent needs that he has. This view came to be held in common by several later schools of thought that were accustomed to thinking of themselves as opposed to one another: for example Heidegger and the modern form of existentialism that developed out of him,

Wittgenstein and the school of analysis that fed on his posthumously published philosophy, and the evolutionary epistemology that grew out of Karl Popper's work.

## LUCID PROSE

Peirce lived and worked in obscurity, read by only a handful of friends and specialists. It was a lifelong friend of his called William James (1842–1910) who made "American pragmatism" known throughout the world. James graduated at Harvard in medicine and became a lecturer there in anatomy and physiology, but then became Professor of Philosophy – and after that Professor of Psychology. He had an exceptionally pleasing prose style, wholly different from that of his younger brother Henry James, the novelist. Whereas Henry was to become famous for the density and slow-movingness of his prose, William's was fast-moving, full of surprise, and, for all its richness of texture and metaphor, lucid. If one had to judge from literary style alone one would take Henry to be the philosopher and William the novelist. William's books acquired an international readership during

### WILLIAM JAMES
*The American psychologist and philosopher William James, brother of the novelist Henry James, was for most of his adult life associated with Harvard University, where he graduated in medicine, and taught successively physiology, philosophy, and psychology.*

s lifetime, and have continued to be widely read
er since. If today you mention the name "James"
the philosophy department of a university
ople will assume you mean William James,
hereas in the literature department they will
sume you mean Henry James. William's best
own books are *The Principles of Psychology*
890); *The Varieties of Religious Experience*
902); and *Pragmatism* (1907).

## THEORY OF TRUTH

hereas Peirce had put forward pragmatism as a
eory of meaning, James treated it as a theory of
ith. He argued that those statements and theories
e true that do all the jobs required of them: first
d foremost fit all the known facts, accord with
her well-attested statements and scientific laws
experience, but also withstand criticism, suggest
eful insights, yield accurate predictions, and so

> # ' NOTHING IS VITAL FOR SCIENCE; NOTHING CAN BE "
>
> CHARLES SANDERS PEIRCE

i and so forth. If a statement meets every such
quirement, he asks, what consideration could
ere be that stops us from calling it "true"?
nfortunately for James, he was widely assumed
be putting forward the crude view that the true
whatever works. The term "pragmatism" was
self most unfortunate in this respect, for it
icouraged the misunderstanding.

Furthermore, a shallow interpretation of James
as encouraged by what he seemed to be saying
out religious belief – that if a religious statement
r system of statements could possibly be true, in
her words could not be disproved, and a given
idividual stood to gain some vital benefit from
elieving it, then he was justified in believing it.
his was a view that was to become more closely
ssociated with the name Jung. Peirce retained good
ersonal relations with James, and was, needless to

THE POWER OF BELIEF
*A superficial interpretation of James was encouraged by what
he seemed to be saying about religious belief – that if a
statement could not be disproved, then one was justified in
believing it if one benefited from it: for instance, a bereaved
mother comforted by believing that her child is in heaven.*

say, not shallow in his understanding of what James
was saying, but he publicly dissociated himself from
James' interpretation of pragmatism. James himself
eventually tired of what came to seem endless and
often repetitive controversy surrounding pragmatism,
and moved the focus of his work on to other

*"What is sometimes called an act of self-expression might better be termed one of self-exposure; it discloses character – or lack of character – to others. In itself, it is only a spewing forth"*

JOHN DEWEY

problems, deliberately leaving the field as far as pragmatism was concerned to a younger philosopher called John Dewey.

## INTERNATIONAL

John Dewey (1859–1952) started out as a shy young New Englander, educated at the University of Vermont. He was a fair but not brilliant student, was twice refused grants to study philosophy at post-graduate level, and in the end had to borrow $500 from an aunt in order to do so. He made the grade, however, and spent the whole of his career as a university teacher, first at the University of Michigan, then Chicago, and finally Columbia University in New York.

JOHN DEWEY
*Apart from being a leading 20th-century philosopher, Dewey is equally recognized as an influential psychologist, educator, and an authentic voice of American democracy.*

He began as a Hegelian, but early on he moved over to pragmatism. In accordance with pragmatic theories he was always involved in a wide range of practical activities, for instance with scientific groups, and political groups, and in the founding of new kinds of school. He was always trying to propagate his ideas to a wider audience, and produced a lot of high-quality journalism as well as many books. He became internationally known and influential. He lectured in Tokyo, Beijing, and

Nanking, and carried out educational surveys of Turkey, Mexico, and Soviet Russia. At the age of 78 he headed an independent commission of enquiry into the charges brought against Trotsky at the Moscow trials: its verdict, after careful investigation, was Not Guilty. When Bertrand Russell's famous *History of Western Philosophy* was published in 1946, only one living philosopher was given a chapter to himself, and that was John Dewey. His output of books was so large that selection is difficult, but perhaps the one that gives the most concentrated expression to his central ideas is *Logic: The Theory of Inquiry* (1938).

His most popular book has been *Reconstruction in Philosophy* (1920), and perhaps his most influential *The School and Society* (1899).

## LEARNING BY DOING

Dewey saw it as an inescapable fact that for several hundred years now, far and away our greatest successes in the acquisition of knowledge have been in the sciences. Two features of this knowledge struck him forcefully: it is more reliable than our knowledge in other fields, and it is also more useful to us in the sense that it makes more difference to the actual lives we lead. As a pragmatist he regarded knowing of every kind as a human activity first and foremost, and from this point of view he examined scientific knowing to see whether what was so special about it was something that could be adapted to other sorts of knowing. He came to the conclusion that it was. Science, he thought, was a highly disciplined, self-critical form of enquiry with a logical structure that could with profit be adapted to most other forms of enquiry. We always begin from a felt difficulty of some kind, so our first requirement is to get this clear, in other words to work on the formulation of our problem. This process may be difficult, and may itself pass through several stages. The next stage is to think

A MAN OF ACTION
*Dewey thought that the two major parties in Congress had failed to deal with the problems in the United States caused by the Depression. He is shown here, in 1936, calling for the foundation of a liberal "third" party.*

a possible solution to the problem. And the next to test this solution experimentally. If our solution refuted by tests we shall have to think again: but it is experimentally confirmed we will have solved e problem, and can move on.

Dewey came to see this as the desirable underlying pattern for all enquiry. This, he thought, how our knowledge and our competence could ow in all areas – though of course the particular ocedures used, type of evidence, testing methods, d so on, would differ in different fields. Because iticism plays an essential role in it he saw it as an escapably social activity. This led him to take a eat interest in institutions, and how they function. also became woven into his conception of emocracy, to which he was deeply committed, and out which he wrote a good deal. He advocated at the education of children should be based on is problem-solving approach – what he called earning by doing" – because it combined being ractical with taking full account of the importance theory, and encouraged children to be imaginative both levels, and above all because it would train them in a general

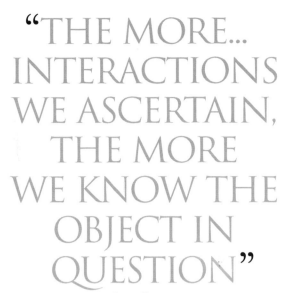

> ❝THE MORE... INTERACTIONS WE ASCERTAIN, THE MORE WE KNOW THE OBJECT IN QUESTION❞
>
> JOHN DEWEY

competence in all fields of human activity. His ideas about education were influential worldwide. At the time when he began writing about it education was thought of almost everywhere as something imposed by strict discipline on a recalcitrant child, against his will. Dewey's proposed methods of enlisting the child's natural energies to drive the education process along had extraordinary effects. He was one of the first great modernists in education theory, and perhaps the best.

**THE SCHOOL AND SOCIETY** In his most notable writing on education, *The School and Society* (1899), Dewey presented the underlying tenets that formed his philosophy of education. These included the role of the teacher as guide and co-worker, and the belief that the educational process must begin with, and build on, the interests of the child.

**JOHN DEWEY'S KEY WORKS**

The School and Society *(1899)*

Studies in Logical Theory *(1903)*

Reconstruction in Philosophy *(1920)*

The Quest for Certainty *(1929)*

Logic: The Theory of Inquiry *(1938)*

PRACTICAL LEARNING

ewey advocated a "learning by doing" approach to ducation, maintaining that children learn more when they re encouraged to be imaginative in both practical and

traditional theory work. In this photograph, two ten-year-old boys, watched by a teacher, experiment to determine what happens to air when it is heated and cooled.

# 20th-Century Philosophy

The 20th century was the first since the Middle Ages in which all the leading philosophers were academics. Partly as a result of this, there was an exponential growth of concern with analysis. In logical analysis and linguistic analysis massive developments occurred, far beyond anything dreamt of in the previous history of the subject. Otherwise the biggest advances were on two fronts. One was a response to 20th-century science, which compelled a radical reappraisal of the nature of human knowledge as such. The other was an attempt to understand the human condition in a universe no longer seen as created by God, or as having any meaning or purpose of its own.

NUCLEAR BOMB OVER BIKINI ATOLL
*Between 1946 and 1963 Bikini Atoll, situated in the north Pacific, was used by the US as a test site for atomic bombs.*

## GIUSEPPE PEANO

*Many of Frege's ideas were first transmitted by other people, including the Italian mathematician Giuseppe Peano. As the founder of symbolic logic, Peano created his own logic notation (as did Frege), and established the basic elements of geometric calculus. Peano also invented his own international auxiliary language, "Interlingua", which was a fusion of vocabulary from Latin, French, German, and English.*

### LETTER TO HUSSERL
Frege perceived a difference between his views on the relationship between words and their significance and those that Husserl expresses in his *Philosophy of Arithmetic* (1891). In the letter above, Frege explains the difference, and sets out his distinction between the sense and the reference of expressions.

# FREGE AND MODERN LOGIC

## LOGIC MOVES TO CENTRE STAGE

*In the early 20th century breakthroughs occurred in logic which affected the whole of the rest of philosophy.*

THE SYSTEM OF LOGIC laid down by Aristotle remained unaltered in its essentials until the 19th century. By that time logic had come to be thought of as consisting of the laws that govern thought. As Schopenhauer put it, we were no more able to think coherently without obeying these laws than we were able to bend our limbs against our joints. However, in the later part of the 19th century a German called Gottlob Frege (1848–1925) had an insight whose consequences were to overthrow this conception of logic and bring about revolutionary developments in the subject.

### LOGIC IS OBJECTIVE
Like so many ideas of major importance, it appears obvious once it is stated, but had never been obvious before. It is this: something either does in fact, or does not, in fact, follow from something else, and whether it does or not cannot possibly depend on anything to do with the psychology of human beings. In other words, logic is not "laws of thought" at all, or indeed anything to do with thought. Logical relationships are independent of human thought. Of course, we human beings can know them, learn them, overlook them, misunderstand them, and so on and so forth, but we can do these things with much else that exists independently of us. The point is that logical propositions are objective truths. We may grasp them, or fail to grasp them, but their existence has nothing to do with any feature of human thinking.

**GOTTLOB FREGE**
*The German mathematician and philosopher Gottlob Frege was the founder of modern mathematical logic and laid the foundations for analytic philosophy. It was not until after his death that he became widely known.*

When this insight was applied to general philosophy it had momentous consequences. Since Descartes, Western philosophy had been dominated by the question "What can I know?" Theory of knowledge, epistemology, had been at the centre; and this was taken to mean that what went on in people's minds was the main subject of investigation. But Frege's insight had the consequence of de-psychologizing philosophy. If what is the case and what follows from what, are both independent of the human mind, then our attempts to understand the world cannot legitimately centre on epistemology. The clear implication is that philosophy ought to be logic-based, not epistemology-based; and Frege's work precipitated changes in that direction which continued unabated in many of the main areas of philosophy throughout the 20th century.

### MATHS IS LOGIC
Frege's other great achievement concerned our understanding of mathematics. Mathematics, of course, consists almost entirely of what follows from what. And mathematical arguments and demonstrations, like all other arguments and demonstrations, have to start from somewhere, from some premises; and they must also have at least one rule of procedure if they are to move beyond their premises. As has been said before, it is not possible for a demonstration to prove the validity of its own premises, or of its own rules of procedure, for if it

ed to do that it would be moving in a vicious circle; for it would already have assumed what it set out to prove. This means that every mathematical demonstration starts from unproven premises, and uses rules of procedure whose validity it does not establish. So what a valid mathematical "proof" actually proves is that, given those rules of procedure, these conclusions follow from those premises. It does not prove that the conclusions are true, because it cannot prove that the premises are true. Since this applies to all mathematical arguments and demonstrations without exception, the whole of mathematics has to be seen as somehow free-floating in mid-air, without any visible means of support.

Starting with arithmetic, what Frege aimed to show was that all the unproven assumptions and rules that sustain this edifice of mathematics could be derived from the most elementary principles of logic. This would have the consequence of validating mathematics as a body of necessary

## "THERE IS NOTHING MORE OBJECTIVE THAN THE LAWS OF ARITHMETIC"

GOTTLOB FREGE

truths derived from purely logical premises. The aim was to set mathematics on solid foundations; but this programme was to have two sets of side-effects which were each of historic importance.

If logic contained the whole of mathematics within itself as a necessary consequence, it was as true to say that logic was part of mathematics as it was to say that mathematics was part of logic. In either case, what had been considered for more than 2,000 years to constitute the whole of logic would turn out to be merely a tiny corner of it. In the light of this probability, the study of logic underwent a transformation into a vast and highly

technical field overlapping with mathematics, and is now taught and researched as such in every major university in the world.

The other great side-effect was that if mathematics was co-extensive with logic, then the de-psychologization of logic automatically involved the de-psychologization of mathematics. Throughout the history of mathematics a dispute about its fundamental nature had been going on between those who saw it as a product of the human mind, like language, and those who saw it as having an independent existence of its own. If Frege's programme could be carried through successfully, their dispute would be settled in favour of the latter option.

### BELATED FAME

Frege was a mathematician, and spent the whole of a long working life in the mathematics department of the University of Jena. Although he published his findings they were not read by members of the philosophy departments of German universities, which at the time were firmly in the grip of German idealism, with its committed belief in the view of mathematics as a product of the human mind. Nor, for many years, did his findings reach philosophers in the English-speaking world either, few of whom could read German in any case. So he spent his most productive years in obscurity. Eventually it was an Englishman, Bertrand Russell, who "discovered" him and made his work known to the world at large – though not before Russell had done a great deal of hard work on his own account re-discovering and re-inventing things that Frege had already done.

Before turning to philosophy, Russell had been trained in Cambridge as a mathematician. And having, as an infant, had a German-speaking nurse he had been able to speak German before he knew any English. All this enabled Russell to amalgamate and develop to the full the work that he and Frege had launched independently. And by developing its implications across the entire range of philosophy he was to become, it can possibly be said, the most influential single philosopher of the 20th century.

CONCEPT SCRIPT
*In 1879 Frege published a pamphlet entitled* Begriffsschrift *(Concept Script). In it, in a little more than a hundred pages, he described a new calculus which has since been at the centre of modern logic. The work also deals with the nature of logic, proof, and language.*

# RUSSELL AND ANALYTIC PHILOSOPHY

## PHILOSOPHY TURNS ITS SPOTLIGHT ON LANGUAGE

*Bertrand Russell used the new logic to analyse statements in ordinary language. This inaugurated a whole new way of doing philosophy.*

> *"There is absolutely nothing that is seen by two minds simultaneously"*
>
> BERTRAND RUSSELL

**LORD JOHN RUSSELL**
Bertrand's grandfather was the liberal politician John, 1st Earl Russell (1792–1878), who entered the House of Commons in 1813 and was twice elected prime minister of Great Britain between 1846 and 1866. Lord Russell supported Catholic emancipation, and led the fight for the great Reform Bill of 1832.

BERTRAND RUSSELL (1872–1970) had one of the most interesting lives among the great figures in philosophy. He was the grandson of Lord John Russell, who piloted the Great Reform Bill of 1832 through the House of Commons, and subsequently became Prime Minister of Great Britain. Both of young Bertie's parents died before he was four, so he was brought up by his grandparents, who educated him at home; and this meant that he grew up in an aristocratic English household at the apex of British society at a time when Britain itself was at the apex of its imperial grandeur as a world power. In due course he was to inherit an earldom from his grandfather, via his elder brother.

### IN LOVE WITH MATHEMATICS
At the age of 11 he fell in love with mathematics. In his autobiography he wrote: "From that moment until Whitehead and I finished *Principia Mathematica*, when I was 38, mathematics was my chief interest, and my chief source of happiness." When he went up to Cambridge as an undergraduate he studied mathematics at first, and then combined it with philosophy. In keeping with this, his first book of lasting significance, published in 1900, was a study of the great mathematician-philosopher Leibniz.

**BERTRAND RUSSELL**
*Russell spent the last 15 years of his life actively campaigning against the manufacture of nuclear weapons. Even at the age of 90, he intervened with heads of state during the Cuban Missile Crisis of 1962, when the USA told the Soviets to withdraw nuclear missiles from Cuba or face nuclear attack.*

It was the only book he ever wrote about another philosopher – though of course his *History of Western Philosophy*, an international bestseller when it was published in 1946, was entirely devoted to the work of other philosophers.

### PIONEER IN LOGIC
Russell engaged with life on a broad front. As a young man he was an active socialist, and stood for parliament as a Labour Party candidate. He was in the forefront of the new thinking about social questions that became influential in the early years of the 20th century, the sort of liberal-radical attitudes to war, empire, legal reform, social class, marriage, morals, and so on whose most conspicuous advocate in the Britain of those days was George Bernard Shaw – a position in which Russell succeeded Shaw in later life. In middle age he poured out books and journals on such topics. He married four times, and after a certain age became a notorious womanizer.

Because of his range of activities, combination of gifts, and social connections, he was constantly travelling internationally; and everywhere he went he met people at the highest levels of politics, literature, the sciences, and the academic world. It was an extraordinary life. He wrote more than 60

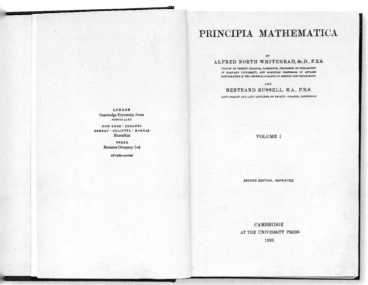

*PRINCIPIA MATHEMATICA*
*The collaboration between Russell and A. N. Whitehead on* Principia Mathematica *(1910–13) marked an unprecedented advance in man's understanding of logical relationships. It has become Russell and Whitehead's most prestigious piece of work, in which they attempted to show that mathematics could be reduced to a branch of logic.*

...ooks, won the Nobel Prize for Literature, and was ...ctive as a public figure until only a couple of years ...hort of what would have been his 100th birthday.

Perhaps surprisingly for a person of this ...escription, his contribution to philosophy began ...t a level of extreme technicality. Independently ...f Frege he had arrived at the view that arithmetic,

> # "THE SECRET OF HAPPINESS IS TO FACE THE FACT THAT THE WORLD IS HORRIBLE, HORRIBLE, HORRIBLE"
>
> BERTRAND RUSSELL

...nd probably the whole of mathematics, could be ...erived from the fundamental principles of logic. ...his was argued in his book *The Principles of ...athematics*, published in 1903. Using Frege's ...roundwork in addition to his own he then

embarked on the mammoth task of proving his case by carrying out all the actual reductions required to demonstrate it. This he did in collaboration with the distinguished person who had taught him mathematics at Cambridge, Alfred North Whitehead. Together they produced the three massive volumes of *Principia Mathematica*, published 1910-13, regarded by many as the greatest single contribution to logic since Aristotle. It was only after these gargantuan achievements in mathematical logic that Russell bent his efforts towards general philosophy. By then he was in his fortieth year.

## THE QUEST FOR CERTAINTY

His first general philosophy book, published in 1912, was *The Problems of Philosophy*. It contained original ideas and yet, unlike his work in mathematical logic, was accessible to the interested beginner. This was characteristic of all his subsequent books, as of course it had been of the writings of nearly all the great philosophers. Of special note among his works was one whose very title encapsulated his programme as a philosopher: *Our Knowledge of the External World as a Field for Scientific Method in Philosophy*, published in 1914. Other important books included *The Philosophy of Logical Atomism* (1918), *The Analysis of Mind* (1921), and *The Analysis of Matter* (1927). Then followed the years in which he was most deeply immersed in his political, social, and educational activities. But then came *An Enquiry Into Meaning and Truth* (1940), and *Human Knowledge – Its Scope and Limits* (1948). He signed off his career in philosophy with a book that critically surveyed his life's work, *My Philosophical Development*, published in 1959.

### RUSSELL AND PACIFISM

*In Britain during World War I all fit men of conscription age were legally required to enlist to fight. Russell's activities as a pacifist and his refusal to join in the war effort resulted in him being fined £100 in 1916, his dismissal from his lectureship at Trinity College, Cambridge, and imprisonment for six months in 1918, during which time he wrote his* Introduction to Mathematical Philosophy *(1919).*

SIT-DOWN PROTEST
*In the 1950s, Russell began to divert his attention away from philosophy to politics. In 1958 he became president of the Campaign for Nuclear Disarmament, but resigned in 1960 to set up the more militant Committee of 100. Above, Russell sits with other demonstrators outside the Ministry of Defence, London, to protest against Britain's nuclear policy.*

**ALFRED NORTH WHITEHEAD**
The English philosopher
and mathematician
Alfred North Whitehead
(1861–1947) was
professor of applied
mathematics at London
University (1914–24) and
professor of philosophy
at Harvard University
(1924–37). His works
include *Principia
Mathematica* (1910–13),
written with Russell, and
*The Concept of Nature*
(1920). In his "theory
of the organism" he
attempted a synthesis of
metaphysics and science.

As a general philosopher Russell felt himself to be
in a direct line of succession of well-known British
empiricists of whom the leading figures were
Locke, Berkeley, Hume, and Mill. (Mill was in fact
Russell's godfather.) He believed that all our
knowledge of the external world – both our
everyday commonsense knowledge and our
scientific knowledge – was derived ultimately from
experience, and what he wanted to do was find a
rational demonstration of the certainty of this
knowledge, to put it on unshakably solid foundations.

### ANALYZING WHAT WE SAY

But whereas his forebears had taken it for granted
that knowledge was a matter of epistemology, and
approached it solely in these terms, Russell brought
to the problems the whole apparatus of logic that
he, Whitehead, and Frege had developed between
them. Just as previously he had tried to provide
mathematics with watertight logical foundations,
so now he tried to provide our knowledge of the
external world, including our scientific knowledge,
with watertight logical foundations, in both cases
the aim being to establish
human knowledge with
absolute certainty. In neither
case did he succeed in the
end; but in both cases he
achieved great things in the
course of trying.

Given Russell's
programme and early work
it came naturally to him
to apply the techniques
of logical analysis to
our ordinary claims to
knowledge. Immediately, he
exposed serious difficulties
concerning meaning and
truth in even apparently
simple statements. If we
say "The heir to the British
throne is bald" the meaning
of our statement seems
obvious; and if we try to
establish its truth by
checking the facts we find
that it is false. But suppose
we change the statement
only ever so slightly to one
that seems of exactly the
same form: "The heir to the
French throne is bald." Is this
true or false? There is no

French throne, and consequently no heir to it, so
there is no-one and nothing to whom the statement
refers. So how could it be said to be either true or
false? In fact, does it even mean anything?

As soon as Russell subjected our ordinary way
of talking about things to this kind of logical analysis
he exposed it as a minefield of problems and traps.
He showed, as in the example above, that two

> ## "MATHEMATICS POSSESSES NOT ONLY TRUTH, BUT BEAUTY – A BEAUTY COLD AND AUSTERE, LIKE THAT OF SCULPTURE"
>
> BERTRAND RUSSELL

statements may have exactly the same grammatical
form and yet two totally different sets of logical
implications, so that in at least one case the linguistic
form of what we are saying is actually hiding its
true logical nature, which may be highly problematic.

### THE BIRTH OF ANALYTIC PHILOSOPHY

This pioneering work of Russell's launched a
development in philosophy which became known
as "analytic philosophy", and which was to come
close to dominating philosophy in the English-
speaking world for most of the 20th century.
In the course of this time it took different forms,
but common to them all was the close analysis
of propositions, or of the individual terms and
concepts they employed, or of their logical
implications both internal and external, with a view
to bringing everything that was hidden in them
to the surface. The overall question always was:
"What are we really saying when we say so-and-so?"

---

**MATHEMATICAL LOGIC**
*In their seminal work, Principia Mathematica, Russell
and Whitehead attempted to show – using a different
notation from Frege's – that the whole of arithmetic
could be derived simply from logical truths. The page
shown above is part of an hypothesis of classification,
from the section of the book dealing with
mathematical logic.*

TRINITY COLLEGE, CAMBRIDGE
Founded in 1546 by Henry VII, Trinity is the largest of the colleges at Cambridge University. Over the years it has produced 20 Nobel Prize winners, six British prime ministers, and several poets, including Byron and Tennyson. Russell entered Trinity in 1890, and it was here that he mixed with some of the finest minds of the 20th century, including G. E. Moore, A. N. Whitehead, and later Wittgenstein, who was his student from 1912–13.

CHECKING THE FACTS
*Members of the Vienna Circle believed that the true meaning of a statement is revealed when we ask ourselves what we have to do to establish its truth or falsehood, that the meaning of a statement can be revealed by its mode of verification. This man at the College of Arms is collecting information to identify the details of heraldic insignia.*

Among the groups that took up Russell's approach and developed it was one that came into existence in Vienna in the 1920s and became known as the Vienna Circle. It consisted more of scientists and mathematicians than of philosophers, and its chief concern was to establish the philosophical foundations of a scientific worldview. Theirs was a philosophy that became known as Logical Positivism. It contended that the true meaning of a statement was uncovered when we asked ourselves: "What would we have to do to establish the truth or falsehood of this statement?" In other words, what observable difference does its truth or falsehood make to the way things actually are?

*"The method consists in an attempt to build a bridge between the world of sense and the world of science"*

BERTRAND RUSSELL

### VERIFIABLE STATEMENTS
*Logical Positivists held that statements that make no difference to anything have no content. Only verifiable statements are meaningful. The advertising slogan "Put a tiger in your tank" is an effective metaphor, but has no meaning empirically.*

A statement that purports to be about reality but whose truth or falsehood makes no observable difference to anything has no content, no meaning – it is not saying anything. In this belief they had something fundamentally in common with the American Pragmatists, but their formulation of it was tighter: only statements that are empirically verifiable are empirically meaningful; and the actual meaning of any given statement is revealed by the mode of its verification.

With this scalpel the Logical Positivists cut away most of the high-flown nonsense they had inherited from the past, not least from the by-now-decadent tradition of German idealism. Its dissection of religious ways of talking about the world, and also of the political discourse of the rising Fascist ideology in the German-speaking world of that day, was ruthless. Here was a philosophy with special appeal to the iconoclastic young. The book that introduced it to the English-speaking world, *Language, Truth, and Logic* (1936), was written by someone still in his early twenties, A. J. Ayer. With the rise of the Nazis to power, in Austria as well as in Germany (the two countries merged under Hitler in 1938), the members of the Vienna Circle were scattered, mostly to the United States and Britain, where they exercised a major influence over a whole generation.

## COMMON SENSE
Meanwhile, in Britain, a near-contemporary and lifelong friend of Russell's called G. E. Moore had been pursuing the analysis of statements in ordinary language using neither science nor technical logic as his yardstick but common sense. This developed, largely through the intermediacy of a figure called J. L. Austin, into a mode of philosophy that was eventually to displace Logical Positivism. It became known as "linguistic philosophy" or "linguistic analysis", and its criterion was the ordinary use of language. The Logical Positivists had been mistaken, said the linguistic analysts, in trying to force the straightjacket of scientific standards on all forms of utterance. Umpteen different sorts of spontaneous discourse go to make up human life, and each one has its own logic. Philosophical problems are conceptual confusions that arise when a form of utterance appropriate to one mode

### MISUSE OF LANGUAGE
*The Logical Positivists were unsparing in their dissection of the bombastic rhetoric of Nazi propaganda (such as the above poster) and they became an effective part of the critique of Fascist ideology. After the Nazis came to power in Austria in 1938, the members of the Vienna Circle were forced to emigrate – mostly to the United States and Britain*

**THE USES OF LANGUAGE**
*Linguistic philosophers argue that many forms of spontaneous discourse – each with its own logic – go to make up human life, and that confusions occur when a mode of utterance is used in the wrong context. For example, these men working on the stock trading floor are using a series of hand gestures that would be entirely inappropriate in a declaration of love.*

**G. E. MOORE**
*The British philosopher George Edward Moore (1873–1958) was professor of philosophy at Cambridge University from 1925–39. In his most famous book,* Principia Ethica *(1903), which was particularly influential on members of the Bloomsbury Group, he analyzes the moral question "What is good?" Moore's analytic approach to ethical problems was very influential among English-speaking philosophers.*

of discourse is mistakenly used in the wrong context. The task of the philosopher is to unpick such confusions, employing as his criterion the ordinary uses of language. When he has shown how any such confusion has arisen he will have not so much solved the problem as dissolved it – all will have been made clear, and there will be seen to be no longer a problem.

## UNDERSTANDING THE WORLD

The attractiveness of linguistic philosophy received its greatest boost of all from the later work of Wittgenstein, a pupil of Russell's, whom we shall consider in the next chapter. But just as Logical Positivism eventually ran its course as the most fashionable philosophy among the Second World War generation in the English-speaking world, so linguistic philosophy ran its course among the generation after that, above all in Britain. Since then, philosophy in both countries has been less fashion-bound, and has taken its problems from an increasingly wide range of subject matter, by no means confined to the sciences. But the prevailing view of philosophy's task has continued to be the logical analysis of formulations in language, with a view to bringing hidden implications to light – and that is a task that was inaugurated by Russell.

Russell himself, however, came more and more to feel that philosophers after him were declining into what was essentially a decadent activity of analysis for its own sake - they had come to think of philosophy

## "THE SENSE OF REALITY IS VITAL IN LOGIC"

BERTRAND RUSSELL

as being analysis - when what he had intended was to apply the new logic of the 20th century to philosophy's traditional task of understanding the nature of the reality external to ourselves.

**RUSSELL'S INFLUENCE**
*Bertrand Russell was one of the most influential intellectual figures of the 20th century. He published books on a wide range of subjects, including philosophy, science, mathematics, ethics, sociology, education, history, religion, and politics. His works on mathematics and logic profoundly affected Western philosophy. In the last decades of his life Russell was active in the campaign against nuclear weapons and the Vietnam War.*

# WITTGENSTEIN AND LINGUISTIC PHILOSOPHY

## A PHILOSOPHY THAT DOES NOT GO BEYOND LANGUAGE AND LOGIC

*Wittgenstein produced two philosophies, both of them influential. In the later one linguistic analysis achieved its ultimate degree of refinement.*

> *"What we cannot speak about we must pass over in silence"*
>
> LUDWIG WITTGENSTEIN

ALTHOUGH LUDWIG WITTGENSTEIN (1889–1951) was born in Vienna, and wrote in German, he spent most of his career as a philosopher in Britain, at Cambridge University, and became a British citizen. Being three-quarters Jewish, he would not have been able to return to Austria in any case during the Nazi era. His father had been the richest steel magnate in Austria, and Ludwig inherited a fortune from him. He was one of five brothers, three of whom committed suicide, and the other, Paul, became an internationally famous pianist. Paul lost his right arm in World War I, whereupon he commissioned piano works for the left hand alone from the leading composers of the day, including concertos from Ravel and Prokofiev.

LUDWIG WITTGENSTEIN
*Before reading Bertrand Russell and going on to study mathematical philosophy at Cambridge in 1911, Wittgenstein studied engineering at Berlin from 1906–08, and did aeronautical research at Manchester from 1908.*

to Cambridge to study philosophy under Russell – who later wrote: "Getting to know Wittgenstein was one of the most exciting intellectual adventures of my life."

### THE BOUNDS OF SENSE
In his teens Wittgenstein had read Schopenhauer and come to the conclusion that Schopenhauer was, as he put it, fundamentally right. For the rest of his life he accepted a view of total reality that saw it as divided between, on the one hand, a realm of which we could have no conceptual understanding and about which we could therefore say nothing, and on the other hand this phenomenal world of our experience, which we could indeed talk about and attempt to understand. Intelligible philosophy, he always thought, had to confine itself to the world we could talk about, on pain of becoming meaningless nonsense if it stepped across the borderline.

PAUL WITTGENSTEIN
Ludwig Wittgenstein was the youngest of eight children, all of whom had artistic and intellectual talent. His brother Paul was a gifted concert pianist with an international reputation who continued to play even after losing an arm while serving as a lieutenant in the Austrian army during World War I. Paul Wittgenstein is pictured here in 1934 on board the SS *Majestic* in New York after arriving for a concert tour.

### EXCITING ADVENTURE
Ludwig grew up fascinated by machinery, and received an education based firmly on physics and mathematics. It was to study aeronautical engineering that he came to England in 1908, and spent three years at Manchester University. While there he became fascinated by what were in fact philosophical questions about the mathematics he was using. This caused him to read Bertrand Russell's *Principles of Mathematics*. It came as a revelation. He paid a visit to Frege in Germany to discuss it, and on Frege's advice he gave up his place at Manchester and went

### LANGUAGE AND REALITY
However, at first he saw in the pathbreaking work of Frege and Russell a possibility of putting Schopenhauer's view of the phenomenal world on more secure foundations, foundations not only of epistemology but of logic. This in turn made it possible to explain how it is that the world is

escribable in language, and thus to explain the relationship between language and reality. And, as a next step, this would make it possible for us to map out in principle what the limits were to what could intelligibly be expressed in language – and therefore what the limits were to intelligible conceptual thought. Given that Schopenhauer was "fundamentally right", these were the only important tasks left for philosophy to perform. Wittgenstein's early philosophy, then, was based on a revised version of the Kantian-Schopenhauerian programme of trying to establish the limits of what is apprehensible to human beings. Wittgenstein set out to work through it again in terms of the new 20th-century developments in logic and the analysis of language.

## LOGICAL FORM

This is the substance of Wittgenstein's first book, *Tractatus Logico-Philosophicus* (1921). The forbidding title was suggested to him by G. E. Moore, and seems to have been an allusion to Spinoza's *Tractatus Theologico-Politicus*. Wittgenstein's book is almost always referred to simply as the *Tractatus*. Wittgenstein honestly believed that with this book he had cleared up all the outstanding problems that remained to be dealt with in philosophy, so he turned away and did other things. His book became the bible of the Vienna Circle, and powerfully influenced a whole generation in philosophy. However, while it was doing this, Wittgenstein himself was coming to the conclusion that it was importantly mistaken. So, with some reluctance at first, he returned to the world of Cambridge philosophy in 1929, and remained there until his death in 1951.

During this second period he published virtually nothing; but after his death a mass of writings appeared, in volume after volume. The most important of these was *Philosophical Investigations*, published in 1953. In Britain, at least, it has probably been the most influential single work of philosophy since World War II. It has spread Wittgenstein's name outside philosophy into fields ranging from

sociology to literary criticism, and has made him one of the intellectual icons of the age. Wittgenstein, then, produced two different philosophies in the course of his life, each of which had great influence.

> ## "NAMING IS SOMETHING LIKE ATTACHING A LABEL TO TO A THING"
>
> LUDWIG WITTGENSTEIN

They are usually referred to as "the early Wittgenstein" and "the later Wittgenstein". What he himself came to feel was most wrong with his early philosophy was its so-called picture theory of meaning. This term rested on an analogy

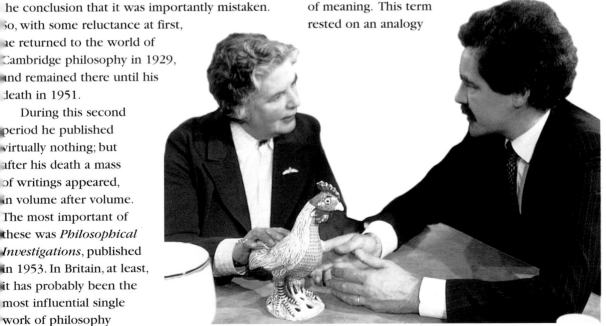

### LANGUAGE AND REALITY
*Wittgenstein used the work of Frege and Russell to formulate a more logical explanation of Schopenhauer's view of the phenomenal world. This enabled him to explain how the world can be described in language, and the relationship between language and reality. It was then possible for him to chart the limits to language and conceptual thought.*

### TRACTATUS
Throughout World War I Wittgenstein wrote down his thoughts on logic and philosophy in notebooks carried in his rucksack. The resulting book, *Tractatus*, was eventually published in 1921. Although only 75 pages long, it covers a vast range of topics, most notably the conception of the limits of language.

### MARGARET STONBOROUGH-WITTGENSTEIN
*Ludwig's parents and his seven siblings were all extremely gifted, both artistically and intellectually. His sister Margaret (1882–1958) in particular was a great influence on him. She introduced him to the work of Schopenhauer, was a patron of the arts, maintained a correspondence with Sigmund Freud, and had her portrait painted by Gustav Klimt in 1905.*

with painting. A small piece of canvas is a totally different sort of object from an expanse of countryside, yet a painter is able to make the former represent the latter with immediate recognizability by placing certain patches of colour on it in the same relationship to one another as corresponding elements are related to one another in the landscape. To this set of internal relationships common to both Wittgenstein gave the name "logical form", and he said that it was because the logical form was the same in both cases that the one was able to represent the other. Similarly, he argued, we are able to assemble words, which stand for things, into sentences that have the same logical form as the states of affairs that the sentences describe, and are thus able to represent reality accurately (or of course inaccurately) in language. So it is logical form that enables us to talk about the world.

## FORMS OF LIFE

Later, Wittgenstein came to feel that he had picked on one of a great many tasks that language is able to perform, and generalized a whole theory of meaning from it. Language can do so many other things besides the picturing of reality: it can give orders (this was his own first counter-example) and do all sorts of other things that cannot be said to picture anything.

To explain how meaning works he dropped this metaphor of a picture and adopted instead the metaphor of a tool. Language, he said, is a tool that can be used for an indefinite number of different tasks, and its meanings consist of all the various things that can be done with it. If you take an individual word or concept, its meaning consists of the sum total of its possible uses, which may be very various. There is not necessarily any "one thing" that it "stands for": its meaning is unlikely to wear a single face, though there will probably be a family resemblance among its many faces. But when you have given a full account of what can be done with it you have exhaustively described its

meaning: there is nothing else left over, so to speak. Such an account rejects two traditional theories of meaning. One is that specific words stand for specific things, and have fixed meanings: the true situation is far more protean and fluid than that. The other is that words derive their meanings from the intentions of their users, so that to understand what someone says you need to know what is in

# "THE MEANING OF A WORD IS ITS USE IN LANGUAGE"

LUDWIG WITTGENSTEIN

his mind. Language is public, Wittgenstein insisted. We learn it, and how to use it, from other people, in social situations. There could be no such thing, he says, as a private language: it would contradict the very nature of language.

In fact, Wittgenstein believed that words derived their meanings ultimately from whole forms of life. There is, for example, a whole world of scientific

**RUDOLPH CARNAP**
*The German philosopher Rudolph Carnap (1891–1970) was one of the leading figures of the Logical Positivist school of thought. He made important contributions to the philosophy of science, logic, and the theory of probability. In 1926 he was invited by Moritz Schlick to join the Vienna Circle – a group who met to discuss philosophical issues, in particular the writings of Wittgenstein – and he became one of its more influential figures. Carnap's most important work is* The Logical Structure of the World *(1928).*

### THE PICTURE THEORY OF MEANING
*Although the canvas is a very different sort of object from that which is being painted, the artist can represent the scene by his use of colour so that the two share the same "logical form". In the same way, Wittgenstein believed, words can represent reality if, again, both share the same logical form.*

**LANGUAGE IS PUBLIC**
*According to Wittgenstein, there is no such thing as a private language; we learn language, and how to use it, from social situations – like the crowd gathered around this orator at Speakers Corner, London.*

activity, and scientific terms derive their meanings from the ways they are used within this world – and these may well shift over time. Similarly there is a whole world of religious activity that has its own language, and a world of musical activity, and a business world, and a military world, and a theatrical world, and so on. What is apparently the same concept may function quite differently in different such worlds. For example, what counts as "evidence" is quite different to a lawyer, an historian, and a physicist. Hearsay is not admissible as evidence in a court of law, whereas it is sometimes the only evidence an historian has, in which case he may make judicious use of it, while for a physicist the question of hearsay does not even arise – there is no hearsay in physics. It was this aspect of Wittgenstein's philosophy that was first seen to be a useful tool by sociologists and anthropologists, and was taken up by some of them.

## PHILOSOPHY AS LANGUAGE

There was a period in the middle third of the 20th century when Wittgenstein dominated philosophy in Cambridge, and J. L. Austin dominated it in Oxford, and their methods overlapped. Both saw philosophical problems not as presented to us by the fundamental mysteries of the world in which we find ourselves – time, space, matter, causal connection, and so on – but as confusions into which we stumble as a result of our misuse of language – as it might be, say, using the term "evidence" in one context in a way that would have been appropriate only in another, and thereby getting ourselves into a logical muddle. The example is a very simple one, to make the point: the kind of confusions philosophers concerned themselves with were on the whole much subtler than this. The philosopher's task, they thought, was to straighten out all such muddles by a painstakingly careful analysis of our use of language. This produced many worthwhile empirical studies of language, and provided opportunities for displays of brilliance and subtlety in analysis, which gave immense pleasure to the people doing it. But the whole approach looked no further than language and logic for its problems. It offered a rationale

THE ANALYSIS OF LANGUAGE
*Wittgenstein saw philosophical problems as the result of confusions caused by the misuse of language. The soldiers above are learning to defuse bombs – any ambiguity here could be fatal.*

THE MEANING OF WORDS
*Wittgenstein believed that words derive their meanings from the worlds in which they are used. What is apparently the same concept in the world of opera may function very differently in the worlds of business, religion, or science.*

for this. Empirical problems, it said, were to be tackled by empirical methods, whether those of common sense, the appropriate science, politics, the judicial system, or whatever. Contrary to what so many people had believed in the past, philosophy had nothing to contribute at this level. Its task was to sort out conceptual problems, to analyse and clarify concepts and their use. On this basis, much philosophy in the English-speaking world came to be involved solely with language, its particular concerns being problems concerning meaning, reference, and truth.

## SPEECH AS ACTION

However, after a certain honeymoon period, more and more people in the world of professional philosophy itself, while fully appreciating the merits of this approach, came to feel that it was unduly narrow, too often inclined to topple over into scholasticism. When A. J. Ayer described J. L. Austin's work as arid there were many colleagues who agreed. The tendency today among analytical philosophers is increasingly to apply their formidable techniques of analysis to problems outside the confines of logic and language – in fact across a whole range of subject matter that

utterance of words. He usually began his analysis of a statement by asking: "What would somebody be doing if he said this? And in what circumstances would it actually be used?" And he contended that if there were no imaginable circumstances in which the statement would be used then it had no meaning. One kind of speech-act that he identified caught peoples' fancy especially, and that was what he called performative utterances. These are statements which themselves perform the actions they describe. Examples are "I thank you", "I congratulate you", "I promise", and "I apologize".

## THE LANGUAGE-CONSCIOUS CENTURY

Austin's name, however, has not entered the general culture, whereas Wittgenstein's has. The ingenuity and subtlety of Wittgenstein's analyses of linguistic meanings endeared him to a number of literary critics, just as his ultimate location of these meanings in forms of life endeared him to sociologists and anthropologists. For reasons that extend far beyond philosophy, and which affect all the arts and all academic subjects, the 20th century has been more concerned with language, and more self-conscious about its use, than any century before. This being so, the linguistic philosophy that developed during the 20th century found itself in keeping with the temper of its time, and received a readier acceptance from the intellectual community in general than it is likely to have done in any former period.

J. L. AUSTIN
The English philosopher John Langshaw Austin (1911–60) was White's Professor of Moral Philosophy at the University of Oxford, from 1952–1960, and the dominating figure in Oxford philosophy. Austin was a pioneer in the investigation of how words are used by ordinary speakers, and his thinking had a great influence in the period following World War II, particularly his notion of speech as behaviour.

hilosophers have rarely considered in the past, ncluding music, sex, and social policies on matters oncerning race and gender, in addition to the more raditional kinds of problem which continue to e pursued. The approach, however, is still through he analysis of concepts and modes of utterance haracteristically used in those fields. To do Austin ustice, he contributed a particularly fruitful idea o philosophy, that of the "speech-act". He pointed ut that every time we say something we are doing

## "IF A LION COULD TALK, WE COULD NOT UNDERSTAND HIM"

LUDWIG WITTGENSTEIN

omething: describing, denying, encouraging, rdering, asking, suggesting, explaining, warning, nd so on and so forth. It may well be impossible o talk at all without doing some such thing; and ustin claimed to be able to distinguish a thousand ifferent actions that people perform by their

In no previous era had any philosopher of name and note believed that the subject matter proper to philosophy was linguistic, and indeed many of the outstanding philosophers of the 20th century did not believe it either. Reference has been made already to the fact that Bertrand Russell, who fathered the approach, declared himself dumfounded that anyone could consider it an adequate conception of philosophy; and there were other major figures, their methods quite different from Russell's, who were pursuing quite different paths.

SAYING AND DOING
One category of speech that Austin differentiated was what he called "performative utterances". These were usually utterances the very making of which performed the act they designated. Common examples are "I thank you", or "I congratulate you".

# EXISTENTIALISM
## FROM KIERKEGAARD TO HEIDEGGER

*The individual finds his own identity a problem, and hopes to uncover meaning in life through investigating the mystery of his own existence.*

> *"Life can only be understood backwards, but it must be lived forwards"*
> SØREN KIERKEGAARD

THE MOST FASHIONABLE philosophy in Europe during the period immediately following World War II was existentialism. It flourished not only in universities but in the worlds of quality journalism and café intellectuals, in poems, novels, plays, and films, even in cabarets and night clubs. It was unquestionably one of the outstanding intellectual movements of the 20th century, and remains a significant element in contemporary thinking, in addition to leaving behind it a number of long-lasting plays and novels.

One curious thing about this is that the fashion came an unusually long time after the philosophy. The leading existentialist philosopher of the 20th century, Martin Heidegger, had produced his most important work during the 1920s; and the thinkers next to him in the line of influence were very much farther back than that, in the 19th century: Kierkegaard and Nietzsche (for Nietzsche see pp. 172–79). The sudden fashion for existentialist ideas that seemed to arise almost out of nowhere in the 1940s and 1950s was in fact rooted in a process of reaction against the experience of Nazi domination and occupation, from which Europe was beginning to emerge.

### ME AND GOD
The founder of existentialism is generally held to be a Danish thinker called Søren Kierkegaard (1813–55). He wrote at a time when the dominant philosopher of the age was the recently dead Hegel. Hegel, said Kierkegaard, explained everything in terms of huge great sweeps of ideas in which actual things,

**SØREN KIERKEGAARD**
*The founder of existentialism was born, and lived most of his life, in Copenhagen. His thought inspired many 20th-century philosophers, particularly the Existentialists. Kierkegaard believed that no system of thought could explain the unique experience of the individual.*

individual entities, are not even so much as mentioned, whereas the fact is it is only individual things that exist. Abstractions, generalizations, do not exist in the same sense: they are helps that we invent for ourselves in order to be able to think an-

> *"THE SUPREME PARADOX OF ALL THOUGHT IS THE ATTEMPT TO DISCOVER SOMETHING THAT THOUGHT CANNOT THINK"*
> SØREN KIERKEGAARD

make connections. But if we want to understand what does exist we have to find some way of coming to terms with uniquely individual entities, because that is all there is. This is especially true of human beings. Hegel had seen the individual as fulfilling himself only when absorbed into the larger and more abstract entity of the organic state, whereas in fact, said Kierkegaard, it is the individual himself who is the supreme moral entity, and therefore it is the personal, subjective aspects of human life that are the most important. Because of the transcending value of moral considerations the purely philosophical tradition of existentialism, the one that makes no appeal to religious faith: humanist existentialism. This too has its 19th-century roots in the work of Kierkegaard, but then also in the work of Nietzsche, who was an atheist. Its most distinguished representative in the 20th century was Martin Heidegger.

## TAINTED BY NAZISM

Martin Heidegger (1889–1976) was born in Baden, Germany, in the year Wittgenstein was born in Vienna. He lived in Germany all his life, and also was an academic all his life. As a student at Freiburg he studied under the renowned Edmund Husserl (1859-1938), and was trained in Husserl's special method, which we shall outline in a moment. He made central use of this method in his masterpiece *Being and Time*, which was published in 1927 and dedicated to Husserl.

Heidegger joined the Nazi party, and when the Nazis came to power in 1933 he became the first National Socialist rector of the University of Freiburg. Husserl, however, was a Jew, or at least partly Jewish; so at that stage Heidegger publicly repudiated his connection with Husserl. This action blotted his personal reputation for the rest of his life. He resigned as rector a year later; but when the Germans were defeated at the end of the World War II he was forbidden to teach for six years because of his Nazi past. This has been controversial ever since, and is much used against him by people who disagree with his philosophy. But in truth being a Nazi no more disqualified him from

**DECISION-MAKING**
*The couple above have decided to get married, one of the most significant personal decisions many people have to make. Kierkegaard proposed that it is the individual that is the supreme moral entity and that decision-making is the most important human activity – through making choices we create our own lives.*

most important human activity is decision-making: it is through the choices we make that we create our lives and become ourselves. For Kierkegaard all this had religious implications: he believed, in the central tradition of Protestant Christianity, that what mattered more than anything else was the relationship of the individual soul to God.

## TWO EXISTENTIALISMS

Many thinkers have gone along with Kierkegaard up to the point at which he brings God in, but have not shared his belief in God. Because of this, two parallel traditions of existentialism have developed side by side: Christian existentialism and humanist existentialism. Both have been at their most productive in the 20th century. This book will not attempt to go into the religious traditions of existentialism, except to remark that some of the most original theologians of the 20th century have been in a significant sense existentialist thinkers who felt themselves indebted to Kierkegaard. These include Karl Barth, Paul Tillich, and Rudolf Bultmann. Our concern in this book is with the

**KARL BARTH**
One of the most influential theologians of the 20th century, Swiss-born Karl Barth (1886–1968) initiated a radical change in Protestant thought. He held chairs of theology in Germany at Göttingen, Münster, and Bonn, vigorously opposing the rise of National Socialism. Barth drafted the Barmen Declaration, which became the doctrinal basis of the anti-Nazi Confessing Church. His *Church Dogmatics* (1932–62) makes Jesus' resurrection the focal point of Christianity.

*"Man alone of all beings, when addressed by the voice of Being, experiences the marvel of all marvels: that what-is is"*
MARTIN HEIDEGGER

**HEIDEGGER'S KEY WORKS**

What is a Thing?
(1926)

Being and Time
(1927)

Kant and the Problem of Metaphysics
(1929)

What is Metaphysics?
(1929)

What is Philosophy?
(1956)

**MARTIN HEIDEGGER**
*A leading exponent of existentialism, Heidegger remains a continuing influence on intellectual thought. He originally trained to be a Jesuit before studying with Husserl and becoming his successor at the University of Freiburg. His support for Nazism damaged his reputation.*

**BEING AND TIME**
Hard to penetrate because of its difficult style, *Being and Time* (1927) is Heidegger's greatest work, in which Heidegger uses Husserl's phenomenology to explore the structures of human existence. His declared purpose was to ask "What is the meaning of Being?" The book strongly influenced Sartre and other existentialists.

being an interesting thinker than others were disqualified from being interesting thinkers by being Communists. The idea that a great thinker must be a morally admirable human being is romantic, indeed childish, and is in any case contradicted by too many examples in the history of philosophy for us to take it seriously.

### EXAMINE ONLY EXPERIENCE

*Being and Time* presented itself as volume one of what was to be a two-volume work, but it was never finished. Instead, Heidegger's philosophy changed direction; so there is what has since become known as "the early Heidegger" and "the late Heidegger". The later Heidegger contains no single masterpiece, and tends to put forward Heidegger's ideas in the process of discussing other peoples', above all those of Nietzsche and the pre-Socratics – though also the work of some poets, especially Novalis. *Being and Time* remains Heidegger's acknowledged masterpiece, and has come to be regarded as the fountainhead of 20th-century existentialism.

The use of Husserl's method is so important to *Being and Time* that before the contents of that book can be discussed this method needs to be

> " **I EXIST, AND ALL THAT IS NOT-I IS MERE PHENOMENON DISSOLVING INTO PHENOMENAL CONNECTIONS**"
>
> EDMUND HUSSERL

understood. It can be approached in the following way. Husserl agreed with Descartes that for each of us there is one thing whose existence is indubitably certain, and that is our own conscious awareness; therefore if we want to build our conception of reality on rock-solid foundations, that is the place for us to start. But he also agreed with Hume that if I look at, say, a table, my awareness is of the table, not of myself having the experience of looking at the table. In ordinary circumstances my consciousness always takes this form: I am directly aware of objects, but not of myself as an object. However, all attempts to prove that these objects exist independently of my awareness seem doomed to failure. It is notoriously impossible to prove the very existence of the external world.

At this point Husserl makes an ingenious suggestion. Do not let us get bogged down, he says, in insoluble problems about the independent existence of the objects of awareness. It is indubitably certain that they exist *as objects of consciousness for us*, whatever other existential status they may have or lack. So let us investigate them as objects of awareness

RENÉ MAGRITTE, *THE TIREDNESS OF LIFE*, 1927
*Husserl agreed with Hume that when one looks at an object, a table for example, one is aware of the object and not of oneself. He proposed that philosophy should base itself on the method of examining what is directly experienced, and should not make unprovable assumptions about the existence of anything else. This approach became known as phenomenology.*

**EDMUND HUSSERL**
*Edmund Husserl is regarded as the founder of Phenomenology, a philosophy that concentrates on what is consciously experienced. Its influence extends to such fields as the philosophy of science, the philosophy of language, the philosophy of religion, and to the social sciences.*

the absolute certainty that they exist as such, without making any other assumptions about them. As objects of awareness they are as directly open to our investigation as anything could possibly be. So let us simply put on one side (in brackets, so to speak) the unanswerable questions, and make progress with what we are so well equipped to investigate.

## OUR LIVED-IN WORLD

Thus Husserl formed a whole new approach to philosophy devoted to the examination of consciousness and its objects. It was a systematic analysis of experience, and became known as phenomenology, because it treated everything as phenomena. The term has acquired also a general use in philosophy: people talk about "the phenomenology" of an activity, any activity at all, and this means a description or analysis of the conscious experiences involved.

To give an example, the philosophy of mathematics is about such questions as the logical foundations of mathematics, and the nature of number, proof, and so on, whereas the phenomenology of mathematics is about mathematics as a conscious activity, and the experiences involved in doing it. And of course there is a phenomenology of everything, not only

of our perception of material objects but also of the arts, religion, the sciences, and indeed of things "internal" to ourselves, such as our own thoughts, feelings, memories, pains, and so on. The sum total of things actually experienced by us is the sum total of what we are indubitably certain of, though only as phenomena, experience. Nevertheless, this is our world, the one we do in fact experience, the one we actually live in; and for this reason the term *Lebenswelt*, which means literally life's-world, was coined for it by Husserl. The sum total of possibility offered by Husserl's philosophy is an exhaustive investigation of our *Lebenswelt*.

## WHAT IS EXISTENCE?

Heidegger studied this approach under Husserl himself. But the specific problem to which he applied it was one that he reached from a different starting point. He was struck by the fact that ever since Descartes the problem of knowledge had been treated by Western philosophy as its central problem. This Cartesian approach saw reality as split into mind and matter, subject and object, observer and observed, knower and known. The young Heidegger may well not have known of the work of the American Pragmatists, but his objection to traditional epistemology had much in common with theirs. He considered it untrue to the realities of the situation. We are not separate from the world,

**SILENT THOUGHTS AND FEELINGS**
*This atmospheric, late 19th-century oil painting by André Collin,* Poor People, *powerfully evokes a mood of introspection. Sitting in silence, the characters appear to have become absorbed in the contemplation of their own inner feelings, without any sense of self-awareness.*

**AWARENESS OF EXISTENCE**
*It was Heidegger's belief that we all have immediate awareness of our own existence. He then suggested that we could not have this conscious awareness unless there were some sphere of activity for it to be happening in. "Being", and some sort of "world", are therefore inseparable.*

looking at it. We are ourselves an integral part of the world; and our being cannot even be conceived of as other than in a world of *some* kind. On deeper reflection the central mystery is not knowledge but being, existence. What is this existence that we find ourselves in, or with? What is it for something to exist? How is it that anything exists at all? Why is there not simply nothing?

### THE ANALYSIS OF BEING

The existence of which we have immediate, indubitable awareness is our own. Therefore, thought Heidegger, the way to address ourselves to the problem of existence is to carry out a phenomenological analysis of what it is we are aware of when we are aware of our own existence. And this is how his book *Being and Time* starts. In a slow, painstaking, systematic, almost deliberately pedestrian way he separates out the distinguishable strands that go to make up our conscious awareness of our own existence. For instance, he shows that we could not have it at all unless there were some sort of field of awareness, some scene, or screen, or setting, some world for it to be happening in; and therefore our being is inherently "worldish". For us, at least, being and some sort of world are inseparable. Also, we could not have it unless there were an

apprehension that something or other was going on; but this necessitates the dimension of time; therefore the existence of which we are aware is inherently temporal. Again, we could not have an awareness of our own existence unless it impinged

## "WE ARE OURSELVES THE ENTITIES TO BE ANALYSED"

MARTIN HEIDEGGER

on our consciousness: it must needs concern us in some way, at least minimally, for us to be aware of it at all: concern is an irreducible element. And so on and so forth. We might have supposed

**BEING IS TIME**
*Heidegger called his most important book* Being and Time *because it comes to the conclusion that being is time. Existence is, so to speak, embodied time, objectified time, and human beings are, literally, time incarnate. When it is put in this way it is easy to see how this philosophy came to exercise a profound influence on Christian theology.*

when we started out that our awareness of our own existence is something so immediate, direct, and transparent that it is not capable of any further analysis, but Heidegger refutes this by producing a rich and deeply insightful analysis of it. The conclusion he finally arrives at is that, in its most important aspects, our mode of being has a three-fold structure whose elements correspond to past, present, and future time, so that in the very last analysis being is time – hence the title of the book.

## BECOMING OURSELVES

From these beginnings Heidegger goes on to analyse the human situation. Far from us starting out as isolated individuals who then face the problem of making contact with other people, our existence from the beginning is a shared and social one, and our problem is that of becoming individuals, finding an authentic mode of personal existence. We are all the time pressing into an unknowable future, and having to make choices without any certainty about their outcomes. Guilt and anxiety fall to our lot, especially anxiety in the face of death. We long for our lives to have some metaphysical ground or foundation, and also to have some meaning; yet we have no assurance that any of these things actually exists objectively; and if they do not exist, our lives may just be ultimately meaningless, absurd – or else any meaning that they have is meaning that we give them.

## MEANING WITHOUT GOD

These themes came to dominate existentialism in the 20th century, which took on Nietzsche's challenge and tried to confront a universe without God. It tried to find a basis for values in a world without any objective significance, and without any goals or purposes of its own. It tried to find ways of discovering or creating meaning in the fleeting lives of individuals who had no afterlife. After World War II these ideas were popularized to a degree that rarely happens with any philosophy. By that time the international centre for them was

EXISTENTIAL ANGST
*We have to make choices, Heidegger argued, without any certainty as to their outcomes – the only thing we can be certain of is that we face a life of guilt and anxiety. The Scream (1893), by the Norwegian painter Edvard Munch, powerfully expresses the artist's anxiety and pessimism, caused by the confusion and loneliness of existence.*

Paris, and most of the well-known existentialist writers, moving on now from Heidegger, were French. The one who made existentialism known all over the world was Jean-Paul Sartre, who was not a philosopher alone but also a novelist and playwright of international standing. We shall continue the story of existentialism with him in the next chapter.

# BERGSON AND RECENT FRENCH PHILOSOPHY

## PHILOSOPHY AS A BRANCH OF LITERATURE

*In France, philosophy has developed in the 20th century as part of the general literary culture, without so much specialist interest in science, logic, and analysis.*

> *"When we think this present as going to be, it exists not yet; and when we think it as existing, it is already past"*
> HENRI BERGSON

HENRI BERGSON (1859–1941) was born in Paris to an English mother and a Polish-Jewish father, and grew up with French as his mother tongue. He spent his working life as a university teacher of philosophy, but was such an attractive writer that he was widely read and influential outside universities. In 1927 he was awarded the Nobel Prize for Literature. Among his best-known books are *Time and Free Will* (1889), *Matter and Memory* (1896), and *Creative Evolution* (1907). In the latter years of his life his thought took a religious turn, and he may have been received into the Roman Catholic church shortly before his death; if so, the move was deliberately delayed and kept secret, because he did not want to seem to desert the Jewish people while they were being persecuted by the Nazis, and while France was under German occupation.

### INTUITION

Bergson believed that human beings are primarily to be explained in terms of the evolutionary process. It seemed to him that from the beginning the function of the senses in living organisms has been not to provide the organism with "representations" of its surroundings but to stimulate reactions of a life-preserving character. First sensory organs, then central nervous systems, then minds, developed across countless ages as part of the organism's equipment for survival, and always as adjuncts to behaviour; and to this day what they provide us with are not objective pictures of our surroundings but messages that cause us to behave in certain ways. Our conception of our

HENRI BERGSON
*During World War I, Bergson undertook several diplomatic missions, including one to America. When the League of Nations was formed in 1920, he became the first president of its Commission for Intellectual Cooperation.*

surroundings is not at all like what a set of detailed photographs would be like: it is highly selective, always pragmatic, and always self-serving. We pay attention almost only to what matters to us, and the conception we form of our surroundings is built up in terms of our interests, the overriding one being our own safety. Only if this is realized can the true nature of human knowledge be understood.

As for evolution, Bergson believed that the mechanical processes of random selection are inadequate to explain what occurs. There seems to be some sort of persistent drive towards greater individuality and yet at the same time greater complexity, in spite of the fact that these always mean increased vulnerability and risk. To this drive Bergson gives the name *élan vital*, which has been freely translated as "life force".

LIFE FORCE
*Within evolution, Bergson argued, there is a persistent drive towards greater complexity and individuality. Bergson called this drive the* élan vital, *or "life force".*

Bergson believes that, because everything is changing all the time, the flow of time is fundamental to all reality. We actually experience this flow within ourselves in the most direct and immediate way, not through concepts, and not through our senses. Bergson calls this kind of unmediated knowledge "intuition". He believes that we also have intuitive knowledge with regard to our decisions to act, and therefore immediate knowledge of our own possession of free will. However, this immediate knowledge of the inner nature of things is quite different in character from the knowledge that our intellect gives us of the world external to ourselves.

## REALITY FLOWS

What our intellect provides us with are always the materials required for action, and what we want to do is to be able to predict and control events, so our intellect presents us with a world we can handle, and use, a world broken up into manageable units, separate objects in marked-off measures of space, and also marked-off measures of time. This is the world of everyday affairs, business, common sense, and also of science. Its extraordinary usefulness to us is displayed in the triumphs of modern technology. But it is all a product of our way of dealing with the world, in exactly the same sort of way, and for the same sort of reasons, as a map-maker will represent a living landscape in terms of a squared-off geometrical grid. It is undeniably useful, prodigiously so, and enables us to do all sorts of practical things that we want to do; but it does not show us reality. Reality is a continuum. In real time there are no instants. Real time is a continuous flow, without separable units, not marked off in measurable lengths. Similarly with space: in real space there are no points, and no separate and specific places. All these are devices of the mind.

## BEING AND TIME

So we live simultaneously in two worlds. In the inner world of our immediate knowledge all is continuum, and all is flux, perpetual flow. In the outer world presented to us by our intellects there are separate objects occupying determinate positions in space for measurable periods of time. But of course that outer time, the time of clocks and calculation, is an intellectual construct, and is not at all the same as the "real" time of whose

**MANAGEABLE UNITS**
*Bergson believed that our intellect presents us with a world we can contend with, one of separate objects in marked-off measures of space and time. However, this manageable world does not show us reality.*

continuous flow we have direct inner experience. At the culminating point of his philosophy Bergson identifies this inwardly experienced flow of time with life itself, and with the life force, the *élan vital* that carries the process of evolution perpetually onward. It will be remembered that the philosophy of Heidegger also culminated in the identification of being and time, though the two philosophers reached the same conclusion independently, and from completely different starting points.

In his own day Bergson had some very distinguished critics among contemporaries such as Bertrand Russell. Their chief complaint was that although Bergson made his ideas attractive with vivid analogies and poetic metaphors he did not

**REALITY IS A CONTINUOUS FLOW**
*Bergson concluded that the separate objects, or units, of the outer world are devices of the mind, and that "real time" is in fact a continuous flow with no separate units.*

> *"The movement of the stream is distinct from the river bed, although it must adopt its winding course"*
> HENRI BERGSON

**MARCEL PROUST**
*During his student days the French novelist, Marcel Proust (1871–1922), was directly influenced by the work of Henri Bergson. Proust's most famous novel, the autobiographical* Remembrance of Things Past *(1913–27), is an exploration of the nature of time, and also a reflection of French provincial life at the end of the 19th century. The book presents human experience not as chronological narrative, but through thought associations and the realization of memory.*

SIMONE DE BEAUVOIR
The French existentialist novelist and essayist Simone de Beauvoir (1908–86), who had a lifelong relationship with Sartre, was one of the founders of modern feminist philosophy. She is best known for her book *The Second Sex* (1949), in which she pleas for the abolition of the myth of the "eternal feminine".

---

SARTRE'S
KEY BOOKS

Nausea *(1938)*

The Psychology of Imagination *(1940)*

Being and Nothingness *(1943)*

Existentialism and Humanism *(1945)*

The Age of Reason *(1945)*

The Problem of Method *(1960)*

---

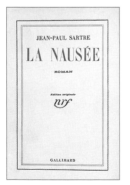

*NAUSEA*
Sartre wrote his first successful book, *Nausea* (*La Nausée*), during his years as a teacher in Le Havre. The book is written in the form of a diary and narrates the feelings of revulsion experienced by the main protagonist when faced with the world of matter – including his own body.

---

support them with much in the way of rational argument. He left them to commend themselves to the reader's intuitions. Furthermore, his critics complained, his ideas did not stand up very well to logical analysis. His defenders replied by saying that he possessed all these characteristics in common with the best creative writers, and that this was because he was offering insights rather than logical arguments. In either case, it is certain that his thought had wide appeal, and remains a distinctive element in 20th-century philosophy.

## NOVELIST AND PLAYWRIGHT

Many of the same characteristics were shared by Jean-Paul Sartre (1905–80), who possessed them in greater abundance. Not only was Sartre a brilliant writer, he was internationally famous as a playwright and novelist, something no other philosopher has achieved: those who came closest were Rousseau, who wrote two highly successful novels, and Camus, whom we shall come to in a moment. In 1964 Sartre was offered the Nobel Prize for Literature, but turned it down. It may be that his fame as a creative writer will outlive his fame as a philosopher.

Sartre was born in Paris and grew up as an exceedingly bookish child – he called an autobiographical volume about his childhood *Words* (1963). Unsurprisingly, perhaps, he became a professional teacher of philosophy. In 1938 he published a novel, *Nausea*, which is really a phenomenological account of a mind in the process of disintegration. In 1940 came his first important work of directly written philosophy. The French title means *The Imaginary*, but an uncomprehending English translation called it *The Psychology of Imagination*. World War II changed Sartre's life. After joining the French army he was captured and imprisoned by the Germans. In prison he studied Heidegger's philosophy, and wrote his first play. On his release he lived in occupied Paris, where he wrote his most important philosophical work, *Being and Nothingness* (1943).

The end of the war found him famous, partly as a philosopher but more for his two plays *Flies* and *No Exit*. His 1945 lecture *Existentialism and Humanism* launched existentialism on its legendary career of fashionability in post-war

## "HELL IS OTHER PEOPLE"

JEAN-PAUL SARTRE

Europe. At this point he renounced his academic career and became a full-time writer. His partner, Simone de Beauvoir, was the first internationally acclaimed feminist writer, with her book *The Second Sex* (1949). His other closest associates included the writer Albert Camus, who was awarded the Nobel Prize for Literature in 1957, and a fine philosopher called Maurice Merleau-Ponty, with whom Sartre founded the journal *Les Temps Modernes*. Sartre became deeply involved in revolutionary left-wing politics, often acting

JEAN-PAUL SARTRE
*Sartre was one of the leading proponents of existentialism. He believed that people's awareness of their own freedom induces in them anxiety, and that they take refuge from this anxiety in "bad faith". Sartre is pictured above at his flat on the Rue Bonaparte, Paris.*

as advocate or apologist for Communism. Calling himself now a historical materialist, he began writing a large-scale work, *Critique of Dialectical Reason*, which was aimed at reconciling existentialism and Marxism. He left it unfinished, but a single volume of it was published.

Sartre's history as a philosopher falls clearly into three distinguishable phases, each of which sits heavily under the influence of one or two other thinkers. Husserl dominates the work of his first period, which includes *Nausea*, *The Imaginary*, and *Sketch for a Theory of the Emotions* (1939). Heidegger dominates the second, which was Sartre's own most influential period, seeing the publication of *Being and Nothingness*

1943) and *Existentialism and
Humanism* (1945). Then Hegel and
Marx came to dominate the long final
period of Sartre's productivity. In the
first two of these periods, he was far
more famous than the people whose
ideas he was propagating, and this had
the result that these ideas came to be
more directly associated with him than
with them in the minds of many people.

## WE CREATE OURSELVES

Sartre's most significant personal
contribution, and the thing his
philosophy became best known
for, was the way he dramatized the
freedom of the individual. In a Godless
world, he said, we have no alternative
but to choose, and in that sense create,
our own values. Yet in doing this we
are laying down the ground-rules of
our own lives. And in doing *that* we are
determining how our own personalities
develop: we are creating ourselves.

Many people find this freedom and this
responsibility too terrifying to face, so they run
away from it by pretending that they are bound
by already existing norms and rules. But this is
what Sartre calls "bad faith". One really does have,
he says, "total choice of oneself"; and living to the
full means making that choice, and then living in
accordance with it: "commitment", as he called this.
Many young people found these ideas thrilling, as
also did large numbers of dissidents who longed
to opt out of society for whatever reason. However,
in his later, more Marxist phase, Sartre said that he
had exaggerated the extent to which the individual
could free himself from the pressures of the
society in which he lived.

## THE ABSURD

Sartre's friend Albert Camus (1913–60) was the
writer who coined the description "absurd" or "the
absurd" for the situation in which human beings
demand that their lives should have significance
in an indifferent universe which is itself totally
without meaning or purpose. It is a demand, Camus
insisted, that can never be met. But in that case
what is the point of living at all, once the sheer
meaninglessness of human life has been fully
understood and assimilated? He famously opened
his essay *The Myth of Sisyphus* (1942) with the
words: "There is but one truly serious philosophical
problem and that is suicide. Judging whether life is

**LIVING TO THE FULL**
*It is often the young who challenge the rules and regulations set out by
society. For this reason, many young people were thrilled by the freedom
conveyed in Sartre's statement that we all have "total choice of oneself".*

or is not worth living amounts to answering the
fundamental question of philosophy." He concludes
that to destroy oneself is a kind of capitulation.
In an open appeal to pride – "there is nothing equal
to the spectacle of human pride" – he calls
for a life of stoic refusal to accommodate
oneself to cosmic meaninglessness, a life
which in that sense is a form of rebellion
against one's cosmic circumstances.
Apart from *The Myth of Sisyphus* and
a book called *The Rebel* (1951) he
developed these ideas chiefly in a series
of novels: *The Stranger* (1942), *The
Plague* (1947), and *The Fall* (1956).
In 1960 he was killed in a car crash.
The novel he was working on at the
time, *The First Man*, was published,
unfinished, in 1994.

Camus, an unusually
attractive character, has
been described as "a saint
without a God". A poor
white from Algeria, when
he was denounced by the
French left for refusing to
support Algeria's National
Liberation Front his reply
was: " I believe in justice,
but I will defend my
mother before justice."

| CAMUS' KEY WORKS |
| --- |
| The Myth of Sisyphus *(1942)* |
| The Stranger *(1942)* |
| The Plague *(1947)* |
| The Rebel *(1951)* |
| The Fall *(1956)* |

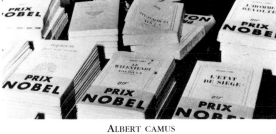

**ALBERT CAMUS**
*Camus' writings reflect the alienation and
disillusionment of the post-war intellectual, and owe
a great deal to existentialist thought. In 1957, at the
age of 44, Camus received the Nobel Prize for Literature.*

*"The world is not what I think, but what I live through"*

MAURICE
MERLEAU-PONTY

To a Communist friend he remarked: "Whatever happens, I would defend you against the firing squad, but you'd be obliged to approve if I were shot." In the end he broke off relations with Jean-Paul Sartre over Sartre's persistent apologetics for Communist terror.

## THE BODY'S VOICE

The least widely known but perhaps the best of the Paris-based philosophers of that time was Maurice Merleau-Ponty (1908–61). His most important books are *The Structure of Behaviour* (1942) and *The Phenomenology of Perception* (1945), especially the latter. His special contribution was to bring to philosophy a much needed acknowledgment of the importance of the human body. Both phenomenologists and existentialists had tended to write as if what each human being is, above all else, is a centre of conscious awareness, and therefore something that can be thought of as abstract or immaterial, though of course none of them actually said that. Merleau-Ponty insisted

MAURICE MERLEAU-PONTY
*Merleau-Ponty was one of the most significant contributors to phenomenology after Husserl. For him, perception was the source of knowledge and had to be studied before the conventional sciences.*

that it is fundamental to our identity as human beings that we are physical objects, each one of which has a different and unique location in space or time. Not only must everything that can ever be experienced by anyone be experienced through the unique physical apparatus of one such object: the whole of the rest of reality can be apprehended only from the perspective of its unique point of view. All this is still true even if we are more than just our bodies: we are perpetually aware of our bodies, and without them we cannot perceive or act. These things being so, is the human body to be regarded as subject or object? It is both – and yet, in a queer way, neither. It is not a disembodied subject of experience, because it is a physical object in the world, and yet it is not an object in the world just like all the other material objects, for it is a self-aware subject having experiences.

Merleau-Ponty wrote with great penetration and insight about the deep philosophical problems involved in subjectivity, including its inescapably perspectival and therefore inherently incomplete character. These problems present profound difficulties, and so his writings inevitably make serious demands on the reader. This has prevented them from achieving the same kind of fame and popularity as those of Camus and Sartre, but it is possible that they may be of higher and more lasting quality.

## ENTER STRUCTURALISM

When Jean-Paul Sartre died in 1980 more than 50,000 people attended his funeral. He had become that rare thing, a philosopher with a mass audience. But by that time he was no longer at the cutting edge of intellectual advance: the *avant-garde* had moved on. In the late 1960s structuralism had become fashionable in Paris, part of a more general approach to philosophy that has been called "the linguistic turn". Put at its simplest, structuralism is the view that any discourse of any kind, philosophical or otherwise, is a structure in language and that is all. The text does not present us with anything other than itself: there is nothing "beyond" the language. This led devotees of

A UNIQUE LOCATION IN SPACE AND TIME
*Merleau-Ponty was responsible for bringing to 20th-century philosophy an acknowledgment of the importance of the human body. In Berthe Morisot's* Woman and Child in a Garden *(1883–84) the two figures appear lost in their own unique location in time and space.*

structuralism to interpret texts primarily in terms of rules governing the various uses of language – to see them as *about* discourse, language, communication, and so on. This critical approach to texts became known as "deconstruction".

## OLD IDEAS RENEWED

In the 1960s and 70s Louis Althusser (1918–90) tried to integrate the dominant ideas of structuralism with Marxism. In doing so he overtook Sartre as the leading Marxist philosopher in the eyes of the intellectually adventurous. At the same time, and in a parallel way, Jacques Lacan (1901–81) brought a structuralist approach to the ideas of Freud and psychoanalysis. Lacan argued that the unconscious is literally "structured like a language", with the consequence that deconstruction provides us with the right way to understand it.

Michel Foucault (1926–84) formed the view that every kind of discourse is an attempt on the part of its user to exercise power over others, so that texts can be deconstructed successfully only if that fact is kept in mind; furthermore, that the personalities of those who exercise such power are shaped by what they do, and therefore that they too can be revealed and understood by a deconstructionist approach to what they say or write.

LOUIS ALTHUSSER
*Althusser was the leading Marxist philosopher of the 1960s and 70s. His most famous works include* For Marx *(1965) and* Reading Capital *(1965). Althusser argued that the ideology of the ruling class is a form of class control.*

JACQUES LACAN
*The French psychoanalyst Jacques Lacan reinterpreted Freud in terms of structural linguistics. As a result he became an important influence on structuralist thought.*

MICHEL FOUCAULT
*Foucault rejected phenomenology and existentialism. He believed that every kind of discourse is an attempt by the user to exercise power over others.*

JACQUES DERRIDA
*Derrida, the founder of deconstruction, came to prominence in the late 1960s. He is particularly concerned with the relationship between philosophy and language.*

These and other Paris-based philosophers stirred wide international interest, as their predecessors had done. But there was one important difference. Whereas Bergson, Camus, and Sartre had been superb writers – all three, for instance, had been offered the Nobel Prize for Literature – the structuralists and post-structuralists tended to write in tortuous prose: dense, intricate, opaque. Their style was derided by the analytic philosophers of the English-speaking world, who alleged that when these complicated sentences were unravelled and analysed they often turned out to be rhetorically hollow, saying something only vaguely focused, or perhaps saying nothing at all, or else something trivial, or false, or self-contradictory. When in 1992 Cambridge University gave an honorary degree to the leading structuralist of the day, Jacques Derrida, there was a public storm of protest from the philosophers who regarded it as a scandal. However, such controversy has helped to keep structuralism in the public eye.

The rhetorical nature of structuralism and post-structuralism, which can alienate other kinds of philosopher, is capable of having great appeal for people whose approach to language is not through logical analysis – for example, to students of literature.

> *"How can we be sure we are not impostors?"*
> JACQUES LACAN

SARTRE'S FUNERAL
Sartre died from a lung tumour on 15 April 1980. On 19 April over 50,000 people witnessed the funeral cortège as it journeyed from Broussais hospital in the south of Paris on its way to Montparnasse cemetery. Among the political and intellectual figures who followed the coffin through the streets were his lifelong companion Simone de Beauvoir and the French film actors Yves Montand and Simone Signoret.

# POPPER

## FROM SCIENCE TO POLITICS

*Scientific knowledge has turned out to be conjectural, permanently open to revision in the light of experience. The same principle seems also to apply to politics.*

> *"The whole of science is nothing more than a refinement of everyday thinking"*
> ALBERT EINSTEIN

FOR AT LEAST TWO HUNDRED years after Newton, most educated Westerners regarded the new science as certain knowledge, hard fact, completely and utterly reliable. Once a new scientific fact or law was discovered, it was not open to change. This certainty was believed to be the distinguishing characteristic of science: scientific knowledge was the most reliable knowledge that human beings possessed, and could be regarded as incorrigible truth. The growth of science, it was thought, consisted in the addition of newly discovered certainties to an ever-expanding body of existing ones, like a treasure-chest whose contents go on increasing over time: what is already there simply stays the same, as new things are added. Those who were familiar with the ideas of Locke and Hume realized that scientific laws had not been proved conclusively; but in view of the apparently unbroken success of their application over long periods of time, such people tended to regard them as what one might call infinitely probable, that is to say as near to being certain as makes no difference for practical purposes.

### UNCERTAIN KNOWLEDGE
At the turn of the 20th century a scientific genius came on the scene who was comparable to Newton, a German Jew called Albert Einstein (1879–1955) – and he produced theories incompatible with Newton's. Like Newton, Einstein was

TECHNOLOGICAL LANDSCAPES
*The modern industrial age was made possible by the application of Newtonian science, allowing Western man to believe that he had discovered a body of reliable knowledge. However, Einstein's theories demonstrated that this "knowledge" was inaccurate. This fact had dramatic consequences for both philosophy and science.*

amazingly fertile of fundamental ideas. What he is best know for are his contributions to relativity theory: his Special Theory of Relativity, published in 1905, and his General Theory of Relativity, made public in 1915. Not surprisingly, these theories were highly controversial at first; but virtually nobody who was knowledgeable in the field could deny that they were deserving of the most serious consideration. And that fact in itself had disconcerting implications, because if Einstein was right then Newton was wrong – and in that case we had not "known" the contents of Newtonian science all along.

And so it was to prove. Crucial experiments were devised to adjudicate between the two sets of theories; and as the empirical evidence mounted it unmistakably favoured Einstein. The consequences of this for philosophy were earthquake-like. Ever since Descartes, the search for certainty had been at or near the centre of Western philosophy; and with Newtonian science Western man believed he had uncovered a vast body of reliable knowledge about his world and beyond, knowledge of fundamental significance and enormous practical usefulness.

ALBERT EINSTEIN
*The German physicist Albert Einstein did not do well at school, but achieved recognition in his own lifetime as a genius who changed the face of history. His theories of relativity revolutionized both the study of science and philosophy.*

civilization; yet now, we discovered, it was inaccurate. This presented us with an utterly baffling situation, for it appeared that we had been mistaken not only about what was knowledge but about what knowledge was.

### A MANY-SIDED UPBRINGING

We have seen how Locke spelt out the implications that the Newtonian revolution in science had possessed for philosophy, and how some of the most important consequences of his ideas then turned out to be in political and social theory. The 20th-century philosopher who carried out this task for the Einsteinian revolution was Karl Popper (1902–94). Popper was born in Vienna in 1902, the son of a prosperous lawyer. His parents had converted from Judaism to Christianity, so he himself received a Lutheran upbringing. In his early and middle teens he was a Marxist, but he grew disgusted with the Communists' willingness to let ordinary people be killed if it happened to suit their tactics; so he moved to the Social Democrats.

He lived his socialism – dressed like a working man, lived among the unemployed, worked with handicapped children. This last brought him into contact with the psychoanalyst Alfred Adler. At the same time he was active in the musical avant-garde led by Schoenberg, and formed a friendship with the composer Webern. For holidays he was addicted to mountaineering. He married one of the student beauties of his generation. Altogether his life in Vienna was exceptionally rich and many-sided, full of enthusiastic commitments and exciting activities.

What is more, the methods by which that knowledge had been gathered had been closely considered and carefully codified, and were thought to guarantee its certainty, to validate it as sure knowledge. And yet now it turned out not to have been "knowledge" at all. What was it, then? Its use had led to immense progress in our understanding of the world; its practical application through technology had brought about a whole new historical age, namely modern industrial

> ## "ONLY DARING SPECULATION CAN LEAD US FURTHER, AND NOT ACCUMULATION OF FACTS"
>
> ### ALBERT EINSTEIN

**ALFRED ADLER**
The Austrian psychoanalyist Alfred Adler (1870–1937) was a member of the Freudian circle of doctors based in Vienna from 1900. However, by 1911 he had parted company with Freud, as he saw the "will to power" as more influential in accounting for human behaviour than the sexual drive. His books include *Organic Inferiority and Psychic Compensation* (1907), and *Understanding Human Nature* (1927). One of his main contributions was the introduction of the term "inferiority feeling", often inaccurately, called "inferiority complex".

**ARNOLD SCHOENBERG**
Before he was nine, the Austro-Hungarian composer Arnold Schoenberg (1874-1951) had begun to compose small pieces for two violins. After early romantic works such as *Songs of Gurra* (1900–11) Schoenberg changed the course of 20th-century music when he formulated the 12-tone method. This was a method of composition whereby all 12 notes within the octave are treated as equals, with no chords or groups of notes dominating as in conventional harmony. Schoenberg's most important atonal works include *Five Orchestral Pieces*, Opus 16 (1909), and the *Violin Concerto*, Opus 36 (1934–36).

**KARL POPPER**
*The Austrian philosopher of science, Karl Popper, was born and educated in Vienna. He was naturalized British in 1945, before becoming Professor of Logic and Scientific Method at the London School of Economics.*

**LONDON SCHOOL OF ECONOMICS AND POLITICAL SCIENCE**
Part of London University, the London School of Economics and Political Science was founded in 1895 by the English social reformers Sidney (1859–1947) and Beatrice (1858–1943) Webb. Many famous academics have been associated with the LSE, including Popper, and the English political theorist Harold Laski (1893–1950). It is now recognized as one of the major European centres for the research and teaching of Social Sciences.

But then came Nazism. In 1937, the year before Hitler took over Austria, Popper accepted a university job in New Zealand, and he was there throughout World War II. When the war ended, in 1945, he went to England, and spent the rest of his career at the London School of Economics, where he became Professor of Logic and Scientific Method. In England he lived a life completely different from that of his youth in Vienna, deliberately isolating himself in order to produce his writings, which covered an exceptionally wide range of subjects. He was still publishing worthwhile new ideas at the age of 92, when he died.

### THERE IS NO CERTAINTY IN SCIENCE

Popper realized that if the centuries of corroboration received by Newtonian science had not proved it to be true, nothing was ever going to prove the truth of a scientific theory. So-called scientific laws were not incorrigible truths about the world after all; they were theories, and as such they were products of the human mind. If they worked well in their practical application then that meant they must approximate to the truth, yet it was always possible, even after hundreds of years of pragmatic success, for someone to come along with a better theory that was closer still to whatever the truth was.

Popper developed this insight into a full-scale theory of knowledge. According to him, physical reality exists independently of the human mind, and is of a radically different order from human

> ## "SCIENCE IS PERHAPS THE ONLY HUMAN ACTIVITY IN WHICH ERRORS ARE SYSTEMATICALLY CRITICIZED AND,...IN TIME, CORRECTED"
>
> KARL POPPER

experience – and for that very reason can never be directly apprehended. We produce plausible theories to explain it, and if these theories yield successful practical results we go on making use of them for as long as they work. Nearly always, though, they run us into difficulties sooner or later by proving inadequate in some respect, and then we cast around for a better theory, a more ample one that explains everything the first one could explain without being subject to its limitations. We do this not only in science but in all other fields of activity, including everyday life. It means that our approach to things is essentially a problem-solving one, and that we make progress not by adding new certainties to a body of existing ones but by perpetually replacing existing theories with better theories. The search for certainty, which obsessed some of the greatest Western philosophers from Descartes to Russell, has to be given up, because certainty is not available.

It is impossible to prove, finally and for ever, the truth of any scientific theory, or to put the whole of science or the whole of mathematics on ultimately secure foundations. "Justificationism", as Popper came to call it, is completely wrong-

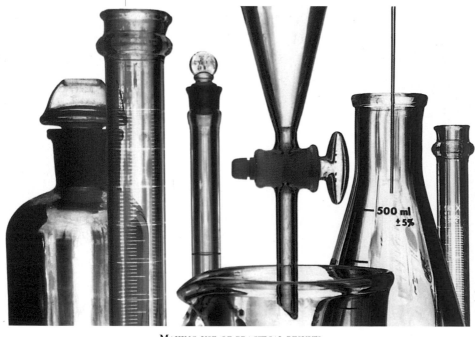

**MAKING USE OF PRACTICAL RESULTS**
*For Popper, physical reality exists independently of the human mind, and so we can never apprehend it. We create theories to explain it, and use them for as long as they work. However, eventually each theory will prove inadequate, and we replace it with a better one.*

...aded. If you build a house on ...les in a swamp, you need to drive ...e piles down deep enough to ...stain the structure, and any time ...u enlarge the house you will ...ed to drive the piles down ...eper, but there are no necessary ...nits to that process: there is no ...ltimate" level of foundations that ...ill hold up anything regardless, ... "natural" or given basis for this ... any other structure.

However, although no general ...eory can be proved, it can be ...sproved, and this means it can ...e tested. As we saw earlier (see ...115) although no number of ...servations of white swans, ...owever large, will ever prove the ...uth of the statement "All swans ...re white", a single observation of ... black swan is enough to disprove ... So we can test general statements ...y searching for contrary instances. ...his being so, criticism becomes the chief means ...y which we do in fact make progress. A statement ...at no observation would falsify cannot be tested, ...nd therefore cannot count as scientific, because ... everything that could possibly happen is ...ompatible with its truth then nothing can be ...egarded as evidence for it. A good example would ...e the statement "God exists": it has meaning, and ...ight be true, but no intellectually ...erious person would regard it as ... scientific statement.

GOD'S EXISTENCE CAN NEVER BE A SCIENTIFIC FACT
*Although a general theory cannot be proved, it takes only one contrary instance in order to disprove it. A declaration such as "God exists" – although it may be be true – is one that cannot be falsified, and therefore cannot be tested and regarded as a scientific statement.*

The most undesirable and indefensible forms of modern society are those in which centralized planning is imposed, and dissent disallowed. Criticism is the chief way in which social policies can be improved before they are implemented; and the noting of undesirable consequences is the promptest cause of their modification or abandonment after they have been implemented.

## THE OPEN SOCIETY
...he seminal book in which ...opper put forward these ideas was *...he Logic of Scientific Discovery*, ...ublished in German in 1934 and ...n English in 1959. Only after he ...ad worked them out with regard ...o the natural sciences did he fully ...ealize that they applied to the ...ocial sciences as well. He wrote a ...wo-volume work called *The Open ...ociety and Its Enemies*, published ...n 1945, in which he applied them ...o political and social theory. ...ertainty, he argued, was no more ...vailable in politics than in science, ...nd therefore the imposition of a ...ingle viewpoint is never justified.

POLICE STATE
*Popper identified the worst kind of society as one which is centrally controlled and where dissent is disallowed. Such a situation is described in George Orwell's novel* Nineteen Eighty-Four *(1949), which portrays the kind of society Orwell believed could develop if man allowed politicians to establish totalitarian rule.*

SIR JOHN ECCLES
*The work of the Australian physiologist John Eccles (1903–97) has done much to aid the treatment of nervous diseases. In 1963 he shared the Nobel Prize (with Alan Hodgkin and Andrew Huxley) for work on conduction in the central nervous system. His books include* The Self and its Brain *(1977), which he collaborated on with Popper.*

*"All we can do is to search for the falsity content of our best theory"*
KARL POPPER

EINSTEIN'S KEY WORKS
On the Electrodynamics of Moving Bodies (1905) *in which Einstein published his Special Theory of Relativity*
The Foundation of the General Theory of Relativity (1916)

PROTEST MARCH
*Popper believed that the criticism and opposition allowed in an "open" society are the principal, and most effective, means by which social policy can be made better. A society where dissent is disallowed is thoroughly undesirable.*

> "*Piecemeal social engineering resembles physical engineering in regarding the ends as beyond the province of technology*"
>
> KARL POPPER

SIR ERNST GOMBRICH
The Austrian-born art historian Sir Ernst Gombrich (1909– ) came to England in 1936, where he joined the Warburg Institute in the University of London. He is best known for his books *The Story of Art* (1950), and *Art and Illusion* (1960), which among much else, apply Popper's ideas to art.

Therefore a society that allows critical discussion and opposition (what Popper calls an "open" society) will almost certainly be more effective at solving the practical problems of its policy-makers than one that does not. Progress will be quicker and less costly. And all this is true regardless of moral considerations.

In politics, as in science, we are continually replacing established ideas with what we hope are better ideas. Society too is in a state of perpetual change, and the pace of that change is increasingly

fast. These things being so, the creation and perpetuation of an ideal state of society is not an option for us. What we have to do is manage a process of endless change that has no stopping place. So what we are engaged in is perpetual problem-solving. We should all the time be seeking out the worst social evils and trying to remove them: poverty and powerlessness, threats to peace bad education and medical care, and so on. Becaus perfection and certainty are unattainable we shoul concern ourselves less with the idea of building model schools and hospitals than with getting rid the worst ones and improving the lot of the peopl in them. We do not know how to make people happ but we can remove avoidable suffering and handica

## THE GRAVEDIGGER OF MARXISM

In the course of putting forward these ideas Popper mounts a massive onslaught on the most influential proponents of an ideal form of society, above all Plato and Marx. His critique of Marxism was widely regarded as the most effective that anyone had produced, and it was this that first made Popper's name known internationally. There was a period after *The Open Society* had been published when something like a third of the human race lived under governments that called themselves Marxist, and this fact alone gave the ideas of that book a global relevance. That aspect of it may be less urgent now, but the book's positive case for democratic openness and tolerance remains probably the most compelling that anyone has produced.

REMOVING SOCIAL EVILS
*Modern society is constantly changing, and as a result it will never be possible to create the perfect society. Popper believed that what we must do is concentrate on removing* *the worst social problems, such as bad education and poverty In Great Britain, the slum clearances of the 1960s were an attempt to improve the living conditions of the urban poor.*

# *The* EINSTEINIAN REVOLUTION

Upheavals in modern science have changed our understanding of what knowledge is, and have therefore changed philosophy. Because scientific knowledge is the most practically reliable and useful knowledge that human beings possess, any view of what knowledge itself is, any account of the nature of knowledge as such, has to apply to science if it is to be plausible. In fact for much of the history of Western philosophy investigations into the nature of knowledge have been science-led. This has been especially true during the last four hundred years.

In the 20th century in particular, profound changes took place in science, which was found to be something radically different from what had previously been supposed. In physics alone, two great upheavals occurred. Einstein's theories of relativity superseded traditional science. Then along came quantum theory, which was logically incompatible with relativity theory and yet produced results that were every bit as accurate. It is not possible for both theories to be correct, indeed it is likely that both are incorrect, yet both are in everyday use and give minutely

accurate results. This led to the realization that even the best of our knowledge consists of man-made theories that are fallible and corrigible – theories that we ourselves hope and expect to replace with better theories sooner or later. Human knowledge is fallible precisely because it is human; and we are now challenged with the realization that it does not consist of cast-iron, unchanging certainties, as people used to believe.

Not only have the scientists radically altered our conception of what knowledge is. They have done more than the philosophers of their day to change our understanding of concepts which are utterly fundamental to our experience of the world, concepts such as "time", "space", "matter", and "physical object". So it may be that when historians in the future look back at our age they will see the path-breaking scientists as having been, in effect, also the path-breaking philosophers, in that it is they who have done the most to change peoples' philosophical understanding of the world.

## SCIENTIFIC KNOWLEDGE IS THE MOST RELIABLE AND USEFUL KNOWLEDGE THAT HUMAN BEINGS POSSESS

# The FUTURE of PHILOSOPHY

## INCREASING ENLIGHTENMENT ON A QUEST TO WHICH THERE MAY BE NO END

NEARLY ALL PHILOSOPHERS who are famous in their own lifetime are forgotten not long afterwards. Only a tiny handful, most notably those discussed in this book, have reputations that survive – not many when you consider that their lives have been spread over a period of more than two and a half thousand years. For this reason we shall make no attempt in this book to discuss philosophers who are living now on the same level as the great ones of the past. We can be fairly sure that only one or two of today's philosophers, if any, will still be known by name a century hence: the rest will have disappeared into the same limbo as that now inhabited by most of the philosophers who were well known in previous centuries. The intellectual fashions of each generation, far from being a pointer to the future, are destined for almost certain extinction.

In this book we have considered only philosophers whose ideas have proved of lasting interest or importance. These are people who, by contrast, have usually exerted their greatest influence after their death. For example, Locke published all his philosophy in the 17th century, but it was in the 18th that it had its historic impact on Europe and America. Marx's life was entirely enclosed within the 19th century, but it was in the 20th that his ideas changed the world. At a humbler level of influence, it is half a century since Wittgenstein died, but he is now a more significant figure in our culture than he was in his lifetime, or looked like ever becoming.

THESE FACTS NATURALLY lead us to suppose that the short-run future of philosophy is likely to see the full impact of the most recently dead of the great figures. There is a rich seam to be worked out of Heidegger in response to the existential challenges posed to us by Nietzsche. And there are rich seams to be worked out of Popper in response to the challenges posed to us by

**A PICTURE OF EARTH**
*In years to come, human beings may spread throughout the universe, and inhabit many worlds. They may then look back on their primitive origins on Planet Earth in much the same way as we now look back on pre-historic man's origins in tropical Africa.*

the ever-changing sciences, and by the formation of increasing numbers of democratic societies. The voracious interest in Popper's work shown by people in emerging democracies is already a striking phenomenon.

But that will still be only part of the scene. What else? What will be new? Presumably philosophers who change the subject irreversibly will continue to emerge in the future just as they have in the past – figures like Descartes and Kant, after whom nothing in philosophy was ever the same again. Because our historical past is so short, and the future before us indefinitely long, the chances are that the biggest and most illuminating innovations ever to occur in philosophy lie ahead of us rather than behind us. Unfortunately, such subject-changing insights cannot be predicted: if we could predict them now we would have

However, there are lesser developments that we can confidently expect, some of which are bound to be interesting. The techniques of philosophical analysis will be brought to bear on an ever-increasingly wide range of subject matter. The most urgent of the problems will be those of public policy, but others will be drawn from a wider range of subjects, from music to sex, than most philosophers of the past would have considered.

THERE SEEMS, ALSO, to be a revival of public interest in philosophy, and an increase in the value people set on it. Philosophy has recently been introduced into secondary education in Britain for the first time. It is also a comparatively recent development for advisors on business ethics to be asked to sit on the boards of companies, and for philosophers to be engaged by governments to scrutinize legislation. These activities are likely to expand. There is also taking place a corresponding shift in the interests of the general reading public towards philosophy. An international best-seller of recent years, Jostein Gaarder's *Sophie's World* (1991), was an introduction to the history of philosophy in the unexpected form of a novel. Such a success for such a book would not have been thinkable a generation previously.

So the outlook for philosophy in our society is buoyant. But philosophy is like music in that, although it has many practical uses, its supreme value lies not in any of them but in what it is in itself. It may be that from within the confines of our human limitations we shall never be able to find the answers to some of our most fundamental questions. But, as

## "SUPERSTITION SETS THE WHOLE WORLD IN FLAMES; PHILOSOPHY QUENCHES THEM"

VOLTAIRE

them now, and they would not be future. But this means that we can no more predict the most important future developments in philosophy than anyone before Kant could have predicted Kant. Difficult though it might be for us to accept, the fact is that the future of philosophy is closed to us in its most important aspects.

this book has tried to show, we can make such worthwhile progress in our understanding of the human situation that even if we never reach any ultimate goal in that respect we shall find that the journey is a hugely enriching experience that is worth undertaking for its own sake. There may be no final answers, but there is a wonderful lot to learn.

# GLOSSARY

## A

**the Absolute** Ultimate reality conceived of as a single, all-embracing principle. Some thinkers have identified this with God; others have believed in it but not in God; others have not believed in it. The philosopher most closely associated with the idea is Hegel.

**Aesthetics** The philosophy of art. Also philosophical questions about beauty.

**the Aesthetic attitude** Contemplating something for its own sake, regardless of any use that can be made of it.

**Agent** The doing self, as distinct from the knowing self; the self that decides or chooses or acts.

**Agnostic** Neither believing nor disbelieving, but suspending judgement.

**Analysis** Seeking a deeper understanding of something by taking it to pieces. The opposite is **Synthesis**, which means seeking a deeper understanding of something by putting the pieces together.

**Analytic philosophy** A view of philosophy that sees its aim as clarification – for instance the clarification of concepts, statements, methods, arguments, and theories by carefully taking them apart.

**Analytic statement** A statement whose truth or falsehood can be established by analysis of the statement itself. The opposite is a **Synthetic statement**, which has to be set against facts outside itself for its truth to be determined.

**Anthropomorphism** The attribution of human characteristics to something that is not human, for instance the weather, or to God.

**Antinomy** Contradictory conclusions from equally good premises.

**A priori** Something that is known to be valid in advance of experience. The opposite is **a posteriori,** which is something whose validity can be determined only by experience.

## C

**Category** One of our basic conceptions. Categories are the broadest classes into which things can be divided. Aristotle and Kant each tried to provide a complete list of them, but philosophers no longer attempt to do this.

**Cognition** Any kind of knowing or perceiving.

**Concept** A thought or idea; the meaning of a word or term.

**Contingent** May or may not be the case, things could be either way. The opposite is **Necessary**.

**Contradictory** Two statements are contradictory if one must be true and the other false: they cannot both be true, nor can they both be false. The opposite is **Non-contradictory**, and applies to statements whose truth-values are independent of one another.

**Contrary** Two statements are contrary if they cannot both be true but may both be false.

**Corroboration** Evidence that lends support to a conclusion without necessarily proving it.

**Cosmology** Study of the whole universe, the cosmos. Questions raised in cosmology can be philosophical, but they can also be scientific.

## D

**Deduction** Reasoning from the general to the particular. For instance, "If all men are mortal then Socrates, being a man, must be mortal." It is universally agreed that deduction is valid. The opposite process of reasoning from the particular to the general is called **Induction**. An example would be "Socrates died, Plato died, Aristotle died, and taking them one by one each other individual man who was born more than 130 years ago has died, therefore all men are mortal." It is agreed that induction does not necessarily yield results that are true. It is therefore disputed whether it is genuinely a logical process. Hume believed it to be a psychological process, not a logical one, and so did Popper.

**Determinism** The view that nothing can happen other than what does happen, because every event is the necessary outcome of causes preceding it – which themselves were the necessary outcome of causes preceding them. The opposite is **Indeterminism**. Dispute between the two is still very alive.

**Dialectic** i) Skill in questioning or argument. ii) A technical term used by followers of Hegel or Marx for the idea that any assertion, whether in word or deed, evokes opposition, the two of which then become reconciled in a synthesis that includes elements of both.

**Dualism** A view of something as made up of two irreducible elements. The most familiar example is the idea of human beings as consisting of bodies and minds, the two being radically unlike.

# E

*Élan vital* The driving principle of the evolutionary process, the life force; that which distinguishes the living from the non-living.

**Emotive** Expressing emotion. In philosophy the term is often used in a derogatory way for utterances that pretend to be objective or impartial while in fact expressing emotional attitudes, as for example in "emotive definition".

**Empiricism** The view that all knowledge of anything that actually exists must be derived from experience. Thus: **Empirical world** The world as revealed to us by our actual or possible experience. **Empirical knowledge** Knowledge of the empirical world. **Empirical statement** A statement about the empirical world, in other words a statement about what is or could be experienced.

**Epistemology** The theory of knowledge, that branch of philosophy concerned with what sort of thing, if anything, we can know, and how, and what knowledge is. In practice it is the dominant branch of philosophy.

**Essence** The essence of a thing is what makes it what it is, that which is distinctive about it. For instance, the essence of a unicorn is that it is a horse with a single horn on its head. This leaves open the question

whether unicorns exist. They do not, of course – so essence does not imply existence. This distinction is important in philosophy.

**Ethics** Philosophical reflection on how we should live, and therefore on questions of right and wrong, good and bad, ought and ought not, duty, and other such concepts.

**Existentialism** A philosophy that begins with the contingent existence of the individual human being and regards that as the primary enigma. It is from that starting point that philosophical understanding is pursued. There are two main strands, religious existentialism and humanist existentialism.

**Fallacy** A seriously wrong argument, or a false conclusion based on such an argument.

# F

**Falsifiability** Property of a statement, or set of statements, namely that they can be proved wrong by empirical testing. According to Popper, falsifiability is what distinguishes science from non-science.

# H

**Humanism** A philosophical approach based on the assumption that mankind is the most important *anything* that exists, and that there can be no knowledge of a supernatural world, if any such world exists. "The proper study of mankind is man" (Pope) is the best-known encapsulation of this view.

**Hypothesis** A theory whose truth is assumed for the time being.

# I

**Idealism** The view that reality consists ultimately of something non-material, whether mind, our minds

and mental contents, or spirits, or one spirit. The opposite is **Materialism**.

**Induction** See **Deduction**.

**Intuition** Direct knowing, whether by sensory perception or by insight; a form of knowledge that makes no use of reasoning.

# L

**Linguistic philosophy** Also known as LINGUISTIC ANALYSIS. The view that philosophical problems arise from a muddled use of language, and are to be solved, or dissolved, by a careful analysis of the language in which they have been expressed.

**Logic** The branch of philosophy that makes a study of rational argument itself – its terms, concepts, rules, methods, and so on.

**Logical positivism** The doctrine that the only empirical statements that are meaningful are those that are verifiable.

# M

**Materialism** The doctrine that all real existence is ultimately of something material. The opposite is **Idealism**.

**Metaphysics** The branch of philosophy concerned with the ultimate nature of what exists. It questions the natural world "from outside", as it were, and its questions can therefore not be dealt with by the methods of science. Philosophers who take the natural world to be all there is use the term metaphysics for the broadest, most general possible frameworks of human thinking.

**Methodology** The study of methods of enquiry and argument – these being different in different fields, as for example in physics, psychology, history, and law.

**Monism** A view of something as formed by a single element; for example, of human beings, the view that they do not consist of elements that are ultimately separable, like a body and a soul, but are unitary, of one single substance.

**Mysticism** Intuitive knowledge that transcends the natural world.

# N

**Naive realism** The view that reality actually is as it appears to us in our daily lives.

**Naturalism** The view that reality is explicable without reference to anything outside the natural world.

**Nature** The empirical world as given to mankind.

**Necessary** Must be the case. The opposite is **Contingent**, i.e. need not be the case. Hume believed that necessary connections existed only in logic, not in the real world, a view that has been upheld by many philosophers since.

**Necessary and sufficient conditions** For X to be a husband it is a necessary condition for X to be married. However, this is not a sufficient condition – for what if X is female? A sufficient condition for X to be a husband is that X is both a man and married. This distinction between necessary and sufficient conditions is exceedingly important. One of the commonest forms of error is to mistake necessary conditions for sufficient conditions.

**Noumenon** The unknowable reality behind what presents itself to human

consciousness, the latter being known as **Phenomenon**. A thing as it is in itself, independently of being experienced, is said to be the noumenon. "The noumenal" has therefore become a term for the ultimate nature of reality. The German for thing-in-itself, *Ding-an-sich*, has also frequently been used in English, and means the same as the noumenon.

**Numinous** (Not to be confused with the Noumenal, see above.) Anything regarded as mysterious and awesome, bearing intimations from outside the natural realm.

# O

**Ontology** The branch of philosophy that asks what actually exists, as distinct from the nature of our knowledge of it. The latter is called **Epistemology**. Ontology and epistemology taken together constitute the central tradition of philosophy and its history.

# P

**Phenomenon** An experience that is immediately present. If I look at an object, the object as experienced by me is a phenomenon. Kant distinguished this from the object as it is in itself, independently of being experienced: this he called the **Noumenon**.

**Phenomenology** An approach to philosophy, begun by Edmund Husserl (1859–1938), which investigates objects of experience without raising what may be unanswerable questions about their independent nature.

**Philosophy** Literally, "the love of wisdom". The word is widely used for any sustained rational reflection about general principles that has the aim of achieving a deeper

understanding of things. Philosophy as an educational subject provides training in the disciplined analysis and clarification of theories, methods, arguments, and utterances of all kinds, and the concepts of which they make use. Traditionally, the ultimate aim of all this has been to attain a better understanding of the world, though in the 20th century a good deal of philosophy became devoted to attaining a better understanding of its own procedures.

**Pragmatism** A theory of truth. It holds that a statement is true if it does all the jobs required of it, i.e. accurately describes a situation, prompts us to anticipate experiences correctly, fits in with already well-attested statements, and so on. The name "pragmatism" makes it sound crude, but in the right hands it is a sophisticated and worthwhile theory.

**Premise** The starting point of an argument. Any argument has to start from at least one premise, and therefore does not prove its own premises. A valid argument proves that its conclusions follow from its premises – but this is not the same as proving that its conclusions are true, which is something no argument can do.

**Presupposition** Something taken for granted but not expressed. All utterances have presuppositions, and these may be conscious or unconscious. If a presupposition is erroneous an utterance based on it may be mistaken for a reason not evident in the utterance itself. Philosophy teaches us to become consciously aware of presuppositions, and to analyse them.

**Primary and secondary qualities**
Locke divided the properties of a physical object into those possessed by the object independently of being experienced, such as its location, dimensions, velocity, mass, and so on, and those that involve the reactions of an experiencing observer, such as the object's colour, taste, and smell. The former he called Primary qualities, the latter Secondary qualities.

**Principle of sufficient reason**
The insistence that every event in the empirical world must be brought about by factors that explain it, whether we manage to discover these factors or not. Leibniz declared this principle fundamental to all reasoning. Schopenhauer wrote his first book about it.

**Property** In philosophy this word is commonly used to mean a characteristic, as in "having a diaphragm is the defining property of a mammal". See also **Primary and secondary qualities**.

# R

**Rationalism** The view that we can gain knowledge of the world by the use of reason, without relying on sense-perception, which is regarded by rationalists as unreliable. The contrary view, that we cannot gain knowledge of the world without the use of sense-perception, is known as **Empiricism**.

# S

**Scepticism** The view that it is impossible to know anything for certain.

**Semantics** The study of meanings in linguistic expressions.

**Semiotics** The study of signs and symbols.

**Solipsism** The belief that only oneself exists.

**Sophist** Someone whose aim in argument is not to seek the truth but to win the argument. In ancient Greece a sophist was a teacher who trained young men aspiring to public life in the various methods of winning arguments.

# T

**Tautology** A statement which is necessarily true. Its denial would be a self-contradiction.

**Theology** Enquiry into scholarly and intellectual questions concerning the nature of God. Philosophy, by contrast, does not posit the existence of God.

**Teleology** A study of ends or goals. A teleological explanation is one that explains something in terms of the ends that it serves.

**Transcendental** Outside the world of sense experience. Someone (e.g. Wittgenstein) who believes that ethics are transcendental believes that ethics have their source outside the empirical world. Thoroughgoing empiricists do not believe that anything transcendental exists, and nor likewise do Nietzsche or humanist existentialists.

# U

**Universal** A concept of general application, like "red" or "woman". It has been disputed whether universals have an existence of their own. Does "redness" exist, or are there only individual red objects? In the Middle Ages philosophers who believed that "redness" possessed real existence were called "realists", while philosophers who maintained that it was no more than a word, a name, were called "nominalists".

**Utilitarianism** A theory of ethics and politics that judges the morality of actions by their consequences, that regards the most desirable consequence as the greatest good of the greatest number, and that defines "good" in terms of pleasure and the absence of pain.

# V

**Validity** A property of arguments. An argument is valid if its conclusion follows from its premises. This does not necessarily mean that the conclusion is true: it may be false if one of the premises is false, though the argument itself is still valid.

**Verifiability** Property of a statement, or set of statements, namely that they can be proved to be true by empirical evidence. Logical positivists believed that the only empirical statements that were meaningful were those that were verifiable. Hume and Popper pointed out that scientific laws were unverifiable.

# W

**World** In philosophy the word "world" has been given a special sense, meaning "the whole of empirical reality", and may therefore also be equated with the totality of actual and possible experience. Thoroughgoing empiricists believe that this is all there is, but some other kinds of philosopher believe that the world does not account for total reality. Such philosophers believe that there is a transcendental realm as well as an empirical realm, and they may believe that both are equally real.

# GUIDE TO FURTHER READING

HAVING BEEN INTRODUCED to philosophy by the present book, readers are strongly recommended now to read the great philosophers themselves rather than books about them by commentators. However, if anyone feels in need of a more extended introduction to a particular thinker before plunging into his work, there is a series of short and inexpensive paperbacks published by Oxford University Press, under the series title *Past Masters,* that contains books about most of the philosophers discussed in *The Story of Philosophy.* They are written for the general reader, and each one contains suggestions for further reading. Another series of short paperbacks with the series-title *The Great Philosophers* is published by Orion. Readers who would like more introductions by the author of *The Story of Philosophy* are recommended to try: *Confessions of a Philosopher: a Journey Through Western Philosophy* (Orion paperback); *Popper* (Fontana paperback); *The Great Philosophers* and *The Philosophy of Schopenhauer* (Oxford University Press paperbacks).

Coming now to the philosophers themselves, the following books are recommended, bearing in mind their accessibility:

## THE GREEKS AND THEIR WORLD
**On the pre-Socratics** *Early Greek Philosophy* edited by Jonathan Barnes (Penguin Books).
**On Socrates** *The Last Days of Socrates,* four dialogues by Plato (Penguin Books).
**By Plato** *The Symposium* and *The Republic* (Penguin Books).
**By Aristotle** *A New Aristotle Reader* (Oxford University Press paperback), *The Nicomachean Ethics* and *Politics* (Penguin Books).
**On Epicureanism** *On the Nature of the Universe* by Lucretius (Penguin Books).
**On Stoicism** *Letters from a Stoic* by Seneca (Penguin Books), *Meditations* by Marcus Aurelius (Penguin Books).
**On Neo-Platonism** *Enneads* by Plotinus (Heinemann).

## CHRISTIANITY AND PHILOSOPHY
**By St Augustine** *Confessions* and *City of God* (Penguin Books).
**By Boethius** *The Consolation of Philosophy* (Penguin Books).
**By Abelard and Héloise** *Letters* (Penguin Books).
**By Maimonides** *Guide for the Perplexed* (Dover paperback).

## THE BEGINNINGS OF MODERN SCIENCE
*The Sleepwalkers* by Arthur Koestler (Penguin Books).
**By Machiavelli** *The Portable Machiavelli* (Penguin Books).
**By Francis Bacon** *Advancement of Learning* and *The New Atlantis* (Oxford University Press paperbacks), *Essays* (Penguin Books).
**By Hobbes** *Leviathan* (Penguin Books).

## THE GREAT RATIONALISTS
**By Descartes** *Selected Philosophical Writings* (Cambridge University Press paperback).
**By Spinoza** *Ethics* and *On the Correction of the Understanding* (Dent paperbacks).
**By Leibniz** *Philosophical Writings* (Dent paperback).

## THE GREAT EMPIRICISTS
**By Locke** *An Essay Concerning Human Understanding* (Oxford University Press paperback), *Two Treatises of Government* (Cambridge University Press paperback).
**By Berkeley** *The Principles of Human Knowledge* and *Three Dialogues* (Penguin Books).
**By Hume** *A Treatise of Human Nature* (Oxford University Press paperback), *Dialogues Concerning Natural Religion* (Hagner paperback).
**By Burke** *A Philosophical Enquiry* and *Reflections on the Revolution in France* (Oxford University Press paperbacks).

## REVOLUTIONARY FRENCH THINKERS
**By Voltaire** *Candide* and *Philosophical Dictionary* (Penguin Books).
**By Rousseau** *The Social Contract* (Penguin Books).

## A GOLDEN CENTURY OF GERMAN PHILOSOPHY
**By Kant** *Prolegomena* (Open Court paperback), *Critique of Pure Reason* (Macmillan paperback), *The Moral Law* (Hutchinson paperback).
**By Schopenhauer** *On the Fourfold Root of the Principle of Sufficient Reason* (Open Court paperback), *The World as Will and Representation* (two vols., Dover paperback).
**On comparisons of East with West** *Presuppositions of India's Philosophies* by Karl Potter (Motilal Banarsidass paperback), *What the Buddha Taught* by Walpola Rahula (One World Publications paperback), *The Tao of Physics* by Fritjof Capra (Harper Collins paperback).
**By Fichte** *The Vocation of Man* (Hackett paperback).
**By Schelling** *Ideas for a Philosophy of Nature* (Cambridge University paperback).
**On Hegel** *Hegel* by Peter Singer (Oxford University paperback), *Hegel: an Introduction* by Raymond Plant (Blackwell paperback).
**By Hegel** *Phenomenology of Spirit* (Oxford University Press paperback).
**On Marxism** *To the Finland Station* by Edmund Wilson (Penguin Books).
**By Marx** *Capital (Das Kapital)* (Penguin Books).
**By Marx and Engels** *Basic Writings on Politics and Philosophy* (Fontana paperback).
**By Nietzsche** *Beyond Good and Evil* (Penguin Books), *Twilight of the Idols* and *Anti-Christ* (Penguin Books), *Ecce Homo* (Penguin Books).

**DEMOCRACY AND PHILOSOPHY**

**By Jeremy Bentham** *Introduction to the Principles of Morals and Legislation* (Methuen paperback).

**By John Stuart Mill** *On Liberty* (Penguin Books).

**On the American Pragmatists** *The Origins of Pragmatism* by A.J. Ayer (Macmillan hardback).

**By William James** *The Varieties of Religious Experience* (Penguin Books).

**20TH-CENTURY PHILOSOPHY**

**On Frege** *Interpretation of Frege's Philosophy* by Michael Dummett (Duckworth paperback).

**By Bertrand Russell** *The Problems of Philosophy* (Oxford University Press paperback), *Our Knowledge of the External World* (Unwin), *My Philosophical Development* (Unwin paperback).

**By Wittgenstein** *Tractatus Logico-Philosophicus* (Routledge paperback), *Philosophical Investigations* (Blackwell paperback).

**On Heidegger** *Heidegger* by George Steiner (Fontana paperback).

**By Heidegger** *Being and Time* (Blackwell paperback).

**By Bergson** *Creative Mind* (Citadel paperback), *Two Sources of Morality and Religion* (University of Notre Dame paperback).

**By Sartre** *Sketch for a Theory of the Emotions* (Routledge paperback), *The Psychology of Imagination* (Routledge paperback), *Being and Nothingness* (Routledge paperback).

**By Camus** *The Myth of Sisyphus* and *The Rebel* (Penguin Books).

**By Merleau-Ponty** *Phenomenology of Perception* (Routledge paperback).

**By Althusser** *For Marx* (Verso paperback).

**By Lacan** *Four Fundamental Concepts of Psychoanalysis* (Penguin Books).

**By Foucault** *Madness and Civilisation* (Tavistock paperback).

**By Popper** *A Pocket Popper* (Fontana paperback), *The Open Society and Its Enemies* (Routledge paperback), *The Logic of Scientific Discovery* (Hutchinson paperback).

**On Relativity Theory** *The ABC of Relativity* by Bertrand Russell (Routledge).

**On Quantum Theory** *In Search of Schrödinger's Cat* by John Gribbin (Black Swan paperback).

**By Dirac** *The Principles of Quantum Mechanics* (Oxford University Press paperback).

**By Heisenberg** *Physics and Philosophy* (Penguin Books).

**By Schrödinger** *What is Life?* and *Mind and Matter* (Cambridge University Press paperbacks).

# INDEX

# Picture Information

1: star cluster **p.2**: Raphael, *The* *hool of Athens*, 16th-C, detail, fresco, **p.3**: detail, see p.59 **p.4t**: see p.20tl. :: see p.20 **4b**: see pp.68-69 **p.5tl**: tail, see p.84t. **5tr**: see p.185tl. **5lc**: e p.102r. **5cc**: see p.123t. **5cr**: see 216br. **5b**: see p.135 **p.6**: embrandt, *The Two Philosophers*, 528, detail, Neth. **p.7**: Auguste odin, *The Thinker*, 1880, bronze, Fr. **8**: William Blake, *The Ancient of* *ays*, 1794, detail, mixed media, Eng. **9**: Salvador Dalí, *Homage to Newton*, 969, bronze, Sp. **pp.10-11**: galaxy 51/Aphrodite, 2nd-C BC, bronze, r. **pp.12-13**: scene depicting ivination, bearing the name of halcnas, a Greek soothsayer, early th-C BC, bronze mirror back/Thales Miletus, 1820, engr., Ger./olive arvest, c.5th-C BC, black-figure mphora, Gr./Anaximander, c.AD200, osaic. **pp.14-15**: detail, see p.2/ xekias, *The Sea Voyage of Dionysos*, 540BC, black-figure bowl, Gr./ ythagoras, marble/silver tetradrachm Athens, c.445BC, coin, Gr. **pp.16-17**: iagio d'Antonio da Firenze, *Allegory f the Liberal Arts*, late 15th-C, It./ lements from Aristotle's *Physics*, 4th-C, Ms./Temple of Olympian eus, Athens **pp.18-19**: Giovanni da onte, *The Seven Liberal Arts*, early 5th-C, panel, It./panathenaic otrace, c.5th-C BC, black-figure mphora, Gr. **pp.20-21**: after Lysippe, ocrates/*School of Athens*, see p.2/ mphalos stone, Gr./tholos in the anctuary of Athena Pronaia, Delphi/ ndré Castaigne, *Socrates walking hrough the Streets of Athens*, from *he Century*, 1897, engr., Fr./Eng./ ocrates, 1st-C AD, fresco, Ephesus, urkey. **pp.22-23**: scene from ristophanes' play *The Clouds*, 19th-C, ngr., Ger./Socrates, Aristotle, Plato, nd Seneca, 14th-C, Ms., It./ ristophanes, 15th-C, detail/Jacques ouis David, *Death of Socrates*, 1787, r. **pp.24-25**: Plato, marble/School of lato, c.100BC, mosaic, Rome. **pp.26-27**: garden mural, Villa of Livia, late st-C AD, fresco, Rome/U. Feuerbach, cene from the Symposium in *Greece and Rome*, 19th-C, engr., Ger./John he calligrapher, *Clarke Plato*, AD895, letail/Plato, Pythagoras, and Solon, 6th-C, fresco, Romania. **pp.28-29**: thlete cleaning himself with strigil, 5th-C BC, red-figure amphora, Gr./ Milo, *Venus*, c.100BC, marble, Gr./ lance of the Maenads before Dionysos, c.395BC, detail, red-figure vase, Gr./Plato, Hippocrates, and Dioscurus, Ms., It. **pp.30-31**: Fra Angelico, *Virgin and Child with Saints*, early 15th-C, triptych detail, It./ Plotinus' tomb, 3rd-C BC, It./detail, see p.25. **pp.32-33**: Aristotle, 4th-C BC, alabaster copy of Greek bronze, It./ Aristotle and Alexander, 14th-C, book cover, detail, ivory/detail, see p.2. **pp.34-35**: Domenico di Michelino, Dante reading from *The Divine Comedy*, 1465, panel, detail, It./G.B. della Porta, Aristotle, from *Book of Physiognomy*, 1616, engr., It./ Philosopher, poss. Aristotle and followers, 4th-C AD, fresco, It. **pp.36-37**: Aristotle's *Rhetoric*, Ms./ Michelangelo, *The Awakening Slave*, 1528, It./*Logic of Aristotle, Rhetoric of Cicero and Music of Tubal*, 15th-C, fresco, Fr. **pp.38-39**: Archimedes measuring the purity of the gold in the crown of Heiron II of Syracuse, from an edition of Vitruvius, 1511, woodcut copy/after Douris, *Young Greeks at School*, 5th-C BC, detail, red-figure vessel, Gr./Graeco-Roman theatre, Taormina, Sicily/Francesco de Ficoroni, *Greek Actor and Masks* from *Le Maschere Sceniche e Figure Comiche d'Antichi*, 18th-C, It. **pp.40-41**: *Ruins of Ptolemy Library at Alexandria*, c.1811, print, Fr./ Alexander the Great exploring under water, 5th-C, Ms., Fr./Diogenes and Alexander, relief, Gr. **pp.42-43**: Carneades, 18th-C, engr./*The Alexander Mosaic*, Casa del Fauno, Pompeii, c.320BC, detail, mosaic copy of Greek painting, c.4th-C BC, It./ Alexander directing the building of a wall of fire against Gog and Magog, c.1600, Ms., India/Pyrrho's *Sexti Empirici*, 17th-C, title page, Eng. **pp.44-45**: Epicurus, bust/ Bacchus and Maenad, fresco, It./ Epicurean symbols, Pompeii, c.100BC, mosaic, It./Lucretius, *De Rerum Natura*, Ms. **pp.46-47**: Zeno of Citium, bust/Mino da Fiesole, *Marcus Aurelius*, late 15th-C, marble relief, It./ Joos van Gent, *Seneca*, c.1475, panel, Neth./Leonardo Alenza y Nieto, *The Romantic Suicide*, early 19th-C, Sp. **pp.48-49**: image of Christ, Hagia Sophia, Istanbul, 12th-C, mosaic, Turkey/the Archangel Michael, from Pala d'Oro (High Altar), San Marco, Venice, c.AD980, detail, enamel and precious materials, It. **pp.50-51**: St Augustine, from his *City of God*, early 15th-C, Ms. detail/baptism of Christ, Baptistry of Arians, Ravenna, 5th-C, mosaic, It. **pp.52-53**: Adam and Eve, from *Speculum Humanae Salvationis*, c.1360, Ms., Westphalia/ Spanish Inquisition burning heretics, 1849, engr., Ger./ Hell, from Augustine's *City of God*, 15th-C, Ms., Fr. **pp.54-55**: Patio de Los Leones, Alhambra, Granada, 1238–1358, Sp./*Boethius listens to the Instruction of Philosophy*, from *The Consolation of Philosophy*, 15th-C, Ms./Angelo Falcone, *Battle of the Romans and Barbarians*, 17th-C, It. **pp.56-57**: crucifixion plaque, 8th-C, bronze open-work, Ir./Pernottin, *Héloise receiving Abelard's Veil*, 18th-C, print, Fr./*The Creation*, 12th-C, detail, tapestry, Sp. **pp.58-59**: *The Trinity*, 1470, stained glass, Ger./interior, La Sainte Chapelle, Paris, 13th-C, Fr./ *The Return of Excalibur*, from *La Morte d'Arthur*, c.1316, Ms., Fr./ Francesco Traini, *The Triumph of St Thomas Aquinas*, Santa Caterina, Pisa, 14th-C, panel, It. **pp.60-61**: *The Microcosm*, Ms./tapestry, see p.57/ Johannes Scotus Erigena, engr./*The Lady and the Unicorn: Sight*, c.1500, detail, tapestry, Fr. **p.62-63**: Camille Flammarion, *The Heavens*, from *L'Atmosphère Meteorologie Populaire*, 1888 in the style of c.1520, woodcut, Fr./orrery, early 19th-C, Eng. **pp.64-65**: Andrea Pisano, *Ptolemy*, c.1335, relief, It./Andreas Cellarius, *Copernican System of the Universe*, from *Harmonia Microcosmica*, 1708, print, Neth./Nicolaus Copernicus, 1967, 10zy coin, Poland. **pp.66-67**: relationship between planet velocities and musical harmony, from Johannes Kepler's *Harmony of the World*, 1619, Ms. detail/*Tycho Brahe in his Observatory*, from Brahe's *Astronomiae Instauratae Mechanica*, 1602, engr./explanation of the planets, from Kepler's *Harmony of the World*, 1619, engr./*Trial of Galileo*, 1632/ Vicenzo Viviani, Galileo's pendulum design, early 17th-C, drawing. **pp.68-69**: Royal Greenwich Observatory, from O. M. Mitchell's *The Planetary and Stellar Worlds*, 1859, engr., Eng./ Camille Flammarion, *Newton discovers the Law of Gravity*, from *Astronomie Populaire*, 1881, engr., Fr./ John Rowley, orrery, 1712, Eng./Isaac Newton's *Principia Mathematica*, 17th-C, title page, Eng. **pp.70-71**: Château and parterre, Vaux-le-Vicomte, nr. Paris, 17th-C, Fr./library, 18th-C, print, Fr./detail, see p.68bl. **pp.72-73**: Lorenzo Bartolini, *Machiavelli*, early 19th-C, sculpture, It./Santi di Tito, *Niccolò Machiavelli*, late 16th-C, detail, It./Niccolò Machiavelli's *The Prince*, 1580, title page, Basel/Giuseppe-Lorenzo Gatteri, *Cesare Borgia leaving the Vatican*, mid 19th-C, It. **pp.74-75**: Francis Bacon's *Essayes*, 1597, title page, Eng./George Vertue, *Gresham College*, 1739, detail, engr., Eng./ Paul van Somer, *Sir Francis Bacon*, early 17th-C, Belgium/John Bettes, *Elizabeth I*, late 16th-C, detail, Eng. **pp.76-77**: arms and crest of Bacon family/existence of valves in veins, from William Harvey's *De Motu Cordis et Sanguinis*, 1628, engr., Eng./ Egbert van Heemskerk, *The Election in the Guildhall, Oxford*, 1637. **pp.78-79**: Sir Godfrey Kneller, *Thomas Hobbes*, mid 17th-C, Eng./ William Dobson, *Charles II as Prince of Wales with a Page*, mid 17th-C, detail, Eng./Sir Christopher Wren, St. Peter's in the Wardrobe, London, late 17th-C, Eng. **pp.80-81**: Hendrik Steenwyck, *View of a Market-place*, late 16th-C, Belgium/Abraham Bosse (attr.), Hobbes' *Leviathan*, 1651, engr., title page, Eng./execution of the regicides, 1660, detail, woodcut, Eng./Abraham Cooper, *Battle of Marston Moor*, 1819, Eng. **p.82-83**: Sebastien Leclerc, *A Geometer's Cabinet*, 1714, print, Fr./Blaise Pascal's calculator, 1642. **pp.84-85**: after Frans Hals, *René Descartes*, 18th-C, detail/ F. de Gaignères, *Collège des Jesuites de la Flèche*, 1655, detail, pen and wash, Fr./Pierre-Louis Dumesnil the Younger, *Christina of Sweden and her Court*, 18th-C, detail, Fr./diagram from Descartes' *Treatise on Man*, 1677, print, Amsterdam. **pp.86-87**: Claude Monet, (l. to r) *Rouen Cathedral: Portal, Morning Sun (Harmony in Blue)*, 1892; *Portal and Alban's Tower, Full Sunlight*, 1893–94; *Sun's Effect, Evening*, 1893, Fr./diagrams from Descartes' *Treatise on Man*, 1664, print, Fr./diagram from Descartes' *Treatise on Man*, 1662, print, Fr./Descartes' universe, from *The World*, 1668, print, Amsterdam **pp.88-89**: Descartes' skull (alleged)/ C.P. Marillier, *Events of Descartes' life*, 18th-C, engr., Fr./Descartes' *Meditations*, 1641, title page, Fr. **pp.90-91**: *Benedict Spinoza*, 17th-C, detail/Rembrandt, *Jews in the Synagogue*, 1648, etching, Neth./ Robert Hooke's microscope and condenser, from his *Micrographia*, 1665, engr., Eng./Heidelberg University, 1900, engr. after a photograph, Ger. **pp.92-93**: statue of Moses Maimonides in Cordoba, bronze, Sp./Caspar David Friedrich, *Ruin in Riesengebirge*, 1815–20, Ger. **pp.94-95**: Jan Havicksz Steen, *Musical Company; the Young Suitor*, mid 17th-C, Neth./Jean Charles François de la Hay, *Baruch Spinoza*, 1762, crayon, Fr./Spinoza's *Ethics*, 1876, title page, USA/George Eliot, mid 19th-C, Eng. **pp.96-97**: *Gottlieb Wilhelm Leibniz*, from *Historie der Leibnitzschen Philosophie* by Carl Gunther Ludovici, 1737, detail, engr., Ger./ Theobald Freiherr von Oer, *Leibniz in Berlin*, 1855, engr., Ger./diagrams from Leibniz's *Mathematische Schriften* Vol.1, by C.I. Gerhardt, 1849, engr., Ger. **pp.98-99**: Charles Jervas, *Caroline of Ansbach*, 1727, Eng./G. Adcock, *Dr. Pangloss*, played by Mr. Harley in a stage version of *Candide*, c.1800, engr., Eng./Leibniz's house, Hanover, Ger./Leibniz's calculating machine, from *Historie der Leibnitzischen Philosophie* by Carl Gunther Ludovici, 1737, engr., Ger. **pp.100-01**: Sebastian Stoskopff, *The Five Senses (Summer)*, early 17th-C, detail, Fr./viola d'amore, 1774 **pp.102-03**: John Locke's *Philosophical Essays concerning Human Understanding*, 1748, title page, Eng./from a painting by Sir Godfrey Kneller, *John Locke*, 19th-C, illustration/Sir Godfrey Kneller (attr.), *William III of England*, late 17th-C, Eng./Sir James Thornhill, *William and Mary in Glory*, ceiling, Painted Hall, Royal Naval College, Greenwich, c.1710, detail, fresco, Eng. **pp.104-05**: Bartolomé Murillo, *The Holy Family with the Little Bird*, 17th-C, Sp./Jan Steen, *A School for Boys and Girls*, c.1670, Neth. **pp.106-07**: letter from Locke, with illustration of his birthplace, 1699, Eng./David Ryckaert III, *The Artists' Workshop*, 1638, Neth. **pp.108-09**: Thomas Rowlandson, *A Bird's Eye View of Smithfield Market*, 1811, aquatint, Eng./detail, see p.105. **pp.110-11**: Bell Tower, Trinity College, Dublin/John Smibert (attr.), *George Berkeley*, early 18th-C, Anglo-American School/Charles Jervas, *Dean Swift*, early 18th-C, detail, Eng./Doolittle, *A View of the Buildings of Yale College at New Haven*, c.1910, etching, USA/Italian School, *Cloth Dyers Demonstrating their Trade and Skills*, 1522, It./Berkeley's *Treatise concerning the Principles of Human Knowledge*, 1710, title page, Ir. **pp.112-13**: Hume's *Treatise of Human Nature*, 1739, title page, Eng./ Allan Ramsay, *David Hume*, 1766, Scotland/James Tassie, *Adam Smith*, 1787, detail, paste medallion, Scotland/Jean Raoux, *A Lady at her Mirror*, 1720s, Fr. **pp.114-15**: James Gillray, *Billiards*, 18th-C, print, Eng./ Joseph Wright of Derby, *A Philosopher Lecturing*, c.1766, Eng. **pp.116-17**: George Willison, *James Boswell*, 1765, Scotland/Jean-Honoré Fragonard, *Le Verrou (The Bolt)*, c.1777, Fr. **pp.118-19**: C.J. Staniland, *Edmund Burke supporting the Parliamentary Motion for the Abolition of Slavery*, c.1880, engr., Eng./James Northcote, *Edmund Burke*, late 18th-C, detail, Eng./Mansion House, London, 1739, print, Fr./Thomas Gainsborough, *Mr. and Mrs. Andrews*, c.1749, Eng./Burke's *A Philosophical Enquiry into the Origins of our Ideas of the Sublime and Beautiful*, 1757, title page, Eng. **pp.120-21**: *Taking of the Bastille*, late 18th-C, watercolour, Fr./first edn. of Diderot's Encyclopedia, 1751-72, Fr. **pp.122-23**: Jean Huber, *Le Lever de Voltaire*, late 18th-C, Fr./*Voltaire in his Study*, late 18th-C, Fr./*The Peasant weighed down by the Nobility and Clergy*, late 18th-C, etching, Fr./Jean-Pierre Houel, *View of a Cell in the Bastille at the Moment of releasing Prisoners, 14.7.1789*, late 18th-C, watercolour, Fr. **pp.124-25**: Carle van Loo, *Denis Diderot*, mid 18th-C, Fr./Robert Benard, (l. to r.) *Percussion Instruments, Cross-section of a Mine, Papermaking*, from Diderot's Encyclopedia, late 18th-C, engr., Fr./after M. Meissonier, *Diderot discussing the Encyclopedia with Colleagues*, 19th-C, engr., Sp./ Daumont, *Le Grand Café d'Alexandre, Paris*, 18th-C, engr., Fr. **pp.126-27**: Jean-Antoine Houdon, *Jean-Jacques Rousseau*, late 18th-C, terracotta, Fr./ Cesare Mussini, *The Death of Atala*, mid 19th-C, It./Charon after Bouchet, *Rousseau in Switzerland, Persecuted and Homeless*, 19th-C, detail, engr., Fr. **pp.128-29**: *Education of Jean-Jacques*, 19th-C, litho, Fr./Charles Cochin le jeune, Rousseau's *Emile*, 1780, title page, Fr./L.L. de Boilly, *Maximilien Robespierre*, late 18th-C, Fr./ *Declaration des Droits de l'Homme*, late 18th-C, detail, panel, Fr. **pp.130-31**: Carl Friedrich Lessing, *The Castle on the Rock, Romantic Landscape*, 1828, detail, Ger./arms of the King of Prussia, Wilhelm I, late 19th-C, detail, book, Ger. **pp.132-33**: Anton Graff, *Johann von Schiller*, 1786, Switz./Gottlieb Doebler, *Immanuel Kant*, 1791, Ger./John Everett Millais, *The Blind Girl*, 1856, Eng. **pp.134-35**: William Henry Fox Talbot, *Fox Talbot at his Establishment near Reading*, c.1845, calotype, Eng./Caspar David Friedrich, *Two Men by the Sea looking at the Moon rising*, 1817, Ger. **pp.136-37**: *Moses Mendelssohn*, late 18th-C, Ger./Phiz, *Footpads attack a Victim*, from Benson's *Remarkable Trials*, mid 19th-C, detail, engr., Eng./Clemens Kohl, *Doctors visit a hospital*, 1794, engr., Ger./Pugin and Rowlandson, *House of Lords*, 1809, drawing and engr., Eng. **pp.138-39**: Schopenhauer's *The World as Will and Representation*, 1819, Ger./Angilbert Göbel, *Arthur Schopenhauer*, 1859, Ger./halfpenny postage stamps, 1880, GB./ Schopenhauer's *On the Fourfold Root of the Principle of Sufficient Reason*, 1813, title page, Ger. **pp.140-41**: *Johanna Schopenhauer*, 1835, engr., Ger./Thomas Eakins, *The Biglin Brothers Racing*, c.1873, USA/ Dwingeloo 1 Galaxy, from Isaac Newton Telescope, Canary Islands, composite visible light image, Dwingeloo Obscured Galaxy Survey/ V. P. Mohn, *Hansel and Gretel*, from *Grimms' Tales*, 1892, book cover, Ger. **pp.142-43**: C. Müller, *Krishna*, from Friedrich Majer's *Mythological Lexicon*, v.2, 1804, engr., Ger./Georg Emanuel Opiz, *A Hungarian Nobleman with a Pupil of the K.K. Theresian Knight Academy in Vienna*, c.1810, aquatint, Austria/George Stubbs, *Lion Devouring a Horse*, 1769, enamel, Eng. **pp.144-45**: *Nikolaevich Tolstoy on the Terrace*, 1905, panel, Russ./Etienne Jeaurat, *A Musical Soirée*, 18th-C, Fr./detail, see p.142r. **pp.146-47**: Guariento de Arpo, *Scenes from the Life of Christ*, 14th-C, altarpiece, It./Basavanagudi Temple, Bangalore, mid 16th-C, India/Buddha, painted rock relief, Tibet. **pp.148-49**: the Buddha Siddhartha Gautama, 13th-C, gilt copper, Nepal/thang-ka, c.1900, detail, painting on cloth. **pp.150-51**: Shiva dancing on Nandi, 12th-C–13th-C, stone, India/Tibetan burial ground, Sichuan Province, China/*Arjuna with Krishna*, from the *Bhagavad Gita*, 18th-C, miniature, India/Friedrich Majer's *Mythological Lexicon*, 1804, title page, Ger. **pp.152-53**: Sun Yat Sen, from *Je Sais Tout* magazine, 1912, print, Fr./ George Curzon, Viceroy of India, c.1900/Indian philosophy students, Baroda State University, 1947/riots in Shanghai, 1948, press photograph **pp.154-55**: Jena University, c.1900, Ger./Friedrich Jügel, *Johann Fichte*, 1808, aquatint, Ger./Nicholls and Allanson, *Liebig's Laboratory at Giessen*, 1845, engr., Eng./Arthur Kampf, *Fichte Addresses the German Nation*, c.1913, fresco, Ger. **pp.156-57**: geology and palaeontology chart, c.1880, print, Eng./Friedrich Schelling, late 19th-C, engr., Ger./Samuel Palmer, *The Magic Apple Tree*, 1830, ink and watercolour, Eng./Schelling's *Philosophy of Nature*, 1799, title page, Ger./E. Finden, *Samuel Taylor Coleridge*, 1837, detail, engr., Eng. **pp.158-59**: Hegel's *Philosophy of History*, 1837, title page, Ger./Jakob Schlesinger, *Georg Friedrich Wilhelm Hegel*, early 19th-C, detail, Ger./ Michail Wrubel, *Christ on the Mount of Olives*, 1887, Russ. **pp.160-61**: Carl Schlösser, *Beethoven Composing*, 1890, print, Ger./*Cotton manufacture: the Doubling Room, Dean Mills*, mid 19th-C, engr., Eng. **pp.162-63**: Elliott and Fry, *Charles Darwin*, 19th-C, Eng./ after Richard Knötel, *Christmas Eve, 1803: William III giving Uniforms to his Sons*, from *Fifty Pictures of Queen Louise*, 1896, chromotype, Ger./ Hitler Youth, c.1938, Ger./Heinrich Olivier, *Young Woman at a Prie-dieu*, 1824, Ger. **pp.164-65**: H. Moczynay, *Karl Marx and Friedrich Engels at the 2nd Communist Party Congress, London (1847)*, 1961, Ger./Karl Marx, 1880, tinted photograph/Marx's *Das Kapital*, 1867, title page, Ger./*The Mob storms and plunders the Arsenal in Berlin, 14 June 1848*, 19th-C, lithograph, Ger. **pp.166-67**: Engels, Marx and Marx's daughters, 1864, Eng./*Life in Golden Lane, London*, 1872, engr., Eng./Sir Henry Cole, *The Dinner Party*, c.1865, watercolour, Eng./family outside their house, Hornsey, London, c.1890/ *Hetton Colliery, Durham*, from Isaac Brick's *Early Railway Relics*, c.1825, engr., Eng. **pp.168-69**: Marx's and Engels' *Communist Manifesto*, 1848, Eng./drawing room, Berkeley Castle, 1890, c.1890, Eng./prisoners in Russian labour camp, c. 1932/Alexander Petrovich Apsit, *The Tsar, the Priest and the Rich Man carried by the Working People*, 1918, poster, Russ./

*British Library Reading Room*, c.1870, print, Eng. **pp.170-71**: soldiers and workers on the streets of Petrograd, Russia, November 1917/Georgy Tikhonovitch Krutikov, *Flying City*, 1928, drawing, Russ./Leon Trotsky, 1917, Russ./detail, see p.164r. **pp.172-73**: H. Varges, *Richard Wagner*, c.1910, copper intaglio print after 1871 photograph, Ger./Friedrich Nietzsche, c.1875, Ger./Mount Olympus, Gr./satire on strict Sunday observance, from *Lustige Blätter*, 1895, magazine cover, Ger. **pp.174-75**: Richard Burton in costume he wore as a pilgrim to Mecca, mid 19th-C, Eng./Job, *Napoleon in the Royal Military Academy at Brienne*, c.1910, watercolour, Fr./Edouard Detaille, *The Trophy*, 1898, Fr. **pp.176-77**: *Zoroaster*, c.1900, print, Maharashtra, India/Henry van de Velde, Nietzsche's *Thus Spake Zarathustra*, 1908, title page, Ger./Gustav Klimt, *The Kiss*, 1908, detail, Austria/Leni Riefenstahl, *Triumph of the Will (Nüremberg Rally)*, 1934, film still, Ger./Lou Andreas-Salomé, late 19th-C, Ger. **pp.178-79**: William Butler Yeats, early 20th-C/Max Brückner, scenery design for Wagner's *Parsifal*, 1896, Ger./detail, see p.176r. **pp.180-81**: Nathaniel Currier after John Trumbull, *Signing the Declaration of Independence*,

1776, mid 19th-C, engr., USA/United Nations Building, NYC. **pp.182-83**: Rudolph Ackermann, *Dartmoor Prison*, 1810, detail, print, Eng./W.H. Worthington, *Jeremy Bentham*, 1823, detail, engr., Eng./M. Egerton, *Dancing the Quadrille at School in Robert Owen's New Lanark, Scotland*, 1825, detail, print, Eng./*The Westminster Review*, 1824, title page, Eng. **pp.184-85**: T. Heaviside, *The Agapemone, or Abode of Love, at Charlinch, Somerset*, 1851, engr., Eng./T. H. Shepherd and H. Melville, *Central Criminal Court, Old Bailey*, 1840, engr., Eng./John Stuart Mill, 1873, engr., Eng./Mill's *On Liberty*, 1859, title page, Eng./suffragette demonstration, London, 1905/*Harriet Taylor*, mid 19th-C, miniature, Eng. **pp.186-87**: C. S. Peirce, from *Collected Papers of Charles Sanders Peirce*, vol. 1, late 19th-C, USA/*Tay Bridge disaster, Diving Operations*, January 1880, engr., Eng./refuelling a car, early 20th-C, USA **pp.188-89**: *William Röntgen examining a Patient*, 1896, book illustration, Ger./*Wright Brothers' First Flight at Kitty Hawk, North Carolina*, 1904, magazine illustration, Fr./Alice Boughton, *William James*, from *The Letters of William James*, vol.1, 1907, USA/A. E. Emslie, *A Mother's Dream*, 1891,

magazine illustration. **pp.190-91**: John Dewey, mid 20th-C, USA/John Dewey at the Convention for the League for Independent Political Action, USA, 1936/elementary science consultant Philip Blough watches an experiment at a school in Winnetka, USA, 1947/Dewey's *The School and Society*, 1900, title page, USA **pp.192-93**: rush hour, Osaka, Japan, c.1989/atomic explosion, Bikini Atoll, 1956. **pp.194-95**: letter from Gottlob Frege to Edmund Husserl, 1894, facsimile, Ger./Gottlob Frege, from *Nachgelassene Schriften*, early 20th-C, Ger./from *Begriffsschrift (Concept Script)*, 1879, Ger. **pp.196-97**: *Lord John Russell*, late 19th-C, engr., Eng./Bertrand Russell, 1950, Eng./A. N. Whitehead and Bertrand Russell's *Principia Mathematica*, Vol.1, 1935, Eng./Bertrand Russell at CND demo., Ministry of Defence, London, February 1961. **pp.198-99**: A.N. Whitehead, early 20th-C, Eng./from *Principia Mathematica* Vol.1, 1935, Eng./ College of Arms, London/Trinity College, Cambridge, Eng. **pp.200-01**: *Put a Tiger in Your Tank*, Esso advert., 1960s, Eng./*The Reich's Labour Service Calls for You*, 1930s, propaganda poster, Ger./stock trading floor, Chicago **pp.202-03**: Paul Wittgenstein in NYC, 1934/Ludwig Wittgenstein,

1930/David Battie and customer, BBC TV's *Antiques Roadshow*, 1989, GB/Wittgenstein's *Tractatus Logico-Philosophicus*, 1922, title page, Eng. **pp.204-05**: Texas Tim painting desert landscape, New Mexico, c.1995/ Speakers' Corner, London, 1933. **pp.206-07**: British Army suitability test, 1942, Eng./Lotfi Mansouri directing Margarita Lilova in *La Gioconda*, San Francisco, 1979/Professor J. L. Austin at joint session of the Aristotelian Society and the Mind Association, Birmingham, Eng., August 1952/Ben Heatley of GB receiving silver medal for the Marathon, Tokyo Olympics, 1964 **pp.208-09**: Kierkegaard's cousin, *Søren Kierkegaard*, c.1840, drawing, Den./bridal couple, 1920s, Eng./Swiss Protestant theologian Karl Barth, c.1960, drawing, Fr./Martin Heidegger, 1950, Ger. **pp.210-11**: Heidegger's *Sein und Zeit*, 1927, title page, Ger./René Magritte, *La Fatigue de Vivre*, 1927, Belg./Edmund Husserl, early 20th-C, Ger./André Collin, *Poor People*, late 19th-C, Belg. **pp.212-13**: giving directions, 1950s, Eng./sundial, Berea, Kentucky, 1996/Edvard Munch, *The Scream*, 1893, Nor. **pp.214-15**: baby girl, 1989, Eng./Henri Bergson, late 19th-C, Fr./Grand Central Station, NYC/Hood River, Oregon. **pp.216-17**: Simone de

Beauvoir, Nov. 1945, detail, Fr./Jean-Paul Sartre's *La Nausée*, 1938, facsimile of 1st edn., Fr./Sartre at his flat, 42 Rue Bonaparte, overlooking the café Les Deux Magots, Paris, 1950s/Kelly's Cellar, Belfast, 1954/Albert Camus at book-signing, 1957, Fr. **pp.218-19**: Maurice Merleau-Ponty, 1950, Fr./Berthe Morisot, *Woman and Child in a Garden*, 1883-34, Fr./Louis Althusser, 1978, Fr./Jacques Lacan, 1950s, Fr./Michel Foucault, 1970s, Fr./Jacques Derrida, 1993, Fr./Sartre's funeral, Paris, 1980. **pp.220-21**: Albert Einstein at astronomy lecture, Pasadena, California, 1931/power station cooling towers, Eng./Karl Popper, mid 20th-C, Eng./Alfred Adler at an international conference for psychology, Berlin, Sept. 1930, detail/P. Gartmann, *Arnold Schoenberg*, 1930, detail, Ger. **pp.221-22**: exterior, London School of Economics and Political Sciences, Eng./glass laboratory apparatus/Joseph Heinemann, *Creation of the World*, from *Picture Bible*, 1906, lith. and pen, Freiburg/ *1984*, 1955, film still, GB. **pp.224-25**: Anti-nuclear march, Berkshire, Eng., late 20th-C/Ernst Hans Gombrich, mid 20th-C/demolition of flats, UK, late 20th-C/detail, see p220bl. **pp.226-27**: earth in space.

# PICTURE CREDITS

## Author's Acknowledgments

Vastly more work goes into a book of this kind than the author realizes when he begins to write it. The whole visual side of it is the creation of others. My heartfelt thanks go to two people in particular: Neil Lockley, who carried out the crucial task of co-ordinating everyone's efforts, and who himself made major contributions to the pictorial content of the book, and also to researching and writing captions and other boxed material; and Rowena Alsey, the person chiefly responsible for the illustrations and their layout. Various sorts of help were provided by Lara Maiklem, Joanna Warwick, Jo Houghton, Claire Legemah, and Tina Vaughan, all of whom merit my thanks.

The idea of writing the book in the first place was brought to me by Sean Moore, who remained the person at Dorling Kindersley ultimately responsible for its dealings with me. At various stages editorial assistance was given by Gwen Edmonds, Anna Kruger, and Luci Collings, and I thank them all. Dorling Kindersley is to be heartily congratulated on helping to bring philosophy to a new generation of readers.

**Dorling Kindersley would like to thank the following people**: Mandie Tsang for the illustration on p.12; Hilary Bird for the index; Edda Bohnsack; Edward Bunting; Michelle Fiedler; Jo Houghton; Joanne Mitchell; Mariana Sonnenberg; Laura Strevens; Nichola Thomasson; Frances Vargo; Joanna Warwick.